C000229759

ROYALS REMEMBERED

STOP PRESS:

Prior to going to press, the following player transfers were made (June to early September 2001). Playing records, etc. of these players remain complete only up to June 2001.

Paul Bodin	Swindon Youth coach summer 2001
Martin Booty	Chesterfield August 2001
Darren Caskey	Notts Co. (free) June 2001
Michael Gilkes	Bristol R. (trial); Slough T. summer 2001
Andy Gurney	Swindon T. (free) June 2001
Alex Haddow	Carlisle U. summer 2001
Phil Hadland	Leyton O. (free) July 2001
Lee Hodges	Northampton T. (trial); Plymouth Arg. (trial); Luton T. (trial) summer 2001
Scott Howie	Bristol R. (free) July 2001
Barry Hunter	Rushden & D. (loan) September 2001
Dylan Kerr	Exeter C. (free) August 2001
Stuart Lovell	Livingston August 2001
Jimmy McIntyre	Dundee U. (free) July 2001
Mark Nicholls	Torquay U. summer 2001
Simon Osborn	Port Vale (loan) September 2001
Neville Roach	Torquay U. (free) summer 2001
Keith Scott	Dover A. (free) August 2001
Ben Smith	Southend U. (free) July 2001
Steve Swales	Halifax T. (free) summer 2001
Nathan Tyson	Swansea C. (loan) August 2001
Martin Williams	Stevenage B. (free) summer 2001

Players illustrated on previous page (top to bottom):

Syd Crawford	*(1920)*
Matt Forster	*(1931)*
Norman Dodgin	*(1950)*
Bill Lacey	*(1960)*
John Hulme	*(1972)*
Tony Rougier	*(2001)*

ROYALS REMEMBERED
The Official Who's Who
of Reading F.C.
1920 -2001

By Alan Sedunary

Published by:
Yore Publications
12 The Furrows, Harefield,
Middx. UB9 6AT.

British Library Cataloguing-in-Publication Data.
A catalogue record for this book
is available from the British Library.

ISBN 1 874427 04 6

Printed and bound by
Bookcraft, Midsomer Norton, Bath.

Dedication

This book is dedicated to my parents, Sid and Vera for giving me my love of football, and to my wife, Sonia, for putting up with it!

FOREWORD

At first glance a book on the players of a football club that has spent most of its League history in the lower divisions might not look too interesting. However, Reading Football Club has been graced by some of the finest players in the country, has had its fair share of 'characters' and, like most clubs, has players who are legends amongst its own supporters.

As well as over 80 internationals from 16 different countries across all five continents, Reading have included five Olympians with three gold medals to their credit, War heroes, match fixers, League record holders and even a player who has had a TV character named after him.

All are included here, along with every Reading player who has made a competitive first team appearance for the club since its entry into the League in 1920, whether their career lasted fifty years or five minutes. Also featured are all Reading's managers over the last 80 plus years, the World War Two guests, and a special group who never played a competitive game but still deserved a mention.

My credentials are that I have supported Reading Football Club for over 45 years and the last 30 of those have seen me contribute a variety of statistical and historical articles to almost every one of the club's programmes during that period. However, my support was pre-ordained long before my first game. My parents had their first date at Elm Park, while I was born a Martin Hicks clearance from the ground, being delivered by the club doctor.

This book has been very much a labour of love and wherever possible all facts have been double checked, even more in the case of the occasional discrepancy. Consequently, this has ensured that this is the most complete and accurate history of Reading's players ever published. My research has also been able to correct a few popular misconceptions and so the details of Reading's first substitute, fastest goal, or first League sending off may surprise even the most knowledgeable Reading fan. I have even discovered a 'missing' manager who seems to have avoided most other record books.

On the other hand, unlike fellow Reading historian, David Downs who pointed out that Adrian Williams had worn every Reading shirt except number 10, only for Adie to play in that shirt the following week, I cannot claim to have influenced team selection - but I should have! During Trevor Senior's record-breaking goalscoring season of 1983-84, I wrote one of my more obscure articles that statistically 'proved' that Reading's goal machine should be dropped to substitute and brought on for the second half. Amazingly, our normally astute manager, the late, great Maurice Evans, ignored my advice and on the day the article was published, Super Trev missed a first half penalty that would have won our FA Cup-tie against Oxford!

And finally...I know Reading purists will point out that the book's title does not reflect the fact that the majority of players featured are really 'Biscuitmen' and not 'Royals' but the need for a punchy title meant that our current nickname got the nod. I hope fans of all ages and all clubs gain as much pleasure from this book as I have had in writing it.

'Up The Biscuits'

'Come On You Royals'

'G'arn URZ'

Alan Sedunary

October 2001

ACKNOWLEDGEMENTS

My thanks to the many people who have offered advice and encouragement throughout the production of this book. Particular thanks to David Downs for the use of his extensive library, Peter Baxter for the loan of his statistics, Boyd Butler and Andy West of Reading Football Club, Dave Twydell of Yore Publications, and to my wife, Sonia, for her help in beating the manuscript into shape .

PHOTOGRAPHS

Every attempt has been made to trace the copyright of all pictures but this has not always been possible, particularly with some of the pre War trade cards. My thanks for the permission given by the following:

Mapson, W. Price and Eaton by courtesy of Topical Times Football Books, Armour Print/Michael Tubbs (Hicks, L. Jones and S. Richardson), David Downs (R. Reeves, Wheeler, K.Dixon), Matchday (Edelston, R. Campbell, Bainbridge and Cox), Garth Dykes (Harston), Panini (Hislop, Francis, A. Williams, S. Taylor, Osborn, D. Kerr), West Midland Collectors (J. Brooks), J. Palethorpe, Patterson, Geldard, Strauss by kind permission of Imperial Tobacco Ltd, England, Bryan Horsnell (Bacon, Dix, and Colin Newton's photo of Best, Senior and Sanchez), Gallaher Ltd (W. Cook, Eggo, G. James and W.Butler), Philosophy Footballers (Busby), Bob Thomas (N. Webb), Colin and Melanie Bishop of Reading Football Supporters' Club (Duckworth, McConnell, D. Evans and F. Richardson). Special thanks to the Reading Chronicle, David Wright of the Reading Evening Post and Reading Football Club for many of the remaining photos.

~ CONTENTS ~

Fred Bartholomew

Alan Scarrott

Linden Jones

George James

Billy Price

Lee Hodges

INTRODUCTION

Players are detailed in alphabetical order by the full name for which they were known. Consequently, Anthony (Tony) Alexander starts the book off, not John Alexander. When a player was always known by another name, e.g. John becoming Jack or Henry preferring Harry, they are recorded under their popular name but nicknames are shown only in the text. The forename by which the player was known is shown in bold, along with his surname. Managers are listed in chronological order.

The statistics and details of this book are correct up to the end of the 2000-01 season, and where + appears after a player's Reading Record or League Career Total it indicates that the player's career is continuing into 2001-01. Where no League Career Total is shown, that player's entire League career was with Reading. Playing careers are shown numerically as starting appearances (substitute appearance) / goals.

The usual abbreviations have been used for clubs and major competitions. Other competitions included are AMC - Associate Members Cup, FLGC - Football League Group Cup, FLGT - Football League Group Trophy, FMC - Full Members Cup, SL - Southern League (Division One only), SPFC - Southern Professional Floodlit Cup, SSC - Third Division Southern Section Cup. Apologies to the various sponsors who fail to get a mention due to lack of space.

In an attempt to avoid confusion following the renaming of the divisions after the launch of the Premier League in 1992, First Division, Second Division, Third Division/Third Division South and Fourth Division has been used for the pre-Premiership divisions and after 1992 they are shown as Premier League, Division One, etc.

Every attempt has been made to trace the dates of death for players but where a player is known to have died but the details are not known this is indicated by recording it as 'd. ?'

ALEXANDER Anthony Alan

b. Reading 8.2.1935
Ht 5ft 7 W 10st 9 (53-54)
Career: READING amateur 22 October 1951, professional 5 August 1952; Yeovil summer 1956; Crystal Palace August 1960; Bedford T. June 1961

Now better known as the father of author and broadcaster, Shelly Webb, and, consequently, Neil Webb's father in law, Tony graduated through Reading's youth teams to sign professional at 17. He made his League debut a week after his 18th birthday and although he had to wait until 29 April 1953 to add to his League total it was worthwhile as he capped his home debut with a goal. Tony was a speedy and determined player but when he returned from National Service in the RAF he was up against fierce competition for the right wing position. Because of this, the next three seasons only produced another nine League appearances and one more goal before he was released by the club.

Reading Record: Lge 11/2

TONY'S CLAIM TO FAME - As a 13 year old, Tony was at Elm Park to watch Notts County's new signing, England centre forward Tommy Lawton, but he never saw much of the great man. In the pre-match kick about a wayward Lawton blockbuster hit Tony in the face and he was carried out of the ground unconscious!

ALEXANDER John Eric

b. Liverpool 5.10.1955
Ht 5ft 11 Wt 11st (78-79)
Career: Ulysses; Millwall from non contact July 1997; READING (£3,000) October 1978; Northampton T. (free) August 1981; Watford secretary; Tottenham H. secretary March 2000

John came to prominence as a speedy striker when he was selected for the British Universities team, coached by Eamonn Dunphy who recommended him to his then club, Millwall. With his degree in Geography at London University secured, John signed professional for the Lions, having already made six League appearances, scoring twice towards the end of the previous season. His appearances in Millwall's Second Division side were restricted and so he signed for Reading in October 1978, again at the recommendation of Eamonn Dunphy who was by now a Reading player. Bought mainly as cover for an already successful Reading side, John again found it difficult to break into the first team but when his chance came he took it sensational fashion. Starting in the League side for the first time in three months against Fourth Division championship rivals, Grimsby, John scored all four goals in a devastating display of finishing.

Not surprisingly, he retained his place in the run-in, scoring three more vital goals as Reading won the title in some style. The following season, John had just fought his way back into the first team when he suffered a badly broken leg at Brentford in November 1979 and, apart from one substitute appearance 14 months later, his Reading career was over.

Reading Record: Lge 22(3)/9, FAC 4/1, LC 1(1)/2, Total 27(4)/12
League Career Total: 53(9)/15

ALLAN Adam McIlroy

b. Glasgow 12.9.1904 d. ?
Ht 5ft 10 1/2 Wt 13st 1 (30-31)
Career: Falkirk; Sunderland (£1,200); READING (£1,500) July 1930; Queen of the South (£400) August 1933

A broad shouldered centre half who, allegedly, 'could head the ball as far as he can throw it', Adam was considered a great capture when he joined Reading to replace the legendary Alf Messer. He had played in half of Sunderland's First Division games in the previous three seasons but found himself trying to shore up Reading's suspect defence in what proved to be their relegation season from the Second Division. He was one of the few successes of that season while his ready wit made him a great asset in the dressing room. Virtually ever-present through his three seasons at Elm Park, there was disappointment at the club when he failed to agree terms and subsequently joined Queen of the South for a substantial fee. After a shaky start he regained his form to become one of the best centre halves in Scotland and in 1934 he scored the penalty that won the Southern Charities Cup for the Queens.

Reading Record: Lge 107/3, FAC 5, Total 112/3
League Career Total: 170/3

ALLAN John

b. Dunfirmline c.1891 d. ?
Ht 5ft 9 1/2 Wt 12st (22-23)
Career: Dunfirmline; East Fife; Bury 1913; READING July 1922

'Jock' played in every first team game during the 1922-23 season so it was a great surprise to Reading fans when he was not retained at the end of the season but the reason soon became apparent. The FA had been investigating a match between Bury and Coventry and found that nine Bury players and officials, including Allan, had been guilty of match-fixing and all were suspended for life. This was a tragedy for both the player and Reading who had lost a reliable defender who could perform equally well in either full back berth.

Reading even tried, unsuccessfully, to reclaim some of the transfer fee paid to Bury. Jock emigrated to America where he was able to continue playing as the States were not at that time a part of FIFA, and although the ban was rescinded in 1929, his career was already over.

Reading Record: Lge 42, FAC 1, Total 43
League Career Total: 144

ALLEN Brynley William

b. Gilfach Goch 23.3.1921
Ht 5ft 9 1/2 Wt 11st (49-50)
Career: Gilfach Welfare; Manchester U. (trial); Swansea T. from groundstaff March 1939; Cardiff C.(Wartime guest); Cardiff C. (£1,250) December 1945; Newport Co. (£5,000) October 1947; Cardiff C. (player exchange) August 1948; READING (£4,000) 12 May 1949; Coventry C. (£7,000) 16 January 1950; Merthyr Tyd; Hereford U; Barry T. (free) summer 1952; Haverfordwest

The War meant that Bryn never got to make any League appearances for his local League club, Swansea, although he played several Wartime games for them. These proved a welcome diversion from his War service that saw him on Royal Navy convoy duty on the hazardous Murmansk run. He also played in several Wartime representative games including an appearance for the British Army of Occupation at the invitation of Field Marshal Montgomery. After the War, Bryn spent short but successful spells with the other South Wales League clubs before venturing out of the Principality to join Reading for 'probably the biggest fee in the history of the club'. Again, the fair haired inside forward made a quick impression, scoring a hat trick in his fifth game, at Exeter. However, Bryn was as much a creator as a scorer - the slightly built player making many chances for his team mates with his clever, skilful play. Coventry were so keen to sign him that their manager drove to Bryn's house and dragged him out of bed at midnight for his signature. Bryn's form with Coventry attracted the attention of the Welsh selectors and by the end of 1950 he had won two caps. In 1952 he quit League football to play for Barry Town, helping them win the Welsh Cup in 1955. He later worked as a postman in his home town and subsequently retired there.

Reading Record: Lge 26/12, FAC 1, Total 27/12
League Career Total: 198/67

ALLEN Denis James

b. Dagenham 2.3.1939 d. 9.7.1995
Ht 5ft 10 Wt 11st (69-70)
Career: Charlton A. from jnrs August 1956; READING (£900) 9 June 1961; Bournemouth (£6,500) 6 August 1970; ASO Ostend player/coach; Cheltenham T. Manager July 1974 to April 1979; Exeter C. director

Spotted by Charlton while captaining a local youth team that included Bobby Moore, Denis failed to make much impression at The Valley and so was allowed to join Reading at a fee that was to be one of the club's all time bargains. Denis played throughout the Sixties, regularly reinventing himself as he grew as a player to be one of Reading's most versatile and popular players. Signed as a centre forward, Denis relied on his skill rather than strength and soon developed into the inside forward berth although he was used in all five forward positions. In his first season he was the club's top scorer and scored a hat trick against Chester in Reading's first win in the League Cup. Although a regular scorer, Denis was converted into a scheming midfielder, particularly adept from deadball situations and then, towards the end of his Reading career he played as a sweeper with some aplomb. If this wasn't versatile enough, Denis was also stand in goalie and performed well on the odd occasion he was needed between the posts.

What made Denis special to Reading fans was his rapport with them. He played the game with a smile on his face, always acknowledging the part fans played, both on and on the pitch, and for some unknown reason was nicknamed 'Daisy'. There was great disappointment when Denis was sold to Bournemouth and his popularity was demonstrated when over 12,000 turned up for his testimonial. A member of the Allen footballing family that includes brother Les, nephews Bradley, Clive and son Martin, Denis sadly died at the age of just 56 after a long illness.

Reading Record: Lge 331(4)/84, FAC 24/6, LC 18/5, Total 373(4)/95
League Career Total: 353(4)/89

DENIS'S CLAIM TO FAME - While doing his National Service in the Far East, Denis gained full international honours when he was capped twice...for Malaya! The only European in the games against Peru and Mexico, Denis made his mark on the international scene by scoring two goals.

ALLEN Ralph Slack Littlewood

b. Newburn 30.6.1919 d. Blyth 9.5.1981
Ht 5ft 11 Wt 12st 7 (36-37)
Career: Walbottle; Sheffield Wed; Wombwell; Dipton U;
Fulham 1928; Brentford (£275) 1930; Charlton A. (£650)
October 1934; READING (£828) 18 June 1936; Northampton
T. 23 October 1936; Torquay U. 1938

A former pit worker, Ralph played for a number of
clubs before hitting form in Brentford's reserve side
where he scored an amazing 149 times in three seasons.
Despite this he was unable to get more than the
occasional first team game with the Bees so he moved to
Charlton where he was an instant success. His 32 goals
in just 28 games during that first season is still a
Charlton record and made him the Third Division South
top scorer as they won the championship. Injury
restricted his appearances the following season but he
still managed 15 goals as he helped Charlton to their
second consecutive promotion. It was, therefore, a
surprise when Charlton accepted Reading's record fee to
move Allen back to the Third Division South. By
October he had scored seven in 10 games yet,
remarkably, Reading then accepted a substantial offer
from Northampton and Ralph was on the move again.
In his short spell at Elm Park, the well built Ralph had
impressed with his powerful shooting with both feet and
his aerial ability. His brother, Jack, was also a
successful forward who played mainly for Sheffield
Wednesday and Newcastle for whom he scored twice in
the 1932 Cup Final.

Reading Record: Lge 10/7, SSC 1, Total 11/7
League Career Total: 172/122

ALLEYNE Andrew McArthur

b. Springtown, Barbados 19.5.1951
Ht 5ft 8 Wt 10st 7 (73-74)
Career: Argyle Yth; READING amateur 1967; Newbury T;
READING amateur October 1971, professional 17 November
1972

Few players have had a more sensational League debut
than Andy. A regular in Reading's youth team from
1967 to 1969, Andy was not taken on as a professional
so he moved to Newbury while working for the GPO.
However, after the sacking of Jack Mansell, caretaker
manager Jimmy Wallbanks invited Andy back to Elm
Park. A series of fine displays at right back for the
reserves saw him selected for the home game against
League leaders, Southport, on 21 October 1972. As
well as becoming the first black player to appear in
Reading's first team and turning in an impressive
performance, Andy scored Reading's equalizer with a
massive punt from inside his own half that eluded
everyone.

Remarkably, Southport's goal in this 1-1 draw was also
scored from 50 yards - surely the only time when both
goals have come from the halfway line. Andy kept his
place for most of that season but the signing of Stewart
Henderson saw his first team chances greatly restricted.
Andy's Elm Park career ended in the same way as it
started but unfortunately in his last home game the goal
went in the wrong net to give Gillingham a first leg
League Cup lead. Released in May 1976, Andy
reverted to local football where his family had built up
a strong reputation.

Reading Record: Lge 46(2)/2, FAC 4, LC 1, Total
51(2)/2

ALLISON John 'Jackie'

b. Stannington 31.7.1922 d 1985
Ht 5ft 10 1/2 Wt 11st 3 (49-50)
Career: Blyth Spartans; Chesterfield April 1947; Blyth
Spartans; READING (£1,500) 15 January 1949; Walsall
(£200) June 1950

Having failed to break into Chesterfield's first team,
Jackie returned to Blyth Spartans where his form
attracted the attention of several League clubs. It cost
Reading a record North Eastern League fee to sign the
player that their manager, Ted Drake, described as
'another Cliff Bastin' and he went straight into
Reading's first team, where his speed, body swerve and
powerful shooting kept him there for the rest of the
season. There was strong competition for the number
11 shirt and although Jackie was a two footed player, he
spent most of the season in the reserves, and was
released to Walsall at the end of 1949-50. There he
scored his only League goal for them with a penalty on
his debut - against Reading!

Reading Record: Lge 29/4
League Career Total: 76/5

AMOR William George

b. Pewsey 6.11.1919 d. 1988
Ht 5ft 10 1/2 Wt 12st (48-49)
Career: Pewsey; Huntley & Palmers; READING amateur
December 1947

Reading have the Royal Marines and the Police to thank
for the services of this most popular amateur. On the
same day as Bill received an invitation for a trial with
Plymouth he was called up into the Royal Marines so
football had to take a back seat. As a commando, he
served in Burma until the end of the War, despite
sustaining a thigh injury. After the War he joined the
police and was stationed in Reading, playing for Huntley
& Palmers and was spotted by Reading when 'The
Factory' reached the Third Round of the Amateur Cup.

Within two months of signing for Reading he was playing in the League and this led to even greater honours. He soon received the first of two Amateur caps for England and then, in the summer, he was part of the Great Britain Olympic squad, playing against Yugoslavia and Denmark in the third place play-off, when he scored a penalty. His police duties meant that he did not play as many games as he might have but his natural stamina and ability made up for his lack of full time training. Although used solely on the left wing by Reading, Bill played left back for Great Britain and for the English Police team while he often turned out at centre forward for Reading police. Bill's last games for Reading came at the end of 1951-52, and after that he concentrated on his police career, eventually retiring in 1975 having spent his entire duty in Reading where he was a popular and respected local personality.

Reading Record: Lge 66/12, FAC 2, Total 68/12

ANDERTON Sylvan James
b. Reading 23.11.1934
Ht 5ft 8 Wt 11st (57-58)
Career: Battle A; READING amateur 1951, professional 2 June 1952; Chelsea (£15,000) 13 March 1959; QPR January 1962

The product of Ted Drake's youth system at Reading, Sylvan was spotted playing for top local youth side Battle Athletic as a centre forward. He progressed quickly through the club's youth ranks to make his debut at Leyton Orient just before Christmas 1952. From then on he was on the fringes of the first team, being used mainly as an inside forward, but it wasn't until November 1956 that he became a regular. By that time he had developed into a right half and was soon being hailed as the best in the division. Sylvan was justifiably described as *'a real artist on the ball'* and it wasn't long before several top clubs were showing an interest. Reading held on as long as they could but eventually Ted Drake, by then at Chelsea, made an offer for the player he had discovered, that Reading could not refuse.

Strangely, Sylvan's last four games for Reading were at his original centre forward position and the fact that he averaged a goal a game in that spell must have influenced his price. He had two good seasons at Stamford Bridge but as 'Drake's Ducklings' progressed he lost his place.

Reading Record: Lge 155/18, FAC 12/1, SPFC 11, Total 178/19
League Career Total: 235/20

ANDREWS Leonard Thomas Alford
b. Reading 9.12.1888 d. Southampton 21.1.1969
Ht 5ft 9 Wt 11st 4 (20-21)
Career: Reading University; Reading Amateurs; READING October 1909; Southampton August 1912; READING (£100) June 1919; Southampton August 1921; Watford August 1924

A local player who turned professional while training to be a teacher, Len was a fine inside forward who had already played for Berks & Bucks at junior and senior level before joining Reading. Although not overkeen on training he still hit 28 goals in his first pro season and was a regular in the Southern League team until he moved to Southampton. Len was their most consistent performer in the pre-War seasons, but after the conflict, where he was promoted through the ranks to Regimental Sergeant Major, he returned to Reading. Able to play in any forward position, Len was at his best on the left side and it was said that he had the hardest and most accurate left foot shot in the game. He used this to good effect from the penalty spot, especially at Southampton where his record of 20 out of 22 earned him the title of "Penalty King". He played in Reading's first league game, at Newport on 28 August 1920, creating the club's first goal in the League and was virtually ever-present in that first League season. Again, he left Reading for Southampton where he helped them to the Third Division South title in 1922.

Reading Record: Lge 33/5, FAC 13/3, SL 67/12, Total 113/20
League Career Total: 130/14

LEN'S CLAIM TO FAME - Len played for the Southern League representative side on five occasions including the side's very last game, v Corinthians, before the league was absorbed into the Third Division.

ARCHER Phillip
b. Rotherham 25.8.1952
Ht 5ft 8 Wt 10st 6 (71-72)
Career: Sheffield U. apprentice 1968; READING (trial) August 1970, professional 12 November 1970; Hillingdon Bor. (free) July 1972; Addlestone November 1975.

Phil was recommended to Reading by Fred Green, a former assistant of Reading manager Jack Mansell, when he was at Rotherham. Initially Phil suffered from home sickness and went back to Yorkshire for a short period, but his return to Elm Park was rewarded with a professional contract. Steady progress in the reserves plus good performances in the pre-season friendlies saw Phil make his League debut at right back at Hartlepool in Reading's first ever Fourth Division fixture. From then on Phil was used in a variety of defensive roles but his first team opportunities diminished when Mansell left the club in October and he was given a 'free' at the end of the season.

Reading Record: Lge 12(5)

ARCHIBALD Steven

b. Glasgow 27.9.1956
Ht 5ft 10 1/2 Wt 11st 6 (90-91)
Career: Crofoot U; Fernhill A; Clyde 1974; Aberdeen (£25,000) January 1978; Tottenham H. (£800,000) May 1980; Barcelona (£900,000) July 1984; Barga A; Blackburn R. (loan) March 1988; Hibernian 1988; Espanol 1990; St Mirren 1991; Clyde 1991; READING (trial) January 1992; Ayr U. 1992; Fulham 1992; East Fife player/manager 1994-1996; Benfica executive director August 1998; Airdrie chief executive

Reading have had few players who have won more varied honours in the game than Steve who, in his wide-ranging career, had won 27 Scottish caps, the Scottish and Spanish Leagues, the FA Cup, the UEFA Cup and played in the 1986 European Cup Final for Barcelona. His short spell with Reading was arranged through the contacts of manager Mark McGhee, a former teammate of Archibald. Steve played just one game for Reading, in January 1992 and was given little opportunity by a well-drilled Huddersfield defence to demonstrate the clever skills and deadly finishing that had made him such a dangerous forward.

Reading Record: Lge 1
League Career Total: 151(3)/64

ASABA Carl Edward

b. Westminster 28.1.1973
Ht 6ft 2 Wt 13st 4 (97-98)
Career: Carshalton; Kingstonian; Dulwich Ham; Brentford August 1994; Colchester U. (loan) February 1995; READING (£800,000) 7 August 1997; Gillingham (£590,000) 29 August 1998; Sheffield U. (£92,500) March 2001

A late starter to the professional game, Carl did not sign for Brentford until he had completed a Banking and Finance course at Middlesex University. Having spent the first season getting accustomed to League football, he made his mark in 1996-97 when he scored 23 League goals, including a seven minute hat-trick against Shrewsbury, as Brentford made it to the Second Division play-offs. His scoring had attracted the attention of several clubs, including Leeds, but just before the start of the 1997-98 season Terry Bullivant paid a club record fee to bring him to Reading and earned Dulwich £40,000. Initially, Carl struggled in Division One, but he was a striker in the Stan Collymore mould - at his most dangerous when running at defences. Unfortunately, he was rarely given the opportunity to display his undoubted skills as Reading finished bottom of the division. The appointment of Tommy Burns sealed Carl's Reading fate as he never made the new manager's starting line-up and in August 1998 he was sold to Gillingham at a loss of £210,000. He was soon back amongst the goals, ending up top scorer with 20 goals, including the winner against Reading, plus another in the play-off final at Wembley.

His success at Gillingham has only fueled the debate as to whether he should have been kept at Reading, with the fans still split down the middle.

Reading Record: Lge 31(2)/8, FAC 3/1, LC 8/3, Total 42(2)/12
League Career Total: 164(22)/74 +

ASHDOWN Jamie Lawrence

b. Reading 30.11.1980
Ht 6ft 1 Wt 13st 5 (00-01)
Career: READING youth academy 1999; Bishop's Stortford (loan) October 2000: Gravesend &Northfleet (loan) March 2001

Jamie showed such promise while playing in goal for Reading's Youth Academy team that the club were able to sell its other promising young keeper, England youth international Shaun Allaway, to Leeds for £250,000. Even so, Jamie was still a long way down the pecking order but retirements and transfers saw him start 2000-01 as Reading's substitute keeper. The commanding young player made his League debut in September 2000 when he was given 16 minutes against Oldham and immediately set up Reading's fifth goal with an astute throw -out.

Reading Record: Lge (1) +

ASHTON John

b. Reading 4.7.1954
Ht 5ft 9 Wt 10st 10 (75-76)
Career: Battle A; READING non contract, professional 1 January 1975; Didcot February 1976; Hungerford T. July 1976

A regular member of Reading's youth sides without being offered an apprenticeship, John progressed to the reserves and was their top scorer when he was given his League debut in the last home game of 1971-72, against Colchester in what was Reading's youngest ever team. He continued on a semi-professional basis while working for a local engineering firm, until January 1975 when his work rate and goals for the reserves persuaded Charlie Hurley to reward the speedy forward with a full time contract and a run in the first team. John had a reputation as a dressing room joker but, unfortunately, despite all his efforts, he didn't quite come up to what the club needed to push for promotion and he was released.

Reading Record: Lge 10(3)/1

JOHN'S CLAIM TO FAME - In August 1977 John scored Hungerford's winner in a friendly against the Kuwait World Cup squad.

AYRE Robert William

b. Berwick 26.3.1932
Ht 5ft 9 Wt 10st 8 (59-60)
Career: Chippenham T; Charlton A. July 1952; READING
(£7,000) 21 May 1958; Weymouth June 1960

Bobby's first honours came in 1950 when, as a member of Berwick's Air Cadet Force, he was picked to play for both the England and Great Britain ACF teams. His National Service in the RAF took him to Wiltshire and, there he was spotted by Charlton. A skilful, nippy centre forward, he made his League debut in 1953 and was soon attracting the attention of other national selectors, being capped at both England B and Under 23 level. His second and last U23 appearance lasted under 60 seconds as he was stretchered off with a dislocated elbow. Fortunately, he recovered in time to be part of the FA tour of South Africa in 1956, scoring four goals in nine games. A regular scorer at Charlton, Bobby continued in the same vein at Elm Park. But although he was rarely short of a goal, his second season with Reading was hampered by a knee injury that caused him to retire from League football at the end of 1960-61. At least this allowed him to concentrate on his other passion, golf, and in 1966 he scored a hole in one at a local course.

Reading Record: Lge 57/24, FAC 6/2, SPFC 2, Total 65/26
League Career Total: 166/72

BACON Arthur

b. Birdholme 2nd qtr 1905 d. Derby 1.1941
Ht 6ft Wt 12st (29-30)
Career: New Tupton Ivanhoe; Chesterfield; Derby Co. 1924; Manchester C. December 1928; READING (£750) 1 June 1929; Chesterfield (£600) 6 June 1932; Coventry C. July 1933; Burton T. March 1937

A big, burly centre forward, Arthur enjoyed his best goalscoring spell at Elm Park - despite playing in a struggling team for the most part - and so gave good value for 'the big fee' he cost. He rarely roamed from the centre of the pitch where his finishing skills and willingness to give goalies a tough time were used to good effect.

This was never better displayed than in 1930-31 when, despite being relegated, Arthur scored 29 League goals in just 32 games. Included in this total was a remarkable six goal haul in a 7-3 win over Stoke on Good Friday that, not surprisingly, remains a club record. Later on, at Coventry he regained his multiple scoring skills, netting five and then four goals in consecutive Saturdays, but Arthur's dominance in the air was to cost him dearly as he lost his sight in one eye when it was damaged by a football lace. Sadly, Arthur was killed during an air raid while serving as a special constable in Derby.

Reading Record: Lge 69/44, FAC 4/1, Total 73/45
League Career Total: 128/71

BACUZZI Reno David

b. Highgate 12.10.1940
Ht 6ft Wt 12st 3 (68-69)
Career: Eastbourne U; Arsenal from amateur May 1959; Manchester C. (£20,000) April 1964; READING (free) 9 September 1966; Cork Hibs player, player-manager summer 1970; Home Park manager 1975

The son of Fulham, England and, as a Wartime guest, Reading full back, Joe Bacuzzi, Dave was spotted by Ron Greenwood while he was manager of Eastbourne. Dave followed the future England manager to Arsenal but delayed signing pro until he had won the last of his seven England Youth caps, playing alongside the likes of Geoff Hurst and Nobby Stiles. Ron had switched Dave from centre half to right back and it was in this position that he made irregular First Division appearances. Dave was a fine athlete but a loss of confidence at Highbury led to him moving to Manchester City before Reading. At Elm Park he quickly established himself as a crowd favourite with his stylish play and devastating sliding tackles. Apart from a spell out with a broken leg in 1967-68 he was virtually ever-present, captaining the side in the following season. However, the arrival of manager Jack Mansell saw him lose his place and in the summer of 1970 he joined Cork Hibernian. Dave was soon appointed their player-manager and won the League and Cup with Cork. He was also selected for the League of Ireland side and was voted Eire's 'Soccer Personality of the Year' in 1974. He is unlikely to be unemployed outside of football as he had completed a printing apprenticeship, trained as a publican and worked as a travel agent.

Reading Record: Lge 107/1, FAC 9, LC 2, Total 118/1
League Career Total: 209(1)/1

BAGGETT Walter John

b. Derby 29.5.1901 d. ?
Ht 5ft 8 Wt 10st 4 (29-30)
Career: Victoria Ironworks; Bolton W.1921; READING (£1,000) February 1928; Colwyn Bay summer 1930; READING (£70.12.11d) March 1931; Tunbridge Wells Rngrs 1933; later Barrow trainer 1964.

Known as 'Jack' at Bolton, and 'Bill' at Reading, this clever inside forward waited three years before making his League debut at Bolton where he was used as a deputy for David Jack. He was particularly unfortunate in 1926 when he played in every round of Bolton's FA Cup run, scoring in the semi-final, but missed out on a Wembley appearance. On moving to Reading Bill was a regular in the Second Division side, but over the next two seasons first team games became less frequent. At the end of 1929-30 he failed to agree terms and played for Colwyn Bay until returning to Elm Park in lieu of the receipts of a friendly between the two clubs, hence a rather unusual transfer fee. Bill regained his first team place for a while, scoring the opening goal on Reading's international tour when they beat Holland 3-1.

Reading Record: Lge 77/20, FAC 2, Total 79/20
Total League Career: 101/30

BILL'S CLAIM TO FAME - While in the RAF, Bill was sent to Greece by the British Council but when the War broke out he escaped to Turkey where he coached Galatasary to two cup triumphs.

BAILEY Danny Stephen

b. Leyton 21.5.1964
Ht 5ft 8 Wt 11st 6 (96-97)
Career: Bournemouth apprentice 1980; Evagoras, Cyprus; Dagenham; Woodford; Walthamstow Ave; Torquay U. non contract March 1984; Grays A; Haringey Bor; Wealdstone; Exeter (free) August 1989; READING (£50,000) 24 December 1990; Fulham (loan) July 1992; Exeter C. (free) 7 December 1992; Slough T. summer 1997; Forest Green 1998

Despite making his League debut with Bournemouth at 16, Danny had to serve a long non-League apprenticeship before finally getting a professional contract with Exeter at the age of 25. He made up for lost time by being an ever-present in his first season during which he won a PFA Divisional award as Exeter won the Fourth Division title. Danny then came to Reading, when new chairman, John Madejski gave a Christmas present to the club by paying £50,000 out of his own pocket to bring the midfielder to Elm Park. He quickly won over the Reading fans with his committed, ball winning displays and spectacular long range shooting but the appointment of Mark McGhee as manager saw his first team opportunities decline.

Reading Record: Lge 49(1)/2, FAC 3, Total 52(1)/2
League Career Total: 259(13)/8

BAILEY Walter George 'Joe'

b. Thame 9.2.1890 d Weymouth 20.7.1974
Ht 5ft 7 1/2 Wt 10st 6 (20-21)
Career: Oxford C; Nottingham For. 1910; READING amateur September 1911, professional August 1912: Bournemouth August 1921; Sittingbourne 1922

Christened Walter, known as Joe, and nicknamed 'Bubbles', Joe Bailey was a great local sportsman who, in addition to being revered at Reading as a goal-scoring inside forward, played cricket for Berkshire, hockey for Oxfordshire and was a qualified referee. In 1913 he won two amateur international caps, against Belgium and Holland, scoring twice in both, but wrote himself into Reading's history books when he scored the club's very first League goal, at Newport on 28 August 1920. That was not the first vital goal Joe had scored for Reading as he and his forward partner, Alan Foster, always seem to raise their games for some great pre World War One cup-ties. A week after his goal at Newport, Joe scored Reading's first League hat-trick, again against Newport, and ended the season top scorer with 18 goals. He left Reading at the end of that first League season to coach cricket at Warwick School but carried on playing non-League football and in 1922 he hit seven goals in a game for Sittingbourne. During World War One, Joe was promoted from private to captain and won the DSO and Military Cross with two bars for acts of bravery.

Reading Record: Lge 41/17, FAC 15/5, SL 145/58, Total 201/80
League Career Total: 45/18

JOE'S CLAIM TO FAME - On a train journey back from Northampton, Joe plucked up courage to sell a ticket for his benefit League game to a fellow passenger, the Prince of Wales. It was just as well that the future Edward VII did not attend the game as a ladies game against Swindon raised more money for Joe than his designated benefit game.

BAILIE Colin James
b. Belfast 31.3.1964
Ht 5ft 11 Wt 10st 11 (86-87)
Career: Swindon T. from apprentice March 1982; READING
(£22,500) June 1985; Cambridge U. (£25,000) summer 1988;
Wycombe W. 1992; Eynesbury R. 1992

Colin graduated through Swindon's youth teams to
make his League debut in their 1981-82 relegation
season as well as earning five Northern Ireland Youth
caps. In 1985 Ian Branfoot signed him at the second
attempt, having offered Lawrie Sanchez in exchange for
the talented young full back a year earlier. In his first
season Colin featured in both full back berths as
Reading won the Third Division title but after that he
was more or less exclusively used at right back. In 1988
he was ever-present in the Simod Cup run to Wembley,
scoring his second goal for the club in the quarter-final
tie against Bradford. That summer he moved to
Cambridge at a tribunal fixed fee and helped them rise
from the Fourth to the Second Division play-offs and
played in their memorable Cup runs. Having just lost in
the play-offs for the Premiership, he surprisingly quit
football to become a policeman in Penrith.

Reading Record: Lge 83(1)/1, FAC 5(2), LC 9, AMC 1,
FMC 8/1, Total 106(3)/2
League Career Total: 292(18)/8

BAINBRIDGE Kenneth Victor
b. Barking 15.1.1921
Ht 5ft 7 Wt 10st (50-51)
Career: Leyton; West Ham U. 1945; READING (player
exchange) 23 June 1950; Southend U. (£500) 9 February 1953;
Chelmsford C. June 1955

The War meant that
Ken did not start his
professional career
until he was 24 when
he joined West Ham.
Then injuries inter-
rupted his career at
Upton Park and in
1950 they swapped
him for Reading centre
half, Vic Niblett. The
injury jinx appeared to
have followed him to Elm
Park as he broke his collar bone after
just three games which
restricted his appearances in
that first season. There were no such problems in
1951-52 when he made the number 11 shirt his own
and played a major part in Reading's record 112 goal
total. A speedy left winger he produced an endless
supply of crosses for Ron Blackman while his

powerful two footed shooting saw him score 19 goals,
a club record for a winger that was to stand for 25 years.
He continued to hold down his place until Reading
signed Wally Hinshelwood in December 1952 and two
months later Ken moved to Southend.

Reading Record: Lge 89/32, FAC 8/3, Total 97/35
League Career Total: 247/73

BALMFORTH George W.
b. Denaby 2nd qtr 1902 d ?
Ht 5ft 8 Wt 11st 7 (29-30)
Career: Sheffield Wed; READING June 1930; Oswestry T.
summer 1932

George was a defensive wing half who, like the rest of
Reading's defence that season, struggled in the Second
Division. Consequently, he was only once on the
winning side in nine appearances as the club was
relegated with 96 goals conceded. Things failed to
improve for George in the Third Division South and he
was not retained in April 1932. Despite his few first
team appearances, George stuck in the fans memories as
he always played with what appeared to be a toothpick
in his mouth.

Reading Record: Lge 10

BARCLAY John Birrell
b. Thornton 22.1.1904 d. ?
Ht 5ft 8 Wt 11st 5 (26-27)
Career: Dundee; READING (trial) August 1926, permanent
September 1926; Accrington Stan. summer 1927; Yeovil
summer 1929

Signed as cover for John Robson, John only got into the
number 11 shirt three times during his one season at Elm
Park as Robson continued to make the left wing slot his
own. Reading were unbeaten in those three games but
in the penultimate game of the season, Barclay was tried
on the inside left position.

Reading Record: Lge 4
League Career Total: 80/11

BARKER Geoffrey Arthur
b. Hull 7.2.1949
Ht 6ft Wt 12st (75-76)
Career: Hull C. 1968; Southend U. (loan) December 1970;
Darlington (free) July 1971; READING (£5,000) 12 February
1975; Grimsby T. (free) July 1977

Geoff came to prominence with Darlington where he
established himself as the strong and reliable kingpin of
their defence.

During 1974-75, he had won by February, six man-of-the-match awards for them, including one against Reading, when Charlie Hurley bought him to replace John Hulme. The balding centre half immediately settled into the team and played an important role the following season as Reading won their first promotion for 50 years by finishing third in the Fourth Division. Unfortunately, Geoff was finding the cost of living in the South too much and in July 1976 he quit football to return to his native Hull as a builder. The lure of football proved too great and six months later he re-signed for Reading. His last appearance for Reading was in Charlie Hurley's last match in charge and he was released by Maurice Evans at the end of the season.

Reading Record: Lge 51(1)/2, FAC 1, Total 52(1)/2
League Career Total: 322(2)/11

GEOFF'S CLAIM TO FAME - Before joining Reading in February 1975, Geoff had already made 34 League appearances for Darlington that season. With Reading he increased his season's total to a record 50 League games in one season.

BARKUS Lea Paul
b. Reading 7.12.1974
Ht 5ft 6 Wt 9st 13 (96-97)
Career: READING YTS 1991, professional 13 August 1992; Fulham (£20,000) 1 July 1995; Hibernian, Malta 1996; Carshalton 1997

Local youngster Lea looked a great prospect as he progressed through Reading's youth ranks, including a hat trick in each half of a 1990 youth match. This appeared to be borne out by a sparkling League debut when, as a 17 year old, he gave Chester's former Manchester United and Scotland's Arthur Albiston a torrid afternoon. A goal in his next home game looked to have set Lea up for a run on the right side of midfield but he began to suffer from a nagging back problem that eventually required surgery in May 1993. This robbed him of the chance of being part of Reading's Division Two Championship team but he was compensated to some extent by helping the club win the Berks & Bucks Senior Cup for the first time in over 100 years. Despite not making a first team appearance for two seasons former Reading boss, Ian Branfoot, was still sufficiently impressed to pay £20,000 to take the youngster to Fulham. Unfortunately, he suffered further injuries and a League career, that had looked so promising for the skilful youngster with an eye for the half chance, was over.

Reading Record: Lge 8(7)/1, FAC (1), AMC 1, Total 9(8)/1
League Career Total: 11(13)/2

BARLEY John Charles
b. Staveley 10.1904 d. 5.9.1962
Ht 5ft 9 Wt 11st 2 (29-30)
Career: Staveley; Arsenal 1926; READING (player exchange) May 1929; Maidenhead U. coach-groundsman summer 1937

"One of the cleverest ball manipulators who has ever donned a blue and white jersey" was how the Reading Supporters' Club notes described Charlie in the run-up to his benefit match against Chelsea reserves in 1934. Charlie had come to Reading from Arsenal in exchange for centre forward Bill Johnstone five years earlier, with the intention that he should replace the club's regular left half, Tommy Meads, who had also moved to North London when he joined Spurs. While at Highbury, Charlie, an ex-miner, won three Combination championships. For his first four seasons he was a fixture in Reading's first team, usually at left half but the signing of Billy Wright saw Charlie only getting the occasional first team game in his less favoured forward position. Charlie's son, Derek, captained England Youth in 1948-49 and, like his father, went on to play for Arsenal although he never made it to their first team.

Reading Record: Lge 194/16, FAC 19, SSC 1, Total 214/16
League Career Total: 202/17

BARNARD Darren Sean
b. Rintein, Germany, 30.11.1971
Ht 5ft 10 Wt 12st (94-95)
Career: Wokingham T; Chelsea (£50,000) July 1990; READING (loan) 18 November 1994; Bristol C. (£175,000) October 1996; Barnsley (£750,000) August 1997

Despite his birthplace and his being a Chelsea man, Darren was very much a local player when he joined Reading on a month's loan in 1994, having played alongside Reading regulars, Stuart Lovell and Adrian Williams, at Wokingham while still a schoolboy. An England schoolboy international at Under 18 level, Darren was only on the fringe of Chelsea's first team so he jumped at the chance of first team football on loan to Reading. Playing on the left side of midfield he proved a competent player with an obviously classy left foot and can claim that his introduction to Reading's away game at Portsmouth, as sub, was Mark McGhee's last act as Reading manager before resigning the following week. Darren became one of Barnsley's successes during their Premiership season, and discovered a Welsh relative to earn him full international honours for them. A season later and five years to the day after his former Wokingham Town and Reading teammate, Stuart Lovell, had a penalty saved in the Division One play-off final, Darren suffered the same fate with Barnsley.

Reading Record: Lge 3(1)
League Record Total: 215(28)/38 +

DARREN'S CLAIM TO FAME - Darren suffered one of football's more unusual injuries, being out for five months after slipping on an 'accident' left by his new puppy!

BARNES Michael Frederick

b Reading 17.9.1963
Ht 6ft 4 Wt 13st (81-82)
Career: Mapledurham; Wokingham T; READING apprentice 14 May 1980, professional 17 September 1981; Northampton T. (free) August 1984; Maidenhead U; Wycombe W. February 1988; Chesham U.

Michael came to prominence in the Reading schools team that reached the quarter-finals of the English Schools trophy in 1978 and was a graduate of his local club's youth policy. While an apprentice with Reading he was picked for the England Youth squad on a couple of occasions and played for an FA XI in their annual fixture against the Public Schools in January 1981. Three months later, the young, tall centre half was making his League debut, but despite his aerial dominance, Hicks, Hetzke and Wood were already established central defenders so first team chances were rare. Strangely, Michael's best season was one of Reading's worst - the 1982-83 relegation season saw him play almost half the games and score a couple of point winning goals. Michael's League career was ended by a knee injury sustained with Northampton.

Reading Record: Lge 29(5)/2, LC 2/1, FLT 2, AMC 1, Total 34(5)/3
League Record Total: 48(5)/3

BARNEY Victor Roy

b Stepney 3.4.1922
Ht 5ft 8 Wt 10st 10 (48-49)
Career: Oxford C; READING August 1946; Bristol C. October 1948; Grimsby T. June 1949

Few players have had a more dramatic rise to fame than Vic. As a 24 year old amateur, Vic turned up unannounced at Elm Park to ask for a trial and within two weeks he was making a starring debut in Reading's record 10-2 win over Crystal Palace. His next game saw another goal and another big win so Vic looked to become a permanent fixture at inside left. However, Reading were well served for inside forwards and Vic found himself playing in either inside berth or at wing half. Although those first two goals were his last in that first season, Vic was a regular scorer from then on and always displayed the necessary skills to ensure that he never let the side down wherever he was used.

At the start of 1948-49 Vic netted four times in seven games, form which inspired Bristol City to move in for his services.

Reading Record: Lge 45/12, FAC 2/2, Total 47/14
League Career Total: 80/16

BARRAS Anthony

b. Billingham 29.3.1971
Ht 6ft Wt 13st (98-99)
Career: Billingham Synthonia; Stockton; Hartlepool U. from trainee July 1989; Stockport Co. July 1990; Rotherham U. (loan) February 1994; York C. (£25,000) July 1994; READING (loan) 19 March 1999, permanent (£20,000) 25 March 1999; Walsall (£20,000) 26 July 1999

After five years as a professional, during which he played for Stockport in the play-off finals and the Auto Windscreen Trophy final, Tony came to his peak at York. There he developed into the kingpin of their defence and his form saw him named their Clubman of the Year in 1997, which resulted in him being valued at £350,000. By March 1999 he only had three months of his contract to go so York's fear of losing him on a Bosman free allowed Reading to sign him for a cut price fee. He immediately displayed his composed defensive skills while his strength in the air saw him head home an equalizer at Luton in his second appearance for Reading. Despite his displays, Reading had several players fighting for the central defensive role and, along with the need to reduce the club wage bill, Tony was surprisingly sold to newly promoted Walsall after just four months. Two years later he was a member of the Walsall team that beat Reading in the play-off final.

Reading Record: Lge 4(2)/1
League Career Total: 331(22)/23 +

BARRON Paul George

b. Woolwich 16.9.1953
Ht 6ft 2 Wt 13st 5 (86-87)
Career: Slough T; Plymouth Arg. July 1976; Arsenal July 1978; Crystal Palace (£300,000) August 1980; West Bromwich Alb. (£60,000) December 1982; Stoke C. (loan) January 1985; QPR March 1985; READING (loan) December 1986; Welling 1988; Birmingham (loan) March 1992; Aston Villa fitness consultant.

A widely travelled goalie who had attracted some big transfer fees, Paul came to Reading on a month's loan to give Gary Westwood a chance to restore his confidence after some heavy defeats. Everything went to plan as Paul was only on the losing side once in four games and Westwood returned more effective in a defence better organised after the loanee's guidance. Paul returned to Elm Park in December 1989 with Welling and it was his form that resulted in Reading taking four games to knock the non-Leaguers out of the Cup.

Reading Record: Lge 4
League Career Total: 242

BARTHOLOMEW Frederick Charles

b. Reading 3.1.1885, d. 24 April 1979
Ht 5ft 7 1/2 Wt 12 st 2 (11-12)
Career: Reading Biscuit Factory; Reading Amateurs; New Inn; READING amateur April 1904, professional June 1906

Arguably Reading's greatest club servant, Fred played for the club in every position although he was usually a centre half and then, later in his career, a full back. In 1923 he retired as a player to join Reading's training staff before becoming the groundsman at Elm Park until he was nearly seventy. This makes Fred's introduction to the club even more remarkable. On Good Friday 1904 he turned up at Elm Park to watch a local cup final but when one of the sides were a man short Fred made up the numbers and scored a hat trick! Not surprisingly, Reading snapped him up straight away. A regular for Berkshire as well, he won a Southern League Division Two Champions medal in 1910-11 while, during the First World War, he won a Divisional Football Tournament Championship medal while with the Footballer's Battalion. He fought in France, rising to the rank of Company Quartermaster Sergeant, before returning to Reading. At the age of 36 he played in Reading's first League season to add to the 150 plus Southern League appearances for Reading. The famous set of Brigham cigarette cards describe him as a *Very consistent and clever player. The hotter the fight the better he plays. He weighs 12 st 3 but he can move'* but to many residents of Reading he was simply known as 'Old Bart'

Reading Record: Lge 6, FAC 14, SL 158/9, Total 178/9

BARTON Douglas Joseph

b. Islington 31.7.1927
Ht 5ft 9 Wt 10st 12 (49-50)
Career: Ford Sports; READING amateur 1947, professional 8 February 1949; Newport Co. January 1953

A dependable right back for five years with Reading, Doug was rarely given the chance of a run in the first team so his best season's total was only four games. Not surprisingly, Doug was keen to get a first team place so he moved to Newport in 1953.

Reading Record: Lge 10
League Career Total: 33

BASHIR Naseem

b. Amersham 12.9.1969
Ht 5ft 6 Wt 10st 6 (89-90)
Career: Marlow; READING YTS July 1986, professional April 1988; Slough T summer 1990; Aylesbury; St Albans 1996; Maidenhead U; Marlow 2000: Yeading joint manager March 2001

One of several YTS players to be offered professional contracts after Reading's Youth team reached the semi-finals of the FA Youth Cup in 1988, Nas was a skilful right-sided midfield player. He was unable to capitalize on that momentum as he suffered a broken ankle at the start of the next season but enjoyed a short run in the first team in September 1989, that included a goal in his only League start, at home to Chester. While at Reading, Nas developed a keen interest in coaching and had begun his FA qualifications, as well as assisting at the club's Centre of Excellence, by the time he was released. He went on to serve a number of local non-League clubs as well as working as Wycombe Wanderer's community officer.

Reading Record: Lge 1(2)/1, LC (1), Total 1(3)/1

NAS'S CLAIM TO FAME - In 1987, Nas played for Reading in a friendly against Brondby IF and scored their consolation goal against the Dane's young keeper who was making his British debut - Peter Schmeichel.

BASON Brian

b. Epsom 3.9.1955
Ht 5ft 9 1/2 Wt 12st (82-83)
Career: Epsom; Chelsea from apprentice September 1972; Plymouth Arg. (£30,000) January 1978; Crystal Palace March 1981; Portsmouth (loan) January 1981; READING (trial) 12 August 1982, permanent September 1982; Three Bridges summer 1983

Brian had the difficult task of taking over Neil Webb's midfield role at Reading after the local favourite had been sold to Portsmouth. He was a far more defensive player than Webb but his experience proved an asset as Reading struggled at the foot of the Third Division while the club's existence was being threatened by the ill-fated 'Thames Valley Royals' merger plans with Oxford. The bulk of the former England Schools international's League experience was with Plymouth where he was virtually ever present for three years but it wasn't until Brian moved to Reading that he was a regular again. He made the second most appearances for Reading in 1982-83 but, although he was initially retained, he was subsequently released and after a spell in non-League football he gave up the game to run a hotel in Truro.

Reading Record: Lge 41, FAC 1, LC 2, AMC 2(2)/1, 46(2)/1
League Career Total: 219(6)/11

BASS David

b. Frimley 29.11.1974
Ht 6ft Wt 12st 2 (96-97)
Career: READING YTS 1991, professional 14 July 1993; Aldershot T. (loan) 1994; Basingstoke T. (loan) September 1996; Colchester U. (loan); Notts Co. (trial) May 1997; Rotherham U.   summer 1997; Carlisle U.   March 1999; Scarborough summer 1999; Kingstonians summer 2000

As a 14 year old David had a trial for the FA National School at Lilleshall but joined Reading as a YTS professional, making his League debut at Bournemouth in April 1992 when he marked Jimmy Case out of the game.   A powerful midfielder, David was voted Reading's Young Player of the Year in 1993 and made steady progress, but a loan spell to Aldershot in 1994 ended in disaster when he suffered cruciate ligament damage that took four operations and two years to repair. Released in 1997 he moved to Rotherham where he suffered his third broken nose and an operation on his hamstring before moving to Carlisle. Here he played in their vital last game of 1998-99 when they secured their League status with a 94th minute goal by their keeper. He subsequently joined Scarborough, the team relegated by that result.

Reading Record: Lge 7(4)
League Career Total: 28 (10)

BATT Victor Thomas

b. Sheppey 13.3.1943
Ht 5ft 7 Wt 10st 2 (61-62)
Career: READING from amateur 9 August 1961; Yiewsley July 1963

Vic was spotted playing in a Kent youth league and played for Reading at a time when the club had a successful youth team. He helped them win an Under 18 tournament in Germany, represented Berkshire Boys Clubs and was in the team that lost in the 1960 Southern Junior Cup final against an all-star Chelsea side. He could play at right back or on the wing and it was in the forward position that he made all his first team appearances, making his debut on the left at Bournemouth on January 1961, but making the rest on the right. Although he signed professional terms for the start of the next season, he was on a part time basis while he completed his printing apprenticeship before leaving for a long career with Yiewsley (later Hillingdon Borough) that included a Wembley appearance with them in the 1971 FA Trophy Final.

Reading Record: Lge 15, LC 1, Total 16

BATTEN Herbert George

b. Bristol 14.5.1898 d. Chelsea 15.5.1956
Ht 5ft 8 Wt 11st 10 (27-28)
Career: Bristol C; Plymouth Arg. 1921; Everton (£2,000) 1925; Bradford C. 1926; READING (£300) June 1927; Clapton O. (£335) February 1928

Having started with his home town team, Bristol City, Bert found fame at Plymouth where he was selected for an FA tour of Australia in May 1925. The top scorer on the tour, he scored six in one game and five out of eight in the unofficial international against Australia. This attracted the attention of several clubs, including Reading, but everyone was outbid by Everton. By the time Reading finally got their man, his fee had dropped to £300 which was still regarded as substantial. Bert never really settled in the Reading first team and the goalscoring skills that were such a feature of his game had deserted the inside forward. He was tried in several positions but the signing of Johnny Hunter for his favoured inside left role left him surplus to Reading's needs.

Reading Record: Lge 12/2, FAC 2/1, Total 14/3
League Career Total: 177/40

BAYLISS Ronald

b. Belfast 20.9.1944
Ht 5ft 9 Wt 10st 10 (66-67)
Career: READING from apprentice 1 February 1965; Bradford C. July 1968; Folkestone July 1970; Yeovil 1971; Folkestone August 1972

Ron progressed through Reading's youth system, making his League debut in the last game of 1964-65. From then his chances were restricted to the odd game at left half but in September 1967 Ron took over at right back when Dave Bacuzzi broke his leg. This gave him a three month run but when Bacuzzi was fit, Ron was back to filling in when others were injured. He was released at the end of that season and became Jimmy Wheeler's first signing as manager of Bradford City. He helped City to promotion from the Fourth Division that season and later won another honour when, in 1970-71, he helped Yeovil win the Southern League.

Reading Record: Lge 35(3)/1, FAC 4, LC 3, Total 42(3)/1
League Career Total: 70(7)/1

RON'S CLAIM TO FAME - Ron was not noted for possessing a powerful shot but during a League Cup-tie at Arsenal in 1967 he hit the bar with a shot of such force that the ball bounced out of the ground and later it was necessary for the crossbar to be re-aligned.

BEAVON Michael **Stuart**

b. Wolverhampton 30.11.1958
Ht 5ft 7 Wt 10st 8 (80-81)
Career: Tottenham H. from apprentice July 1976; Notts Co (loan) September 1979; READING (£35,000) July 1980; Northampton T. August 1990, assist player manager April 1992; Newbury T. summer 1993; Chesham U. September 1995; Kintbury; Reading T. January 1998

Although born in the Midlands, Stuart's family moved to Oxford when he was only five weeks old following his father, Cyril's, transfer from Wolves to Oxford United. A member of the Oxford Schools side at every age, Stuart made his debut at Elm Park at the age of 10 when he played for Oxford's primary schools against Reading as centre forward, being marked by Lawrie Sanchez. By the time he had helped Oxford U15s to the final of the English Schools Trophy he had moved into the midfield and was on Spurs' books.

Stuart netted 42 goals in 102 reserve games for Spurs but only made three first team starts and, after turning down £50,000 from Notts County after a loan spell, they let him join Reading. A scoring debut heralded the start of a 10 year stay in which he was a mainstay of the club's midfield, playing an average of 40 League games a season, providing a rare element of stability in a turbulent decade. 1985-86 saw Reading win their first 13 League games of the season as they ran away with the Third Division title, with Stuart scoring the opening goal of the record breaking game at Newport. Stuart was also on target in the club's greatest moment, equalizing from the penalty spot in Reading's Simod Cup thrashing of the, then, First Division Luton. That was not Stuart's first penalty success at Wembley - in 1974 he scored five out of six against Gordon Banks in a pre Cup Final schoolboy competition. After 10 years of skilful prompting on the right side of Reading's midfield that produced countless goals, many of them from his floated dead ball kicks, Stuart was released to Northampton but returned to Elm Park in January 1991 for a well deserved testimonial match.

Reading Record: Lge 380(16)/44, FAC 31(1)/3, LC 26(2)/2, AMC 15(2)/3, FMC 8/3, Total 460(21)/55
League Record Total: 484(20)/58

STUART'S CLAIM TO FAME - Stuart played a starring, but uncredited role, in the TV series The Manageress that was filmed at Elm Park. The fictitious team had to stop a penalty, taken by Stuart, to win promotion and it took 10 attempts before the actor/ goalie could make a save to the satisfaction of the director. Back in the League, Stuart's next penalty was saved and he blamed this on having to practice missing spot kicks for the TV programme!

BEDFORD Noel **Brian**

b. Ferndale 24.12.1933
Ht 5ft 11 Wt 11st 5 (54-55)
Career: Beddau Youth Club; READING amateur 27 February 1954, professional April 1954; Southampton July 1955; Bournemouth August 1956; QPR (£750) July 1959; Scunthorpe U. September 1965; Brentford September 1966; Atlanta Chiefs April 1967; Bexley U. November 1968

Despite scoring seven goals on his Reading youth debut, Brian's start as a professional with, first Reading and then Southampton, did little to suggest that the young centre forward would develop into the most feared goalscorer of his day in the Third Division. The goals started going in at Bournemouth but it was when he moved to QPR for just £750 that his true form became apparent. Their top scorer in all six seasons at Loftus Road, he scored a club record 38 goals in 1961-62 and then equalled it the next season, ending up with 180 for Rangers in 283 first team games. After a 14 year football career, Brian worked as a tennis coach and then as a maintenance engineer back at Loftus Road.

Reading Record: Lge 3/1
League Career Total: 399/229

BELL Terence John

b. Sherwood 1.8.1944
Ht 5ft 10 Wt 10st 10 (70-71)
Career: Burton Alb; Nottingham For. (trial) August 1964; Manchester C. (trial) October 1964; Portsmouth; Nuneaton Bor. 1965; Hartlepools U. July 1966; READING (£11,000) 26 February 1970; Aldershot (free) July 1973; Wokingham T. 1978; Hillingdon Bor. (trial) February 1981.

After several false starts, Terry finally made his League debut with Hartlepool after he was spotted by their manager, Brian Clough. His strong, skilful centre forward play saw him finish 'Pool's top scorer in their 1967-68 promotion season while the following campaign he scored two stunning goals against Reading. His transfer to Reading was for a record Hartlepool fee but, more importantly, it saved them from going into receivership. Despite his transfer in February, Terry remained Hartlepool's top scorer that season.

The end of the 1970-71 season saw mixed emotions for Terry - shortly after he was voted the fans Player of the Year he had the misfortune to score the own goal at Villa Park that relegated Reading to the Fourth Division. The next two seasons saw Terry often used in a deeper role so his goal scoring return was reduced but he was, none the less, always an effective player for Reading.

Reading Record: Lge 82(5)/20, FAC 7/1, LC 2(1), Watney Cup 1, Total 92(6)/21
League Career Total: 305(23)/103

TERRY'S CLAIM TO FAME - Terry was closely involved in the formation of the now successful Reading Ladies football team and his wife, Ann, was the side's first captain.

BENCE Paul Ian
b. Littlehampton 21.12.1948
Ht 5ft 9 Wt 11st (69-70)
Career: Brighton from apprentice May 1967; READING (free) 20 June 1968; Brentford July 1970; Hillingdon Bor. (loan) November 1973; Torquay U. (loan) November 1976; Wokingham T. player/coach 1977; QPR youth team manager June 1978; Wycombe W. manager 1984 to January 1986

Paul made just one appearance as sub during his spell with his local League club, Brighton, before he became the only player to be signed for Reading by Jimmy Wheeler. He was given a run at left half towards the end of his first season and rewarded the club with some stylish performances plus a stunning long range winner against Rotherham. The arrival of Jack Mansell saw the flame haired Paul rarely used in the first team and he was released in May 1970, moving to Brentford. Here, he became a first team regular, being voted their Player of the Year in 1972-73 having helped them to win promotion the previous season.

Reading Record: Lge 12(2)/2
League Career Total: 255(9)/8

BENNETT John H
b. c.1900 d. ?
Ht 5ft 8 Wt 11st 10 (21-22)
Career: Brechin Nomads; READING September 1921

Little is known of John, an inside forward who played for Reading during 1921-22. He made his debut at inside right in the club's biggest win of the season, 5-0 over Merthyr, but that was an untypical bout of scoring in a season in which Reading failed to average a goal a game. A couple of brief runs at inside left failed to impress and a broken leg against Charlton reserves on Good Friday 1921 ended his Reading career.

Reading Record: Lge 9

BENNETT Paul Reginald
b. Southampton 4.2.1952
Ht 6ft Wt 12st 9 (77-78)
Career: Southampton from apprentice November 1969; READING (£8,000) July 1976; Aldershot (£25,000) August 1979; Road Sea Southampton player/coach July 1982; Salisbury summer 1987; Eastleigh manager April 1989; Andover October 1989

After a successful schoolboy career that saw him captain Southampton U15s to the semi-finals of the 1966 English Schools Trophy, it was logical that Paul should join Southampton, where he progressed through to their first team. From his debut in April 1972 he played more games than he missed and was a member of the Southampton squad that won the Cup in 1976. However, Paul had now been overtaken by Jim Steele at the Dell and so Reading were able to sign him at a bargain price. Paul quickly established himself as a classy addition to the centre of Reading's defence but he was unable to prevent the club from returning to the Fourth Division in his first season. In October 1977 he found himself in dispute the club over the effect a part time job was having on his availability but this was resolved and he was made club captain by March 1978. This proved the catalyst for both Paul and the club as he led Reading to the Fourth Division title in 1978-79 where his leadership and defensive skills played a major part, particularly in the run in when the team went the last 11 games without conceding a goal. Unfortunately, he could not agree terms with Reading at the end of that season so he joined Aldershot before going on a tour of Hampshire non-League clubs.

Reading Record: Lge 105/3, FAC 8, LC 11, Total 124/3
League Career Total: 333(1)/6

PAUL'S CLAIM TO FAME - When Paul made his Southampton debut, at Spurs, he marked Martin Chivers who had gone to the same school as him. The same game saw Mike England mark Ron Davies and, by coincidence, they had both attended the same school as well.

BERNAL Andrew

b. Canberra 16.5.1966
Ht 5ft 10 Wt 12st 5 (95-96)
Career: Sporting Gijon; Jerez (loan); Ipswich T. September 1987; Heracles; Sydney Olympic; READING (£30,000) 26 July 1994; European agent for SFX

Born in Australia of Spanish parents, Andy was a product of the famous Australian Institute of Sport where he played in the same cricket team as the Waugh twins. Although he had played for Sporting Gijon and Jerez in Spain, it was while on tour with the Institute that he was spotted by Ipswich. Just as he began to establish himself in their first team, work permit problems ended with him being deported. Strangely, his last start for Ipswich was at Reading the week after the Simod Cup triumph.

By 1994 the European Union work regulations had changed so Andy's Spanish passport enabled Reading to sign him. An accomplished full back, Andy soon settled into the right back spot where he used his strength and fitness to good effect as Reading went on to finish second in Division One. Forced to face the play-offs, Andy's injury in the final when Reading were leading Bolton 2-0, was seen by many as the turning point as Reading eventually lost 4-3. Andy also proved a fine central defender and has been used in the holding midfield role. His form brought him back into Australia's international team, winning his 22nd cap and playing in trial matches for European based Aussies, organised by Terry Venables. On occasions Andy's strength has worked against him in that he has suffered no fewer than eight red cards (although one was later rescinded) and some of these were due to his opponent coming off worse than Andy regardless of the legality of the challenge. By no means a dirty player, 'Skippy', as he was unimaginatively nicknamed, was always a crowd favourite and captained Reading on a number of occasions. In January 2000 he suffered a knee and foot injury that ended his career and he returned to Australia as a players agent.

Reading Record: Lge 179(8)/2, FAC 14/1, LC 17(2), AMC 3/1, Play-offs 3, Total 216(10)/4
League Career Total: 183(13)

BERTSCHIN Christian Frederick

b. Kensington 7.9.1924 d. 1995
Ht 5ft 11 Wt 11st 7 (49-50)
Career: Ilford; READING amateur 1945, professional 18 August 1947; Snowden Colliery 1951

Chris won a series of representative honours during the War and his amateur career, including an appearance for The Navy v Russia, plus games for the Isthmian League and Essex.

He was almost 23 when he was recommended to Reading by Bill Robson but within three months he was celebrating a scoring debut with Reading's final goal in a 3-3 FA Cup draw at Bromley. This was the start of a 10 match run on the left wing for the long striding player and then later in the season, Chris had a spell at outside right. In 1948-49 he was tried at centre forward for one game but in the next match a young Ron Blackman was given a chance and his hat-trick sealed the fate of both players. Despite topping the reserves scorers with 18 goals the following season, Chris was released into non-League football.

Reading Record: Lge 12/1, FAC 4/1, Total 16/2

BEWLEY David George

b. Bournemouth 22.9.1920
Ht 5ft 9 Wt 11st 6 (49-50)
Career: Wolverhampton W. amateur; Poole T; Bournemouth September 1937; Wartime guest for Aldershot, Southampton and Gravesend; Fulham May 1945; READING 14 March 1950; Fulham November 1951; Watford (£500) May 1953; Folkestone June 1956; Hemel Hempstead coach October 1957 to January 1959; Fulham scout April 1963

One of many players whose League career was delayed by the War, former England Schoolboy international, David, was 26 when he made his League debut for Fulham. Initially a full back, he had moved to left half by the time he joined Reading. He went straight into the first team and his cool and cultured play saw him keep his place to the end of the season, scoring his only goal in a 1-1 draw against Walsall. The summer signing of Jimmy Johnstone left David to make just one more League appearance before he returned to Fulham and then on to Watford where he made over 100 League appearances.

Reading Record: Lge 11/1
League Record Total: 141/3

BIBBO Salvatore

b. Basingstoke 24.8.1974
Ht 6ft 2 Wt 14st (96-97)
Career: Bournemouth apprentice; Crawley T; Sheffield U. August 1993; Chesterfield (loan) February 1995; Ards (loan); READING (free) 1 August 1996; Basingstoke T. summer 1998; Havant & Waterlooville 1999; Bath C. summer 2000

A solid keeper, Sal took a roundabout route to play for his nearest League club. His three years with Sheffield Utd produced just two Anglo Italian Cup appearances plus a substitute appearance while on loan with Chesterfield. Having been released by United in 1996, Sal impressed in pre-season friendlies for Reading and he was signed as cover for Bobby Mihailov.

He soon got his chance and in his third game he kept his first clean sheet in the televised local derby against Oxford. The signing of Steve Mautone pushed Sal down to third choice keeper but, ironically, Sal reserved his best performance for his last first team game for Reading, against his former club, Sheffield United, in the FA Cup.

Reading Record: Lge 7, FAC 2, Total 9
League Career Total: 7(1)

BILL Roger James
b. Cresswell 17.5.1944
Ht 5ft 7 Wt 10st 7 (62-63)
Career: Chelsea amateur; READING September 1962; Amersham T. summer 1963

A young right winger who joined Reading from Chelsea, Roger was one of five players to be tried in the right wing role during 1962-63 but, while he finished top scorer in the reserves, he met with less success in the first team. In fact, he was never on the winning side in the League and was released by the club at the end of his first season.

Reading Record: Lge 4

BISHTON Dennis Roy
b. Windsor 22.9.1950
Ht 5ft 9 Wt 10st 9 (69-70)
Career: READING apprentice 25 July 1966, professional 23 September 1968; Hillingdon Bor. August 1970; Basingstoke T. May 1971

Dennis was a nimble right back who progressed through Reading's youth teams to be signed as a professional on his 18th birthday. Six weeks later he was making his League debut, replacing Dave Bacuzzi but as soon as Bacuzzi was available, Dennis went back to the reserves and his League career was over, being released at the end of the following season.

Reading Record: Lge 2

BLACKMAN Ronald Henry
b. Cosham 2.4.1925
Ht 6ft Wt 11st 9 (51-52)
Career: Gosport Bor; READING (£10 + friendly) part time 27 February 1947, full time August 1947; Nottingham For. (£6,600) July 1954; Ipswich T. July 1955; Tonbridge July 1958

Thought by many Reading fans to be the club's best ever centre forward, Ron has the statistics on his side with only the equally popular Trevor Senior being able to match his record. Ron came to Reading's attention when he scored 93 goals for Gosport in just 67 games and his services were secured after his local League club, Portsmouth, rejected him. In his first full season he was mainly a reserve player, scoring 21 goals for the second XI as well as getting off the mark in his third League game.

The retirement of Tony MacPhee gave Ron his chance and a hat-trick in his first game of the 1948-49 season secured his first team place. From then on it was goals all the way - nine in 17 games that season were followed by 22, 35, 39, 24 and 28 in the League. The 39 in 1951-52 was the best in the Third Division South that season and remains a club best as does his total of 158 Reading League goals. He also scored five goals on two occasions, against Brighton in November 1950 and Southend April 1952. Brave and strong with a powerful shot in each foot, Ron was particularly deadly in the air, a fact borne out by the fact that 96 of his 167 Reading goals came from headers. It was inevitable that other clubs would be interested in such a prolific scorer and in the summer of 1954 Reading accepted an offer from Nottingham Forest amid great protests from the fans. The move to Forest did not work out and while a spell at Alf Ramsey's emerging Ipswich went better, Ron was troubled by a series of injuries including a damaged shoulder that eventually ended his career. Ron remains an extremely popular personality at Reading and his rare appearances before the crowd always guarantee him a great reception even though the majority present never saw him play.

Reading Record: Lge 228/158, FAC 12/9, Total 240/167
League Career Total: 266/173

RON'S CLAIM TO FAME - When Reading played a friendly under Swindon's new lights in 1951, Ron scored the only goal of the game and so became the first Reading player to score a floodlit goal.

BLATHERWICK Steven Scott
b. Nottingham 20.9.1973
Ht 6ft 1 Wt 14st (97-98)
Career: Notts Co. jnrs; Nottingham For. August 1992;
Wycombe W. (loan) February 1994; Hereford U. (loan)
September 1995; READING (loan) 27 March 1997; Burnley
(£150,000) July 1997; Chesterfield (loan) September 1998,
permanent (£50,000) December 1998

Never able to play more than a handful of first team
games for Forest in his five years with them, Steve had
to rely on loan spells to enhance his experience and this
was the case when he came to Reading to stand in for the
injured Barry Hunter. A solid central defender who was
rarely beaten in the air, Steve played an important part
in one of Reading's most memorable victories. A goal
down to arch rivals Wolves, Steve was pushed into the
forward line and created an injury time equalizer for
Stuart Lovell before Reading won the game, and
secured Division One survival, with a 96th minute
winner. At the end of his loan spell Steve returned to
Forest but only for a short time since he moved to
Burnley in the summer as new manager Chris Waddle's
first signing.

Reading Record: Lge 6(1)
League Career Total: 127(14)/3 +

BODIN Paul John
b. Cardiff 13.9.1964
Ht 6ft Wt 13st 1 (96-97)
Career: Chelsea jnrs; Newport Co. January 1982; Cardiff C.
August 1982; Bath C. summer 1985; Newport Co. (£15,000)
January 1988; Swindon T. (£30,000) March 1988; Crystal
Palace March 1991; Newcastle U. (loan) December 1991;
Swindon T. (£225,000) January 1992; READING (free) 8
July 1996; Wycombe W. (loan) September 1997; Bath C.
(free) player manager 21 April 1998; Swindon T. youth coach
summer 2001

Another player whose career appeared to be over when
he drifted into non-League football in his early twenties.
But Paul re-established his League career when he
joined Swindon at the age of 23. He won a PFA Second
Division award in 1990-91, and was a member of the
Swindon squad that won the Division Two play-offs but
were denied promotion because of financial irregularities.
A big money move to Palace did not work out and he
returned to Swindon. Paul won another play-off final
and another PFA award, but despite playing in 35 of
Swindon's 1995-96 Second Division championship
season he was allowed to join Reading. At Elm Park,
Paul had the unenviable task of following crowd
favourite, Dylan Kerr into the left back spot. He was
defensively sound but lacked Kerr's cavalier attacking
style and rapport with the crowd which made it hard for
Paul to win over the Reading supporters.

Despite the uncertainty of some fans, Paul's form was
good enough to win a recall into the Welsh squad
although he did not add to the 23 caps he had won with
Swindon. The following season was a torrid time for
both club and player with Paul only making three starts
in a relegation season, one of which, against Wolves,
ended with his first ever sending off following a
ridiculous case of mistaken identity. Nicknamed
'Zippy' by his teammates, Paul was popular within the
club, being named Reserve Player of the Season in his
final campaign . Unlike many footballers, who play
cricket during the summer, Paul played baseball for
Tavistock.

Reading Record: Lge 40(1)/1,FAC 1, LC 3,Total 44(1)/1
League Career Total: 360(21)/43

PAUL'S CLAIM TO FAME - A regular and successful
penalty taker, particularly during his second spell with
Swindon, Paul is best remembered for one that didn't go
in. In 1993 he missed the spot kick against Romania at
a crucial stage of Wales' World Cup decider as the
Principality just missed out on qualifying for the 1994
finals.

BOLAND George 'Dicky'
b. Marley Hill 6.10.1902 d. Durham summer 1977
Ht 5ft 6 1/2 Wt 11st (28-29)
Career: White le Head Rngrs; Gateshead 1922; Hartlepools U.
1925; READING August 1928; Fulham summer 1929;
Gateshead 1931; Crewe Alex. 1934

Left winger Dicky played in his native North East,
winning two North Eastern League medals with
Gateshead, then made good progress in the League with
Hartlepools before moving to Reading as cover for Bert
Oswald. His first team chances in the Second Division
were limited to just one game, a 4-0 defeat at Port Vale
and Dicky was released. Despite this apparent set back
he kept his League career going until the mid-Thirties.

Reading Record: Lge 1
League Career Total: 181/27

BOOTY Martyn James
b. Kirby Muxloe 30.5.1971
Ht 5ft 8 Wt 11st 2 (96-97)
Career: Coventry C. from trainee May 1992; Crewe Alex.
(free) October 1993; READING (£75,000) 18 January 1996;
Southend U. (loan) 7 January 1999, (free) 11 February 1999;
Chesterfield summer 2001

Having chosen football over cricket, he was on the
groundstaff of Leicestershire, Martyn's career was
nearly ended at an early stage with a serious cruciate
injury at Coventry.

This restricted his first team appearances to a handful of games but a move to Crewe soon saw him getting regular League action. His neat, crisp tackling full back play fitted in well with Crewe's ball playing style and after two years virtually ever present at Gresty Road he joined Division One Reading. Again, he proved a popular addition with his new club, helping them stave off the threat of relegation with his skilful displays and he scored a vital goal at Luton in a relegation clash. The following season a series of niggling injuries reduced Martyn's first team appearances but he still became the first winner of the Reading Evening Post's 'Player of the Month' in September 1996. He could not help Reading avoid relegation and, like several others, Martyn found himself out of first team contention with the appointment of Tommy Burns as manager.

Reading Record: Lge 62(1)/1, FAC 7/1, LC 10(1), Total 79(2)/2
League Career Total: 239(6)/6 +

BOWEN Jason Peter
b. Merthyr Tydfil 24.8.1972
Ht 5ft 6 Wt 9st (97-98)
Career: Swansea C. from apprentice July 1990; Birmingham C. (£350,000) July 1995; Southampton (loan) 1997; READING (£250,000) 24 December 1997; Cardiff C. (free) 12 January 1999

Jason was a talented young player who has come close to hitting the big time on several occasions. Capped by Wales at Schools, Youth, Under 21, B and twice at full international level, Jason's form at Swansea attracted the attention of Kevin Keegan's Newcastle and a three day trial at St James Park in February 1994 led to talk of a £1 million move. Eventually he moved to Birmingham and while he was never a regular there he still showed enough form as a pacey, skilful winger for City to turn down a £600,000 bid from Huddersfield. Eventually, he joined Reading on Christmas Eve 1997 but after a promising start he found himself embroiled in an unsuccessful relegation battle. The arrival of Tommy Burns saw Jason make just two starts as he was relegated to 'the Death Row Five' - a group of players marginalised by the manager. This unsatisfactory situation came to an end when he moved on a free to Cardiff, scoring two vital winners as his new club won promotion to Division Two. The following season he scored another vital, and personally satisfying winner as Cardiff won at Reading in a relegation battle.

Reading Record: Lge 12(3)/1, FAC 5, LC 1(1), Total 18(4)/1
League Career Total: 218(68)/60 +

BOWEN Mark Rosslyn
b. Neath 7.12.1963
Ht 5ft 8 Wt 11st 11 (99-00)
Career: Tottenham H. from apprentice December 1981; Norwich C. (£97,000) July 1987; West Ham U. (free) July 1996; Shimizu SP, Japan (free) March 1997; Charlton A. (free) September 1997; Wigan A. (free) 1999; READING non contract 7 December 1999; Wales coaching assist. December 1999

Mark, a versatile player at his best at full back or midfield, was capped by Wales at all levels including 41 full caps as well as playing for the Football League against the Italian League in 1991. Beginning with Spurs, he was part of their 1984 UEFA Cup winning squad but, unable to get a regular run in their first team, Mark was sold to Norwich in 1987. At Carrow Road he was a member of the Norwich team that were one of the most attractive in the top division. He played a major role in their memorable 1993 UEFA Cup run, scoring their second goal in what was probably the club's greatest win - 2-1 away to Bayern Munich. Relegated with Norwich in 1994-95 and released a year later he kept returning to the Premier League, first with West Ham and then with Charlton. Released by Wigan earlier in the season, Mark was offered a non contract deal at Reading on his 36th birthday, playing against Leyton Orient in the Auto Windscreen Shield the next day. He then left the club a day later to end the shortest ever Reading career. Mark was searching for a permanent contract and shortly after joined Mark Hughes' Welsh coaching staff.

Reading Career: AMC 1
League Career Total: 397(16)/27

BOWMAN Richard David
b. Lewisham 25.9.1954
Ht 5ft 6 Wt 10st 1 (78-79)
Career: Charlton A. from apprentice January 1973; READING (£10,000) 16 December 1976; Gillingham summer 1980

One of the best midfielders in the lower divisions during the seventies, Richie represented Kent Boys before joining Charlton from school. He was voted their Player of the Year for their 1974-75 Third Division promotion season and it took three months of negotiations before Reading secured his signature. Richie became the driving force of the team, his prompting from midfield and goalscoring knack never being better displayed than in Reading's Fourth Division title win in 1978-79. This was recognized by the fans who voted him their Player of the Year for the second season running while his fellow professionals voted him into the PFA Divisional side.

The following season he was club captain and was again honoured, this time by the Sunday People who named him the best player in the Third Division which won him a £500 cheque plus a silver salver presented by Bobby Charlton. Unable to agree terms at Reading, Richie moved to Gillingham but injuries greatly reduced his appearances for them until he retired in 1984.

Reading Record: Lge 194(1)/30, FAC 11/1, LC 16(1)/1, Total 221(2)/32
League Career Total: 313(4)/43

BOYLE Michael John

b. Bearpark, Co Durham 11.10.1908 d. ?
Ht 5ft 9 Wt 12st 3 (33-34)
Career: Bearpark Colliery; Bolton W. 1928; READING (free) 1 June 1933; Southend U. summer 1935; Exeter C. 1936; Darlington summer 1937; York C.1939

Having played in the same village team that produced England international, Sammy Crooks, Michael spent five years with Bolton during which time he made just 14 first team appearances. In 1933 he became one of a long list of players to move from Burnden Park to join former Bolton hero, Joe Smith, who was in charge at Reading. Michael found it difficult to break into the first team during his first season at Reading and was actually given a transfer but was then re-signed for 1934-35. He then had his best run in the League, playing six of the first seven games before finally leaving Elm Park. Away from football, Michael was a keen pigeon racer and can be considered a little unlucky not to have played more games at Reading since he was only once on the losing side in his 15 League matches for the Biscuitmen.

Reading Record: Lge 15, SSC 2, Total 17
League Career Total: 125/3

BRAITHWAITE Edward

b. Salford 12.12.1902 d. Birchington 2.4.1990
Ht 5ft 7 1/2 Wt 10st 12 (27-28)
Career: New Cross; Bradford C. 1922; READING 10 July 1924; Swindon T. (£100) June 1929; Margate 1933

Teddy was a very skilful inside forward who, whilst being right footed, could operate on the left as well. Initially there was some concern over his eyesight and it took him the first half of his initial season at Reading to secure his position, but from then on he made it his own. He was ever-present in Reading's 1925-26 Third Division South championship season during which he scored the campaign's opening goal. That was to be Teddy's best scoring season with 11 in total despite the assertion of 'Wanderer' in the club programme that he *passed too often when in a shooting position.*

The following season injury robbed him of a place in the side that played in the FA Cup semi-final, and from then on his place was under threat as his first team appearances reduced each season. In the summer of 1929 he moved to Swindon where he was a regular in their first team for four seasons.

Reading Record: Lge 133/22, FAC 17/4, Total 150/26
League Career Total: 292/30

BRAYSON Paul

b. Newcastle 16.9.1977
Ht 5ft 4 Wt 10st 10 (98-99)
Career: Newcastle U. from YTS August 1995; Swansea C. (loan) January 1997; READING (£100,000) 26 March 1998; Cardiff C. (loan) 16 March 2000, (free) July 2000

A prolific scorer for Newcastle with over 100 goals at youth and reserve level Paul earned nine England Youth caps at U17, U18 and U19 as well as the title of 'the Michael Owen of the North East'. His promise seemed to be borne out by five goals in 11 League games while on loan to Swansea. Unable to break into Newcastle's first team, he joined former Newcastle youth coach, Tommy Burns, as one of seven transfer deadline signings made in a fruitless attempt to avoid relegation in 1997-98. Paul scored Reading's last goal of that season but as Burns struggled to find the right format at Reading, Paul found goals difficult to come by and his confidence sank. Although he played in 28 League games during 1998-99, Paul only completed the full 90 minutes in two of them. More of the same followed the next season, and although he was on target for the reserves that next League goal would not come, and when the young striker was loaned to Cardiff in March 2000 he had gone an amazing 23 months without a first team goal.

Reading Record: Lge 15(19)/1, FAC 1, LC (1), AMC 1, Total 17(20)/1
League Career Total: 41(34)/21 +

BREBNER Grant Iain

b. Edinburgh 6.12.1977
Ht 5ft 10 Wt 12st (98-99)
Career: Hutchinson Vale B.C; Manchester U; Cambridge U. (loan) January 1998; Hibernian (loan) February 1998; Reading (£300,000) 15 June 1998; Hibernian (£400,000) 19 August 1999; Stockport Co. (loan) October 2000

A product of Manchester United's famous youth system, Grant had already won the FA Youth Cup with United and been capped for Scotland at U21 level before he had made a League appearance. This persuaded Tommy Burns to pay an initial £200,000 followed by another £100,000 based on appearances for the promising young midfielder. Grant made an immediate impact, having the distinction of scoring the first goal at Reading's new Madejski Stadium. He proved to be one of the few successes of a disappointing season as he scored 10 goals from well timed runs as well as showing a steely determination when winning the ball. He increased his international experience with more U21 caps, several as captain, and in June 1999 he led Scotland's U21 to victory in the President's Cup. Having started the new season with Reading's first goal it came as a shock when the popular young star was transferred to Hibs, the club he had supported as a boy.

Reading Record: Lge 41(6)/9, FAC 1, LC 3/1, 45(6)/10
League Career Total: 44(3)/10

BREMNER Kevin Johnston

b. Banff 7.10.1957
Ht 5ft 9 1/2 Wt 12st 3 (86-87)
Career: Deveronvale; Keith; Colchester U. (£25,000) October 1980; Birmingham C. (loan) October 1982; Wrexham (loan) December 1982; Plymouth Arg. January 1983; Millwall (£25,000) February 1983; READING (£35,000) 13 August 1985; Brighton (£65,000) July 1987; Peterborough U. (£18,000) July 1990; Dundee (free) summer 1991; Shrewsbury (loan) March 1992; Inverness (free) summer 1992; Brora Rngrs; Deveronvale; Gillingham youth coach 1995

It was just as well Reading signed Kevin since he had almost single handedly been responsible for their relegation in 1982-83 by scoring against them for Wrexham, Plymouth and Millwall that season.

He came to prominence with Colchester when he scored 21 goals in 1981-82, and then played a major role in Millwall's Third Division promotion campaign of 1984-85. He was considered to be a bargain buy when he joined Reading, and although he was injured in his first game for the club he became a firm favourite with their fans who nicknamed the all action inside forward 'Mad Max'. Injuries restricted his appearances in that season but he still made a major contribution to the Division Three title win, never more so than in Reading's home game against title challengers Plymouth. 3-0 down just after half time, Kevin was pushed forward from his midfield role and immediately began terrorizing the visitor's defence. Amazingly, Bremner inspired a complete turnaround as Reading scored four times in the last 25 minutes with Kevin getting the winner. While he had been seen as the perfect foil for the freescoring Trevor Senior, Kevin almost matched the top scorer for goals the next season and deservedly was voted 'Player of the Year'. Unable to agree terms, he moved to Brighton in 1987, thereafter becoming a soccer nomad before settling at Gillingham as their youth coach. There Kevin, the younger brother of Scotland international, Des, came out of retirement to make an appearance at the age of 39 in the Auto Windscreen Shield.

Reading Record: Lge 60(4)/21, FAC 6, LC 4/1, AMC 1, FMC 1, Total 72(4)/22
League Career Total: 393(27)/127

BRICE Gordon Henry John

b. Bedford 4.5.1924
Ht 5ft 11 Wt 12st 11 (49-50)
Career: Bedford St Clements; Luton T. from jnrs October 1944; Wolverhampton W. (£11,000) May 1947; READING (£5,000) March 1948; Fulham 5 November 1952; Ayr U.

Gordon was signed by Wolves as a successor to their international centre half, Stan Cullis, after playing for Luton Town throughout the War. Within a year he was on his way to Reading where he made his debut in front  of an Elm Park crowd of 8,241 - in a reserve game!

From the start of 1948-49 to his transfer in December 1952 he missed just two games and set a then club record of 148 consecutive League appearances. Although the majority of these games were at centre half, he had a 10 match run at centre forward in place of Ron Blackman and scored twice in his first game up front. He was a truly dominant defender, both on the ground and in the air, and was selected for the Football Combination against the Diable Rouge in Liege in February 1950. His successful association with Reading was ended when Fulham paid a big fee where he earned the nickname 'Whiz', playing at Craven Cottage until 1956. As well as being a tough but classy footballer, Gordon also played cricket for Northamptonshire while he was with Reading, taking 72 wickets as a medium fast bowler.

Reading Record: Lge 198/9, FAC 12/1, Total 210/10
League Career Total: 310/10

BRIDGER David James

b. Hartley Wintney 8.11.1941
Ht 5ft 10 Wt 11st 4 (64-65)
Career: READING amateur 3 September 1958, professional 5 March 1962; Thorneycrofts summer 1965, manager; Fleet August 1972

David progressed through the juniors at Reading to eventually earn himself a professional contract while Harry Johnston was manager. Although he made his debut against Bournemouth in October 1962, at his preferred centre half position, the majority of his subsequent first team appearances were at full back. In his three seasons as a professional his best total was five first team outings, and in 1965 he was given a free transfer.

Reading Record: Lge 10, LC 2, Total 12

BRIGGS Frederick

b. Wombwell 1.5.1908 d. Reading 1999
Ht 5ft 8 1/2 Wt 11st 6 (36-37)
Career: Mexborough T; Wombwell 1932; Rotherham U. May 1932; READING 12 June 1935; Southampton May 1938; Wartime guest for Fulham, Wrexham, Watford & Accrington Stan.

One of 14 children in a family that also included Plymouth's George Briggs, Fred had two good seasons with Rotherham before being relegated to the reserves for much of 1934-35 and then becoming one of Reading manager Joe Smith's last signings. At Reading he had to content himself with mainly reserve appearances although he had three short runs in his first two seasons at Elm Park.

A strong right winger or occasional wing half, Fred probably deserved to make more than 27 first team appearances, especially as only five of those games ended in defeat. A hat-trick for the reserves against Southampton secured a move to the Dell and he was their top scorer in the season prior to the War. During the hostilities Fred worked for Supermarine Aviation in Southampton and Reading making Spitfires.

Reading Record: Lge 27/6
League Career Total: 139/28

FRED'S CLAIM TO FAME - In his later years Fred would take great delight in mentioning that the usually accurate Association of Football Statisticians had reported his death in 1985, some 14 years before he passed away.

BRITTEN Martyn Edward Walter

b. Bristol 1.5.1955
Ht 5ft 7 Wt 10st 5 (77-78)
Career: Bristol R from apprentice May 1973; READING (£8,000) 6 August 1977; Bath C. (loan) January 1979; Taunton (free) summer 1979

Martyn was a product of Bristol Rovers' youth system and made his League debut in November 1984. Having made just 17 starts in three seasons he moved to Reading just before the start of 1977-78, and went straight into the first team playing in the first ten games. Just when the clever left winger's career appeared to be taking off he suffered a serious ankle injury from which he never really recovered. Martyn was loaned to Bath City in an attempt to regain full fitness but he never played another League match after that injury.

Reading Record: Lge 6(2), LC 3, Total 9(2)
League Career Total: 23(5)/2

BRITTON Gerald Joseph

b. Glasgow 20.10.1970
Ht 6ft 1 Wt 11st (91-92)
Career: Celtic from jnrs; READING (loan) November 1991; Partick Thistle (£10,000) summer 1992; Dunfermline 1997; Livingstone 1999

With Trevor Senior out of the Reading first team, manager Mark McGhee tried several alternatives to stand in for his star striker and one was Gerry, a young striker from Celtic. A big, bustling player who was good in the air, Gerry had already built up a formidable scoring record in Celtic's reserves with 102 goals in four seasons and had won a Scottish Youth cap.

His first team experience at Celtic had been mainly as a sub and it was to be the same at Reading where he did not complete a full ninety minutes during his loan spell. On leaving Celtic 18 months later he developed into a regular scorer in Scottish football.

Reading Record: Lge (2), FAC 1(1), Total 1(3)

BROMLEY Brian
b. Burnley 20.3.1946
Ht 5ft 8 Wt 11st (73-74)
Career: Burnley Boys; Bolton W. from jnrs March 1963; Portsmouth (£25,000) November 1969; Brighton (loan) October 1971, permanent (£20,000) January 1972; READING (£8,000) 14 September 1973; Darlington (loan) February 1975; Wigan A, 1975; Waterlooville player/manager 1977

Only 16 when he made his First Division debut for Bolton, Brian established himself in their first team the following season as an industrious midfielder and was capped at Youth level for England. Brian was sold to Portsmouth in 1968 before moving on to Brighton where he experienced both promotion and relegation. His next move was to Reading where he got off to a flying start by scoring a stunning equalizer against Peterborough on his home debut, to maintain Reading's unbeaten start to the season. Unfortunately for Brian that was as good as it got at Reading as he found his first team chances gradually reduced so that he was allowed to join Darlington on loan before being released at the end of 1974-75.

Reading Record: Lge 13(1)/1, FAC 2/1, Total 15(1)/2
League Career Total: 316(6)/33

BROOKE Garry James
b. Bethnal Green 24.11.1960
Ht 5ft 6 Wt 10st 5 (90-91)
Career: Tottenham H. from apprentice October 1978; Norwich C. July 1985; Groningen (Holland); Wimbledon August 1988; Stoke C. (loan) March 1990; Sweden; Brentford August 1990; Colchester U. (loan) February 1991; READING non-contract March 1991; Wyvenhoe

Gary's best period was his time at Spurs where, if not a regular first teamer, he was a part of their first team squad and as such was involved in some big matches. From then on the dynamic midfielder tried a number of clubs but despite displaying his trade mark powerful, long range shooting, he never again got into double figures for League appearances with any of them. His month's contract at Reading in March 1991 proved to be his last chance at League football but it only produced one start and he moved into the non-League world from then on.

Reading Record: Lge 1(3)
League Career Total: 77(45)/18

GARY'S CLAIM TO FAME - While with Spurs, Gary set a unique record for the days of just one substitute when he came on as sub in three consecutive FA Cup finals, in 1981 and then twice in 1982.

BROOKS John
b. Reading 23.12.1931
Ht 5ft 9 1/2 Wt 10st 8 (49-50)
Career: Mount Pleasant Youth Club; Coley Boys; Castle Street Inst; READING groundstaff 26 February 1949, professional 23 April 1949; Tottenham H. (£15,000) 3 February 1953; Chelsea (player exchange) December 1959; Brentford (£6,000) September 1961; Crystal Palace (£3,000) January 1961; Toronto C; Stevenage October 1964; Cambridge C; Knebworth coach.

The first Reading born player to be capped by England, Johnny can rightly claim to be one of the club's greatest ever players. He was one of the first players produced by Ted Drake's youth plan, making his debut in April 1950 and he would have played many more games for Reading had his spell with the club not been inter-rupted by his National Service. He won a number of representative honours while in the Army and played for the FA against Cambridge University. It was only in 1952-53 that he was able to play regularly in Reading's first team but it soon became clear that Reading would not be able to hold on to this skilful, creative inside right with a memorable body swerve and so it turned out to be. Soon, Spurs offered Dennis Uphill, Harry Robshaw plus £3,000 cash and Johnny was on his way.

With Spurs he developed into the complete inside forward and added a regular flow of goals to his other talents. On 14 November 1956 he made his England debut at Wembley against Wales, and in the following three weeks he gained another two caps but despite scoring two goals and helping his country to win all three games Johnny was never chosen again. He moved to Chelsea in exchange for Les Allen and subsequently played for a number of home counties sides, including Stevenage when, at the age of 35, he helped win promotion to the Southern League Premier Division.

But that was nothing for 'young' Johnny because in 1998 he turned on a typically classy display in Elm Park's last game, a veterans tournament - at the age of 66.

Reading Record: Lge 46/5, FAC 3/1, Total 49/6
League Career Total: 348/93

JOHNNY'S CLAIM TO FAME - In a Reading Minor Cup-tie in November 1945, Castle Street Institute beat Suttons 44-1 with Johnny scoring 19 of their goals.

BROOKS Norman Harry
b. Reading 28.5.1920 d. 1973
Ht 5ft 9 Wt 10st 10 (46-47)
Career: READING (Wartime guest); Huntley & Palmers; READING amateur 1946

Norman was a well known local player who guested for Reading during the War on the left wing. His best season was his first for the club when, in 1940-41, he scored five goals in seven games and helped the club reach the final of the London Cup but missed out on a place in the final and, therefore, a winners Savings Certificate. His one League appearance came in November 1946 in Reading's 5-1 defeat at Port Vale when he replaced the injured Jackie Deverall.

Reading Record: Lge 1, Wartime 11/5, Total 12/5

BROSKOM George Richard
b. Rotherham c.1898 d. ?
Ht 5ft 7 Wt 10st 6 (20-21)
Career: Coventry C; READING 1920; Halifax T. 1922

A strong player, George was Yorkshire Weightlifting champion at the age of 17 and during Reading's first League season he shared the right wing duties with Derek Spence. Although Spence played slightly more games, George scored two special goals for the club. First he had the honour of scoring Reading's first League goal against local rivals, Swindon, on Christmas Day, and then two weeks later he netted Reading's second equalizer in a shock FA Cup replay draw at First Division Chelsea.

Reading Record: Lge 17/1, FAC 3/1, Total 20/2
League Career Total: 18/1

BROWN Arthur Ivor
b. Aberdare 10.10.1903 d. Aberdare 3.4.1971
Ht 6ft Wt 12st 8 (30-31)
Career: Aberdare A; READING (£50) May 1927; Port Vale (£100) June 1929; Crewe Alex. October 1929; Merthyr Tyd. summer 1933

When Reading snapped up goalie Joe Duckworth in 1924, Aberdare signed Arthur Brown as his replacement. While Duckworth was becoming one of Reading's all time great keepers, Arthur was doing the same at the Athletic Ground where a series of fine displays earned him a Welsh cap against Ireland in February 1926, just seven months after turning pro. Unfortunately, he could not save Aberdare from finishing bottom of the League in 1926-27 and, when they were not re-elected he followed Duckworth to Reading. It took Arthur a season to displace Duckworth from the first team but his 11 match run came to an end with a 7-0 reverse at Blackpool. His next chance ended in a 5-0 defeat and in 1929 he moved on to Port Vale.

Reading Record: Lge 14
League Career Total: 180 apps

BROWN Henry Summers 'Harry'
b. Kirkaldy 18.9.1907 d. 1963
Ht 5ft 8 Wt 12st (38-39)
Career: Wymyss A; Hibernian; Darlington 1932; Chesterfield February 1934; Plymouth Arg. (£3,000) 1937; READING 16 November 1938; Wolverhampton W. (Wartime guest)

Harry appears to have been gradually moving South in his career but it was with Chesterfield that he enjoyed his best spell. There, he followed up an ever present season with his best goal haul of 15 in the League by playing a major role in Chesterfield's 1935-36 runaway Third Division North championship win. 18 months after his move to Plymouth, Arthur started moving back North when he joined Reading. At Elm Park he was used in both inside forward berths and at left half but was probably at his best at inside right where he scored in three consecutive games in February 1939. Harry saved his best display for the Southern Section Cup, scoring twice in the 4-0 win over Clapton Orient. Like so many players, the War brought an end to Harry's League career.

Reading Record: Lge 26/4, SSC 2, Total 28/4
League Career Total: 240/60

BROWN Kenneth James
b. Upminster 11.7.1967
Ht 5ft 8 Wt 11st 6 (96-97)
Career: Norwich C. from jnrs 1985; Plymouth Arg. (free) August 1988; West Ham U. (£175,000) August 1991; Huddersfield T. (loan) September 1995; READING (loan) October 1995; Southend U. (loan) March 1996; Crystal Palace (loan) 28 March 1996; READING (loan) September 1996; Birmingham C. (£75,000) December 1996; Millwall (£40,000) July 1997; Gillingham March 1999, Barry T. player coach July 2000

A highly experienced right back, Kenny's early career followed that of his father, also Kenny Brown, who was manager at Norwich and Plymouth at the same time as his son. Any accusations of nepotism against Brown senior were dispelled when he sold his son for a big fee although, admittedly, Kenny junior moved to Ken senior's old club, West Ham. He spent five seasons at West Ham but during the last two he spent more time out on loan than he did at Upton Park. Two of those loan spells were with Reading, the first for two months and then again in September 1996. He was ever-present throughout both spells and, as with all his clubs, Kenny gave excellent, committed performances while his surging, overlapping runs made him a great favourite with the fans. One of his subsequent loan spells saw him help Crystal Palace through the play-offs while a permanent transfer to Gillingham saw a similar successful situation with his new club.

Reading Record: Lge 17/1, LC 3, Total 20/1
League Career Total: 296 (12)/12

KENNY'S CLAIM TO FAME - In the six months from March 1996 Kenny played at Elm Park for four different club's - Southend, Crystal Palace, West Ham and Reading.

BROWN Roy Eric

b. Brighton 5.10.1945
Ht 6ft 1 Wt 12st 10 (69-70)
Career: Tottenham H. from apprentice October 1962; READING (£5,000) 18 July 1969; Dartford (loan) 23 March 1970; Notts Co.(£2,000) July 1970; Mansfield T. non contract November 1975

In his six years with Spurs, Roy was understudy to Pat Jennings and so only made one first team appearance for them during that time. He made up for that after he joined Reading where he went straight into the first team and made 70 consecutive appearances. He was a safe, steady goalie who never let the club down, but Reading's new manager, Jack Mansell, was keen to get his own men in and after Reading signed Steve Death, Roy only played one more first team game, in the ignominious FA Cup defeat at Brentwood. Roy eventually left for Notts County where he enjoyed much greater success, helping them to the 1970-71 Fourth Division Championship and then promotion to the Second Division two years later. At County he developed a knack of stopping penalties, and kept 41 clean sheets in only 113 games for them.

Reading Record: Lge 63, FAC 5, LC 3, Total 71
League Career Record: 178

BRUCE Henry 'Harry'

b. Coundon 5.1905 d. Durham
Ht 5ft 10 Wt 12st (31-32)
Career: Durham C; Bishop Auckland; Birmingham summer 1925; Gillingham 1928; Torquay U. 1929; Bankhead Alb; Rochdale 1930; Darlington 1930; Colwyn Bay; READING May 1931; Colwyn Bay April 1933; Macclesfield

Harry came from the hotbed of English football, having played his early football around the mining villages of the North East before signing professional for Birmingham. He joined them as a left back but played many games, mainly in their reserves, on the other flank. After five seasons in the League he drifted into non-League football where he helped Colwyn Bay win the Welsh Combination and two cups, scoring 14 goals from his defensive position. This persuaded Reading to sign Harry who had by now moved to centre half. He proved an enthusiastic player but only had a seven match run near the start of his first season in Reading's League side. Harry was a popular player at the club, keeping his teammates amused with the tricks he learned through being a member of the Magic Circle. He spent much of his second and final season at Elm Park coaching the reserves who were said to be 'as game as pebbles'!

Reading Record: Lge 7
League Career Total: 75

BUCK George William

b. Abingdon 25.1.1941
Ht 5ft 9 Wt 10st 8 (59-60)
Career: READING amateur 6 September 1956, professional 3 February 1958; Stockport Co. (free) July 1962

Although predominantly a left footed player, George made his League debut for Reading at QPR in December 1958, and several subsequent appearances on the right wing. In 1959-60 and in the following season he had a couple of good runs on the left wing in the first team but he never quite established himself as a regular despite having the happy knack of being on the winning side every time he scored.

Reading Record: Lge 31/4, FAC 1, Total 32/4
League Career Total: 34/4

BURGIN Terence

b. Nottingham 9.10.1938
Ht 5ft 10 Wt 11st 7 (60-61)
Career: READING November 1959

Terry had a short but unusual professional career with Reading. Signed as a 21 year old centre half, he was converted in his second season to a centre forward with some success in the reserves where he finished second highest scorer with 13 goals.

He also contributed to the second XI's impressive scoring record of 90 goals in 38 games that saw them finish as runners up in the Combination. His form in the reserves earned Terry a first team call up on New Year's Eve 1960 at Colchester, and he got a second chance six weeks later. Unfortunately for Terry, the need to cut the number of professionals to cope with the increase in the wage bill brought about by the abolition of the maximum wage meant that he was not retained at the end of 1960-61 and his professional career was over.

Reading Record: Lge 2

BURNS James
b. Dromore c.1899 d. ?
Ht 5ft 9 1/2 Wt 11st (24-25)
Career: Glenavon; READING (£60) July 1924

Sparkling form with Glenavon had earned James a cap for Ireland, against England in 1923 and so he was considered a good capture when he moved to Reading during the 1924 close season. He started the season in his usual left wing position but after four games was replaced by the popular local player, George Springell, and never recovered his first team place, eventually returning to Ireland.

Reading Record: Lge 4

BURNS Phillip Martin
b. Stockport 18.12.1966
Ht 6ft 3 Wt 13st 10 (89-90)
Career: Huddersfield T. YTS 1983; Army 1984; READING March 1989; Ipswich T. (trial); Slough T; Aidrie November 1991

After failing to make Huddersfield's first team, Phil gave up his dreams of becoming a professional goalie and joined the Army. He continued to play football, winning a number of representative honours and it was in one of these games, while he was stationed at Aldershot, that he was spotted by Reading. After two trial games, he was offered a professional contract and made his first team debut in an FA Cup-tie against Welling, keeping a clean sheet in that game and in the second replay. His League debut came in September 1990 and produced another shut-out, at Huddersfield, the club that had rejected him seven years earlier. That game saw the start of a 12 match run that was to be the total of his League career at Reading, since the giant keeper was given a free transfer in May 1991.

Reading Record: Lge 12, FAC 2, AMC 1, Total 15

BURVILL Glenn
b. Canning Town, 26.10.1962
Ht 5ft 9 Wt 10st 5 (85-86)
Career: West Ham U. from apprentice September 1980; Aldershot August 1983; READING (£12,500) March 1985; Fulham (loan) March 1986; Aldershot (free) July 1986 to March 1992; Newhaven T; Saltdean manager July 2000

Although Glenn never made any first team appearances for his local club, West Ham, he did help them win the 1981 FA Youth Cup before his eventual transfer to Aldershot. There he established himself as an industrious player with a knack for goalscoring from his position on the right side of midfield, and this brought about a move to Reading 18 months later. At Reading Glenn was a first team regular for the rest of that season but found himself replaced by Jerry Williams at the start of what was to be the club's Third Division championship season. An injury to Williams gave Glenn his chance in the middle of the season, but Williams' recovery, plus the record signing of Terry Hurlock, restricted Glenn to the occasional substitute appearance. After a loan spell at Fulham, Glenn was allowed to return to Aldershot where he stayed until March 1992, playing in their last League game before their bankruptcy.

Reading Record: Lge 24(6), FAC 4(1), LC (1), AMC 2, Total 30(8)
League Career Total: 267(32)/40

BUTCHER Reginald 'Ron'
b. Shirley 1916 d. 1996
Ht 6ft 3 Wt 12st 8 (37-38)
Career: Shirley T; Aston Villa 1933; Shrewsbury (loan) then permanent; READING 4 May 1936

A giant goalie who played much of his football in the Midlands, winning county honours for Shropshire, Ron had to move to Reading before starting his League career. It took him nine months before he got his first team chance but when it came he took it, literally, with both hands. An amazing start saw him play his first four games in a five day Easter spell without conceding a goal and, not surprisingly, he kept his place to the end of the season. Ron started the next season in the first team goal, keeping out the fans' favourite, Percy Whittaker, and this led to a section of the crowd subjecting him to some unfair barracking. Unfortunately, this affected Ron to such an extent that he lost his first team place and walked out on the club, telling friends that he was fed up with football. He returned after four days but the fact that the story had been leaked to become a front page story in the News of the World resulted in the club suspending him for two weeks and his Elm Park career was effectively over.

Reading Record: Lge 18, SSC 1, Total 19

BUTLER Dennis George

b. Compton, Berks 4.8.1952
Ht 5ft 9 Wt 11st (69-70)
Career: READING amateur then apprentice 1 August 1969,
professional 11 May 1970; Hillingdon Bor. June 1971

In making his League debut for Reading on Easter
Monday 1970, Dennis became the club's youngest
player for 14 years. A week later he scored against
Barnsley in an impressive display that saw him
eventually go off injured as the opposing defenders
struggled to control the lively youngster. Dennis was a
slim, graceful player who looked to have a great future
but he found it difficult to break into the first team after
his initial success and he was released by Reading at the
end of 1970-71.

Reading Record: Lge 7(3)/1, LC (1), Total 7(4)/1

DENNIS'S CLAIM TO FAME - When he came on as
substitute at Rochdale in September 1970, Dennis
completed a reporter's nightmare as he became the third
Dennis Butler on the pitch, alongside Reading's Dennis
M and Rochdale's Dennis A.

BUTLER Dennis Michael

b. Parsons Green 7.3.1943
Ht 5ft 8 Wt 11st 3 (70-71)
Career: Surrey Boys; Chelsea from groundstaff June 1960;
Hull C. (£40,000) June 1963; READING (£14,000) 11
December 1969; Margate July 1974

Although he
was brought up
in Woking,
Dennis began
his career with
the club nearest
his birthplace,
helping Chel-
sea win the FA
Youth Cup
twice and was
a member of
the side that
beat Reading
in the final of
the Southern
Junior Floodlit
Cup in 1960.
First team appearances were in short supply at Stamford
Bridge so in 1963 Dennis moved to Hull for a hefty fee
and soon established himself as one of the best, and
fastest, full backs in the division.

After almost 250 first team appearances, and a Third
Division championship medal in 1966, Dennis returned
South to join Reading where he became a fixture in their
defence. Predominantly a left back, Dennis could
perform equally well on the right and his awesome
tackling power made him a great favourite of the fans,
some of whom nicknamed him 'Demolition Den'. In
addition to his full back skills, Dennis played the first
few minutes of the promotion clash with Luton in goal
when Steve Death was delayed in heavy traffic. Dennis
was club captain from December 1972 and spent the
summer of 1973 redecorating the Supporters' Club
Social Club, but a year later he announced his
retirement from League football as he could no longer
support his family on Fourth Division wages. He never
scored a goal in over 400 League games.

Reading Record: Lge 169, FAC 17, LC 8, Watney Cup
1, Total 195
League Career Total: 402(2)

BUTLER Martin Neil

b. Wordsley 15.9.1974
Ht 5ft 11 Wt 11st 9 (99-00)
Career: Walsall from trainee May 1993; Cambridge U.
(£20,000) August 1997; READING (£750,000) 1 February
2000

Having begun his career with Walsall, Martin really
found his goalscoring touch when he moved to
Cambridge in 1997. The top scorer in his three seasons
with them, he was their Player of the Year in their
promotion season of 1998-99 and was also voted into
the PFA Divisional team that season. The goals
continued in 1999-00 despite the fact that Cambridge
were struggling and several clubs were showing interest
in the lively, hard working, Butler but Cambridge
would not listen to offers until another of their famous
gaintkilling Cup runs was over. True to their word,
United's FA Cup exit heralded a big money move to
Reading where he immediately scored in his first two
games, the first at Preston, one of the clubs whom
Reading had beaten for his signature. He was in
devastating form in 2000-01 and as well as his goals,
Martin's hardworking style meant that even when he hit
a dry spell mid-season he was always a valuable asset to
the team. Consequently, it came as no surprise when he
won another PFA Divisional award and was similarly
honoured by the Royals' fans, ending the season with 28
goals, including two in the play-offs.

Reading Record: Lge 59(3)/28, FAC 3/2, LC 1(1),
AMC (1), Play-offs 3/2, Total 66(5)/32 +
League Career Total: 202(37)/77 +

BUTLER William C

b Atherton 27.3.1900 d. Durban 11.7.1966
Ht 5ft 7 1/2 Wt 11st 8 (33-34)
Career: Royal Navy; Atherton Colliery; Bolton W. April 1920;
READING (£600) 2 June 1933
See 'The Managers' section for Billy's managerial career.

Billy was the son of a well known rugby player who, remarkably in view of his successful playing career, did not start playing football until he was 19. After World War One he made up for lost time as centre forward for Atherton Town, once scoring nine goals in a game, and within a year of starting playing he was signed as a professional by Bolton. Wanderers considered him too small to lead the attack and so switched him to the right wing and it was here that Billy achieved his success.

He was a member of the great Bolton side of the Twenties, winning three FA Cup winners medals and scoring in the 1929 final as well as being capped for his country. After almost 450 first team games at Burnden Park, Billy was allowed to join his former team-mate, Joe Smith, at Reading. Although now near the end of his illustrious career, he was still able to show the dribbling skills and turn of speed that were the hallmarks of his play. When Joe Smith left Reading to manage Blackpool in August 1935, the Elm Park board had no hesitation in appointing Billy as the club's new manager, at which point he retired as a player.

Reading Record: Lge 56/13, FAC 8/3, SSC 2, Total 66/16
League Career Total: 463/78

BILLY'S CLAIM TO FAME - Billy appears to have an affinity for Wembley firsts - he played in the first Wembley Cup Final, made his England debut in the stadium's first international and, sadly, he died on the day it staged its first game in the 1966 World Cup finals.

BUTLIN Barry Desmond

b. Roslington 9.11.1949
Ht 5ft 11 1/2 Wt 11st 7 (76-77)
Career: Derby Co. from jnrs; Notts Co.(loan) January 1969;
Luton T. (£50,000) November 1972; Nottingham For.
(£122,000) January 1977; Brighton (loan) September 1975;
READING (loan) January 1977; Peterborough U. (£20,000)
August 1977; Sheffield U. August 1979

Barry played for several of the top Midland clubs and attracted some big fees along the way. Beginning at Derby, he only played four League games but won the Central League and the Texaco Cup with them and had a lengthy loan spell at Notts County before joining Luton for a record fee for both clubs. He scored the Hatters first goal back in the First Division and enjoyed the best goalscoring spell of his career before another record fee took him to Forest. While at Forest he had a five match loan spell with Reading that produced no goals although some publications incorrectly credit him with a goal at Walsall. A tall centre forward who was good in the air, Barry was unfortunate that his spell with Reading coincided with a low period at the club that saw only one point secured during his stay.

Reading Record: Lge 5
League Career Total: 284(8)/80

BYRNE David Stuart

b. Hammersmith 5.3.1961
Ht 5ft 8 Wt 10st 9 (91-92)
Career: Southall; Hounslow; Chiswick Alb; Harrow Bor;
Hounslow; Kingstonian October 1983; Gillingham July 1985;
Millwall (£5,000); Cambridge U. (loan) September 1988;
Blackburn R. February 1989; Plymouth Arg. (free) March
1989; Bristol R. (loan) February 1990; Watford (£50,000)
November 1990; READING (loan) August 1991; Fulham
(loan) January 1992; Shamrock R. (free) January 1993; St
Johnstone March 1993; Partick Thistle (free) July 1993;
Walsall (loan) February 1994; St Mirren February 1995;
Tottenham H. (non contract) June 1995; Ayr U. August 1995;
Albion R. player/coach January 1996

Few players can have had a more varied career than David who has played for at least 23 clubs. After doing the rounds of London non-League clubs, his break came with Gillingham but his next move, to Millwall, brought his best spell. While with the Lions, David scored Millwall's goal in their 1-0 win over Reading in Elm Park's first Second Division game for 55 years. David had been a winger, capable of performing on either flank, but at Watford he played some games at full back where he could still use his pace and long throw to good effect. At the start of 1991-92 David joined Reading on loan and performed well on the right wing, scoring twice but Reading could not agree terms and he returned to Watford.

He soon continued his nomadic ways that took in spells in Ireland and Scotland during his amazing career, even playing four Inter Toto Cup games for Spurs, managed by his brother in law, Gerry Francis.

Reading Record: Lge 7/2
League Career Total: 163(26)/15

DAVID'S CLAIM TO FAME - On 23 March 1991, Watford were fixed at the bottom of the Second Division when David scored a late winner against Middlesbrough for their first win in three months. This sparked a revival that saw Watford climb out of the relegation zone yet David was never picked again during the rest of his two year career with them so he had the unique distinction of actually scoring with his very last kick for Watford.

CAMERON Duncan
b. Menstree c.1898 d. ?
Ht 5ft 10 Wt 12st (20-21)
Career: Stenhousemuir; READING (£120) October 1920; Stenhousemuir summer 1921; Rotherham Co. summer 1921

Duncan began his career in his native Scotland, before joining Reading in their first season in the League. He could play in either the inside left or centre forward positions with his Reading League career split between the two. He was clearly more a creator of chances since he only managed one goal, at Swansea on Good Friday 1921, in his 28 first team games for Reading. The club's need for more firepower led to his returning to Stenhousemuir before joining Rotherham in a move that cost them a fee to both his previous clubs.

Reading Career: Lge 25/1, FAC 2, Total 27/1
League Career Total: 30/1

CAMPBELL Charles J
b. Dublin c.1903 d. ?
Ht 5ft 11 Wt 11st 7 (26-27)
Career: Pembroke Dock; QPR 1925; READING May 1926

Charles started the 1925-26 season in QPR's first team and scored what was to be his only League goal in his second game for them - against Reading at Loftus Road. At the end of that season Reading clearly recalled that performance and signed the inside right as cover in their first season in the Second Division. His Reading career was delayed after he was taken ill with gall stones during the summer. After that Charles only managed one appearance that season, at Bradford, when he was played at left half and was released at the end of that campaign.

Reading Record: Lge 1
League Career Total: 5/1

CAMPBELL Robert Inglis
b. Glasgow 28.6.1922
Ht 5ft 10 Wt 11st (54-55)
Career: Glasgow Perthshire; Falkirk 1941; QPR (Wartime guest); Chelsea (£9,000) May 1947; READING (£2,000)29 August 1954; Dumbarton manager April 1961; Bristol R. coach 1962, manager November 1977 to December 1979; Gloucester C. manager November 1980; Bristol City Council coach 1982

Bobby made his name with Chelsea as a typical Scottish winger who combined natural ball skills with a good turn of speed which earned him over 200 first team appearances for them, plus five caps for Scotland between 1947 and 1950. He had already toured India with the Services XI during the War and similarly covered Europe with Scotland in 1954. Shortly after that tour Bobby joined Reading, having failed to agree terms with Chelsea. At Elm Park Bobby was used mainly as an inside forward but displayed his adaptability by playing in any forward position, wing half and even full back. His main skill was in providing chances for his colleagues, especially with wickedly inswinging corners, but Bobby had an eye for a goal as well and all of this made him a great favourite at Reading. With his experience, Bobby, an FA qualified coach, assisted coaching at Elm Park and after he hung up his boots in 1958 he joined the club's coaching staff. He had been part of the committee that managed Reading while Jack Smith was unwell in 1955 and in the summer of 1958 he coached the US Army in Germany as well as helping the Scottish FA Summer School. It was obvious that Bobby's future lay in coaching and in April 1961 he became Dumbarton's manager and then began a 17 year association with Bristol Rovers.

Reading Record: Lge 94/12, FAC 15/1, SFC 2, Total 111/13
League Career Total: 282/48

CANOVILLE Paul Kenneth
b. Hillingdon 4.3.1962
Ht 6ft Wt 11st 5 (96-87)
Career: Millford; Hanwell Celtic; Hillingdon Bor. July 1979; Southampton (trial); Chelsea December 1981; READING (£60,000) August 1986; Enfield; Burnham; Maidenhead U.1990; Flackwell Heath; Northwood; Erith

As a regular in Hillingdon's Southern League side at the age of 17, Paul soon attracted the attention of other clubs, including Southampton, who declined to sign him despite Ian Branfoot's recommendation. Eventually he joined Chelsea, making over 80 first team appearances before Ian Branfoot finally got his man, signing him for Reading just before the start of his newly promoted sides' Second Division campaign. Paul was an immediate success on the left wing where his speed, strength and skill added a new dimension to Reading's play. He soon found his shooting boots, scoring in three consecutive games but just as Reading fans were acclaiming a new hero, Paul was the victim of a horrific tackle at Sunderland that dislocated his knee and kept him out for almost a year. He received a tremendous reception when he finally returned to the first team and although he scored in that comeback game it was clear that all was not right with his knee. He bravely persevered but by March 1988 Paul was forced to concede that his League career was over. He was able to continue in non-League circles but the circumstances of his curtailed League career were a constant disappointment to him.

Reading Record: Lge 16/4, LC 4 (1), Total 18(1)/4
League Career Total: 69(26)/15

CAREY Alan William

b. London 21.8.1975
Ht 5ft 7 Wt 10st 10 (95-96)
Career: St Patricks, Tipperary; READING YTS summer 1993 then professional; Weymouth (loan) March 1995; Basingstoke T.1997

Alan was as Irish as they come despite being born in London, having been brought up in South West Ireland, and it was there that he was recommended to Reading, after scoring 28 goals while playing as a sweeper. Converted to a forward, he began scoring regularly for the youth and reserves and hit four goals for an FA Youth XI against SW Counties in March 1993. A year later he made his League debut, coming on as substitute against Wrexham. Although Alan had pace, silky skills and was very dedicated his small build proved too big a drawback for him and he could not compensate for his lack of strength. At least he helped Reading win the Berks & Bucks Cup in 1995 before being released by the club in December 1996. He joined Basingstoke and played a major role in their 1997-98 cup run, scoring the penalty shoot out goal that beat Wycombe and then getting the equalizer against Northampton in the next round.

Reading Record: Lge (3)

CARNABY Bryan James

b. Plymouth 14.12.1947
Ht 5ft 8 Wt 10st 8 (73-74)
Career: Plymouth Arg. amateur; Bristol R. amateur; Brentford amateur; Charlton A. amateur; Bexley U; Arcadia U. (South Africa) 1969; 1971; READING (trial) 6 October 1971, professional summer 1972; Carshalton; Ringwood C. (Australia) April 1978; Wokingham T. November 1979; Butlins coach; READING physiotherapist 7 July 1980; University College of Atlanta (USA)1981; Brisbane C. (Australia) 1981; Millwall physiotherapist November 1984

Few players have ever shown more determination to become a professional footballer than Bryan. After several attempts and a spell in South Africa, Bryan returned to the UK and wrote to all 92 League clubs requesting a trial. Only four replied, and after unsuccessful trials at Bristol City and Brentford he arrived at Reading. Bryan turned in a series of fine performances in the reserves that eventually earned him a professional contract after an eight month trial that involved three managers. Given his debut in the opening game of 1972-73, Bryan waited just 12 minutes to repay the club with his first goal. From then on he settled into the side's midfield, his phenomenal workrate enabling his team mates to display their skills, knowing that Bryan was there to cover them. Although not a regular in 1975-76, Bryan made a major contribution by scoring one of the goals in the 2-2 draw at Cambridge that clinched the club's first promotion for 55 years. Released by the club at the end of the following season, Bryan returned to his nomadic career but returned to Elm Park as physiotherapist for 1980-81, when he became probably the only person to join a League club from Butlins!

Reading Record: Lge 136(9)/10, FAC 8(1), LC 15, Total 159(10)/10

BRYAN'S CLAIM TO FAME - Born in Devon, brought up in London, you would not expect Bryan to be capped by South Africa at full international level and being only 5 ft 9 it is even more surprising that his international honours were won at basketball.

CARNEY Eugene Francis

b. Bootle 1895 d. Bootle 4.12.1952
Ht 5ft 7 1/2 Wt 11st (23-24)
Career: Pontypridd; Rochdale 1921; New Brighton; READING May 1923; Mold 19 January 1924; New Brighton 1924; Caernarfon; 1926, New Brighton

A lively character who, when asked by a local reporter what his role was, replied *'to protect the linesman from the crowd on my side of the pitch'*. Gene joined Reading having already had some League experience during his spell with Rochdale. By-mid January he had only missed three first team games for Reading but had not scored in any of his 22 first team appearances. Consequently he lost his first team place to George Springell and shortly after was allowed to join Mold.

Reading Record: Lge 21, FAC 1, Total 22
League Career Total: 77/9

CARR James Edward Charles

b. Maryhill 19.12.1893 d. Harrow 26.6.1980
Ht 5ft 7 1/2 Wt 10st 6 (21-22)
Career: Watford O. 1912; Watford from amateur August 1913; West Ham U. May 1914, Wartime guest for Portsmouth & Kilmarnock; READING summer 1919; Southampton (£25) July 1923; Swansea T. May 1926; QPR October 1927; Southall 1928

A founder member of Watford Orient, Jimmy turned pro with Watford before joining West Ham and then, after World War One, Reading. Here, 'the clever little player' formed an exciting left wing partnership with Len Andrews as Reading moved into the League. While Andrews moved on to Southampton, Jimmy made the number 11 shirt his own and only missed 10 games in the first three seasons in the League although he was rarely amongst the goals. Jimmy was released by Reading in 1923 when he took the unusual step of placing an advert in the sporting paper, The Athletic News, offering his services in exchange for a business, and as a result he joined Southampton. This led to him replacing Len Andrews in their first team and in 1925 he helped them to an FA Cup semi-final appearance.

Reading Record: Lge 116/7, FAC 5, SL 35/1, Total 156/8
League Career Total: 209/18

JIMMY'S CLAIM TO FAME - Jimmy reached the height of his sporting career at the age of 61 when he represented England at bowls in the 1954 Empire games in Vancouver.

CARTER John Henry 'Jack'

b. Aylesbury 11.11.1910 d. Reading 2.7.1992
Ht 5ft 11 Wt 11st (35-36)
Career: Hazels; Aylesbury U; Watford from amateur November 1931; READING (trial) May 1935, professional September 1935; Ipswich T. July 1936; Yeovil August 1938

Jack must have made a good impression at Watford, signing professional just a few days after joining them as an amateur.

He was used mainly as understudy to former Reading centre forward Billy Lane, but when Jack was called upon he never let Watford down with an average of a goal every two games. In 1935 he joined Reading on trial and, again, got off to a flying start by scoring five goals in a reserve match. This led to him being given a game in the Southern Section Cup and again Jack hit the target by scoring twice against Aldershot. Jack was subsequently given a couple of Leagues games, and although both were lost and he failed to score, it was, perhaps, a little surprising that he was not given a further opportunity to display his goalscoring skills. Despite this disappointment Jack could still be found at Elm Park 40 years later, working as a steward at the ground.

Reading Record: Lge 2, SSC 1/2, Total 3/2
League Career Total: 17/7

CASKEY Darren Mark

b. Basildon 21.8.1974
Ht 5ft 8 Wt 11st 9 (96-97)
Career: Tottenham H. from trainee March 1992; Watford (loan) October 1995; READING (£700,000) 28 February 1996; Notts County summer 2001

A brilliant youth career that saw Darren capped at England Schools and Youth level, culminated in him captaining the likes of Fowler, Scholes, Butt and Campbell as England U18s won the 1993 UEFA Youth Championship with Darren scoring the winning goal in the final. He had been with Spurs from the age of 11 and, having graduated from the FA School of Excellence, Darren signed for them and scored on his debut against Arsenal in August 1993.

First team chances came occasionally but soon after the disappointment of losing his place after a brilliant display in a 4-1 win over Manchester United, Darren agreed to move to Reading for a club record fee. He was soon established as the playmaker in the centre of the field and although he was playing well the general opinion was that Reading had not always seen the best of him. A broken leg in pre-season training saw him miss the start of 1997-98 and this played a part in the club's relegation that season. However, the move to the club's new, impressive, Madejski Stadium seemed to inspire Darren and after a good season he hit sensational form in 1999-00.

Raking, long range passes, determined midfield play and creativity were added to a new found scoring touch. He led the club's scorers all the way, ending up with an impressive 23 goals from midfield, several which came from a series of inch perfect free kicks. He was slightly less effective in 2000-01 and, no longer certain of a place in the starting line up, Darren was released on a 'Bosman' at the end of that season.

Reading Record: Lge 180(22)/35, FAC 9(1)/5, LC 10(2)/4, AMC 7/1, Play-offs 1(1), Total 207(26)/45
League Career Total: 206(34)/40 +

CASPER Christopher Martin
b. Burnley 28.4.1975
Ht 6ft Wt 12st 2 (98-99)
Career: Manchester U. from YTS February 1993; Bournemouth (loan) January 1996; Swindon T. (loan) September 1997; READING (loan) 16 September 1998, permanent (£300,000) 4 November 1998

As a contemporary of David Beckham and Gary Neville, Chris was a member of the all conquering Manchester United youth team that won the 1992 FA Youth Cup and the 1993 European Youth Cup. Chris's father was the former Burnley favourite, Frank Casper, and his pedigree showed in his classy defensive play but, apart from the odd cup appearances, his first team experience came in loan spells. It was at such a loan spell that he came to Reading, immediately settling down a shaky defence from a sweeping role and it came as no surprise that the club were willing to meet United's price to make the move permanent. Although he sometimes looked less comfortable when playing in a back four, Chris was coming to terms with the physical demands of Division Two football when he suffered a broken leg from a terrible tackle at Cardiff on Boxing Day 1999 that saw him sidelined for 15 months and led to legal action.

Reading Record: Lge 46(1), FAC 3, LC 4, AMC 1, Total 54(1) +
League Career Total: 70(4)/2 +

CHANDLER Frederick Ernest John
b Hythe, Southampton, 2.8.1912
Ht 5ft 10 1/2 Wt 11st (35-36)
Career: Portsmouth; Newport (Isle of Wight); READING May 1932; Blackpool (£250) September 1935; Swindon T. May 1936; Crewe Alex. May 1937

A fine, if erratic, left footed player, Fred had a season in Portsmouth's reserves before moving to Newport (IoW) where he was spotted by Reading. A series of strong performances in the reserves led to his League debut in January 1933 and he celebrated with a goal in Reading's 7-1 win over Swindon. Initially used on the wing, Fred moved to inside left where he enjoyed his best season, scoring eight times in 27 starts in 1934-35. He had just won back his first team place in September 1935 when his old manager, Joe Smith, took him to Blackpool.

After the transfer it was discovered that Fred had a broken jaw so his debut for Blackpool was delayed. At Reading, Fred was in demand for his fine fiddle playing and once provided the entertainment at a Supporters' Club smoking evening.

Reading Record: Lge 41/13, SSC 1, Total 42/13
League Career Total: 158/44

CHANDLER Sidney Ellis
b. London 30.5.1901 d. London 16.12.1961
Ht 5ft 7 Wt 10st 10 (29-30)
Career: Aston Villa; Preston N.E. summer 1926; READING (£750) November 1928; Canterbury Waverley 1931

After two years in Aston Villa's reserves, Sid got his chance with Preston and only missed one game in his first season with them, scoring 12 goals. While his brother, Arthur, was scoring freely at Leicester, Sid's chances at Preston were diminishing and in November 1928 he joined Reading. He could not have had a worse start, with Reading losing 7-0 at Blackpool on his debut, but Fred then helped his new club to a 14 match unbeaten run. Fred was ever-present in his right half position until September 1930 when another big defeat, 8-1 at Burnley, saw him lose his place and although he had another couple of short runs he was released at the end of Reading's relegation season. During that season he suffered a broken nose following a heated discussion with Adam Allan over the merits of the Players Union.

Reading Record: Lge 83/1, FAC 7, Total 90/1
League Career Total: 148/14

CHAPMAN John
b. Sacriston 24.5.1945
Ht 5ft 9 Wt 11st 4 (67-68)
Career: Durham amateur; Stockton; Workington February 1963; READING (£2,000) 7 May 1966; Stockport Co. July 1969

John developed a reputation as a tough tackling left sided defender at Workington and his move to Reading did nothing to reduce the power of his play. He added much needed steel to Reading's defence, either at left back or in the centre of the defence, earning him the nickname 'Chopper'. He overcame an unsettled spell that led to a transfer request to regain his first team place and John's last few months at Elm Park saw him used in midfield before leaving the club to join Stockport.

Reading Record: Lge 102(1)/2, FAC 7, LC 3, Total 112(1)/2
League Career Total: 217(3)/8

JOHN'S CLAIM TO FAME - With such a combative style, getting sent off was almost inevitable for players like John, and yet no one could imagine the reason for his dismissal at Colchester in a 1967 League Cup-tie. With a Reading player injured, manager Roy Bentley called John over for tactical instructions. The ref. called John back on to the pitch and promptly sent him off for leaving the pitch. Not surprisingly, the FA did not impose any suspension for this 'offence'.

CHAPPELL Leslie Alan

b. Nottingham 6.2.1947
Ht 5ft 8 Wt 10st 10 (70-71)
Career: Rotherham U. from apprentice February 1965;
Blackburn R. (player exchange) May 1968; READING (free)
10 July 1969; Doncaster R. (£8,500) December 1974; Swansea
C. (free) July 1976 then reserve manager and coach;
Farnborough T. manager October 1984; Basingstoke T.
manager July 1985; Torquay U. assist. manager July 1986

Brought up in Rotherham, Les joined his local club and
soon became a regular goalscorer which attracted a
move to Blackburn in exchange for Alan Gulliver. His
stay at Ewood was such an unhappy one that Les
considered giving up football, but Jack Mansell, his old
manager at Rotherham, persuaded Les to join him at
Reading. An important part of Reading's free scoring
attack of 1969-70, Les was top scorer with 24 League
goals which included a nine minute hat-trick against
Barnsley, completed with a spectacular diving header
that is regarded as one of Elm Park's greatest goals.
Goals were much harder to come by for Les and
Reading in the following seasons, but in 1973-74 he was
the League's top scorer at Easter, before an ankle injury
kept him out for the rest of that season. His 28 goal haul
included a club record equalling four League hat-tricks.
Les had been unsettled in the South for some time and in
December 1974 Reading reluctantly sold the nippy
inside forward to Doncaster. A move to Swansea saw
him play in their record League win, against Hartlepool
in 1978, having played in Reading's record equaling 8-
0 over Southport eight years earlier.

Reading Record: Lge 193(8)/78, FAC 18/7, LC 11/5,
Watney Cup 1, Total 223(8)/90
League Career Total: 428(13)/130

CHEETHAM Hugh David

b. Manchester 3.2.1958
Ht 5ft 8 Wt 11st (80-01)
Career: Manchester U. amateur February 1973; Crewe Alex.
from apprentice February 1974; READING (£25,000) 23 July
1979; Wokingham T. (free) May 1981

A product of Crewe's youth system, Hugh made his
League debut for them on the day he signed professional
and helped his side to a 4-0 derby win over Stockport.
From then on he gradually established himself, making
over a hundred first team appearances before Reading
broke their nine year old transfer record to secure his
services. Hugh started the first seven first team games
on the left side of midfield but then lost his place.
Recalled as substitute for a game at Blackpool in
December 1979 Hugh broke a bone in his foot and was
out for the rest of the season. He was tried at left back
but his last run in the first team was back in midfield.

He never reached the heights expected of him and two
years after that record fee Hugh was given a free
transfer.

Reading Record: Lge 10(2), LC 5, Total 15(2)
League Career Total: 100(8)

CHITTY Wilfred Sidney

b Walton on Thames 10.7.1912 d. 1997
Ht 5ft 11 1/2 Wt 11st 12 (39-40)
Career: Wycombe W; Woking; Chelsea from jnrs March 1930;
Plymouth Arg. December 1938; READING August 1939;
Wartime guest for Clapton O. & Fulham; READING scout;
West Ham U. scout January 1958

Wilf spent eight and a half years with Chelsea, making
a handful of League appearances until 1937-38 when he
scored a very creditable 11 goals in 19 games.
Strangely, shortly after his best season, Chelsea let the
tall, speedy winger go to Plymouth, and then he moved
on to Reading just before the War. Although he had to
wait until after the War to make his League debut for
Reading, Wilf was a regular thoughout the hostilities
and was ever-present in Reading's 1941 London War
Cup triumph. During that period his accurate centres
made him a great favourite at Reading but no one
appreciated him more than centre forward Tony
MacPhee, who was the beneficiary of most of Wilf's
crosses. Towards the end of the War Wilf even played
some games at full back but by the time League football
recommenced he was back in his favoured right wing
spot and he carried on in the first team until beyond his
35th birthday. He was also a fine tennis player, once
giving Fred Perry a close game.

Reading Record: Lge 23/7, FAC 3/1, Wartime 221/46,
Total 247/54
League Career Total: 71/24

WILF'S CLAIM TO FAME - Wilf was a scout for West
Ham well into his seventies, spotting many talented
youngsters including Trevor Brooking and Harry
Redknapp plus one who was to become as popular at
Reading as Wilf himself - Steve Death.

CHRISTIE Alexander Gray

b. Paisley 27.6.1896 d. Reading 22.5.1981
Ht 5ft 10 Wt 12st (20-21)
Career: Larkhall Thistle 1913; Hamilton Acc. 1914;
READING summer 1919; Walsall June 1921; Southampton
May 1922; Norwich C. July 1923; Rochdale July 1924; Exeter
C. May 1928; Aldershot player manager summer 1929

Alec won his first honours with Larkhall Thistle when
they won the Scottish Junior Cup in 1914.

The First World War interrupted his career but he represented the Combined Services XI while working as a decoder in the Navy. Upon his demob, Alec joined Reading in the Southern League and was a regular in the club's first season in the League, playing in his favoured right half position for Reading's first game in the League, at Newport. A very cool, long striding player, Alec left Reading in 1921, and after three clubs in three seasons he spent four very productive campaigns with Rochdale. In 1929 he moved back South to become player/manager at Aldershot and in his last season as a player Alec guided them to the Southern League title.

Reading Record: Lge 33/1, FAC 1, SL 30/2, Total 64/3
League Career Total: 216/7

CHRISTIE Derrick Hugh Michael
b. London 15.3.1957
Ht 5 ft 8 Wt 11st (84-85)
Career: Northampton T. from apprentice March 1975; Cambridge U. (£50,000) November 1978; READING July 1984; Cardiff C. (free) October 1985; Peterborough U. July 1986; Corby T. July 1987; Cambridge C.

Derrick built up a reputation as a skilful midfield player around the lower divisions, giving particularly good service with Northampton, the club that developed him from a schoolboy, and Cambridge with whom he won promotion to the Second Division in 1977-78. He joined Reading to help them consolidate after promotion from the Fourth Division but was only on the fringe of the first team, often being used as a substitute. His only run in the first team came in April 1985 and it was during this period that Derrick scored his only Reading goal. The following season saw Reading running away with the Third Division title but there was no place for Derrick and so he was released in order to join Cardiff.

Reading Record: Lge 8(6)/1, AMC 2, Total 10(6)/1
League Career Total: 280(37)/40

CHUNG Cyril 'Sammy'
b. Abingdon 16.7.1932
Ht 5ft 9 Wt 11st 6 (63-64)
Career: Abingdon; Headington U; READING professional 19 November 1951; Norwich C.(£5,000) 7 January 1955; Watford June 1957 player/coach 1963; Bournemouth coach; Ipswich T. coach 1964; Wolverhampton W. coach 1967, manager June 1976 to November 1978; IFK Vasten (Sweden) manager 1980; United Arab Emirates national coach 1982; Stoke C. assist manager summer 1985; Coventry C; Colchester U. assist manager 1990; Blackburn R; Oldwinford manager; Tamworth manager 1991 to January 1993; Doncaster R. manager 1994 to August 1996

After a free scoring amateur period, Sammy made a sensational start to his professional career with Reading by scoring a hat-trick on his Hampshire League debut and hitting 30 goals in his first eight games. While working to complete his carpentry apprenticeship, Sammy was being groomed as a replacement for Ron Blackman and he made his debut alongside Blackman in April 1953, scoring four goals in his first five games to stake his claim. Blackman was sold during that summer and Sammy started the new season in the number nine shirt but soon moved to inside right. By January 1955 hard-up Reading were forced to sell Sammy to Norwich where a broken leg hindered his progress, but the need to raise funds brought about another transfer, to Watford. There he developed into a fine inside forward and forged a management partnership with Bill McGarry that lasted 12 years. Sammy guided Wolves to the Second Division title in 1976-77 but was sacked shortly after they were knocked out of the League Cup by Reading in 1978. He finally retired from management after being sacked by Doncaster minutes before the start of the 1996-97 season and replaced by Kerry Dixon.

Reading Record: Lge 22/12, FAC 3/1, Total 25/13
League Career Total: 289/43

CHURCHILL Trevor
b. Barnsley 20.11.1923
Ht 6ft Wt 12st 7 (46-47)
Career: Sheffield U. amateur; Corinthian Casuals; READING from amateur October 1946; Dartford (loan) August 1946; Leicester C. August 1947; Rochdale January 1949; Swindon T. May 1953

As a schoolteacher in the Navy, Trevor had to wait for his demob before he could sign professionally for Reading, and so his debut, in September 1946 at QPR, was as an amateur. A series of fine displays in goal earned him his pro contract but after conceding five at Port Vale he lost his place and only played one more League game for Reading. After a spell with Leicester's reserves, Trevor won himself a regular place in Rochdale's first team.

Reading Record: Lge 10
League Career Total: 131

CLARK Paul Peterson
b. Benfleet 14.9.1958
Ht 5ft 10 Wt 12st 5 (81-82)
Career: Southend U. from apprentice July 1977; Brighton (£40,000) November 1977; READING (loan) 1 October 1981; Southend U. (free) August 1982, caretaker manager March 1987, player manager September 1987 to May 1988, player assist. manager to July 1991; Gillingham July 1991; Chelmsford C. summer 1994; Cambridge U. October 1995 assist. manager; Leyton O. September 2000 assist. manager

After a successful schoolboy career that saw Paul play for England at U15 and Youth level, he joined his local League club to make his first team debut at 18. A transfer to Brighton saw Paul help them win promotion to the First Division but three years later he was loaned to Reading where the all-action midfielder made two appearances but, unfortunately, both ended in home defeats. The following summer Paul moved back to Southend where his eight year spell included a period as caretaker manager and player manager during which he led them to promotion. Released in 1991 he had a spell with Gillingham and then Chelmsford before coming out of retirement as a player in 1995 to become the second oldest Cambridge player.

Reading Record: Lge 2
League Career Total: 458(24)/14

CLEMENT Neil

b. Reading 3.10.1978
Ht 6ft Wt 12st 3 (98-99)
Career: Chelsea from trainee October 1995; READING (loan) 19 November 1998; Preston N.E. (loan) March 1999; Brentford (loan) November 1999; West Bromwich Alb. (loan) March 2000, permanent (£200,000) summer 2000

Although born in Reading and the son of QPR and England right back, Dave Clement, Neil joined Chelsea as a trainee after winning England Schools and Youth caps. Chelsea's multi-national squad meant that chances were restricted to just one League appearance by the time he joined Reading on loan. He made an initial impact, solving Reading's left sided defensive problems and scoring on his home debut, against Lincoln. Neil was also used in midfield and although he failed to maintain his exceptional early form he still made a valuable contribution during his three month loan spell.

Reading Record: Lge 11/1, AMC 1, Total 12/1
League Career Total: 75(2)/6+

CLOVER William Arthur

b. Bracknell 19.2.1920 d. 11/1971
Ht 6ft 1 Wt 12st 7 (49-50)
Career: Woodley; Hurst Old Boys; READING from amateur 27 January 1946

A well built right back, Bill was stationed just outside Reading with the RAF police during the War and played once for Reading reserves as well as helping the RAF win the Inter Services Summer Cup in a final played at The Heysal Stadium. Bill became a regular in Reading's first team from January 1946 and played in the first League game after the War.

Strangely, after a few games in that first season he had to wait until January 1949 for his next chance and he stayed in the first team until September, during which time he scored from four penalties. Sadly, Bill then suffered a serious knee injury at Exeter and although he tried to make a comeback, the injury was so severe that he was forced to retire at the end of the 1949-50 season. Bill went into the licensing trade and ran several local pubs but was best known as the landlord of the Spread Eagle, the pub at the corner of Elm Park.

Reading Record: Lge 44/4, FAC 1, Wartime 19, Total 64/4

COCKERILL Henry 'Harry' Leslie

b. Ryhope 27.6.1896 d. 1960
Ht 5ft 9 Wt 12st (23-24)
Career: Arsenal; Luton T. 1920; Mid Rhonda; Bristol C. 1922; READING May 1923; Merthyr T. July 1925

A tough tackling left half, Harry made a handful of League appearances before a move to Reading saw him given a real chance. Between September 1923 and December 1924 he missed just one first team game, scoring twice in a brief spell at inside left. Then Reading signed Dai Evans, and apart from one game at left back he never played another league game for the club. In 1925 Harry moved to Merthyr, the victims of his first League goal, but after four games his League career was over.

Reading Record: Lge 55/2, FAC 4, Total 59/2
League Career Total: 83/3

COCKRAM Allan Charles

b. Kensington 8.10.1963
Ht 5ft 8 Wt 10st 8 (91-92)
Career: Tottenham H. from apprentice January 1981; Bristol R. (non contract) August 1985; USA; Farnborough; Crystal Palace (trial) 1986; St Albans C. January 1987; Brentford March 1988; Brighton (trial) August 1991; Woking; READING (non contract) 4 September 1991; Woking March 1992; St Albans C. player manager March 1992; Chertsey T. to January 1997

Despite having progressed through Spurs' youth system to make a couple of League appearances, Allan found it difficult to maintain a career in League football. He appeared to have resurrected his career with Brentford where he made almost 100 first team appearances but, on being released from Griffin Park, Allan went out of the League, apart from a short spell with Reading. Playing on a non contract basis Allan actually scored on his Reading debut, coming on as sub to equalize at Wigan. Despite this flying start he was only used occasionally over the next four months and after a three match run in February he was released in March 1992.

Reading Record: Lge 2(4)/1, FAC (1), AMC (1), Total 2(6)/1
League Career Total: 71(28)/15

CODNER Robert George
b. Walthamstow 23.1.1965
Ht 5ft 11 Wt 11st 8 (95-96)
Career: Tottenham H. jnrs; Leicester C. (free) September 1983; Dagenham; Barnet; Brighton (£125,000) September 1988; Birmingham C. (trial); READING (free) 22 September 1995; Peterborough U. March 1996; Barnet March 1996; Southend U. March 1997; READING August 1997; Stevenage October 1997; Kettering T. August 2000

Another player who found his way back to the League via non-League football, Robert established his reputation as a skilful midfielder with Barnet when he won five England Semi Pro caps. Despite the big fee for a non-League player, Brighton got good value their money with well over 300 first team appearances, several as captain. Released in the summer of 1995, Robert joined Reading on a three month contract after a trial with the club. Although his class was apparent he just lacked the necessary pace to establish himself in the first team and, not having completed the full 90 minutes in his five first team games, his contract was not renewed. Robert returned to Reading for a short spell to help out the reserves at the start of 1997-98 and played a couple of pre-season friendlies for them in 2000.

Reading Record: Lge 3(1), LC 1, Total 4(1)
League Career Total: 292(16)/40

ROBERT'S CLAIM TO FAME - Early in 1994 Robert was charged with possessing cocaine but, partly thanks to character evidence from his long time friend, Michael Gilkes, the jury quickly found him not guilty. When he joined Reading his team mates showed the typical subtlety for which footballers are famed by nicknaming Robert 'OJ'!

COLGAN Nicholas Victor
b. Drogheda 19.9.1973
Ht 6ft 1 Wt 13st 6 (97-98)
Career: Drogheda U; Chelsea from trainee October 1992; Brentford (loan) October 1997; READING (loan) 27 February 1998; Bournemouth summer 1998; Hibernian July 1999

With just one League appearance to his credit with Chelsea, Nick made the majority of his first team appearances on his two loan spells although he had been capped by the Republic of Ireland at every level except full international. The young goalie came to Reading in place of the injured Nicky Hammond but the team's fragile confidence was further damaged when Nick was caught in possession nine minutes into his debut to concede the only goal in a relegation battle at Crewe.

Worse was to follow as Nick conceded another 15 goals in his next four games before returning to Chelsea although, in fairness, no keeper could have done much to shore up Reading's suspect defence at that stage.

Reading Record: Lge 5
League Career Total: 11

COLLINS John William
b. Chiswick 10.8.1942
Ht 5ft 9 Wt 10st 10 (67-68)
Career: QPR from jnrs August 1959; Oldham A. October 1966; READING (£6,360) 5 August 1967; Luton T. (£10,000) August 1969; Cambridge U. February 1971; Fulham reserve coach 1975; Watford coach 1975 to summer 1977; Brighton assist. manager August 1982

John made his name as a nippy inside forward with QPR, spending seven successful seasons with them before a surprise move took him to Oldham for nine months. He returned south with Reading and gave excellent service for the club, where his skill and experience helped bring out the best of fellow forwards, John Sainty and Peter Silvester. Not that John neglected his own goalscoring duties as he topped Reading's scorers in 1968-69. Amazingly, the appointment of Jack Mansell meant that there was no place for the previous season's top scorer and John was allowed to join Luton.

Reading Record: Lge 82(3)/28, FAC 9/1, LC 3/1, Total 94(3)/30
League Career Total: 407(10)/108

CONROY Michael Kevin
b. Glasgow 31.12.1965
Ht 6ft Wt 12st 7 (88-89)
Career: Coventry C. jnrs; Clydebank (free) 1984; St Mirren (£80,000) December 1987; READING (£50,000); Burnley (£35,000) 16 July 1991; Preston N.E. (£85,000) August 1993; Fulham (£75,000) August 1995; Blackpool (£50,000) March 1998; Chester C. (loan) December 1998; Chester C.(loan) March 1999, Eastern Pride (Australia) January 2001

Having been released by Coventry, Mike went part time with Clydebank and topped their goalscorers in each season with them, netting 38 goals in 92 League starts, before St Mirren took him to the Scottish Premier. There he only managed one goal in 10 games but he wasted no time when moved to Reading, netting in his first start, at Cardiff. Mike had always been a centre forward but the arrival of Ian Porterfield at Elm Park saw him also used as a defender and in midfield. He enjoyed a varied relationship with the Reading fans who, while recognizing his talents, jokingly nicknamed him the 'White Pele'!

The arrival of Mark McGhee saw Mike sold to Burnley where he topped their scorers in their 1991-92 Fourth Division championship season. From then on Mike moved to several clubs, scoring his fair share of goals for each of them to provide a good return on the fees spent on him.

Reading Record: Lge 65(15)/7, FAC 8(2)/1, LC 3(2), AMC 2(2), Total 78(21)/8
League Career Total: 302(35)/94

COOK Maurice
b. Berkhampstead 10.12.1931
Ht 5ft 11 Wt 11st 10 (64-65)
Career: Potten End; Berkhampstead; Watford from amateur May 1953; Fulham (£15,000) February 1958; READING (free) 4 May 1965; Banbury T. player coach July 1966

Spotted while playing on the right wing by Watford, Maurice proved a versatile and successful signing for them, playing in all five forward positions and only missing three games in four and a half seasons. Maurice also became the only Watford player to represent the Third Division South in the annual fixture against the Northern section. His form as a hard running centre forward was such that Fulham broke Watford's transfer record to take him to Craven Cottage and in his first full season he helped them regain their First Division status. Despite this, and being a regular in their First Division side, Maurice once put in a transfer request because he felt he was not good enough to play in the same team as Johnny Haynes! After seven years with Fulham he was allowed to leave on a free transfer and was signed by his old Fulham teammate, Roy Bentley, for Reading. After a run in the League during September, scoring twice, Maurice was rarely in the first team and a four match spell in the spring heralded the end of his League career. When not in the first team, Maurice was a part of Reading's Football Combination promotion winning side but at the end of his first season he was released by the club.

Reading Record: Lge 12/2, LC 1/1, Total 13/3
League Career Total: 441/159

MAURICE'S CLAIM TO FAME - Nine minutes into Fulham's League Cup-tie against Bristol City on 26 September 1960 Maurice opened the scoring with what was the very first goal in this new competition.

COOK William Lawrence
b. Dundee 11.3.1906 d. 6.1981
Ht 5ft 4 Wt 9st 4 (35-36)
Career: Dundee North End; Forfar 1924; Dundee 1925; Bolton W. (£4,000) December 1928; Blackpool May 1936; READING (£500) 30 April 1937; Dundee May 1938; Canoustie Panmure (Wartime guest)

After a successful start to his career in Scotland that saw him twice play for the Scottish League, Billy was the subject of a big transfer move to Bolton in 1928. There, he was an immediate success, helping Wanderers win the 1929 FA Cup and his consistent form earned him three Scottish caps in 1934 plus selection for Scotland's tour of Canada. Although he always played on the left wing for Bolton, his international honours were at outside right. After more than 260 first team appearances for Bolton, Billy joined his old inside forward partner and former Reading manager, Joe Smith, at Blackpool where he promptly helped them win promotion to the First Division. A season later he joined another old Bolton teammate, Billy Butler, at Reading and after his first team debut was delayed until October 1937 he was ever-present to the end of the season. Given a free transfer at that time, Billy returned to play for Dundee and later ran a pub there. Billy was highly regarded in his day but a contemporary cigarette card hinted at why he only won three caps - *'another of football's great midgets. A dazzling winger up to every trick with twinkling feet. Sometimes inclined to over elaborate'.*

Reading Record: Lge 33/2, FAC 1, SSC 3/1, Total 37/3
League Career Total: 286/38

COOPER Adrian Stanley John
b. Reading 16.1.1957
Ht 5ft 9 Wt 10st 10 (75-76)
Career: Tottenham H. apprentice October 1972; Reading apprentice 25 July 1973, professional 17 January 1975; Bracknell T. May 1976; Basingstoke Town

A brilliant schoolboy career saw Adrian play for Reading Schools at all levels and win eight England Schools caps which attracted the attention of a number of top clubs. Adrian chose Spurs but could not settle and returned to play local football before being tempted back to the professional game with Reading. His progress was more obvious and after a consistent run in the reserves he was given his League debut at home to Stockport, three months after his 17th birthday.

Adrian was a striker in his schoolboy career, converted to midfield at Spurs while at Reading his versatility was demonstrated by the fact that his first six League games were in five different positions. The start of 1975 saw him given a regular first team spot in January and February, that produced his two League goals, but he was rarely used after that and was released at the end of 1975-76. Although Adrian had the far more spectacular career during his schooldays, it was his younger brother, Leigh, who had the more successful League record with over 350 appearances, mainly for Plymouth.

Reading Record: Lge 14/2

COOPER Horace George
b. Maidenhead 2nd qtr 1899 d. ?
Ht 5ft 9 Wt 11st (22-23)
Career: Reading Phoenix; Southampton; Reading Liberal Club; READING summer 1920

Horace could claim to be Reading's best goalkeeper since he never conceded a goal during his entire League career. The catch is that his career amounted to just one game - away to Exeter in April 1921. A local player, Horace got his game following an injury to Syd Crawford but he continued playing for the reserves as a part-time player, while working for Thames Conservancy.

Reading Record: Lge 1

COOPER Neale James
b. Darjeeling 24.11.1963
Ht 6ft 1 Wt 12st 7 (91-92)
Career: King Street; Aberdeen 1979; Aston Villa (£350,000) July 1986; Glasgow Rngrs (£250,000) October 1988; READING (free) July 1991; Dunfermline November 1991; Ross Co. manager December 2000

Despite being born in India, Neale was a typically Scottish tough tackling midfielder who was capped at schools, youth and 13 times at U21 level. He was a member of Alex Ferguson's all conquering Aberdeen side that won two championships, four Scottish Cups, a League Cup plus the European Cup Winners Cup and Super Cup in 1983. A big money move to Aston Villa proved a disaster for Neale as a series of leg and knee injuries restricted his appearances. Another big fee saw him move to Rangers in 1988 but, given a 'free' two years later, he joined up with former Aberdeen colleague, Mark McGhee at Reading. His spell with Reading was not a happy one and after a sending off in his second game, Neale failed to show his true form which led to his contract being cancelled by mutual consent so he could return to Scotland.

Reading Record: Lge 6(1), LC 2, Total 8(1)
League Career Total: 25(2)

COOTE Stanley A
b. Harpenden c.1912
Ht 6ft Wt 12st 10 (35-36)
Career: Arden Wed; Luton T. from amateur autumn 1932; READING (£300) 17 October 1935

A butcher by trade, Stan was signed by Luton from a local amateur club and made over 80 appearances in their reserves plus one in the League. Described as 'a dashing defender', full back Stan became Billy Butler's first signing as Reading manager, but was used as a centre half in the first team. He got an early taste of first team football at Reading in the Southern Section Cup but had to wait until the end of March before he got a chance in the League. Although the team only conceded four goals in that spell, Stan was never selected for the first team again and was given a free transfer at the end of 1936-37.

Reading Record: Lge 6, FAC 1, SSC 2, Total 9
League Career Total: 7

COURT Colin
b. Winchester 25.3.1964
Ht 5ft 11 Wt 12st (80-81)
Career: Andover T; READING non contract July 1981

Although Colin only made one appearance in goal for Reading he helped set a League record. He had only made a handful of reserve appearances and was third choice keeper when, on 20 February 1982, he was thrown into the first team for Reading's local derby against Swindon, due to injury to John Turner and Steve Death being in dispute with the club. Colin acquitted himself well, despite his inexperience, but was unfortunate to score an own goal when he deflected a cross into his own net. As if to make Colin feel better, the vastly more experienced Swindon goalie, Jimmy Allan, scored Reading's equalizer - surely the only time that both goals in a League game have been scored by goalkeepers. That proved to be Colin's only first team appearance and he returned to Andover.

Reading Record: Lge 1

COWLING David Roy
b. Doncaster 27.11.1958
Ht 5ft 9 Wt 11st (87-88)
Career: Mansfield T. apprentice; Huddersfield T. August 1977; Scunthorpe U. (loan) November 1987; READING (loan) 24 December 1987; READING (free) March 1988; Scunthorpe U. summer 1988; Doncaster R. manager 1997

David was a fixture in Huddersfield's first team after writing for a trial, making nearly 400 first team appearances for them.

During his spell with them, he won the Fourth Division title and then scored the goal that clinched promotion to the Second Division. He was loaned to Reading during Christmas 1987 and, although David returned to Huddersfield after two games, he later joined Reading on a 'free' on transfer deadline day. He proved something of a lucky charm for Reading in what was a disastrous League campaign for the club. His two loan games produced two away wins and after his permanent signing he scored on his Elm Park debut. His nine Reading starts saw only two defeats which gave him happier memories of his spell with Reading than his previous visit to Elm Park, with Huddersfield, since that ended with a rare sending off for the tall left winger. Released at the end of that season, he joined Scunthorpe, and, in helping them to the 1988-89 play-offs, he scored the first League goal at Glandford Park.

Reading Record: Lge 9(1)/1
League Career Total: 426(14)/49

DAVID'S CLAIM TO FAME - During 1997-98, David was appointed as manager of troubled Doncaster Rovers to complete a hat trick of ex-Reading players in charge at Belle Vue, the other two being Sammy Chung and Kerry Dixon. David's spell was almost over before it had begun, lasting just 10 days - the fifth shortest on record.

CRAWFORD James
b. Chicago 1.5.1973
Ht 5ft 11 Wt 11st 6 (98-99)
Career: Bohemians; Newcastle U. (trial) August 1994, permanent (£75,000) March 1995; Rotherham U. (loan) September 1996; Dundee U. (loan) February 1998; READING (£50,000) 26 March 1998; Shelbourne (free) July 2000

Jimmy and his family moved to Ireland when he was six and played for Bohemians where he came to the attention of Kevin Keegan who offered him a trial at Newcastle. He eventually signed for Newcastle and although he only made three substitute appearances for them, he still won four U21 caps for the Republic. On transfer deadline day of 1997-98 he was one of seven signings made by new Reading manager, Tommy Burns, in an attempt to keep the side in Division One. A skilful player capable of playing in midfield or defence, Jimmy was used mainly at right back at Reading. Although he scored a spectacular late winner against Bristol City on the opening day of 1999-00, the appointment of Alan Pardew as Reading manager saw his first team chances reduce and Jimmy was placed on the transfer list midway through that season.

Reading Record: Lge 17(4)/1 FAC 1, LC 2(2), AMC 1(1), Total 21(7)/1
League Career Total: 28(6)/1

CRAWFORD Harold Sydney
b. Dundee 7.10.1887 d. Tynemouth 21.4.1979
Ht 5ft 10 1/2 Wt 11st 3 (21-22)
Career: North Shields; Hebburn Arg; Woolwich Arsenal 1911; READING July 1913; Millwall (£50) summer 1922; Workington 1925

Syd was spotted by Arsenal playing in the North East, where he was brought up and played 26 First Division games in goal for them before joining Reading prior to World War One. He soon became a great favourite at Elm Park as a fearless keeper, and also because of his uncanny ability at saving penalties. Syd had a unique style for spot kicks, standing to one side of the centre of his goal in order to tempt the kicker to aim for the bigger gap. It clearly worked as Syd saved over 50 penalties in his nine years with Reading. His most famous save came in the last minute of an FA Cup-tie against First Division Chelsea in 1921 that earned Reading a replay. This caused his wife and a club director to faint in the excitement! Syd played in the majority of Reading's first two seasons in Third Division South but in 1922 he was sold to Millwall.

Reading Record: Lge 73, FAC 5, SL 76, Total 154
League Career Total: 176

CROMBIE Dean Malcolm
b. Lincoln 9.8.1957
Ht 6ft Wt 11st 12 (86-87)
Career: Rushton Bucyrus Sports; Lincoln C. February 1977; Grimsby T. August 1978; READING (loan) November 1986; Bolton W. August 1987; Lincoln C. January 1991; Bolton W. youth team manager and assist. manager

A solid, steady left sided defender who could also play in midfield, Dean gave consistency to all the teams he represented in a career of nearly 500 first team appearances. Dean spent nine years with Grimsby during which time they won the Third Division title, in 1980. While he was with Grimsby he was loaned to Reading, playing five times in his one month spell, but was only on the winning side once. In 1987 he began a long association with Bolton, the playing highlight of which was his scoring in their 1988 Sherpa Van Final triumph at Wembley in a season that saw him voted the fans Player of the Year. Since then he has served Bolton in a number of different coaching roles.

Reading Record: Lge 4, FMC 1, Total 5
League Career Total: 443(10)/4

CRONIN Thomas Patrick
b. Richmond 17.12.1932
Ht 5ft 10 Wt 11st 1 (56-57)
Career: East Sheen A; Fulham from amateur September 1950;

READING (£1,750) 30 May 1956; Guildford C. summer 1958; Yiewsley October 1958; Ramsgate June 1959

For much of his career with Fulham, Tommy was the understudy of Johnny Haynes and Bobby Robson so it is, perhaps, not so surprising that he only made two League appearances in his six years at Craven Cottage. Eventually Tommy moved to Reading in search of first team football which, initially, he found. Starting at inside left, he was used at wing half mid season and then had a run on the left wing towards the end of his first season. It was on the wing that his three goals came during that period, but he only managed four League appearances in 1957-58 and left to join Guildford.

Reading Record: Lge 30/4, FAC 1, SPFC 2, Total 33/4
League Career Total: 32/4

CROSS John 'Jack'
b. Bury 5.2.1927
Ht 5ft 10 1/2 Wt 12st (55-56)
Career: Hendon; Guildford C; Blackpool amateur; Bournemouth from amateur 1949; Northampton T. October 1953; Sheffield U. (£12,000) February 1954; READING (£2,600) 29 September 1955; Weymouth May 1958; Headington U.

Jack was one of the first professional footballers to combine his playing career with academic studies and the novelty was such that he was often referred to as 'Jack Cross B.Sc.', in match programmes. A former guardsman, Jack didn't turn professional until he was 22 when he signed for Bournemouth. He was a cultured centre forward and after a short but successful spell with Northampton he joined First Division Sheffield United for a big fee. Shortly after this transfer he played for the Navy against the RAF at Elm Park and 18 months later he was back, having signed for Reading. He scored in his first two games, and soon switched from his central position to inside forward, but after three months in the first team he lost his place. The following season he topped the reserves' goalscorers but failed to make the first team, and Jack was released in May 1957 following difficulties in fitting training in with his work at nearby AERE, Harwell.

Reading Record: Lge 15/6, FAC 3/1, SFC 2, Total 20/7
League Career Total: 206/94

CROSSLEY James John
b. Belfast 19.7.1922
Ht 5ft 10 Wt 12st (46-47)
Career: Cliftonville; Distillery; Portsmouth April 1945; READING July 1946

After a career in Northern Ireland, James came to England as a PT instructor during the War and signed for Portsmouth near the end of the hostilities. He played 12 first team games for Pompey but before League football restarted he moved to Reading. As a right back James played mainly in the reserves and his one League game ended in a home defeat by Ipswich. At the end of his only season with Reading, James was put on the transfer list and quit League football.

Reading Record: Lge 1

CROWN David Ian
b. Enfield 16.2.1958
Ht 5ft 10 Wt 11st 4 (86-87)
Career: Barking; Grays Ath; Middlesex W. 1980; Brentford July 1980; Portsmouth November 1981; Exeter C. (loan) March 1983; READING August 1983; Cambridge U. summer 1985; Southend U. (£50,000) November 1987; Gillingham June 1990; Dagenham & Redbridge; Purfleet; Billericay Town; Purfleet asst. manager

Another late starter as far as League football is concerned, David had played for several top non-League sides before turning professional with Brentford at 22. His pacey left wing play brought him to the attention of several clubs, including Reading who tried to exchange him for Stuart Beavon, but he moved to Portsmouth in stead. It was a missed signing that was to come back to haunt Reading because, during a loan spell with Exeter, his late winner in the last game of 1982-83 kept Exeter up at Reading's expense. The following season David finally joined Reading, having made his last appearance for Pompey as a sub against Reading, and he made amends for relegating them by missing just one game as the Royals regained their Third Division status. As well as his seven goals, David made many more with his crosses for his former Portsmouth colleague, Trevor Senior, as he topped the country's scorers. David was a regular on the left wing the following season but was tried in a more central role on a couple of occasions. In one such game he scored twice at Cambridge and when he was released in May 1985 they snapped him up. There, he revelled in his new striking role and set Cambridge's scoring record with 24 League goals in his first season. Moves to Southend and Gillingham saw the goals continue to flow at the rate of approximately one every other game, a record that earned him a Player of the Year award at Southend in 1989. David then continued playing non-League football while he built up his accountancy practice.

Reading Record: Lge 87(1)/14, FAC 6/1, LC 4/2, AMC 2(1), Total 99(2)/17
League Career Total: 464(10)/170

CRYLE George
b. Aberdeen 10.4.1928
Ht 5ft 8 Wt 10st 10 (49-50)
Career: Wolverhampton W. from jnrs February 1946; READING (£250) 17 June 1948; Ayr U. (£750) 1 August 1951; Swindon T. August 1952

George spent three seasons with Wolves without making it to their first team and was also working as a 'Bevin Boy' down a coal mine up to six weeks before signing for Reading. He was signed as a left half but made his League debut on the wing at Swansea over Christmas 1948, in what must have been a memorable match. Not only did he score in front of a then record crowd, the game saw three players sent off - unheard of in those days. That was the start of a four match run that accounted for half of George's League career in his three seasons at Elm Park. After spells with Ayr and Swindon, George returned to Reading in 1961, where he worked in Maurice Edelston's sports shop as well as helping coach youngsters at Elm Park.

Reading Record: Lge 8/2
League Career Total: 20/2

CULLEN Shane **Jonathon** Raymond
b. Oxford 9.10.1962
Ht 5ft 7 1/2 Wt 10st 10 (81-82)
Career: Didcot T; Oxford U. (trial); READING from apprentice 9 October 1980; Larnaca (Cyprus) summer 1982

Reading signed Jon from under the nose of his local club after he had played for Oxford and the South of England at schoolboy level. Capable of playing in either full back position, Jon only made three appearances in his first two seasons but was selected to play for an FA XI v The Public Schools in December 1979. Jon was used more frequently during 1981-82, mainly at left back or as substitute but, despite it being his best season with Reading, Jon was released at the end of the campaign.

Reading Record: Lge 14(6), FAC 1, Total 15(6)

CULLEN William M
b. Glasgow c.1900 d. ?
Ht 5ft 8 Wt 11st (23-24)
Career: Third Lanark; READING August 1923

Initially a centre forward, William had the misfortune to make his League debut for Reading on the left wing during a 5-1 defeat at Swansea.

More misfortune followed shortly after when he broke his leg in a friendly and his career was over.

Reading Record: Lge 1

CUMMING Gordon Robert Riddell
b. Johnstone 23.1.1948
Ht 5ft 6 Wt 9st 4 (70-71)
Career: Inverness Cal; Glasgow U; Arsenal from groundstaff January 1965; READING (£12,000) 11 December 1969

Gordon played for Arsenal's nursery team, Glasgow United, before moving to Highbury in 1964 where he won a number of youth honours. He played for Young Scotland in the 1967-68 Little World Cup, won the FA Youth Cup in 1966, and was second highest scorer for Arsenal reserves as they won the Combination championship in 1968-69. Despite these successes, Gordon appeared no closer to a first team place so he moved to Reading as a replacement for fans favourite, Tom Jenkins, having signed on in Euston Station.

Gordon wasted no time in winning over the fans by scoring three goals of his first four home games. Gordon's arrival also saw a remarkable turnaround in Reading's form as his skilful play on the right wing saw Reading finish the season as the League's top scorers. Although the club struggled in the next couple of years, Gordon remained on form and finished top goalscorer in both seasons as well as being the runaway winner of the fans Player of the Year vote in 1971-72. The arrival of Charlie Hurley as manager saw Gordon converted from a traditional winger to a more gritty midfielder and although his goal tally reduced his effectiveness didn't. His new role was not always appreciated by the fans, but he played a major part in Reading's 1975-76 promotion season. Following Reading's relegation the following season, Gordon decided to quit League football to help run the family restaurant business.

Reading Record: Lge 277(18)/51, FAC 21(1)/8, LC 13(1)/2, Watney Cup 1/1, Total 312(20)/62

CURETON Jamie

b. Bristol 28.8.1975
Ht 5ft 8 Wt 10st 7 (00-01)
Career: Norwich C. from trainee February 1993; Bournemouth (loan) September 1995; Bristol R. (£250,000) September 1996; READING (£250,000) 21 August 2000

A former England youth international, Jamie originally played out wide on the left but his career changed dramatically when he switched to a striking role after Bristol Rovers sold Barry Hales in November 1998. From then on he became one of the most prolific scorers in Division Two, forming a deadly partnership with fellow Rovers striker, Jason Roberts. Jamie ended that season with 29 goals and the division's Golden Boot award. Another 22 League goals followed the next season but Rovers' lack of success lead to Jamie becoming unsettled and, after scoring on the opening day of the season, he was sold to Reading for a bargain £250,000. It was a significant signing as Jamie had scored six goals against the Royals while with Rovers, including an amazing four second half goals in Reading's 6-0 home defeat in January 1999. At the time of joining Reading, Jamie was still the only player to score a hat-trick at the Madejski Stadium, but within three weeks of his transfer he became the first Reading player to claim the match ball at the new ground with a trio against Brentford. He maintained his scoring record to again finish the top scorer in Division Two, ending with 31 goals. Undoubtedly the bargain of the season, Jamie got his revenge against a vicious hate campaign from some Rovers fans by scoring the winner against them at the Madejski Stadium.

Reading Record: Lge 37(6)/26, FAC 2(1)/1, LC 2/1, AMC 2/1, Play-offs 3/1, Total 46(7)/30 +
League Career Total: 215(36)/104 +

CURLE Keith

b. Bristol 14.11.1963
Ht 6ft Wt 12st 7 (87-88)
Career: Bristol R. from apprentice November 1981; Torquay U. (£5,000) November 1983; Bristol C. (£10,000) March 1984; READING (£150,000) 23 October 1987; Wimbledon (£350,000) 21 October 1988; Manchester C. (£2.5 m) August 1991; Wolverhampton W. (£650,000) August 1996; Sheffield U. summer 2000

Having started his career as a winger with Bristol Rovers, Keith was converted to a defender after his move to Torquay. He moved back to Bristol with City where he quickly developed into one of the most promising defenders in the division and in October 1987 Ian Branfoot broke Reading's transfer record in order to add some much needed pace to his defence. Keith was unable to prevent Reading from relegation from the Second Division but he did complete a remarkable Wembley hat trick - having played in two Associate Members Cup finals, winning in 1986, Keith was a member of the Reading team that won the Simod Cup in 1988. The 4-1 victory was so comfortable that Keith was able to forego his usual 'role' of going down injured whenever Reading scored! Clearly, Keith was too strong for the Third Division and after a year at Elm Park he moved to Wimbledon for a Reading record fee.

Three years later Keith was breaking more transfer records when Manchester City paid the Dons £2.5 million to make him the country's most expensive defender. His speed and calmness at the centre of City's defence earned him three England caps although Graham Taylor used him at right back. Another big money move to Wolves was initially hampered by injury but he became a regular as club captain and in December 1998 became part of their coaching staff while still a first team regular.

Reading Record: Lge 40, LC 8, FMC 5, Total 53
League Career Total: 623(25)33 +

CURTIS Frank

b. Llanelli 1890 d. ?
Ht 5ft 10 Wt 12st 7 (20-21)
Career: Llanelli; Wolverhamton W. 1914; READING August 1920; Bridgend; Bilston 1921; Kidderminster Harriers

Initially a centre forward, Frank must have cursed the start of the First World War as he was in tremendous form for Wolves during the 1914-15 season scoring 25 goals in 37 Second Division games. After the War he only managed three games for them and a move to Reading did little to change his luck. Frank managed just one League appearance for Reading and that was at centre half in a 2-2 draw at Portsmouth. Unable to oust Mavin or Getgood from the centre half role at Elm Park and sent off in a friendly against Oxford University, Frank quit League football at the end of 1920-21.

Reading Record: Lge 1
League Career Total: 41/25

DALE Harold James
b. Woolwich 2nd qtr 1899 d. ?
Ht 5ft 9 Wt 11st 7 (20-21)
Career: READING 1921

For the last two games of their first season, Reading tried a couple of local goalies and for the visit to Millwall on 7 May 1921, Harry got his chance. He acquitted himself quite well but was beaten twice as they lost that game 2-0 and Harry never played for Reading again.

Reading Record: Lge 1

DALTON Bryan L
b. Arundel 9.1.1917
Ht 5ft 9 Wt 11st 7 (36-37)
Career: Littlehampton; Portsmouth (trial) 1936; READING 23 October 1936; Gillingham summer 1937

Bryan made his League debut with Portsmouth during a two month trial with them and the following season he was more successful at Reading, converting his one month trial into a contract. A traditional left winger, Bryan got off to a flying start by scoring on his Elm Park debut in the middle of a three match run in November 1936. He got a further chance in the first team later in the season and got another home goal but was not retained at the end of that season.

Reading Record: Lge 7/2
League Career Total: 14/2

DAND Robert 'Reggie'
b. Ilford c.1900 d. ?
Ht 5ft 7 Wt 11st (21-22)
Career: Ashford RW; Ilford; READING from amateur November 1921; QPR July 1924

A successful amateur career that included an England appearance against Ireland saw Reggie join Reading in the summer of 1921. He impressed in the pre-season friendlies but it took Reading until November to persuade him to give up his job as a stockbroker's clerk and become a professional. Reggie had to wait until the following March to make his League debut but he then became a fixture in Reading's half back line, missing just one game in the next 14 months. Although he joined Reading as a left half, he played in all three half back positions, making the most appearances on the right berth. During the summer, Reggie was cricket coach at Douai College.

Reading Record: Lge 56, FAC 1, Total 57
League Career Total: 57

DARNELL Leonard
b. Irchester 14.5.1905 d. Wallingford 11.1968
Ht 5ft 11 1/2 Wt 11st 2 (30-31)
Career: Rushden T; West Brom Alb. 1926; READING (£500) June 1930; Carlisle U. player coach 1934

A tall, elegant wing half, Len spent four and a half years with West Brom where his best season was 1928-29 when he made 27 appearances. When he became available, Reading wasted no time in bringing him in to Elm Park and he started the 1930-31 season at left half. Like several other Reading players, Len lost his place after the club's record 8-1 defeat at Burnley but won it back at Christmas and kept it to the end of the season when he scored the club's last goal in the Second Division for 55 years. Although Reading were relegated he was virtually ever-present, usually at right half, until February 1933 at which point his first team career with Reading was over. Given a free transfer at the end of 1933-34, Len had a spell as player coach at Carlisle before returning to Reading where he ran The Saracen's Head which he advertised for several seasons in the club programme.

Reading Record: Lge 84/4, FAC 7, SSC 1, Total 92/4
League Career Total: 120/4

DAVEY Hugh H
b. Belfast 1.1.1890 d. ?
Ht 5ft 8 1/2 Wt 11st 4 (25-26)
Career: Glentoran; Blackburn R. (loan); Bournemouth (£100) 1923; READING (player exchange) January 1925; Portsmouth (player exchange + £300) November 1927

It took a tribunal to sort out Hugh Davey's transfer to England because Bournemouth were a non-League side at the time so they were not liable to pay a transfer fee, but shortly after they were elected into Third Division South, Glentoran demanded a hefty £250 fee. Eventually the Anglo-Irish League Board set a fee of £100 which looked good value as Hugh finished Bournemouth's first ever League top scorer in 1923-24, including two at Elm Park, and had previously received a winners medal in the Irish FA Cup in 1921. Consequently, Reading could hardly believe their luck when Bournemouth accepted reserve back, Rob Marshall, in exchange for the prolific scorer.

Hugh started his Reading career at inside left and it wasn't until the last game of the 1924-25 that he moved to centre forward and he celebrated with a hat trick. The following season a knee injury kept him out for almost half the season but he still topped Reading's scorers with a remarkable 23 goals in only 24 League games, that included another final match hat trick as Reading clinched the Third Division South championship.

In October 1925 he earned the first of four Irish caps he won while with Reading and a year later he scored against England. Hugh continued to score regularly in the Second Division, netting Reading's first ever goal in that division and with 13 goals from his first 12 games of 1927-28 he was sold to Portsmouth where he added one more cap before injury curtailed his career. Reading fans who saw him play rate Hugh Davey as one of the very best centre forwards the club had and, because he was on the small side, he was more skilful than many of his contemporaries who tended to rely more on strength than skill.

Reading Record: Lge 61/45, FAC 5/3, Total 66/48
League Career Total: 111/69

DAVIDSON Douglas Bell
b. Dundee 2.12.1918 d. 1968
Ht 5ft 7 1/2 Wt 11st (50-51)
Career: East Fife; Blackpool October 1948; READING (£1,750) 4 May 1950; Birmingham C. trainer/coach August 1954; Portsmouth trainer 1964

Even though Douggie missed his best years as a player due to the War he still managed to win a Scottish B Champions and League Cup medal with East Fife before moving to Blackpool. His first team appearances were limited but at least when he did get a game at inside left, he had the opportunity to play alongside Stan Mortenson and Stanley Matthews. Douggie was 31 when Reading signed him and although he went straight into their first team by November 1950 and from then on he concentrated on coaching. He was made player coach the following season and then assistant trainer in August 1953 before leaving Elm Park.

Reading Record: Lge 11/1
League Career Total: 25/1

DAVIES Gareth Melville
b. Hereford 11.12.1973
Ht 6ft 1 Wt 11st 12 (97-98)
Career: Hereford U. from YTS April 1992; Crystal Palace (£120,000) July 1995; Cardiff C. (loan) February 1997; READING (£100,000) 12 December 1997; Hibernian (trial) January 1999; Swindon T. (free) 2 March 1999

The cousin of Republic of Ireland international, Kevin Sheedy, Gareth won eight U21 caps for Wales as he established himself as a promising central defender at Hereford. His form brought him a move to Crystal Palace where he was a highly regarded squad player even if he was only on the fringe of the first team, and Reading were thought to have got a bargain when he joined their battle for Division One survival.

Gareth immediately won over the Reading fans with some committed displays and surging runs into the attack. Although Reading continued to concede too many goals, Gareth was considered one of the few successes of the season so it was a surprise when new manager, Tommy Burns, failed to use him as Reading were relegated. The following season things got much worse for Gareth - after just one game it was clear that he did not feature in Burns' plans and he was forced to train alongside the youth team with four other out of favour players who became known as the 'Death Row Five'. Gareth refused to accept this unhappy situation and, amidst rumours of dressing room bust ups, he called in the PFA to mediate but the matter was resolved when he joined Swindon in March 1999.

Reading Record: Lge 18(1), FAC 3, LC 1, Total 22(1)
League Career Total: 160(10)/5 +

DAVIES Roy
b. Ealing 25.10.1953
Ht 5ft 7 1/2 Wt 11st 4 (77-78)
Career: Maidenhead U. 1973; Leatherhead; Hendon; Slough T; READING (£5,000) 1 October 1977; Torquay U. (£11,000) 24 August 1978; Wimbledon August 1980; Wealdstone; Malta 1985

After a varied non-League career, Roy made up for lost time when he joined Reading at the age of 24. He went straight into the first team and within a month his infectious personality and forceful displays on the left of Reading's midfield had earned Roy the captaincy. He remained ever-present for the rest of that season although he asked to be relieved of the captaincy in March as he believed it was affecting his form. Roy started the 1978-79 season on the subs bench and was sold to Torquay just after the start of the season. He proved a popular player for United even though, as the Torquay programme tactfully put it, 'discipline was not his forte'.

Reading Record: Lge 37/2
League Career Total: 108(8)/8

DAVIES Royston
b. Penydarren 19.10.1903 d. Gloucester 15.10.1944
Ht 5ft 7 Wt 11st 7 (1929-30)
Career: Aberamen A; Merthyr T. March 1925; Manchester U. May 1925; Southport (£600) November 1925; Cyfartha Stars October 1926; Barry T. March 1927; Bristol R. May 1927; Ebbw Vale summer 1928; Wolverhampton W. May 1929; READING 2 October 1929; Guildford C. summer 1932

Roy played a handful of League games as he flitted between League and non-League clubs but a run on the right wing for Wolves came to a premature end when his contract was cancelled by mutual agreement shortly after he was sent off against Hull.

He was snapped up by Reading where he at last became a first team regular, having several good runs in his three seasons at Elm Park, the best being 1930-31 when he played 30 Second Division games on either wing. That season also saw Roy's best goal tally, although three of his four goals were scored against Barnsley. Released by Reading, Roy moved to Guildford who were managed by Andrew Wylie, the man who had signed him for Reading. Sadly, Roy died with his boots on, expiring in an ambulance after being taken ill during an amateur game.

Reading Record: Lge 69/7, FAC 1, Total 70/7
League Career Total: 85/7

DAVIES William
b. Middlesbrough 16.5.1930
Ht 5ft 11 Wt 12st 7 (59-60)
Career: South Bank Jnrs; St Marys COB; Hull C. April 1949; Leeds U. August 1950; Scarborough; Bloxwich Strollers; READING 19 January 1953; Dover July 1961

Missed by Hull and Leeds, Bill became one of Reading's most consistent performers in the Fifties. Dominant in the air and clean in the tackle, he was an ideal centre half as well as being a non-smoking teetotaler. Several times it seemed that he would be replaced by another defender but each time Bill fought his way back. Although he was only ever-present in 1958-59, he averaged over 30 games a season after making his League debut at Bristol City on Christmas Day 1954. His calm play earned him several representative honours including a place in the Football Combination side that played a Dutch XI in Amsterdam in April 1959 and for the Third Division South side in the last annual fixture against the Northern Section in May 1958. Bill was also a member of the Reading team that reached the final of the 1958 Southern Professional Floodlit Cup. While at Reading Bill also coached Wallingford Town, but in 1961 he retired to concentrate on his engineering firm although he returned to Elm Park to run the reserves in 1971-72.

Reading Record: Lge 202, FAC 15, LC 1, SPFC 8, Total 226

BILL'S CLAIM TO FAME - No Reading outfield player has played more first team games for the club without scoring than the 226 goalless appearances Bill made.

DAVIS Joseph Frederick
b. Walsall 23.5.1929 d. 1996
Ht 5ft 9 Wt 10st 2 (53-54)
Career: Talbot Stead Tube; Bloxwich Strollers; READING (£350) 23 January 1953; Wrexham (£500) summer 1955

Right half Fred came to prominence playing for his works team and was twice picked for the Wolverhampton Works League representative side which led to a professional contract with Bloxwich Strollers. Further progress earned him a move to Reading and after seven months in their reserves he made his League debut at home to Southend. A run of three defeats in December cost him his place and he did not get it back until April. Basically a defensive player, Fred only scored once for Reading but at least he made it count as it was the winner at Norwich. He was released at the end of 1953-54 and joined Wrexham where Fred played nearly 250 first team until he retired in 1961.

Reading Record: Lge 63/1, FAC 7, Total 70/1
League Career: 293/13

DAVIS Herbert
b. Nottingham 1st qtr 1902 d. ?
Ht 5ft 8 Wt 10st 10 (24-25)
Career: Boston U; READING May 1923; Mansfield T. May 1925

An inside forward with an eye for goal, Bert joined Reading from Boston and made his League debut on the opening day of the 1923-24 season. He started on the right side but after losing his place in October, Bert came back at inside left where he showed an inclination to score goals in consecutive games. As fixtures were paired together in those days, with a home game being followed by the away match against the same club the following week, this resulted in Bert scoring doubles against Gillingham, QPR and Norwich. The signing of Ted Braithwaite and Walter Tinsley restricted Bert to just one appearance the following season and he was released in May 1925.

Reading Record: Lge 33/8, FAC 1, Total 34/8

DAWTRY Kevin Austin
b. Hythe 15.6.1958
Ht 5ft 6 Wt 8st 13 (82-83)
Career: St Mary's College; Southampton from apprentice June 1976; Crystal Palace May 1980; Bournemouth March 1981; READING (loan) 13 September 1982; RS Southampton July 1984; Salisbury summer 1985; Fareham T. October 1986; Gosport Bor. summer 1987; Salisbury September 1988; Blackfield & Langley April 1990; Exon Fawley manager

With just one substitute appearance for his home town club, Southampton, and none for Palace, Kevin at last made his mark at Bournemouth. The tiny winger helped them to win promotion to the Third Division in his first season but, having scored in their 4-2 Football League Trophy pre-season defeat at Reading, Kevin returned to Elm Park a month later on loan.

It was an eventful four game spell as it included a remarkable 7-5 defeat at Doncaster and the club's lowest ever League attendance for what proved to be Kevin's last game for Reading. Released by Bournemouth in 1984, Kevin served a number of Wessex clubs, including Salisbury where he won promotion in the Southern League and topped their scorers in 1985-86.

Reading Record: Lge 4
League Career Total: 62(8)/11

DEAN Cyril George
b. Bournemouth 27.7.1915 d. Bournemouth 9.1997
Ht 5ft 7 1/2 Wt 11st 2 (35-36)
Career: Bournemouth; Aston Villa; READING 22 January 1937; Southampton summer 1938; Wartime guest for Fulham, Lincoln & Millwall; Gloucester C. player manager 1946; Cheltenham T. player manager & secretary; Trowbridge; Swindon T. youth coach; Dursley T. player manager August 1955

After a successful schoolboy career that saw him capped at U15 and Junior level, Cyril started his professional career with his home town side, Bournemouth. He then spent four years at Villa Park before a foggy night brought him his chance in the League. Villa were travelling to Aldershot when they were held up in Reading because of a heavy fog. One of Villa's directors took the opportunity to meet up with an old friend, Reading director T W Stone, and during their conversation he recommended Cyril. Reading manager, Billy Butler, followed up the tip and as a result Cyril joined Reading. Capable of playing in either inside forward role, he played in both for Reading, making his League debut in February 1937 at home to Crystal Palace. While with Reading, Cyril was troubled with a knee injury that greatly reduced his appearances for the club and he was released at the end of 1937-38. Initially he was planning to join Reading colleague, Billy Wright, at FC Rouen, but Southampton persuaded him to stay in England although he never added to his League total. As an FA qualified coach he was constantly in demand but he also carried on playing into his forties, helping Dursley Town win their league championship in 1955-56.

Reading Record: Lge 16/3, FAC 1, SSC 1, Total 18/3

DEAN Raymond George
b. Steventon 15.12.1945
Ht 5ft 11 Wt 11st 8 (66-67)
Career: Cheltenham T; READING amateur 5 October 1963, professional 7 May 1966; Aldershot (free) July 1969; Margate 1975; Cheltenham T. 1976

Like many of his contemporaries, Ray came to the fore at Reading during the reserve's 1965-66 promotion season and he was rewarded with a professional contract. Throughout his career at Elm Park, Ray was in competition for the centre half role with the vastly experienced Dick Spiers and it is to Ray's credit that he made as many first team appearances as he did. The two were of a similar style - they both liked to attack the ball, were good in the air and calm under pressure so that even though football was moving towards two central defenders, they rarely played alongside each other. Ray was given a free transfer in 1969 and joined Aldershot where he became a fixture at the centre of their defence, making over 250 League appearances. In 1976 he returned to Cheltenham where he was Player of the Year in their 1977 promotion season.

Reading Record: Lge 50(4), FAC 6, LC 1(1), Total 57(5)
League Career Total: 306(4)/7

DEATH Stephen Victor
b. Elmswell 19.9.1949
Ht 5ft 7 1/2 Wt 11st (77-78)
Career: West Ham U. from apprentice May 1967; READING (loan) 6 November 1969, permanent (£20,000) 11 August 1970

It is hard to imagine that the goalkeeper that many regard as Reading's greatest, only went in goal by chance after he injured his knee playing on the wing. Steve progressed to win three England Schools' caps, sharing the role with Peter Shilton, and never conceded a goal. He was spotted for West Ham by former Reading favourite, Wilf Chitty, but having made just one first team appearance, at Manchester City in April 1969, he was loaned to Reading. Steve was Reading's first loan player under the new system and, typically, kept a clean sheet in his first game. He stayed for the rest of the season, making such an impact that he won the first of his four Player of the Year awards even though he was still a West Ham player. It took a club record £20,000 to bring Steve to Elm Park permanently but he was still one of the club's biggest bargains.

For the next 12 years he was a fixture in Reading's goal where he rewrote the record book. Steve won two promotions with Reading, the second seeing him ever-present in the 1978-79 Fourth Division championship side that set a League record of 1,074 minutes without conceding a goal. In 1972-73 he conceded just seven League goals at Elm Park and the next season saw him lower his own record to 37 conceded in 46 games. His record of 536 first team appearances has since been beaten by Martin Hicks but no one has come close to his 156 consecutive games from August 1978 to April 1981. Steve was also a winner of the first PFA Divisional awards in 1974 and again in 1979. All of this was achieved as the shortest goalie in the League, a fact that he overcame with great agility and bravery. Sadly Steve's great career came to an unhappy end when a dispute over a club house ended with him walking out on the club he had served so well in February 1982, and he became a greenkeeper at a local golf course.

Reading Record: Lge 471, FAC 33, LC 32, Watney Cup 1, Total 537
League Career Total: 472

DENNINGTON Leslie Arthur
b. West Bromwich 6.1902 d. ?
Ht 5ft 10 1/2 Wt 11st (27-28)
Career: Wolseley Motors; Aston Villa 1924; READING June 1926; Exeter C. (free) November 1928

Les made one League appearance for Villa before joining Reading as cover for centre half, Alf Messer. Unfortunately for Les, Messer was a fixture in the Reading defence at that time so he had to make do with the occasional game at wing half. He was highly thought of at Reading, captaining the reserves on many occasions, but although he was a clever player, Les' slim build put him at a disadvantage against Twenties centre forwards as this was usually a physical battle.

Reading Record: Lge 11
League Career Total: 76

DEVERALL Harold Reginald 'Jackie'
b. Reading 5.5.1916 d. 11.6.1999
Ht 5ft 8 Wt 10st 3 (38-39)
Career: Christchurch Jnrs; Prospect Alb; Simmonds A; Maidenhead U; READING amateur June 1931, professional November 1937; Wartime guest for Southport & Chelsea; Leyton O. (£1,750) August 1948

Jackie was a very versatile player from his schoolboy days when he won two England U15 caps at left half even though he was left back for Reading Schools and centre half for Norcot School.

He then helped Maidenhead reach the Amateur Cup semi-finals before turning professional with Reading. By this time Jackie had moved to the forward line, making his League debut on the left wing at home to Newport in January 1939. The War interrupted his career and as he spent most of the duration with the RAF in Rhodesia he was not able to play regularly until the restart of League football making him one of only four Reading players to appear both sides of the War. He was a regular on the left wing that season and Jackie scored twice in the club's record victory over Crystal Palace in September 1946. He had a ferocious shot but the following season Jackie played more at left half and joined Leyton Orient at the start of 1948-49 as a part-timer. After retiring from League football he ran a newsagents in Reading for many years.

Reading Record: Lge 74/9, FAC 4/1, SSC 3, Wartime 36/18, Total 117/28
League Career Total: 189/11

DILLEY Ernest Edward
b. London c.1898 d. ?
Ht 6ft Wt 10st 6 (20-21)
Career: QPR; READING 1919

Ernie joined Reading as a centre forward but clearly the club weren't quite sure what to do with him as he played one League game at centre half and the other at centre forward. His debut came in a goalless draw at home to QPR in September 1920, after he had scored five for the reserves, and four weeks later he was in the defence at Brighton for the his League game. Soon after he was suspended by the club and transfer listed.

Reading Record: Lge 2, SL 3/1, Total 5/1

DILLON Kevin Paul
b. Sunderland 18.12.1959
Ht 6ft Wt 12st 7 (92-93)
Career: Birmingham C. from apprentice July 1977; Portsmouth (£200,000) March 1983; Newcastle U. July 1989; READING (trial) August 1991 then permanent; Newbury T; Stevenage T. 1994; Yeovil assistant player manager July 1995; READING youth scout September 1996, youth development officer March 1998, reserve manager October 2000

A sparkling schoolboy career that saw Kevin play for Sunderland and Durham Schools, led to a successful apprenticeship with Birmingham. There Kevin was capped at U21 level for England and had the honour of being the last player to be given his League debut by Sir Alf Ramsey who thought so highly of Kevin that he described him as being better than Martin Peters.

Portsmouth broke their transfer fee record to buy the talented midfielder and he became the playmaker in Pompey's midfield. Having helped Portsmouth back to the First Division in 1986-87 he moved on to Newcastle where he teamed up with Mark McGhee and captained United in 1989-90.

When Kevin was released by United, Reading's new boss, McGhee, signed him on after a successful trial period. Kevin proved an immediate asset to Reading, bringing steel and guile to Reading's midfield while his raking passes produced many goals for his teammates. Although occasionally in trouble with referees, Kevin was a key member of McGhee's side and this was borne out as he played a major role as Reading won the Division Two championship in some style in 1993-94. Unfortunately Kevin was troubled with injuries towards the end of that season and, disappointed with the club's requirement to prove his fitness before offering a new contract, Kevin quit League football. Two years later he returned to Elm Park, initially as Youth Scout, and then helped as the club achieved Academy status in 1999. In 2000-01 he took charge of the reserves and guided them to their most successful season for over 30 years.

Reading Record: Lge 100(1)/4, FAC 4, LC 8/1, AMC 6, Total 118(1)/5
League Career Total: 549(15)/64

KEVIN'S CLAIM TO FAME - Kevin's first goals for Portsmouth solved Pompey's problem with missed penalties as he converted two in the same game - against Reading. In November 1986 he went one better when he became one of only 11 players to score a hat-trick of penalties in first class English football when he put three past Millwall. That win was in the Full Members Cup which makes Kevin the only player to have scored a trio of spot kicks in that competition.

On 3 March 1928 Ronnie scored in Bristol Rover's win over Norwich at the age of just 15 years 180 days, making him the League's youngest ever goalscorer. It wasn't until 1930-31 that he established himself as a first team regular and soon after Ronnie began a nomadic career. In November 1938 he was capped by England for the only time, despite scoring in their 4-0 win over Norway. In the same month, he netted twice for the Football League against the Scottish League. The War saw Ronnie guest for several clubs, most notably Blackpool with whom he won the League North Cup in 1943 and a runners-up medal in 1944, as well as playing in numerous representative games. The War meant that Ronnie only played one season for Spurs before joining Reading for 'several thousand pounds' even though he was 35 by then. He proved good value, scoring on his debut and forming an effective partnership at inside left with 33 year old centre forward Tony MacPhee - between them they scored 37 goals in the 30 games they played together. Ronnie retired in 1949 to run a local business in Bristol, having been described by *The Century of English International Footballers* as '*a stocky, cleverly constructive inside forward of high consistency*'.

Reading Record: Lge 44/13, FAC 7/2, Total 51/15
League Career Total: 410/130

DIXON Cyril
b. Rawmarsh 1.2.1901 d. Rotherham 1978
Ht 5ft 8 1/2 Wt 11st 8 (32-33)
Career: Rawmarsh A; Barnsley 1924; READING (£150) June 1932; Scarborough summer 1933

In his eight seasons with Barnsley, Cyril was their regular full back, making well over 250 first team appearances on either side of the defence. He moved to Reading after Barnsley's relegation from the Second Division but found it much harder to break into the Elm Park side's first team. Cyril had to wait until December 1932 to get his chance but after four games he was dropped and subsequently put on the transfer list at the end of the season.

Reading Record: Lge 4
League Career Total: 256/7

DIX Ronald William
b. Bristol 5.9.1912 d. Bristol 2.4.1998
Ht 5ft 9 Wt 12st 7 (35-36)
Career: Bristol R. from amateur September 1927; Blackburn R. (£3,000) May 1932; Aston Villa May 1933; Derby Co. (£4,875) February 1937; Tottenham H. (£8,500) June 1939; Wartime guest for Blackpool, Bristol C, Chester, Liverpool, Middlesbrough, Totttenham H, Wrexham & York C; READING (£2,750) 6 November 1947

It was clear from his spectacular schoolboy career, culminating in him captaining England Schools twice, that Ronnie was going to make an impact on League football but no-one could have guessed how quickly he would strike.

DIXON Kerry Michael
b. Luton 24.7.1961
Ht 6ft Wt 13st (82-83)
Career: Luton T. youth; Chesham U; Tottenham H. from apprentice part-time professional July 1978; Dunstable summer 1979; READING (£20,000) 22 July 1980; Chelsea (£175,000) 4 August 1983; Southampton (£575,000) July 1992; Luton T.(free) February 1993; Millwall (£5,000) March 1995; Watford (£25,000) January 1996; Doncaster R. player manager August 1996; Basildon U. October 1997; Boreham-wood player coach; Letchworth coach manager 2000

Kerry was turned down by Luton and Spurs, despite scoring 27 goals in 37 games for them, but re-awoke interest by scoring 52 for Dunstable Town in 1979-80. Reading manager, Maurice Evans, had been watching the prolific young centre forward for four months before signing him as one for the future. Despite this, and the fact that Kerry was still only part-time while completing his toolmaking apprenticeship, he still finished as Reading's top scorer in his first season. More goals and experience were gained the following season but in 1982-83 everything came together for Kerry.

The first 22 games had produced 21 goals for him, despite playing in a side struggling at the foot of the table and unsettled by the fact that the club was up for sale. Unfortunately Kerry had to cope with a pelvic injury for several games and by the end of December it was too serious for him to carry on. He missed 11 games and, even though Kerry came back before he had fully recovered, he still scored another five goals to end up as the Third Division's top scorer, despite Reading being relegated. Kerry was the complete centre forward - strong and pacey, with a good shot in either foot and powerful in the air, so it was clear that Reading would not be able to hold on to their prized possession. In the end Chelsea paid a Reading record to beat off several other top clubs and Reading lost one of the most spectacular and popular players the fans had seen. Chelsea's faith was fully justified. In his first season he topped the Second Division scorers as Chelsea won promotion, and then completed a unique hat-trick by finishing as the First Division's top scorer with a total of 36 first team goals. This feat earned Kerry an England U21 cap and, in the summer of 1985, he joined the England tour of Mexico and the USA.

Having come on as sub against Mexico, Kerry celebrated his first international start with two goals against West Germany and then another brace against the States, his caps earning Reading another £25,000 from Chelsea. In total he won eight caps to add to the three Golden Boots and PFA Divisional awards as well as becoming the second highest scorer in Chelsea's history. Gradually, Kerry moved down the football ladder, ending his League career as player manager at the ill-fated Doncaster Rovers before combining the running of a pub in Dunstable with assisting local clubs.

Reading Record: Lge 110(6)/51, FAC 2(1), LC 6(1), FLT 6(1)/6, Total 124(9)/57
League Career Total: 560 (33)/231

> KERRY'S CLAIM TO FAME - As well as being only one of two players to top his division's scorers in a relegated side (Blackpool's Bob Hatton was the other), Kerry is also the first England player to score two goals against West Germany in 90 minutes of play!

DIXON Michael George
b. Reading 12.10.1943 d. 1993
Ht 5ft 10 Wt 11st (67-68)
Career: READING from apprentice 9 August 1961; Aldershot (free) July 1969; Salisbury July 1971; Wokingham T. coach, secretary & treasurer summer 1975

Having played alongside Martin Peters in the England Schools side that beat West Germany at Wembley in April 1959, and winning several other youth honours, Mike joined his local club, Reading, from school. The young goalie made his League debut in September 1962 and from then on he was in a straight battle with Arthur Wilkie for the green jumper at Reading. Although Wilkie held the slight edge in appearances, there was little to chose between them even though they were very different in style. While Wilkie was probably the more accomplished shot stopper, Mike was one of the bravest players ever to appear for Reading, fearlessly throwing himself at the feet of opposing players and invariably coming out with the ball, and he won the Player of the Year in 1967-68 whilst a part-timer. Strangely, having shared the goalkeeping duties for six years, both Mike and Arthur left the club at the same time with the former continuing his career with Aldershot. After his League career was over Mike ran a newsagent's shop in Reading, and although he assisted local clubs, he became better known in the town area as a referee - something he had taken up while recovering from an arm broken while making a typically brave stop. Mike's bravery was a feature of his personal life as well but, sadly, it was not enough to pull him through a serious illness and he died at the young age of 49.

Reading Record: Lge 113, FAC 9, LC 12, Total 134
League Career Total: 151

DIXON Thomas Charles

b. Newcastle 8.6.1929
Ht 6ft Wt 11st 9 (57-58)
Career: Newcastle U. amateur; West Ham U. February 1951; READING (£2,750) 5 March 1955; Brighton (£4,250) 11 October 1958; Workington July 1960; Barrow October 1961

A traditional centre forward who built up a reputation as a powerful, freescoring player, Tommy actually began his career as a full back and played in that position as a youth for the Boys' Brigade. It was during his National Service that the Army converted him to a centre forward and there that he was spotted by Newcastle, who signed him as an amateur. A professional contract was then offered by West Ham and two years later Tommy made his League debut, while his best run in their first team came in 1953-54 when he netted 25 goals. Tommy's move to Reading was hampered by an injury on his debut. The 1955-56 season saw him moved around the forward line but he ended the season with a goalscoring flourish that continued for the next two seasons during which he scored a total of 65 goals. At that point his goal touch deserted him and after going on the list at his own request in October 1958, Tommy joined Brighton.

Reading Record: Lge 123/63, FAC 10/6, SPFC 10/7, Total 143/76
League Career Total: 312/136

DIXON Wilfred Edward

b. Wood Green 20.2.1950
Ht 5ft 8 Wt 10st 6 (70-71)
Career: Arsenal from apprentice May 1968; READING 7 July 1969; Colchester U. (trial) August 1973; Swindon T. September 1973; Aldershot July 1977; Woking; Wokingham T; Watford coaching staff 1996

Although Will had a successful youth career, he never got close to a first team appearance in his one professional season at Highbury. He joined Reading on a two month trial and ended that first season with more League appearances than any other player at Elm Park. As a solid right back with considerable attacking flair, Will fitted in perfectly with Jack Mansell's style of play and he built up a great rapport with Reading's fans, particularly at away games where he was always quick to acknowledge the travelling support. He was a first team regular up to March 1973, occasionally being used in midfield, from where he scored his only goal for Reading in their 1972-73 FA Cup win at Gillingham, as well as his more usual right back position. Although Will never cost any of his clubs a transfer fee he gave his best performances against two of the game's most valuable player.

In Reading's Watney Cup-tie against Manchester United, he marked George Best out of the game and then, 18 months later, did the same thing to the most expensive player in Britain - Arsenal's Alan Ball. Having lost his place to Andy Alleyne he was released and joined Swindon where he suffered relegation from the Second Division in 1973-74.

Reading Record: Lge 150(3), FAC 14/1, LC 6, Watney Cup 1, Total 171(3)/1
League Career Total: 398(15)/16

DOCHERTY John

b. Glasgow 29.4.1940
Ht 5ft 5 Wt 9st 4 (68-69)
Career: St Roch's; Brentford July 1959; Sheffield U. March 1961; Brentford December 1965; READING (£10,200) 2 February 1968; Brentford 11 March 1970; QPR player coach July 1974; Brentford manager January 1975; Cambridge U. coach September 1976, manager January 1978 to December 1983; Brentford assist manager February 1984; Millwall manager July 1986; Bradford C. manager March 1990; Slough T. manager 1992

John had a rather unusual playing career that saw him spend most of his time on the M1, travelling between Brentford and Sheffield! It only took a handful of games with Brentford, who spotted John playing in Scottish Junior football, to persuade Sheffield United to sign the tiny winger. After 41 First Division games, John made the return journey to Griffin Park where he hit his best scoring form before interrupting his Brentford/Sheffield United career to join Reading. His signing was funded from the proceeds from Reading's two FA Cup games against the 1967-68 League Champions, Manchester City, and he was ever-present for the rest of that season. Despite his lack of inches, John proved to be a determined player who was not easy to knock off the ball and provided good service with accurate crosses from either wing. He played in about half of the next season's matches but was barely used following the arrival of Jack Mansell, and in March 1970 he returned to Brentford where he ended his playing career. John then established himself as a successful manager with a strong character that enabled him to instill discipline and build strong teams on a small budget. He was particularly successful at Cambridge, whom he kept in the Second Division against the odds for several seasons, and Millwall where he guided them to First Division football in 1987-88. Needless to say, John's managerial career included two spells at Brentford, making it a total of five in all.

Reading Record: Lge 45(1)/8, FAC 1, LC 1, Total 47(1)/8
League Career Total: 337(5)/83

DOCHERTY Thomas

b. Penshaw 15.4.1924
Ht 5ft 8 Wt 11st (53-54)
Career: Sunderland amateur; Murton Colliery Welfare 1945; Lincoln C. July 1947; Norwich C. (£1,500) June 1950; READING (£750) June 1953; Newport Co. 15 July 1955

After playing for a number of North Eastern clubs, Tommy was finally offered a professional contract with Lincoln for whom he played on the left wing. In 1950 he moved to Norwich but after two seasons on their wing, that included two goals in an FA Cup win over Liverpool, Tommy was converted to left half and it was in this position that he joined Reading. Almost immediately Reading converted him back to his forward position and he scored both his Reading goals as an inside left, the first being in a 4-4 draw against his old club, Norwich. Although Tommy was a first team regular in his first season, he then lost his left wing spot to Jimmy Wheeler and, having then moved back to left half, he lost that role to Eddie McLaren.

Reading Record: Lge 53/2, FAC 1, Total 54/2
League Career Total: 291/10

DODGIN Norman

b. Gateshead 1.11.1921 d. 2000
Ht 5ft 11 Wt 11st 12 (50-51)
Career: Whitehall BC; Newcastle U. August 1940; READING (£5,000) 17 June 1950; Northampton T. (£850) September 1951; Exeter C. August 1953

As a regular right half in Newcastle's post War side that won promotion back to the First Division in 1948-49, Norman was considered a great capture for Reading and he cost *one of the biggest fees in our history*. He was made club captain and started well, scoring Reading's winner against Watford, but this was followed by a run that saw the club gain just one point from five games. Norman was one of five players to lose his place and when the new look line-up won their next game, he faced an uphill battle to regain his first team place. He only played three more first team games in the next 12 months, at which point he was sold on to Northampton. Norman is a member of a footballing family, the best known being his younger brother, Bill, who became a well known manager.

Reading Record: Lge 13/1
League Career Total: 149/4

NORMAN'S CLAIM TO FAME - While playing for his regiment in Italy during the War, Norman's displays so impressed AC Milan that they tried to sign him.

DOHERTY Michael

b. Liverpool 8.3.1961
Ht 5ft 7 Wt 10st (82-83)
Career: Basingstoke T; READING (trial) then permanent (£1,500) October 1982; Slough T. summer 1983; Weymouth; Maidstone (£10,000) summer 1987; Farnborough 1990

Mike won England Semi professional honours before joining Reading on trial at the start of 1982-83, eventually signing for a small fee in October 1982. Reading were already a club in turmoil, up for sale and heading for relegation, so it was hardly the ideal environment for a player to start his League career but Mike did his best for the club. A slightly built, left sided midfielder, he scored the winner against Wigan on his home debut which was the first of five goals, all of which earned vital points for the club. Reading's relegation at the end of Mike's first season saw him become a victim of the inevitable clear out and he continued his career in non-League football.

Reading Record: Lge 23(2)/5, FAC 1, FLT 3(2)/1, Total 27(4)/6

DOLLERY Horace Edgar 'Tom'

b. Reading 14.10.1914 d. Birmingham 20.1.1987
Ht 5ft 10 1/2 Wt 12st (1935-36)
Career: West Bromwich Alb. Colts; St Mark's Wednesday, Reading; READING July 1934

Which Reading player made just one League appearance but went on to play for his country? The answer is Tom Dollery, while the reason for this anomaly was that Tom gave up football to become a top class cricketer. As a pupil of Reading School he became known as 'the Boy Wonder' because of his talents at all sports. He had made his cricketing debut for Berkshire at 17 and had already scored a double century when he joined Reading as a centre forward. His scoring prowess had previously been displayed when an 11 youth match spell at West Brom in 1933-34 produced 16 goals. Tom made just one first team appearance for Reading, against QPR in January 1936, and although he made their goal it was not enough to prevent Reading's first home defeat in 55 League games at Elm Park. At the end of the season Tom was released so he could join Warwickshire full time. There he scored over 24,000 runs, including 50 centuries and was regarded as the best and most consistent right hand batsman in the country. This led Tom to winning four Test caps after the War and on his retirement he was Warwickshire's coach and served as a Test selector.

Reading Record: Lge 1

TOM'S CLAIM TO FAME - In 1949-50 Tom became the first professional cricketer that century to captain his team to the County Championship.

DONCASTER Richard Arthur

b. Barry Dock 13.5.1908 d. ?
Ht 5ft 7 1/2 Wt 11st 4 (35-36)
Career: Barry T; Bolton W; Exeter C. 1928; Crystal Palace summer 1932; READING (free) July 1933; Gillingham summer 1934; Yeovil summer 1936

As a former Welsh Schoolboy international, Dick had to wait until he moved to Exeter before making his League debut in 1928. He was a regular on their left wing for four years but his season at Crystal Palace was less successful so Dick moved to Reading in an attempt to regain regular first team football. The move failed as Dick made just two appearances in September 1933 and, with both games ending goalless for Reading, his career in Reading's League attack was over. Fortunately for Dick, a close season move to Gillingham revitalized his League career for a couple of seasons before he move back to the non-League game.

Reading Record: Lge 2
League Career Total: 211/52

DONE Robert

b. Runcorn 27.4.1904 d. Chester 9.1982
Ht 5ft 10 Wt 12st (35-36)
Career: Runcorn; Liverpool 1926; READING (£150) 15 May 1935; Chester summer 1937; Accrington Stan. 1938; Bangor 1939

Bob made over 150 first team appearances for Liverpool at right back and, occasionally, on the left. He had built up a reputation for powerful kicking and as well as being considered to have one of the longest kicks in football, it was also one of the hardest. He used this to good effect from free kicks and scored 13 League goals for Liverpool in a time when full backs rarely crossed the half way line. It took a club record fee for a full back to bring Bob to Reading, but after an eight match run at the start of 1935-36, that saw him score a penalty against Clapton Orient, first team chances were restricted by injury and a loss of form. Given a 'free' at the end of 1936-37 he regained his first team place with a move to Chester.

Reading Record: Lge 13/1
League Career Total: 203/13

DONNELLAN Gary

b. Kensington 3.7.1961
Ht 5ft 8 Wt 12st (82-83)
Career: Chelsea apprentice September 1978; Watford (free) December 1978; READING (£5,000) November 1981; Wealdstone summer 1983; Yeovil; Enfield (£10,000) 1990; Slough T; Hendon June 1992

Gary was understudy to John Barnes at Watford so, not surprisingly, his first team chances were limited to one substitute appearance. A move to Reading gave him first team football and for his first 12 months at Elm Park he was a regular on the left wing where he used his strength and determination to good effect. In Reading's 1982-83 relegation season he found the going tougher but, with his first team position under threat, he produced the performance of his career. 3-1 down in the Football League Trophy to his old club, First Division Watford, with only minutes to go, Gary inspired a remarkable fightback to win 5-3 in extra time by scoring a hat-trick. Gary was one of several players released at the end of that season and he developed into a combative midfielder, helping Wealdstone to the non-League double in 1984-85, and had a long non-League career which he combined with his job as a button salesman.

Reading Record: Lge 33(8)/5, FAC 1, LC 2, FLT 5/4, Total 41(8)/9

DORAN Samuel

b. Bradford 22.12.1912
Ht 5ft 11 Wt 13st (38-39)
Career: Bradford C. (trial); Sunfield R; Bradford P.A. 1934; READING 10 September 1938; Halifax T. summer 1939

Sam spent four seasons with Bradford Park Avenue after being rejected by his home town's other League club and although he was never a regular in their first team he was considered a good capture when he joined Reading. The Elm Park programme described him as a *'tricky winger who brought considerable punch to the right wing'*, and he was regarded as the fastest player at the club. Unfortunately, Sam found the move south unsettling and went on the transfer list in January 1939. Although this affected his form for a while, Sam fought his way back into the first team where he continued to find the net fairly regularly.

Reading Record: Lge 27/8, FAC 2, SSC 4, Total 33/8
League Career Total: 81/12

DOUGALL James H

b. Wishaw 3rd qtr 1903 d. ?
Ht 5ft 7 1/2 Wt 10st 11 (26-27)
Career: Clelland Jnrs; Motherwell; Coventry C. 1919; READING (£605) July 1926

As a tricky right winger who was a creator of chances rather than a prolific scorer, Jimmy had been capped twice at Scottish Junior level and had come close to getting a full cap while with Coventry, being chosen as a reserve on one occasion.

After his first season with Coventry he hardly missed a game and was seen as a great asset when he joined newly promoted Reading in 1926. Just as he was establishing himself in Reading's first team, disaster struck. In Reading's FA Cup-tie against Manchester United, a powerful tackle left him with a compound fracture of his leg and this terrible injury saw him spend six months in hospital and, with the leg shortened by an inch, his playing career was obviously over.

Reading Record: Lge 11, FAC 1, Total 12
League Career Total: 237/14

DOUGALL Robert
b. Falkirk c.1910
Ht 5ft 9 1/2 Wt 11st 8 (38-39)
Career: Forth Rngrs; Hamilton Acc; Blackpool September 1933; READING 9 June 1937

A former steelworker, Robert was an attacking right half who made his name during three successful seasons with Hamilton before moving to Blackpool. There his first team opportunities were reduced each season and in 1937 he joined Reading. His constructive play made him a favourite at Elm Park and he played a major part in the club's 1938 Southern Section Cup winning run. The War ended his League career although he carried on playing for Reading until he retired in 1941.

Reading Record: Lge 74/7, FAC 2, SSC 6, Wartime 53/3, Total 135/10
League Career Total: 148/9

DOUGLAS Edward Alfred C
b. Hebburn 26 March 1899
Ht 5ft 10 Wt 11st (29-30)
Career: Crook T; Crystal Palace 1922; Crook T; Washington CW; Brentford 1925; READING (player exchange) June 1929; Bristol R. (loan) October 1931

Edward enjoyed a successful spell with Brentford where he made over 100 appearances, including the 1927 fifth round Cup-tie at Reading that set Elm Park's attendance record. Left winger Edward came close to scoring an equalizer in that game and so in 1929 the two agreed a player exchange with Billy Lane moving to Griffin Park. This exchange proved a disappointment for both Edward and Reading since his two seasons produced just five first team appearances, each one ending in defeat with a goal aggregate of 5-21 against. Edward scored his one goal for Reading in the 5-1 FA Cup reverse at Aston Villa in 1930.

Reading Record: Lge 4, FAC 1/1, Total 5/1
League Career Total: 108/22

DRAPER William
b. c.1899 d. ?
Ht 5ft 10 1/2 12st 2 (20-21)
Career: READING August 1920; Southampton November 1920

William played just three games at left back for Reading in September 1920, including the club's very first League win at Elm Park. As a part-timer, he was only a temporary replacement for George Horler and once the regular left back was available, William's League career was over although he did move to Southampton but failed to make their first team.

Reading Record: Lge 3

DRYSDALE Brian
b. Wingate 24.3.1943
Ht 5ft 7 Wt 11st (77-78)
Career: Lincoln C. from amateur September 1960; Hartlepools U. (free) July 1965; Bristol C. (£10,000) May 1969; READING (loan) 24 February 1977; Oxford U. July 1977

Although Brian began his League career with Lincoln, it was with Hartlepool that he established himself, helping them to their first promotion, in 1967-68, under the astute management of a young Brian Clough. On the down side he was a member of the Hartlepool team that lost 7-0 at Reading the following season. In 1969 Brian moved to Bristol City where he made over 300 appearances, and helped City to the First Division in 1975-76. By 1977, Brian was no longer a regular for City, so he was loaned to Reading on his 34th birthday but even with all his experience he could not have anticipated his start with them. In his first game at Reading, their manager, Charlie Hurley, resigned at half time and two days later Brian was made Reading's captain. He kept the captaincy and the left back shirt to the end of the season and although he could not prevent Reading's return to the Fourth Division the club were keen to sign the quick, tough defender. As it was, Brian decided to join Oxford but after a season with them he retired from League football.

Reading Record: Lge 16
League Career Total: 501(3)/5

DUCKWORTH Joseph Cullen
b Blackburn 29.4.1898 d. ?
Ht 5ft 10 Wt 12st 4 (29-30)
Career: Blackburn R. 1914; Aberdare A. 1921; READING June 1924; Brighton (free) June 1930; York C. July 1932

One of the most popular players to appear for Reading, Joe began his career as a 16 year old goalie in Blackburn's reserves.

After four years in the Army during the First World War, Joe returned to Ewood Park and played five First Division games for them before joining Aberdare. Here he turned in a series of fine performances and in 1923-24 Joe kept three clean sheets against Reading. This persuaded Reading to sign him and he became a fixture between the posts during one of Reading's most successful periods. Joe missed just one League game in his first four seasons at Elm Park as Reading won the Third Division South championship in 1925-26, and then reached the FA Cup semi-finals a year later. His bravery in the far more physical days of the 1920s was legendary at Elm Park and when, in 1929, he found himself playing second fiddle to Lance Richardson, the fans were quick to remind the management who their favourite was. At the end of 1929-30 Joe was allowed to leave Reading for Brighton but he is still held in the highest regard by those Reading fans lucky enough to have seen him play. His playing days over, Joe eventually became a deckchair attendant on Blackpool beach.

Reading Record: Lge 202, FAC 23, Total 225
League Career Total: 335

DUNCAN Colin John
b. Plymouth 5.8.1957
Ht 5ft 10 Wt 11st 12 (84-85)
Career: READING amateur 1972; Oxford U. from apprentice December 1974; Gillingham (£50,000) January 1981; READING September 1983; Aldershot May 1985; Sittingbourne July 1992

Although born in Plymouth, Colin was brought up in Wantage and had a season with Reading in their Middlesex Border League side. He was only offered non contract terms so he joined Oxford and had a trial for Scotland Youth as his father was Scottish. In his six years as a professional at Oxford he played nearly 200 first team games as a powerful, tough tackling midfielder with enviable stamina built through a successful cross country career as a schoolboy. Gillingham had to break their club record to secure his services in 1981, but Colin was plagued with back problems that cost him a year of his spell with them.

He returned to Reading after a trial to ensure his fitness and he became the final part of the jigsaw that saw the club regain its Third Division status at the first attempt. Colin was still having occasional problems with his back and the signing of Glenn Burvill in March 1985 signalled the end of his first team career with Reading. In that summer Colin moved to Aldershot to fill the vacancy left by Burvill's transfer to Reading.

Reading Record: Lge 56/3, FAC 4, LC 2, AMT 1, Total 63/3
League Career: 342(3)/14

DUNPHY Eamonn Martin
b. Erin Isle 3.8.1945
Ht 5ft 7 3/4 Wt 8st 13 (75-76)
Career: Manchester U. from apprentice 1962; York C. August 1965; Millwall (£9,000); Charlton A. (£16,666) November 1973; READING (free) July 1975; Shamrock R. player coach July 1977

Although he did not play in Manchester United's first team, Eamonn played a major role in their success as, during his time at Old Trafford, he befriended a homesick Irishman and helped persuade a young George Best to stay with the club. Eamonn's fame was to be achieved elsewhere - initially with York where his scintillating form took less than half a season to attract other clubs, including Reading, before he joined Millwall. He had already become the first York player to be capped and the 22 Eire games he played while with Millwall still makes him their most capped player. With the Londoners he immediately won promotion to the Second Division and was a part of their team that went 59 games unbeaten at home, thus breaking Reading's 30 year old record. After nearly 300 first team games at the Den, Eamonn was sold to Charlton. It was not a completely happy move even though he helped them win promotion to the Second Division, and in 1975 he joined Reading. Again the Dunphy magic worked and his first season ended with the club's first promotion for 50 years. Eamonn's skill and experience provided constant impetus from midfield and he captained the team in the tense run-in at the end of the season.

Unfortunately, Eamonn did not always see eye to eye with manager, Charlie Hurley, and shortly after signing a new contract for the next season he was put on the transfer list. Despite this, Eamonn still played 33 games that season but was unable to recapture his exciting form of the previous campaign and he was released in the summer. After a spell in Irish football Eamonn concentrated on his blossoming writing career, that included his acclaimed 'Only A Game' and biographies of U2 and Sir Matt Busby before becoming an often controversial broadcaster who has graduated to hosting Ireland's version of 'The Weakest Link'.

Reading Record: Lge 74(3)/3, LC 2, Total 76(3)/3
League Career Total: 402(13)/33

EAMONN'S CLAIM TO FAME - Before Millwall's away game at Blackburn, Eamonn brought a Golden Goal ticket and went on to score with two minutes to go from his usual inside left position. When he returned to the dressing room he realized that his ticket was for the visitor's no 10 after 88 minutes and so he had scored to make his own ticket a winner!

EARLES Patrick John
b. Titchfield 22.3.1955
Ht 5ft 7 Wt 11st 6 (80-81)
Career: St Mary's College; Southampton from apprentice November 1972; READING (£15,000) 10 January 1977; Road Sea Southampton summer 1983; Bognor Regis T. 1987

A successful schoolboy career in which he was capped against Scotland, meant it was inevitable that Pat would join his local League club. He was at Southampton when they had some great forwards and although Pat was a regular scorer in the reserves he found it difficult to get a first team game. Having come on as sub in 1974, Pat had to wait another 16 months before getting his full debut, and although he came on during two of Saint's European games, he had the disappointment of being dropped after both his first team goals.

Two months after playing in the final of the Anglo Italian Cup against Napoli, Pat took the chance of regular first team football with Reading. He scored on his home debut but although he scored some vital goals, Pat could not save Reading from relegation. The next three seasons saw the player hit double figures in the League and he was top scorer in 1978-79 as Reading won the Fourth Division championship. In addition he was a regular cup scorer and his 11 in the League Cup was a club best until overtaken by Trevor Senior. It might have been this cup success that lead to him being the first Reading player to be the subject of a random drug test in 1979!

Pat also created goals for his colleagues from his position on the right of Reading's forward line where he combined nippy skills with strength on the ball. Pat decided to retire from League football after the club's relegation back to the Fourth Division, in order to concentrate on a career in the probation service. He continued playing in the Southern League and in 1984 was top scorer for Road Sea Southampton as they won their division.

Reading Record: Lge 240(7)/68, FAC 8(1)/6, LC 22/11, FLGC 6, Total 276(8)/85
League Career Total: 244(15)/69

PAT'S CLAIM TO FAME - As well as scoring the very first goal in the Tennants Caledonian Cup, against Manchester City, Pat was also successful in that game's penalty shoot-out. This must have set some sort of record as all 22 players were successful from the spot and Southampton eventually won on the toss of a coin.

EATON Frank
b. Stockport 12.11.1902 d. 1979
Ht 5ft 9 Wt 11st 2 (30-31)
Career: New Mills; Cressbrook; Barnsley 1925; READING (£1,750) June 1930; QPR July 1933

Frank was a goalscoring inside right who scored over seventy first team goals for Barnsley, including 21 in his first full season. It took weeks of negotiations and a club record fee to persuade Barnsley to let him move to Reading. He got off to a flying start, scoring Reading's first five goals of the season, and although the goal flow slowed after that, Frank still ended the season with 15 in the League - a particularly creditable total as Reading were relegated. Despite this he was 'the butt of jokes and ribald remarks one would expect to hear from a third rate comedian, not a so called sportsmen', comments which forced a public apology from one of the local papers.

Even so, the next two seasons in Division Three South saw Frank again playing in three quarters of the first team games, but in 1932-33 he only found the net seven times and failed to agree terms with Reading at the end of that season. Initially put on the transfer list at £850, he eventually moved to QPR but, unable to regain his form, he quit League football after one more season.

Reading Record: Lge 101/33, FAC 9/1, Total 110/34
League Career Total: 267/94

EDELSTON Maurice

b. Hull 27.4.1918 d. Reading 30.1.1976
Ht 5ft 8 Wt 11st 10 (49-50)
Career: Fulham May 1935; Brentford amateur December 1937; Wimbledon; London Univ; READING amateur summer 1939, club secretary February 1946 to 1947, professional July 1947; Wartime guest for Aldershot, Brentford & Watford; Northampton T. (£1,250) July 1952

Without doubt, Maurice Edelston was one of Reading's all time great players and had the War not interrupted his career he would almost certainly have been capped for England. As it was he had to settle for 10 amateur caps, dating back to the 1936 Berlin Olympics, and five Wartime caps plus numerous representative honours. Maurice played for both Fulham and Brentford as an amateur while his father, Joe, was on their coaching staffs, and when Joe was appointed Reading's manager in April 1939, Maurice again followed his father. Maurice played in the first three games of the aborted 1939-40 season before joining the Army Physical Training Corps. He was in constant demand for a variety of representative teams and this restricted his appearances for Reading although he still hit over 100 Wartime goals for them, including one in the final of the 1941 London War Cup. The War over, Maurice was at last able to make his League debut for Reading and what a start he made, scoring hat-tricks in his first two games, as Reading beat Crystal Palace 10-2 and Southend 7-2 to become the only amateur to score consecutive League hat-tricks.

He continued to play as an amateur, teaching classics at the local Bluecoat School and even having a spell as Reading's secretary in 1946, eventually turning professional to become Ted Drake's first signing. A goalscoring inside right, Maurice combined natural skill and a high level of fitness with the soccer brain that you would expect from the son of a former player and manager. He was a vital part of the free scoring Reading side of the post War years and it is no coincidence that two of Reading's greatest centre forwards, Tony MacPhee and Ron Blackman, scored the majority of their goals while playing alongside Maurice.

It came as a great shock to Reading's fans when Maurice was sold to Northampton in July 1952 after one of the club's best seasons. Again, he got off to a flying start by scoring just 10 seconds into his Northampton debut but quit League football in 1954 to concentrate on his blossoming broadcasting career. Maurice had been introduced to the BBC by Reading supporter, John Arlott, and became their top tennis commentator on the radio as well as covering football. He was BBC's radio summariser for the 1966 World Cup final and continued to work for them until his premature death from a heart attack at the age of 57.

Reading Record: Lge 202/70, FAC 21/10, Wartime 132/107, Total 355/187
League Career Total: 265/93

EDWARDS Matthew David

b. Hammersmith 15.8.1971
Ht 5ft 10 Wt 9st 8 (90-91)
Career: Tottenham H. from apprentice July 1989; READING (loan) 28 March 1991; Peterborough U. March 1992; Brighton August 1992

Although he had not made any first team appearances for Spurs, Matt had been consistently impressive for their reserve and youth sides so he was loaned to Reading to gain League experience in a joint deadline day loan deal that also included Brian Statham. Almost immediately Reading dismissed Ian Porterfield so Matt's loan spell was during an unsettled period that saw the club struggling to score goals. Even so he did well enough on the left wing, making eight appearances before returning to White Hart Lane. A year later a permanent transfer to Peterborough failed to increase Matt's League total but a subsequent two season spell with Brighton was more successful.

Reading Record: Lge 6(2)
League Career Total: 55(13)/6

EGGO Robert Mollison

b. Brechin 22.11.1895 d. Sheffield 1977
Ht 5ft 9 Wt 11st 8 (21-22)
Career: Heart of Midlothian; Sheffield Wed. 1919; READING June 1921

Bert was just establishing himself as Sheffield Wednesday's first team right back when a bout of pleurisy cost him his place but it was something of a surprise when they let him join Reading in 1921. He proved a great signing for Reading, but the deal was less successful for Wednesday, a contemporary cigarette card commenting that they *were very hasty when they transferred him to Reading for the price of an old song*.

A remarkably consistent player who was always calm under pressure and relied on skill rather than brawn, Bert formed a perfect full back pairing with Billy McConnell and rarely missed a game in his first seven seasons. As captain of the 1925-26 Third Division South Championship side and the semi-final side a year later, Bert was a kingpin of one of the great eras of Reading Football Club. His displays also earned him an appearance for the Southern League against the Welsh National League in 1922. In 1928, Bert lost his place and retired in 1929 after a career that saw him make more pre World War Two appearances than any other Reading player and he is generally regarded as the club's best ever right back.

Reading Record: Lge 289/2, FAC 23, Total 312/2
League Career Total: 312/2

BERT'S CLAIM TO FAME - In September 1934 Bert played in a charity match for the Ancient Order of Foresters at the old Reading Greyhound Stadium that became the first floodlit game staged in the town.

ELLISON Samuel Walter
b. Leadgate 27.8.1923 d. 1994
Ht 5ft 9 1/2 Wt 11st 2 (49-50)
Career: Middlesbrough Crusaders; Sunderland 1946; Consett 1948; READING 23 June 1949; Guildford C. summer 1950; Brighton August 1951

Having made his League debut for Sunderland while still only 18, Sam looked to have a long career ahead of him, but he was released and joined North Eastern League side Consett. There he was spotted by Reading and spent a season at Elm Park, playing mainly in the reserves where he scored eight times. Just before Christmas 1949 Sam was given his chance in the first team but could not displace Bill Amor from the number 11 shirt, and he left Reading at the end of the season. Although he later had a spell with Brighton, Sam never added to his League total.

Reading Record: Lge 4
League Career Total: 7

ELSEY Karl William
b. Swansea 20.11.1958
Ht 5ft 11 Wt 12st 7 (88-89)
Career: Pembroke Bor; QPR January 1979; Newport Co. July 1980; Cardiff C. September 1983; Gillingham August 1985; READING (player exchange) August 1988; Maidstone U. (£20,000) July 1989; Gillingham August 1991; Sittingbourne 1992; Margate joint manager 1995

With over 450 first team appearances with six different League clubs, Karl had a much longer career than his father, John, who managed just one League game for Swansea in 1956-57. Part of Karl's success was due to his versatility for, although his best position was on the right of midfield, he could also play at full back or in the centre of defence. After a brief spell with QPR, where he made his League debut, Karl moved to Newport and was part of that club's last successful spell, during which he played in the European Cup Winners Cup. When Karl moved to Gillingham he found Kent to his liking, but suffered the first of the Gills play-off disappointments when they lost out on a Second Division place in 1986-87. A year later he joined Reading in exchange for Jerry Williams and, like Williams, Reading used Karl in a number of roles so that he wore seven different shirts that season. He was used predominantly in midfield but Karl did not want to move from Kent and as he found commuting around the M25 difficult, Reading reluctantly allowed him to move to Maidstone.

Reading Record: Lge 41(3)/3, FAC 7/2, LC 4, AMC 3, Total 55(3)/5
League Career Total: 441(19)/44

EVANS David 'Dai' Gethin
b. Abercanaid 28.1.1902 d. Sully 15.12.1951
Ht 5ft 7 Wt 11st 6 (24-25)
Career: Tredyrhiw Stars; Merthyr 1922; Nelson; Bolton W. October 1923; READING August 1924; Huddersfield T. (£6,200) 6 June 1928; Bury (£5,200) May 1929; Merthyr T. August 1930; Burton T. November 1932

'A clean and clever player admired by friend and foe alike' is how the Reading programme described Dai and that would seem to be the case. Having failed to make Bolton's League team, Dai made his debut at Exeter in the first match of 1924-  25 and, although he had to wait until December for his next game, he then established himself as a regular. The following season proved a strange one for him.

He had made the left half spot his own when an injury crisis saw Dai used as an experimental centre forward, but having scored six goals in his first three games up front he failed to regain his half back spot. Dai's sparkling form, back at left half, attracted the attention of the Welsh selectors who capped him for the game in Ireland in 1926 and then twice more while he was with Reading. Dai was also ever-present in Reading's run to the FA Cup semi-final and his good form continued the following season, so in June 1928 mighty Huddersfield broke their and Reading's transfer record to take him to Leeds Road. Although he added one more Welsh cap to his collection, he only played 18 times in the First Division.

Reading Record: Lge 122/11, FAC 19, Total 141/11
League Career Total: 159/11

DAI'S CLAIM TO FAME - Many footballers retire to run pubs but Dai must be the only one to be named after a pub - his parents inn, 'The Dai Gethin'.

EVANS Maurice George
b. Didcot 22.9.1936 d. Reading 18.8.2000
Ht 5ft 7 Wt 10st 10 (63-64)
Career: Didcot A; READING groundstaff September 1952, professional 22 September 1953 (See also The Managers)

Another player who is rightly regarded as one of Reading's all time greats, Maurice remains one of the most popular personalities the club has ever had and served the club in virtually every capacity since first joining them from school. A member of the Berkshire Boys Club side that reached the NABC final, Maurice also represented England Boys Clubs against Germany before progressing through Reading's youth teams. He made his League debut against Southampton in October 1955 at left half, the position he was to make his own from the next season. From then on he was the picture of reliability, allying skill and determination with a passion and understanding of the game that has been a hallmark of all his many roles in football.

Maurice also managed to play the game in a fair and sporting way and was never booked in his career, a fact that further endeared him to Reading's fans. He was rewarded with a selection for the Football Combination against the Dutch XI in November 1957 two weeks after being reserve for the Division Three South team against the Northern section. In view of his continued good form it was surprising that no other club was able to prize Maurice away from Elm Park. By the mid Sixties Maurice was being used more frequently as a full back and although he only made 13 first team appearances in 1966-67 it was still a surprise when the club gave him a free transfer.

Reading Record: Lge 407/13, FAC 26/3, LC 15, SPFC 11, Total 459/16

EVANS Samuel
b. Bridgetown, Glasgow 8.2.1905 d. ?
Ht 5ft 8 Wt 11st 4 (27-28)
Career: St Mirren; Clydebank; READING (£100) June 1927; Ballymena (£100) February 1929; York C. 1929; Darlington 1932

Sam was a typical Scottish winger with an eye for a goal that was borne out by the 24 goals he had scored for Clydebank in 1926-27. Up to then he had been a right winger but when Sam moved to Reading they played him at right half in the reserves but used him on the left wing in the first team. This might help explain why the goals dried up at Elm Park as Sam failed to score in any of his 13 first team games and he was released after two years.

Reading Record: Lge 13
League Career Total: 81/12

EVERS Sean Anthony
b. Hitchin 10.10.1977
Ht 5ft 9 Wt 9st 11 (98-99)
Career: Luton T. from trainee May 1996; READING (£500,000) 25 March 1999; St Johnstone (loan) October 2000; Plymouth Arg. (free) 8 March 2001

Sean was a highly regarded young player who was developed via Luton's youth system and turned down the chance to represent Eire so he would remain eligible for England. His form with Luton as an attacking midfielder was such that he was selected to play for the Nationwide League U21s against the Italian Serie B side, scoring in the 1-1 draw in November 1998. Luton were keen to hold on to one of their prized assets but a dire financial position that saw them go into administration, forced them to sell him to Reading on the 1999 transfer deadline.

Still recovering from a stomach injury at the time of his transfer, Sean's Reading debut was delayed until the last match of that season and further injury problems meant that Reading never saw the best of their big money purchase. A loan spell with St Johnstone failed to help and he eventually left on a 'free'.

Reading Record: Lge 8(10), FAC 4, LC 1(1), AMC 2(1), Total 15(12)
League Career Total: 53(24)/6 +

FAIRCHILD Michael Peter
b. Northampton 24.11.1942
Ht 5ft 10 Wt 10st 12 (65-66)
Career: Lowestoft T; Luton T. November 1960; READING (free) 1 July 1964; Cambridge U. summer 1966; Hillingdon Bor. July 1967; Lowestoft T. May 1972

A pacey winger who could play on either flank, Mike spent three and a half seasons with Luton where he was on the fringes of their first team before moving to Reading. Although Mike started the season in the first team and scored on his home debut, he had to wait until January to get a regular start after fine performances in Reading's fourth round FA Cup-ties against First Division Burnley. This run saw him get amongst the goals more regularly and he ended his first season with six goals in 18 League games. 1965-66 saw an eight match run in September but after that Mike had to be content with assisting the reserves to win the Combination Second Division championship. After Mike left Reading he assisted a number of non-League clubs and played in Hillingdon's 1971 FA Trophy defeat at Wembley.

Reading Record: Lge 24/6, FAC 2, LC 2/2, Total 28/8
League Career Total: 45/7

FARQUHAR Douglas Methven
b. Methil 11.6.1921
Ht 5ft 7 Wt 10st 8 (50-51)
Career: St Andrews U; Arsenal May 1944; READING (£250) 19 September 1950; Hereford U. 1952; Bedford T. 1956

Doug played at centre half in Scottish junior football during the War before joining Arsenal in 1944 but in his six years at Highbury he did not make it to their first team. His move to Reading saw him spend the majority of his first season on the right wing in the reserves but he was given his League debut at Easter and, although Doug was never a prolific scorer, he opened his account in his second game. 1951-52, again, saw Doug mainly in the reserves and, having been released at the end of that season, he moved into non-League football and later emigrated to the States where he played several senior representative games.

Reading Record: Lge 9/1

FAULKES Brian Keith
b. Abingdon 10.4.1945
Ht 5ft 9 Wt 10st 10 (66-67)
Career: READING from apprentice 11 September 1963; Northampton T. July 1967; Torquay U. July 1969; Bath C. March 1970; Wallingford 1976; Hungerford summer 1976

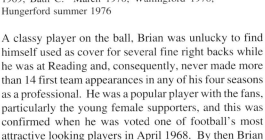

A classy player on the ball, Brian was unlucky to find himself used as cover for several fine right backs while he was at Reading and, consequently, never made more than 14 first team appearances in any of his four seasons as a professional. He was a popular player with the fans, particularly the young female supporters, and this was confirmed when he was voted one of football's most attractive looking players in April 1968. By then Brian had moved to Northampton and he later continued his career in non-League football, playing for the Hellenic League against the Isthmian League in October 1976.

Reading Record: Lge 23(2), FAC 1, LC 2, Total 26(2)
League Career Total: 80(3)/2

FEALEY Nathan James
b. Aldershot 12.3.1973
Ht 6ft Wt 12st 2 (91-92)
Career: READING YTS July 1991; Aldershot T. summer 1992

A strong defender, Nathan got his one League game just before his 18th birthday when he replaced the suspended Floyd Streete at the centre of Reading's defence at Peterborough. It proved an eventful game, ending 5-3 in Peterborough's favour, including such rare events as a player scoring for both sides on his debut (David Lee) and the even rarer sight of a Steve Richardson goal. Nathan, substituted in that game, never got another chance and was released in the summer.

Reading Record: Lge 1

FEARON Ronald Thomas
b. Romford 19.11.1960
Ht 6ft Wt 11st 12 (80-81)
Career: Ipswich T. (trial); West Ham U. (trial); QPR from apprentice 1977; Luton T. (trial); Cambridge U. (trial); Bristol C. (trial); Dover T; READING 23 February 1980; San Diego Sockers summer 1983; Mansfield T. (trial); Sutton U; Ipswich T. September 1987; Sutton U. February 1989; Brighton (loan) September 1988; Witchita Wings summer 1990 & 1991; Walsall (loan) February 1992; Southend U. October 1993; Ashford 1994; Leyton O. August 1995, Hendon October 1999

Released by QPR even though he helped their youth team win three trophies, Ron kept goal regularly for Dover as they won the Southern League South Division championship.

His form earned him yet another trial, this time with Reading, and after six weeks he was offered the contract he had waited for. Signed as cover for the legendary Steve Death, Ron had to wait until April 1981 before getting his first team chance but the following season he had taken over from Death as Reading's first choice keeper. His reign at Elm Park was comparatively short-lived as Alan Judge was bought in, initially on loan, early in 1982-83. Ron then began a nomadic career that included appearances with four more League clubs, two American sides and several non-League clubs.

Reading Record: Lge 61, FAC 2, LC 4, FLGC 6, Total 73
League Career Total: 115

FEATHERBY Walter **Leonard**
b. King's Lynn 28.7.1905 d. King's Lynn 22.2.1972
Ht 5ft 7 1/2 Wt 11st 19 (30-31)
Career: Whitefriars; King's Lynn; Norwich C. 1925; Northfleet U; Millwall; Merthyr T. 1928; Wolverhampton W. 1929; READING June 1930; QPR June 1931; Mansfield T. 1931; Crewe Alex. 1932; Plymouth Arg. March 1934; Notts Co. August 1935

At the age of 16 Len was chosen to play for Norfolk against the touring South African international side and was soon making his League debut with Norwich. After a couple of seasons he drifted out of the League until he joined Merthyr for a short spell that revitalized his career. The skilful inside left joined Reading after two fine performances against them with Wolves. Despite joining the club already engaged in an unsuccessful battle against relegation, Len had the best League season of his career by playing in 23 games. Although he was a creative inside forward rather than a regular scorer, Len netted on his debut in Reading's second win of the season. His Reading career ended after he was suspended by the club for getting drunk on the way back from a game at Port Vale.

Reading Record: Lge 23/3
League Career Total: 127/21

LEN'S CLAIM TO FAME - During Reading's game at Bury in December 1930, Len committed an innocuous challenge but the referee sent him off. As Len trudged towards the dressing room the players protested that the ref had made a mistake and persuaded him to change his mind. Len was called back to complete the game and was not banned. The referee, Mr Cox, was not so lucky. When the FA got to hear of his indecision, they suspended him instead!

FERGUSON Archibald **Daniel**
b. Flint 25.1.1906 d. ?
Ht 5ft 9 Wt 11st (28-29)
Career: Buckley U; Manchester U. 1926; READING (free) May 1928; Accrington Stan. June 1929; Chester March 1932; Halifax T. July 1933; Rotherham U. September 1934; Stockport Co. July 1935; Macclesfield T. 1936

Danny played eight first team games for Manchester United in his two years with them, mainly at right half or centre forward, before joining Reading. Although he was initially signed with the centre forward role in mind, Reading gave him his League debut at inside right. Unfortunately, that game was the 7-0 defeat at Preston in August 1928, and the following game, another defeat, was to be his last in Reading's first team. Released at the end of that first season, Danny moved to Accrington Stanley where he became a first team regular.

Reading Record: Lge 2
League Career Total: 232/17

FERGUSON William A
b. Willenhall 2.3.1900 d. 1986
Ht 5ft 10 Wt 11st (24-25)
Career: Sunbeam Motor Works; Oldham A. 1922; READING June 1924; Rochdale (free) July 1925; Rotherham U. summer 1926; Worcester C.

As reserve centre forward for Oldham, William only got a handful of first team chances with them but his 16 goals in the Central League in 1923-24 persuaded Reading to sign him. He averaged a goal a match in his first three games for them but, despite being the club's most frequent scorer, he had a couple of lengthy spells out of the first team that season. William finished top scorer in 1924-25 with 10 out of the club's 41 goals, which he scored in only 27 games. The signing of Hugh Davey in March ended William's Reading career and in the summer he moved to Rochdale, scoring 19 times in 21 League games in his first season with them.

Reading Record: Lge 24/8, FAC 3/2, Total 27/10
League Career Total: 70/31

FIELDING Horace L
b. Castleton 14.10.1906 d. Peterborough, 14.6. 1969
Ht 5ft 10 Wt 11st 6 (35-36)
Career: Mossley; Stockport Co. 1926; Grimsby T. 1930; READING (£600) 22 June 1933; Crystal Palace 12 March 1937; Peterborough U. summer 1938

Horace began his League career with Stockport in 1926-27 and played alongside Joe Smith before he became Reading's manager.

A move to Grimsby saw Horace playing First Division football and he scored against Manchester United on his debut for them in 1930-31. Gradually the number of his appearances increased until he linked up again with Joe Smith, this time at Reading. Although not as fast as many contemporary wingers, Horace was a reliable crosser of the ball and became a fixture on Reading's left wing where he also scored regularly. While with Reading he also built up a reputation as a fine cricketer and once scored centuries in consecutive games to win a bat awarded by a local paper for the week's best performance. During his last season, Horace was joined at Reading by a forward named Howard Fielding, and, although the newcomer never made it to Reading's first team, there was still plenty of confusion over the two.

Reading Record: Lge 132/36, FAC 15/5, SSC 5/1, Total 152/42
League Career Total: 314/67

FISHER Frederick
b. Hetton le Hole 28.11.1924
Ht 5ft 5 Wt 9st 2 (49-50)
Career: Slough T; Chelsea (Wartime guest); READING amateur March 1944, professional August 1944; Shrewsbury T. (£350) July 1952; Leyton O. July 1954

If fans and historians were confused over Reading's two Fieldings, it was even worse during the last two War seasons when the club frequently played two Freddy Fishers. One, a right back, was a guest player from Grimsby while the other came via Slough and signed permanently for the club after appearing on the right wing for the last few games of 1944-45. During that amateur spell he was one of seven Reading players who were in a Berks & Bucks XI that held a strong FA XI to a draw. He gradually established himself as Reading's first choice on the right wing during the first League season after the War and held on to it until the start of 1950-51 when a broken leg in the first game of the season that virtually ended his first team career. Freddy did have the consolation of helping Reading's reserves win the Combination championship in his final season.

Reading Record: Lge 139/23, FAC 13/1, Wartime 23/3, Total 175/27
League Career Total: 205/33

FITZGERALD Michael Alfred
b. Conisborough 25.11.1911 d. 1981
Ht 5ft 9 Wt 11st (35-36)
Career: Denaby U; READING (trial) July 1934, professional August 1934; QPR May 1936; Aldershot November 1945

A strong tackling left half Alf spent the majority of his two season stay at Reading in the reserves waiting for the club's regular number 6, Billy Wright, to be injured, so he only played seven first team games in that time. Alf even had the disappointment of losing his place after he had scored the winning goal against Millwall on Boxing Day 1934 and then suffered a cartilage injury. He enjoyed much more success on leaving Reading, making over 100 first team appearances for QPR before the War and another 60 plus for Aldershot after the League programme restarted.

Reading Record: Lge 6/1, SSC 1, Total 7/1
League Career Total: 159/45

FLANNIGAN Raymond John
b. Margate 15.3.1949
Ht 6ft 1 Wt 12st (71-72)
Career: Margate; READING (£1,500) 5 February 1970; Ramsgate summer 1972; Cambridge C. 1975

Ray spent four years playing for Margate, playing mainly on the left wing while Tom Jenkins was on the right. The success of Jenkins at Reading encouraged them to go back for Ray and they beat several other clubs with a fee of £1,500 that doubled after 10 League appearances. In September 1970 he made his League debut on the left wing but from then on he was converted to a stylish left back whose attacking runs, with his long hair flowing behind him, were one of the few promising features of a disappointing relegation season. The dismissal of Jack Mansell saw Ray reverting to his forward position but, with his first team appearances reducing in number, he was given a 'free' at the end of the season, having a spell in Canada in between playing non-League football.

Reading Record: Lge 36(4), FAC 5/1, LC 1, Total 42(4)/1

FLECK Robert William

b. Glasgow 11.8.1965
Ht 5ft 7 Wt 11st 7 (98-99)
Career: Possil YM; Glasgow Rngrs July 1983; Partick Thistle (loan) November 1983; Norwich C. (£580,000) December 1987; Chelsea (£2.1 m) August 1992; Bolton W. (loan) December 1993; Bristol C. (loan) January 1995; Norwich C. (£650,000) August 1995; READING (£60,000) 26 March 1998; Gorleston coach March 1999

Robert's reputation was built on two high scoring seasons, one with Rangers and the other during his first spell at Norwich. These earned him six Scottish U21 caps and four full caps plus several large money moves of which the biggest, the £2.1 million move to Chelsea was the least successful as he only scored four times in 43 first team starts. In 1995 Robert returned to Norwich where he continued the rapport he had established with their fans and there was disappointment at Carrow Road when he left to join Reading. Robert was the first of new Reading manager, Tommy Burns' seven transfer deadline day signings and he saw the determined, experienced scorer as the type of player to help in Reading's relegation fight. Although he could not help Reading avoid the drop, Robert had the consolation of scoring in the opening game at the new Madejski Stadium. Sadly for Robert he was already troubled with a back injury and in February 1999 he was forced to retire from League football.

Reading Record: Lge 5(4)/1, LC 1, Total 6(4)/1
League Career Total: 279(34)/62

ROBERT'S CLAIM TO FAME - Before he played for Reading in the final League game at their old ground, Elm Park, Robert was presented with the Player of the Year award - for his part season with Norwich !

FORRESTER George Larmouth

b. Cannock 8.6.1927 d. Reading 9.1981
Ht 5ft 7 Wt 11st 1 (55-56)
Career: West Bromwich Alb; Gillingham August 1947; READING (£25) July 1955; Headington U. July 1956; Ashford U; Wokingham T. manager; Wingate manager

After a youth career that saw him win the FA Youth Trophy with Staffordshire and play for England Youth, George failed to secure a contract with West Brom and so joined Gillingham. He helped the Gills win the Southern League title in 1948-49 and then played for them as they regained their League status in 1950. In 1955 George moved to Reading where he played only a handful of games but became one of the select band of players to score in their last League game when he scored Reading's winner against Crystal Palace in April 1956. Two days later he scored in the semi-final of the Southern Floodlit Cup against West Ham.

Released in the close season, George then played for a number of non-League clubs but never moved away from Reading, and in 1964 he was influential in the growth of Sunday League football in the town. Sadly, George collapsed while jogging in Prospect Park and died within yards of Elm Park at the age of 54.

Reading Record: Lge 6/2, SPFC 2/2, Total 8/4
League Career Total: 106/5

FORSTER Matthew

b. Newburn on Tyne 24.8.1900 d. St Albans, 18.10.1976
Ht 5ft 10 1/2 Wt 11st 10 (30-31)
Career: Newburn; Tottenham H. 1920; READING (£750) 3 July 1930; Charlton A. summer 1933; Bexleyheath

In his 10 years with Tottenham, Matt gradually established himself as their regular right back so that in the four seasons from 1925-26 he only missed 17 games. During this period he played in two international trials but never made it to the England team. Matt joined Reading for what was to be a relegation season but even so, he was one of the few successes of that season. Although he was used less frequently after Joe Smith became manager at Elm Park, he was a popular personality off the pitch, being a keen golfer and also a fine pianist who, apparently, could play anything.

Reading Record: Lge 69, FAC 10, Total 79
League Career Total: 306

FORSTER Nicholas Michael

b. Caterham 8.9.1973
Ht 5ft 10 W 11st 5 (99-00)
Career: Holland Sports; Horley T. 1991; Gillingham May 1992; Brentford (£100,000) June 1994; Birmingham C. (£700,000) January 1997; Reading (£750,000) 25 June 1999

Snapped up by Gillingham from non-League football, Nicky soon displayed a natural scoring ability that persuaded Brentford to buy him in the summer of 1994. He hit 24 goals in his first season, earning Nicky a PFA Divisional award, a place in the Endsleigh League side that played the Italian Serie B team, and four England U21 caps. In 1996-97 he formed a devastating partnership with Carl Asaba that attracted a lot of attention as Brentford were at the top of Division Two but, while the inevitable sale of Nicky to Birmingham brought them a large fee, it is generally thought that it cost them automatic promotion that season. Nicky's spell with Birmingham was hampered by injuries but, even when he was fit, he was rarely given a good run in the first team so he went on the transfer list in January 1999.

Reading were interested in him from that time, eventually getting their man six months later for another big fee. Despite suffering from an injury in pre-season training that delayed his debut and troubled him for the first half of the season, Nicky quickly became a crowd pleasing and effective player, his devastating speed and close control catching out many Division Two defences (as well as quite a few assistant referees!) and he ended the season as second highest scorer. Unfortunately, a cruciate injury sustained in a pre-season friendly in August 2000 kept him out for eight months. He still made a tremendous impact on Reading's season, his ninth minute substitute appearance in the play-off semi-final earned him the man of the match award after he made Reading's first goal and then scored the last minute winner.

Reading Record: Lge 31(14)/11, FAC 2, LC 3, AMC 2(1), Play-offs (3)/1, Total 38(18)/12 +
League Career Total 217(72)/85 +

FOSTER Deane
b. Reading 22.8.1966
Ht 5ft 10 Wt 10st 9 (85-86)
Career: READING apprentice 1983, professional 1985; Farnborough T. 1987; Maidenhead U. 1988

Reading almost missed out on Deane as he had trials for Rotherham and Bury before joining his home town club after leaving school. Deane turned professional at the time Reading were running away with the Third Division Championship and so the slightly built right back had little chance of breaking into the League side. His first professional season saw him build up his strength and go over the 10 stone mark as well as getting a couple of games in the Freight Rover Trophy. His debut saw him up against one of the division's top forwards, Bournemouth's Colin Clarke, and although he did well, a basically Reading reserve side lost 5-0 while his second game ended in a 3-0 home defeat. Deane never got to play another game and was released in 1987.

Reading Record: AMC 2

FOSTER Ronald Edmund
b. Islington 22.11.1938
Ht 5ft 9 Wt 10st 10 (67-68)
Career: Clapton; Leyton O. March 1957; Grimsby T. (£11,500) December 1962; READING (£5,250) 25 July 1966; Dallas Tornados (£3,000) summer 1968; Brentford March 1969; Dover July 1969

Ron was a skilful, creative inside forward whose early form with Leyton Orient, which included promotion to the First Division in 1961-62, prompted Grimsby to pay their record fee to boost their Second Division side.

He was a fixture in their first team, captaining the side for much of 1965-66, before moving to Reading the day before England reached the World Cup final. After starting the season in midfield, and scoring on his home debut, Ron lost his place in November but his return in April saw Reading win their last eight games and come close to sneaking a promotion place. He was less successful the following season but at least Ron had the satisfaction of scoring his last goal for Reading against his old club, Grimsby. After a spell helping to try to launch football in the States, Ron returned to the League for a three game spell with Brentford.

Reading Record: Lge 44(1)/5, FAC 5, LC 4/1, Total 53(1)/6
League Career Total: 248(2)/46

FOSTER Thomas Curtis
b. Sunderland c.1913
Ht 5ft 9 Wt 11st 4 (35-36)
Career: READING December 1933; Clapton O. 1935; Swansea T. 1936; Crewe Alex. 1937

A renowned sprinter, Tom made his League debut when he was selected at centre forward for Reading's home game against Newport in January 1934 and although he did not get on the scoresheet, they won 4-0. The next season he moved to Clapton Orient where he scored 10 goals in 11 games in his first season which proved to be his best spell in a career that was ended by the War.

Reading Record: Lge 1
League Career Total: 95/41

FRANCIS Stephen Stuart
b. Billericay 29.5.1964
Ht 5ft 11 Wt 11st 5 (96-97)
Career: Chelsea from apprentice April 1982; READING (loan) 27 February 1987, permanent (£20,000); Huddersfield T. (£150,000) 1 August 1993; Northampton T. January 1999

Steve was capped at England Youth level while at Chelsea where he made his League debut in goal for them at the age of 17 and kept his place to the end of the season. In March 1986 he helped Chelsea win the Full Members Cup against Manchester City at Wembley but a year later he joined Reading after a short spell on loan. Three clean sheets in his first four games helped move Reading clear of the relegation battle but it was his performance in the last home game of that season that finally assured Reading's Second Division status. Down to 10 men against champions elect, Derby, Steve turned in one of the best goalkeeping displays seen at Elm Park that culminated in a penalty save.

The following season Steve could not save Reading from relegation but he was ever-present as they won the Simod Cup at Wembley. Steve remained the number one keeper with Reading until 1993, with injuries being responsible for most of his absences. It was, therefore, something of a surprise when he was then sold to Huddersfield for a tribunal fixed fee and despite conceding three on his home debut, against Reading, he stayed with Huddersfield until January 1999 when he moved to Northampton. Again he made his debut against Reading and kept a clean sheet as Northampton got a shock win at the Madejski Stadium. His performance was no surprise to the Reading fans who recognized the brilliant shot stopper as one of the best keepers in the club's history.

Reading Record: Lge 216, FAC 15, LC 15, FMC 6, AMC 7, Total 259
League Career Total: 476

FRANKLIN Paul Leslie
b. Hainault 5.10.1963
Ht 6ft 2 Wt 12st 2 (87-88)
Career: Birmingham C. assoc. schoolboy; Waltham New Town; Watford from apprentice August 1981; Shrewsbury T. (loan) October 1986; Swindon T. (loan) November 1986; READING (free) July 1987; Wycombe W. player coach August 1989; Norwich C. assist manager July 1995; Leicester C. assist manager December 1995

A central defender who was ever-present as Watford won the 1982 FA Youth Cup, Paul graduated to their first team and, as well as League and cup appearances, he played four times in their European campaigns. A couple of loan spells helped increase his experience but he moved to Reading in an attempt to get regular first team football. Paul was soon converted to right back but after January, when he scored the winner in an FA Cup-tie against Tranmere, he only made one more appearance. That game was the last of the season, at Chesterfield, and proved eventful as Reading were 2-0 down at one stage and heading for their second consecutive relegation before they scored four second half goals to avoid the drop.

At the end of that season he joined Wycombe where he teamed up with Martin O'Neill as assistant manager and they continued the partnership at Norwich and Leicester.

Reading Record: Lge 17(3), FAC 5/1, LC 3, AMC 3, Total 28(3)/1
League Career Total: 60(3)/1

FREEMAN Andrew James
b. Reading 8.9.1977
Ht 5ft 10 Wt 10st 6 (96-97)
Career: Crystal Palace YTS; READING from YTS 15 March 1996; Kingstonian (loan) October 1997; Yeovil (loan) December 1997; Basingstoke T. summer 1998

On 16 April 1996, new club professional Andy Freeman wrote himself into Reading's records when he came on as substitute for the last five minutes of their game at Watford. That proved to be Andy's only first team appearance and so he has the shortest League career of any Reading player. Andy looked at one stage to have a bright future and he was noted for his hard working midfield displays and his passing ability in the reserves. He was loaned out to a couple of non-League clubs to gain more experience but was eventually released in the summer of 1998 and now runs a Brazilian 'futeball de salas' soccer school in Bracknell.

Reading Record: Lge (1)

FREEMAN Ronald Peter Percy
b. Stourbridge 4.7.1945
Ht 6ft 2 Wt 14st (72-73)
Career: Stourbridge; Alvechurch; West Bromwich Alb. (£2,500) April 1968; Lincoln C. June 1970; READING (£11,000) 9 January 1973; Lincoln C. (£3,500) January 1975

A former night club bouncer, Percy was understudy to Jeff Astle at West Brom so he only made two first team starts before moving to Lincoln where he became a great favourite of the fans.

He averaged almost a goal every other game for them before he moved to boost Reading's shot shy forward line. Percy proved an instant hit at Elm Park where his barnstorming centre forward play livened up many a game. His game was all about power and strength, both of which he had in abundance, and although Percy might not have been the most skilful player he was always a handful for Fourth Division defences. Unfortunately, the cost of living in the South on Fourth Division wages caused Percy to quit football for a while, in 1974, to work as a scaffolder. Although he returned to Reading after a few months, the club realized he wanted to move away and he returned to Lincoln. There he helped the Imps win the Fourth Division title while his goals and play saw him top the Sunday People's Divisional Merit Marks. During that summer Spurs offered £35,000 for Percy but, although the club agreed, Percy preferred to stay with Lincoln where he remains popular with their fans to this day.

Reading Record: Lge 53(7)/13, FAC 1(1), LC 3, Total 57(8)/13
League Career Total: 193(22)/77

PERCY'S CLAIM TO FAME - The power of Percy's shooting is legendary but his accuracy was not all it could have been. On one occasion, a wayward shot put Elm Park's electronic scoreboard out of action while at the other end of the pitch a Percy blockbuster sailed out of the ground and brought down a line of washing in a nearby garden!

FRENCH Graham Edward
b. Wolverhampton 6.4.1945
Ht 5ft 10 Wt 11st 5 (73-74)
Career: Huddersfield T. apprentice; Shrewsbury T. from apprentice November 1962; Swindon T. (£11,500) August 1963; Watford (£1,250) August 1964; Wellington (free) November 1964; Luton T. October 1965; READING (loan) 7 November 1973; Boston Minutemen June 1974; Southport March 1976

Graham was a talented right winger who seemed to lack the necessary discipline to play at the high level his ability could have supported. He won three England Youth caps and attracted a lot of attention when he broke into Shrewsbury's first team at 17 but Graham failed to reach his potential until Luton rescued him from non-League football. In August 1973, Luton agreed to sell Graham to Reading but the player could not agree personal terms and, although the deal fell through, he joined Reading three months later on loan. Injured in his third game at Elm Park, Graham returned to Luton, making almost 200 appearances for the Hatters. Graham occasionally courted controversy and was once jailed following a shooting incident in Luton, and subsequently changed his name to Lafite.

Reading Record: Lge 3
League Career Total: 221(2)/23

FRIDAY Robin
b. Hammersmith 27.7.1952 d. Ealing 31.12.1990
Ht 5ft 10 Wt 12st (75-76)
Career: QPR (trial); Chelsea amateur; READING (trial) 1968-69; Walton & Hersham; Enfield; Hayes; READING (trial) November 1973, professional 6 February 1974; Cardiff C. (£35,000) December 1976

It is remarkable to think that Robin Friday's amazing talent was missed by several League clubs, including Reading in Jack Mansell's days, and that he was 21 before he got his chance. He seemed destined to spend his playing career around London non-League clubs until the 1973-74 FA Cup draw put Reading up against Hayes, and Robin rose to the occasion to show what he could do. Reading manager, Charlie Hurley, invited Robin for a trial and after two months he was given his League debut. His first two games were away from home, but he made such an impression that a larger than normal home crowd saw him produce a sensational, two goal performance against Exeter. That performance turned out to be standard for Robin, who combined the traditional centre forward assets of strength, bravery and aerial ability with brilliant ball skills and a totally unique style. In his first full season he finished as Reading's top scorer and was runaway winner of the Player of the Year vote, a feat he repeated in 1975-76 as Reading won promotion to the Third Division. His goal against Tranmere in March 1976, a thunderous 20 yard volley, is widely regarded as the best ever scored at Elm Park while his goal celebration after scoring a late winner against Rochdale was equally memorable - especially for the policeman he kissed! Robin's bravery was almost as legendary as his skill - Robin would torment defenders with his talent and could, and did, give as good, physically, as he got.

But if Robin's discipline on the pitch was causing some concern, the real worry surrounded his lifestyle. Robin lived life as hard as he played with the town being filled with rumours of his wild ways involving drinking and other excesses.

While these did not appear to affect his play it was clear that it was only a matter of time before they did. In December 1976 Reading decided to let Robin move to Cardiff, and although he made a typically sensational debut, scoring twice against Fulham while being marked by an, apparently, shell-shocked Bobby Moore, his playing career quickly went into decline. Within a year his contract was cancelled and Robin quit football as his life went into freefall.

Drug and alcohol related convictions followed until, on New Year's Eve 1990, Robin was found dead in his flat. He was 38.

Subsequently, Robin has become part of football's folklore and he has been immortalized in the best-selling book by Oasis guitarist, Paul McGiugan, entitled *'The Greatest Footballer You Never Saw'*. To many Reading fans, he remains the greatest player they did see, and in November 1999 Robin Friday was voted Reading's Player of the Millennium

Reading Record: Lge 121/46, FAC 3/2, LC 11/5, Total 135/53
League Career Total: 141(1)/52

FRIEL George Patrick
b. Reading 11.7.1970
Ht 5ft 8 Wt 10st 11 (90-91)
Career: READING from apprentice July 1989; Woking summer 1991; Peppard: AFC Wallingford; Henley Town

George was succeeding at Elm Park long before he joined Reading as an apprentice. In 1981 he won the Junior Royals under 10 Superstars competition and a year later he won a Roy of the Rovers penalty shoot out at the ground. His progress through the youth ranks included four goals in the club's 15-0 away win at Weymouth in the 1987-88 FA Youth Cup and by October 1989 he had made his League debut, at Wigan. By then George had developed into a wide midfielder but he hadn't lost his eye for a goal, scoring in his first home game of 1990-91. He was used intermittently through that season but was released at its end.

Reading Career: Lge 10(6)/1, FAC 1, LC (1), AMC 1, Total 12(7)/1

FULLWOOD James
b. Ilkeston, 17.2.1911 d. Wokingham 1981
Ht 6ft Wt 12st 3 (38-39)
Career: Thorne Colliery; Tottenham H. October 1934; READING 26 August 1938

A well built left back who 'never gets flurried', Jimmy made only 34 League appearances for Spurs in four seasons but it still took a lot of persuading to get him to move to Reading in 1938. He played in every game that season and, because the competition ending had been held over from the previous season, he was able to captain Reading to victory in the two legged final of the Southern Section Cup against Bristol City. Although the War ended Jimmy's League career he was one Reading's most frequent players during the hostilities and played in the 1941 London War Cup victory. All of Jimmy's games for Reading were at left back except one, when he played on the left wing at Crystal Palace in January 1945 and scored his only goal for the club. Jimmy retired from football at the end of the War and went into business locally but still found time to show his other sporting skills at cricket, golf and tennis.

Reading Record: Lge 42, FAC 2, SSC 6, Wartime 178/1, Total 228/1
League Career Total: 76/1

GAMBLE Frederick C
b Charing Cross 29.5.1905 d. Lambeth 15.5.1965
Ht 5ft 11 Wt 11st 12 (33-34)
Career: Southall; Brentford 1928; West Ham U. 1931; Aldershot summer 1932; READING (£500) 16 March 1933

Having scored regularly for several London clubs without gaining more than a few first team starts, Fred moved to Aldershot shortly after they were elected into the League. The son of music hall comedian, Fred Gamble, he played in the Shots first ever League game and started finding the net regularly, including four against Reading, Later that season Reading sold their own star centre forward, Jack Palethorpe, and bought Fred the following day. A fast and courageous player, he scored in three of his first four Reading games but after that the goals dried up. During that summer Fred made his debut as a medium pace bowler for Surrey and when he was given a transfer at the end of 1933-34 he quit football to concentrate on his cricketing career. In total, Fred took 40 wickets while batting was obviously not a strength as he ended with an average of 8.8 runs in his 25 innings.

Reading Record: Lge 10/3
League Career Total: 49/25

GAMBLE Joseph Finbar
b. Cork 14.1.1982
Ht 5ft 7 Wt 11st (00-01)
Career: Cork C; Ipswich (trial) summer 2000; READING August 2000: Crawley T. (loan)

After a series of sparkling performances in Reading's pre-season friendlies, the club had to beat off several Premiership clubs to secure Joe's signature. He was a regular for the Republic of Ireland's U18 team and was likened to a young Roy Keane so it was no surprise that Joe didn't have to wait long for his League debut, coming on as substitute at Port Vale at the beginning of September 2000.

Reading Record: Lge (1), FAC (1), LC (1), Total (3) +

GARDINER Robert
b. Motherwell c.1896 d. ?
Ht 5ft 8 Wt 12st (21-22)
Career: Motherwell; READING (£300) November 1921

When Reading paid £300 for Robert it was regarded as such a large fee that the club had to hold dances, a concert, and a Christmas raffle to pay it off. Initially, they must have wondered if he was worth it as his first four games in Reading's attack failed to produce any goals for the team, but after Robert opened his scoring account in January 1922 he began to display the skills that the club had paid for. In 1922-23 the skilful inside right was joint top scorer with 13 goals and ever-present but was less successful the following season and was released by Reading.

Reading Record: Lge 102/23, FAC 3, Total 105/23

GARDINER William Silcock
b. Lambert 15.8.1929
Ht 6ft 1 Wt 12st 1 (59-60)
Career: Glasgow Rngrs 1951; Leicester C. August 1955; READING (£5,000) 17 November 1958; Sudbury T. June 1961

Willie was capable of prolific scoring and won a Scotland B cap while with Rangers for whom he hit four goals in a game against Stirling Albion in October 1954. This sort of form saw him move to Leicester and helped then win the Second Division title in 1956-57. With 48 goals in 69 League games for Leicester, Willie was considered a fine signing for Reading but a broken leg sustained in only his seventh game for them all but ended his playing career. After one comeback game, 11 months later, the blond centre forward was forced to retire from League football.

Reading Record: Lge 8/2
League Career Total: 77/50

GARRATT Frederick C H
b. Wolverton c.1900 d. ?
Ht 5ft 7 Wt 11st 6 (22-23)
Career: Wolverton T; READING 1922

Fred was given a couple of games at centre forward in Reading's home and away fixtures against Portsmouth in October 1922. Reading had a goalscoring problem throughout that season and had failed to net in five of their first 10 games but Fred was unable to solve this as Reading drew a blank in both of his games and he was never selected for the first team again, his career being hampered by 'a tendency to suffer from boils'.

Reading Record: Lge 2

GAUNT (Goldberg) Leslie
b. Leeds 3.1.1918
Ht 5ft 10 1/2 Wt 11st 9 (49-50)
Career: Leeds U. from groundstaff May 1935; READING Wartime guest, trial July 1946, permanent 15 March 1947; Newbury T. manager 1955; READING coaching staff 1969 to 1971

Born Goldberg, Les played twice for England Schools before beginning a 15 year association with Leeds although, because of the War, he only made 31 League appearances in three seasons. During the War, Les guested regularly for Reading while stationed nearby, making a strong impression with the club and its fans as a consistent and skilful right back. When it became apparent that he was not commanding a first team place at Leeds, Reading spent a record fee to sign him on a permanent basis. For his part, Les only agreed to drop to the Third Division because of his happy spell with Reading during those Wartime games. It continued to be a happy association with Les a permanent fixture at right back, although he did confuse the statisticians by changing his name to Gaunt during the summer of 1948. He was injured at Brighton in November 1948 and it took him almost a year to regain his first team place, but in his third game back he suffered a badly broken leg at Norwich and his playing career was over. Les stayed in the area, helping out local clubs, and returned to Elm Park as administration and technical assistant to Jack Mansell in the early Seventies.

Reading Record: Lge 71, FAC 7/1, Wartime 80, Total 158/1
League Career Total: 102

GERNON Frederick Anthony John **'Irvin'**
b. Birmingham 30.12.1962
Ht 6ft 1 Wt 12st 8 (89-90)
Career: Ipswich T.   from apprentice January 1980;
Northampton T. (loan) November 1986; Gillingham (£30,000)
March 1987; READING (£20,000) 19 September 1988;
Northampton T. (£25,000) October 1989

A promising career that saw Irvin capped at England
Youth and U21 level never reached its full potential due
to a catalogue of injuries. Having made his debut for
Ipswich in March 1982, Irvin would have made many
more than the 76 League appearances he achieved but
for those injuries.   18 months at Gillingham were
followed by a move to Reading where went straight into
the first team.   Irvin and his cultured left foot were
mainly used at left back but his height and unflustered
style meant he was also able to operate in the centre of
defence.   A return to fitness by Steve Richardson
eventually saw Irvin drop out of the first team in
February and he only had another three first team starts
before he moved on to Northampton.

Reading Record: Lge 21(4), FAC 5/1, AMC 1, Total
27(4)/1
League Career Total: 186(7)/2

GETGOOD (Goodman) **George**
b. Coylton 15.11.1892 d. Kidderminster, 22.7.1970
Ht 5ft 8 Wt 11st (20-21)
Career: Ayr U. 1912; READING July 1914; Withenhall Swifts
July 1921; Birmingham (£600) August 1921; Southampton
March 1922; Wolverhampton W. January 1923; Kidderminster
Harriers March 1925; Aberdare A. July 1926; Shrewsbury T.
November 1926; Bathgate 1927; Bo'ness 1928; Nuneaton T.
February 1929

George began his career in the Army and then moved to
Ayr United where he led their forward line. Shortly
before the War, he moved to Reading who almost
immediately converted him to a half back while he
changed his name to Getgood. His versatility was
demonstrated by the fact he played in five different
positions during Reading's first League season,
including the club's first ever League game.   At
Southampton he was centre half as they won the original
Third Division South title.   After a year at the Dell,
George moved to Wolves and there he completed a rare
double when he won a Third Division North
championship medal in 1923-24. From 1925 he ran the
Great Western Hotel near Kidderminster but carried on
playing until his late thirties.

Reading Record: Lge 36/1, FAC 4, SL 72/4, Total 112/5
League Career Total: 141/3

GIAMETTEI Aaron Pietro
b. Reading, 11.10.1973
Ht 5ft 10 Wt 10st 10 (91-92)
Career: READING from YTS July 1992; Newbury T. October
1992; Abingdon 1995

Despite his Italian sounding name, Aaron was a local
lad who was with Reading as a schoolboy and played
through the youth and reserves to get his first team
chance in 1992. A lively midfielder, Aaron came off the
subs bench twice and although he nearly scored with his
first touch in League football when he shot just over
against Fulham he never got a first team start. His
second appearance, at Bradford, was unusual in that,
having come on as sub, he was then replaced himself so
that his League career lasted just 54 minutes in total.

Reading Record: Lge (2)

GILHESPY Thomas William **Cyril**
b. Fencehouses 18.2.1898 d. Lancaster 3.1985
Ht 5ft 8 1/2 Wt 11st 12 (30-31)
Career: Chester le Street; Sunderland 1920; Liverpool 1921;
Bristol C. 1925; Blackburn R.1929; READING June 1930;
Mansfield T. summer 1931; Crewe Alex. summer 1932

Cyril's well travelled League career only took off after
a move to Bristol City saw him become a first team
regular where his powerful right wing play produced a
regular supply of goals.   It also generated a record
transfer fee when he moved to Blackburn but this
proved a disappointing move for both Cyril and his new
club and so he was allowed to join Reading, having
made just five League appearances for Rovers.   At
Reading it was a case of out of the frying pan into the
fire as the club had already conceded 14 goals before
Cyril made his debut in their fourth game, and after his
first two games the total was up to 26. At least he was
getting first team football but at the end of that season he
was on the move again.

Reading Record: Lge 21/3, FAC 3/1, Total 24/4
League Career Total: 200/37

GILKES Michael Earl Glenis McDonald
b. Hackney 20.7.1965
Ht 5ft 8 Wt 10st 10 (91-92)
Career: Leicester C. youths; READING (free) 10 July 1984;
Chelsea (loan) January 1992; Southampton (loan) March 1992;
Wolverhampton W. (£150,000) 27 March 1997; Millwall (free)
July 1999; Slough Town summer 2001; Bristol Rovers (trial)

A three month spell with Leicester did not produce a
contract but shortly after Michael began his 13 year
spell with Reading.

He became one of the most popular players in recent years - nothing would get the Elm Park faithful going more than the sight of 'Gilksie' leaving a trail of de-fenders in his wake as he set off on another scorching run down the left wing. Initially, Michael lacked the consistency to go with his searing pace but in August 1987, Ian Branfoot experimented by playing him at left back and three months later Michael was given his chance in this role in the League. Revelling in the space he got from starting his runs from a deeper position Michael was ever present from then on and capped his season with a sensational performance in the Simod Cup Final at Wembley when he ran First Division Luton ragged in a rare game in the forward line.

From then on Michael was rarely out of the first team, apart from a spell following a broken leg sustained at Southend in February 1991. A year later he finished third in the Ladbroke Sprint Final prior to the League Cup Final with a time of 11.62 seconds, having led for the first 60 yards. That Wembley appearance coincided with an unsettled spell for Michael when he had loan spells with Chelsea and then Southampton before re-establishing himself in Reading's first team, finishing 1992-93 with his best goal tally of 12. Although Michael invariably wore either the 7 or 11 shirt he was used equally on the wing and at full back. Having helped Reading win the Division Two title in 1993-94, he hit sensational form the following year as Reading reached the Division One play-off final. As well as scoring eight times, he switched to full back for the run-in and was equally effective. On transfer deadline day 1997, his former manager, Mark McGhee, made a deal worth £150,000 to take Gilksie to Wolves but he still had a fine turn out for his testimonial at the last first team game to be played at Elm Park, in August 1998. In July 2000 he was picked for Barbados in a World Cup qualifier v Costa Rica.

Reading Record: Lge 348(45)/43, FAC 31(3)/1, LC 25(7)/6, Play-offs 3, FMC 7(1)/1, AMC 16(1)/1, Total 430(57)/52
League Career Total: 413(57)/46 +

MICHAEL'S CLAIM TO FAME - At 10.38 pm on 2 March 1988, Michael had the responsibility of taking the last kick in the Simod Cup semi-final penalty kick shoot-out. In converting the penalty he won for Reading at their first ever Wembley visit and wrote himself into the record books by scoring the latest first class goal in this country.

GIRVAN Hector
b. Glasgow 10.12.1901 d. ?
Ht 5ft 7 1/2 Wt 11st (27-28)
Career: Parkhead Jnr; Bo'ness; READING (£75) August 1926; Swindon T. (£300) May 1929; Margate August 1934

Hector joined Reading from Bo'ness, a regular source of players for the Biscuitmen in manager Andrew Wylie's days. Previously he had won a number of honours with Parkhead Juniors, including four winners medals in 1922-23. At Reading he had the unenviable task of trying to displace Billy McConnell from the left back spot and so he only made the first team when the great Irish defender was injured or on international duty. When he did get in the first team he let no one down, being described in the club programme as being a *'fearless defender who tackles well and has good speed'* although he did have a tendency to balloon clearances when under pressure. At the end of 1928-29, Hector moved to Swindon where he hardly missed a game in four seasons.

Reading Record: Lge 33
League Career Total: 181

GLASGOW Byron Fitzgerald
b. Clapham 18.2.1979
Ht 5ft 4 Wt 9st 7 (98-99)
Career: Arsenal assoc schoolboy; READING from YTS 24 August 1996; Crawley T. 1999; Luton T. (trial) August 2000, St Albans C. February 2001, Carshalton 2001

A small but tenacious midfielder whose size three boots were reported to be the smallest in the League, Byron has his mother to thank for his start in football. At the age of seven, Byron was considered too small to be picked for any of his local teams in Battersea so his mother formed a team specially to showcase her son's talent. The plan worked, not only for Byron, but for several other of his team mates who went on to win League contracts. Reading beat several clubs for his signature on YTS terms and Byron made a handful of promising first team appearances before being given an extended run by Tommy Burns in a wide midfield position. His high workrate and gradually improved distribution earned him 32 League games in 1998-99 so the future looked bright for Byron when a bombshell was dropped.

On 8 July the club cancelled his contract after it had been revealed that he had tested positive following a random drugs test. The club provided financial support for his rehabilitation and his FA ban was subsequently lifted but he has yet to make it back into League football.

Reading Record: Lge 31(8)/1, FAC 1(1), LC 2, AMC 1, Total 35(9)/1

BYRON'S CLAIM TO FAME - Byron scored Reading's last competitive goal at Elm Park when he netted for their reserves against Rushden and Diamonds in August 1998.

GLIDDEN Gilbert Swinburne
b. Sunderland 15.12.1915 d. 1988
Ht 5ft 9 Wt 11st 8 (49-50)
Career: Sunderland; Port Vale 1935; READING May 1936; Tranmere R. (Wartime guest); Leyton O. (free) 12 June 1950; Stoke C. physio 1952 to 1954

One of three brothers who played League football, Gilbert, like his more famous brother, Tom, was capped for England Schools and joined Sunderland at 14, initially as an office boy. Although he made it on to the playing staff, Gilbert had to wait until he moved to Port Vale to get his League debut. After a season in the Potteries he moved to Reading where, although he was never really a first team regular, he still enjoyed a 14 year career. Of course, the War intervened when he also played for Tranmere, and he was picked for the RAF v the Army in February 1941. Prior to the War, Gilbert had played in both legs of Reading's 1938 Southern Section Cup final triumph. Gilbert was a hard working utility player who could perform equally well as inside forward or half back but his trademark was his legendary fitness. He was reported to *train unsparingly for physical perfection'* so it is not surprising that he set up one of the town's first keep fit studios and advertised it in the Reading programme. When his playing days were over, Gilbert qualified as a physiotherapist.

Reading Record: Lge 111/24, FAC 8/1, SSC 3/1, Wartime 34/8, Total 156/34
League Career Total: 117/25

GILBERT'S CLAIM TO FAME - On 9 April 1949 Gilbert had double cause to celebrate when he scored the first goal to be conceded by Norwich at Carrow Road in four and a half months on the day his son was born.

GOLDBERG Leslie - see GAUNT

GOLDIE Alexander
b. Ayrshire c.1901 d. ?
Ht 5ft 8 1/2 Wt 11st 7 (23-24)
Career: Nuneaton T; READING summer 1923

Alex's brief League career came to a quick end when he asked for his contract to be cancelled after he lost his first team place after just four games for Reading. He had joined the club in the summer of 1923 and his short run at inside left came in September but with one goal to his credit he left the club the following month.

Reading Record: Lge 4/1

GOODALL Bernard
b. Islington 4.12.1937
Ht 5ft 10 Wt 11st 4 (59-60)
Career: READING amateur September 1953, professional 4 July 1959; Carlisle U. (free) July 1963; Halifax T. November 1964; Hillingdon Bor. July 1965

National Service interrupted Bernie's career with Reading, delaying his signing professionally and his League debut until 1959. Having come into the first team eight games into the 1959-60 season he kept the right back position until he lost it to Gordon Neate after a 4-3 win over Bournemouth on Boxing Day 1960. Bernie regained his place before the season was over and was ever-present when, in March 1962, he suffered a broken leg at Crystal Palace. By coincidence, that game also finished as a 4-3 Reading win in a game that is regarded as one of the club's greatest performances. Sadly for Bernie, that injury spelt the end of his Reading career but not of his footballing success. In 1963-64 he played one game for Carlisle in their Fourth Division promotion season and two years later he helped Hillingdon Borough to promotion as well. After his playing career was over, Bernie became a successful local businessman with interests ranging from welding firms, office furniture and a local hotel. In addition he had a spell as Leyton Orient's chief executive in the Nineties.

Reading Record: Lge 98, FAC 8, LC 3, SPFC 1/1, Total 110/1
League Career Total: 122

GOODCHILD Gary Dean
b. Chelmsford 27.1.1958
Ht 6ft 2 Wt 12st 3 (77-78)
Career: Arsenal from apprentice January 1975; Hereford U. June 1976; Sheffield Wed. (loan); READING (loan) 1 September 1977; Kramfors (Sweden); Crystal Palace December 1979; Wycombe W. youth team manager 1998

An England Schoolboy international, Gary was a free scoring centre forward who once scored four against Reading in the South Eastern Counties youth league. Form like that won him a contract with Arsenal but no first team games. Consequenly, he moved to Hereford in 1976 but even including loan spells at Sheffield Wednesday and Reading he only managed one League start plus six sub appearances. Gary's one appearance for Reading came at Torquay where he came on at half time but could not prevent a 3-0 reverse.

Reading Record: Lge (1)
League Career Total: 1(6)

GOODING Michael Charles
b. Newcastle 12.4.1959
Ht 5ft 9 Wt 10st 7 (93-94)
Career: Warsent T; Bishop Auckland; Rotherham U. July 1979; Chesterfield (player exchange) December 1982; Rotherham U. August 1983; Peterborough U. (£18,000) August 1987; Wolverhampton W. (£85,000) September 1988; READING (£65,000) 24 December 1989; Southend U.1998; Henley Town 2001
See 'The Managers' for details of Mick's managerial career.

A late start to his professional career did Mick no harm as he was still able to make over 700 League appearances and was still playing when aged 40. He scored on his first team debut for Rotherham, back in 1979, and helped them win the Third Division title in 1980-81. At Peterborough he was regularly amongst the goals, with 27 in 60 games, form that encouraged Wolves to buy him where, again, he won a Third Division champion-ship medal.

There was some surprise at Reading when Ian Porterfield, the manager who gave Mick his start at Rotherham, paid £65,000 for the 30 year old midfielder, but any doubts were quickly dispelled by Mick's driving play from midfield. The player that Porterfield described as *'the Third Division's Bryan Robson'* proved every bit as good as that claim and the fans agreed, voting Mick Player of the Year in 1992, 1993 and 1996.

For much of 1992-93, Mick was used as a full back but the club's two most successful seasons - the 1993-94 Division Two championship and the following season's run to the play-off final, saw him back in midfield. Since the end of 1995, Mick had been combining his playing duties with that of joint manager but the added responsibility and work load had no affect on his performances on the pitch. The oldest, yet fittest player at the club, Mick hardly missed a game until he and Jimmy Quinn were released by the club as managers and players in May 1997. Although he was 38 by then, Mick was in demand by several clubs but an accident to his knee while playing football with his children kept him out of the game for a year. It speaks volumes for Mick's determination and overall fitness that he was able to come back from that to play for Southend as their oldest ever debutante and continued well past his fortieth birthday. There he continued to be a credit to every club he represented and to the game itself.

Reading Record: Lge 303(11)/26, FAC 19/2, LC 19, Play-offs 3, AMC 16/2, Total 360(11)/30
League Career Total 663(37)/94

GOODMAN George- see GETGOOD

GOODWIN Harry B
b. Glasgow 4.12.1903 d. ?
Ht 5ft 9 Wt 10st 12 (29-30)
Career: Bo'ness; Portsmouth 1925; READING December 1927; Dolphin summer 1930

Harry spent two and a half seasons with Portsmouth before joining Reading and for the next two years Harry was a fixture on Reading's right wing where he displayed good ball control at speed, along with a fierce shot. He started 1929-30 with four goals in three games, but by February he had lost his first team place and was released in the summer. Surprisingly, in view of his good record up to that date, Harry never played League football again.

Reading Record: Lge 89/15, FAC 6, Total 95/15
League Career Total: 127/23

GORDON Colin Kenneth
b. Stourbridge 17.1.1963
Ht 6ft 1 Wt 12st 12 (86-87)
Career: Wolverhampton W. jnrs; Stourbridge; Worcester C. 1981; Bromsgrove R; Halesowen Harriers; Lye T; Cradley T; Oldbury U. 1982; Swindon T. October 1984; Wimbledon (£80,000) July 1986; Gillingham (loan) February 1987; READING (£80,000) 17 July 1986; Bristol C. (loan) March 1988; Fulham (£80,000) 7 October 1988; Birmingham C. (£80,000) June 1989; Hereford U. (loan) September 1990;

Walsall (loan) December 1990; Bristol R. (loan) January 1991; Leicester C. July 1991; Kiddermister Harriers player coach; Gloucester C. 1993; Stourbridge player manager May 1996

After doing the rounds of Midlands non-League clubs, Colin was finally spotted by Lou Macari who signed the big, strong centre forward for Swindon. In Colin's first full season his goals played a major part in their Fourth Division championship of 1985-86. A big money move to Wimbledon was hampered by a shin injury so he only made three League appearances for them before moving to Reading a year later. This gave Colin the toughest role in football at that time - replacing fans favourite, Trevor Senior. A poor start to the season by the club did nothing to help Colin and even an eight goal burst, including two at Stamford Bridge in a League Cup aggregate win, could not win over the fans. In truth, this goal bonanza could not disguise the fact that Colin was not quite skillful enough for Second Division football although he certainly tried his hardest. Towards the end of that season he was loaned to Bristol City and he scored the goal that clinched their play-off place. In October 1988, Colin was transferred to Fulham and, to prove the strange ways of football, was replaced at Reading by the returning Trevor Senior.

Reading Record: Lge 23(1)/9, FAC 1, LC 6/2, FMC 1, Total 31(1)/11
League Career Total: 167(27)/60

COLIN'S CLAIM TO FAME - While with Birmingham, Colin sustained one of football's more unusual injuries, getting blood poisoning after being accidentally bitten by a Swansea player.

GORDON Neville Spencer Damian
b. Greenwich 15.11.1975
Ht 5ft 9 Wt 10st 12 (96-97)
Career: Charlton A. assoc. schoolboy; Millwall from YTS May 1994; Blackpool (trial); READING (free) 11 August 1995; Woking (loan) 1996; Honka (Finland) summer 1996, Whitstable T. 2000

Neville was a prolific scorer for Millwall's youth team, netting 57 South Eastern Counties goals in two seasons as well as being in their teams that won the Southern Floodlit Youth Cup and reached the final of the FA Youth Cup. Despite this, Neville failed to get a first team chance and was released after one year as a professional. Having impressed during a trial period, he joined Reading and in October he came off the bench to replace Jimmy Quinn for the last 10 minutes at West Brom. Never selected again, those 10 minutes for Neville provided Reading's shortest League career until Andy Freeman halved that total six months later.

Reading Record: Lge (1)

GORRINGE Frederick Charles
b. Salford 4th qtr 1903 d. 1965
Ht 5ft 8 Wt 11st 2 (31-32)
Career: Manchester Dock; Manchester C. September 1926; Lincoln C. January 1928; Crewe Alex. 1929; Bolton W. December 1929; READING May 1931

Looking at the statistics of Fred's career he would seem to have been hard done by at several clubs. A docker before becoming a goalscoring outside left, Fred scored twice on his League debut with Manchester City yet he never got another first team chance with them. Fred got back amongst the goals with eight in his first 17 games of 1929-30 for Crewe which prompted a transfer bid from Bolton. Despite scoring 25 times for their Central League side he only got one first team game before joining former Bolton colleague, Joe Smith, who was now manager at Reading. Unfortunately for Fred, this move did little to establish his career. At Reading he was converted to a left half and it was in this position that he appeared in what proved to be his last League game, a 2-1 home win over Coventry on Boxing Day 1931.

Reading Record: Lge 1
League Career Total: 26/12

GRAHAM Harry
b. Edinburgh 16.12.1887 d. Scotland
Ht 5ft 8 1/2 Wt 11st 6 (25-26)
Career: Granton Oakvale; St Bernard's; Bradford C. 1910; Birmingham 1911; Raith R; Hearts; Leicester C. 1920; St Bernard's; READING July 1925

A skilful, scheming inside left who was also a dentist, Harry spent much of his career going backwards and forwards across the Scottish border during his 17 years as a professional. His English career began at Bradford City and he was with them when they won the Cup in 1910-11, although he only played 10 games during that season. He returned to the League with Leicester where he enjoyed his best spell and his best season - six goals from 39 League games in 1922-23. Another spell in Scotland followed before, at the age of 37, he joined Reading. Harry was never a regular in their first team but he did make nine appearances in the 1925-26 Third Division South championship side and the following season he made his final League appearance at South Shields. He was 39 years and three months old at the time and so became the second oldest player to appear in the League for Reading.

Reading Record: Lge 12, FAC 2, Total 14
League Career Total: 145/18

GRANT David Bell

b. Edinburgh 31.5.1943
Ht 5ft 9 Wt 11st (63-64)
Career: Third Lanark 1961; READING 20 May 1963; Trowbridge T. summer 1966; Stirling Alb.

David was a classy centre forward who had scored nine goals in 21 games for Third Lanark before joining Reading for a small fee in a joint deal that also brought Peter Kerr to Elm Park. Unfortunately, the start to David's Reading career was delayed when he broke a bone in his neck in a swimming pool accident before the season had even begun and so he did not make his League debut until Christmas. On the small size for a Third Division centre forward, David never got a long run in the first team but when he got his chance he added a different dimension to Reading's forward line. Despite missing the start of the season he topped the reserves goalscorers in 1963-64 and he had his moment of glory in the League Cup, scoring twice at Craven Cottage as Reading knocked out First Division Fulham in October 1965. Released in the summer of 1966, David eventually returned to Scotland where he switched to the right half position with Stirling Albion.

Reading Record: Lge 17/3, FAC 2, LC 3/2, Total 22/5

GRANT Leonard

b. Reading c.1893 d. 1967
Ht 5ft 8 Wt 11st 8 (21-22)
Career: Reading U; READING amateur 1921, professional August 1921

Len was one of the most famous local footballers in Reading, having helped the schools U15s to the semi-finals of the English Schools Shield even though he was only aged 11. He later played for England Schools against Wales at Walsall in 1907 but, despite playing for a

number of top local amateur clubs, it was another 14 years before he made it to Reading's first team, having acquired the nickname 'Cabby'. From his League debut in October 1921 Len was ever-present until an injury kept him out for a season.

He appeared in every match again in 1923-34, despite switching from his favoured right back position to the left flank in order to accommodate Bert Eggo, and Len captained Reading to victory over Brighton in the end of season Royal Berks Hospital Charity Cup. The start of 1924-25 saw Len lose his first team place due to a recurring knee injury and by the end of that season the injury had forced him to retire from football. Although Len died over 30 years ago there is still a family connection with Reading FC as his nephew, Ron Grant, is kit manager at the Madejski Stadium.

Reading Record: Lge 77/1, FAC 2, Total 79/1

> **LEN'S CLAIM TO FAME** - Len played in the very first schoolboy international in the world and so was justifiably proud of the cap he was awarded. No wonder, then, that he was horrified to be forced to wear his precious trophy throughout a Reading Schools game at a muddy Elm Park a few weeks later. Equally unsurprising were contemporary reports which stated that Len was less willing than usual to head the ball during this match!

GRANT Peter

b. Glasgow 30.8.1965
Ht 5ft 10 Wt 11st 9 (99-00)
Career: Celtic from jnrs July 1982; Norwich C. (£200,000) August 1997; READING (free) 20 August 1999; Bournemouth (free) player coach 1 July 2000

In over 470 appearances for Celtic, Peter helped them qualify for Europe 14 times in his 15 seasons with them. Capped at every level for Scotland, including two full international appearances in 1989, Peter's trophy cabinet also includes medals from three Scottish championships and four Scottish Cup victories. At the start of 1997-98 he moved to Norwich where his experience in midfield proved a great asset to their emerging team of youngsters and his hard working, tough tackling style provided a perfect example to his teammates. Four days before his 34th birthday, Peter's former Celtic colleague, Tommy Burns, recognized those same qualities and signed him to assist his struggling Reading side. Although Peter was used mainly as a substitute after Burns' dismissal, he fought his way back into the first team and it was no coincidence that his return saw an upturn in the team's performances in the second half of the season. Reading were keen to retain Peter's services but he was looking to move into a coaching role and, having helped in this way at Reading's Academy and been linked with a return to Celtic alongside Burns, he moved to Bournemouth as player coach at the end of 1999-00.

Reading Record: Lge 27(2)/1, FAC (4), LC 3, AMC 2, Total 32(6)/1
League Career Total: 105(7)/4 +

81

GRAY Andrew

b. Southampton 25.10.1973
Ht 5ft 6 Wt 10st 10 (96-97)
Career: Bournemouth YTS; READING from YTS 3 July 1992; Woking (loan) October 1993; Leyton O. (free) 20 July 1994; Enfield (loan); Slough T. March 1996; Wokingham T. summer 1996; Hampton February 1998; Thatcham T. summer 2000

Andy developed into a promising young striker who scored regularly for Reading's youth and reserve teams but was up against the formidable Quinn-Lovell striking partnership and so he was generally only on the fringe of the first team. This is borne out by the fact that he only played the full 90 minutes in five of his 20 games for Reading. His best run came in February and March 1993, a spell that saw all but one of his first team starts and produced his three goals, which were scored in consecutive matches. This form indicated that if he could get into the first team, Andy could have done a good job as a wide striker but at the end of 1993-94 he was released.

Reading Record: Lge 8(9)/3, LC (1)/1, AMC 1(1), Total 9(11)/4
League Career Total: 24(25)/6

GRAY Stuart

b. Harrogate 18.12.1973
Ht 5ft 11 Wt 11st 2 (98-99)
Career: Giftrock AFC; Celtic Boys Club; Celtic 1992; READING (£100,000) 26 March 1998; Rushden & Diamonds March 2001

Like his father, Leeds legend Eddie Gray, Stuart possessed a glorious left foot but was a more defensive player than his father, being used in midfield or at left back. Despite his connection with Leeds and the fact that he played for Leeds and North Yorks Schools, Stuart linked up with Celtic from 14 years old, even though this meant weekly journeys from Leeds to Glasgow. Stuart was rewarded for all this traveling with a contract at Celtic Park that led to 30 first team games and seven Scotland U21 caps before his former Celtic boss, Tommy Burns, brought him to Reading on transfer deadline day 1998. At Reading he was used predominantly at left back but a groin injury then back trouble restricted his appearances. Comfortable on the ball and a good passer with a powerful long range shot, Stuart just lacked that extra yard of pace in defensive situations and the arrival of Matt Robinson in January 2000 effectively spelt the end of his Reading career and he was put on the transfer list soon after.

Reading Record: Lge 46(6)/2, FAC 1(1), LC 8, AMC 2, Total 57(7)/2

GREEN Albert

b. Rickmansworth 7.10.1892 d. ?
Ht 5ft 9 1/2 Wt 11st (23-24)
Career: Rickmansworth 1908; Watford from amateur 1914; Crystal Palace 1919; Sheppey U; Charlton A. 1921; Millwall May 1922; READING 12 July 1923

Albert captained Rickmansworth before moving to Watford where he helped them to the Southern League championship in 1914-15 and took part in a trial for England Amateurs. In total he made 62 appearances for Watford, scoring 14 goals from his inside left position before playing for several South East London clubs. Albert moved to Reading for the 1923-24 season where he was in and out of the first team up to Christmas but never played after the turn of the year and his League career was at an end. Although Albert only scored twice for Reading, one was an important goal as it was the winner against local rivals, Swindon.

Reading Record: Lge 10/2
League Career Total: 27/5

GREEN George Frederick

b. Northowram 22.12.1914 d. 1995
Ht 5ft 8 1/2 Wt 11st 13 (48-49)
Career: Yeovil; Bradford P.A. 1936; Huddersfield T. October 1944; READING October 1947

By the time George joined Reading from Huddersfield he had only made 11 League appearances since making his debut for Bradford P.A. in the 1936-37 season. George scored on his League debut for Reading, a feat he repeated for them in his first FA Cup game a month later, but an injury on Boxing Day cost him his first team place for a while. The following season saw him switch from his usual right half position to left half, again scoring on his first game in that new position, but at the end of that 1948-49 season George retired from League football.

Reading Record: Lge 44/6, FAC 4/1, Total 48/7
League Career Total: 55/7

GREEN Roy

b. Loughborough 8.6.1931
Ht 5ft 6 Wt 10st 7 (55-56)
Career: Birmingham C; Derby Co; Bloxwich Strollers; READING (£350) 23 January 1953; Hastings U. summer 1957

One of five footballing brothers, Roy played in Birmingham's youth side but he had moved to Bloxwich Strollers when he was recommended to Reading by a former player, Jack Lewis.

National Service then intervened and although Roy represented his Command team in Germany it meant that his League debut was delayed until March 1956, over three years after he signed for Reading. As often happens, Roy made up for lost time by scoring in his first two home games and retained his place at inside right until the end of the season. The signing of Jimmy Whitehouse that summer cost Roy his inside right spot and so his three remaining first team appearances before he was released at the end of 1956-57 were at inside left.

Reading Record: Lge 14/3

GREGORY Charles **Frederick**
b. Mexborough 24.10.1911 d. 1985
Ht 5ft 10 1/2 Wt 12st 9 (35-36)
Career: Brodsworth Colliery; Doncaster R. 1929; Manchester C. (£2,000) March 1930; READING (£1,000) 28 February 1934; Crystal Palace 15 December 1937; Hartlepools U. June 1946; Rotherham U. February 1947

Versatility was the name of Fred's game. He made his League debut at 17 with Doncaster as a centre half but after a big money move to Manchester City, Fred was converted to a centre forward. Although Reading had tried to sign him as a defender in 1933, they subsequently saw him as the ideal replacement for free scoring centre forward, Frank Newton, and so paid 'a four figure fee' to bring him to Elm Park. Despite scoring on his Reading debut, Fred was the subject of another positional change after just three games in the attack when he was converted to a fine right back. In addition he was a useful stand in goalie! The next three and a half seasons saw him as a fixture at right back where his strong and fearless play made him a favourite of the fans, as did his powerful kicking. Fred was fast for a full back, but manager Billy Butler thought he had failed to reach his full potential due to a tendency to panic under pressure and so he was sold to Crystal Palace for a large fee. With them, Fred made 104 appearances, the majority in War games, and scored a creditable 23 goals.

Reading Record: Lge 129/6, FAC 14/1, SSC 4, Total 147/7
League Career Total: 228/20

GRIEVE David
b. Selkirk 15.2.1929
Ht 5ft 8 1/2 Wt 10st 11 (53-54)
Career: Dalroy Thistle; Elgin C; READING (£400) 28 January 1952; Elgin C. (loan) January 1952; Crystal Palace (£2,000) 24 April 1954

Spotted playing in Scottish junior football, David's early professional career was restricted by his National Service duties that kept him in Scotland until May 1952. He managed a couple of League appearances on Reading's right wing during that first season but had to wait until March 1953 for an extended run. The next season was his last and although first team games were rare David managed nine goals for the reserves and netted his only League goal for Reading in his last game at Elm Park, a 4-1 win over Crystal Palace. That performance impressed the visitors who almost immediately signed the young winger for the following season.

Reading Record: Lge 19/1, FAC 1, Total 20/1
League Career Total: 41/5

GROVES Kenneth Ernest Leonard
b. Eton 9.10.1921
Ht 5ft 11 Wt 11st 10 (46-47)
Career: Windsor & Eton; Preston N.E. March 1939; Wartime guest for Lincoln, Southport, Brentford & Fulham; READING amateur July 1946

Ken was spotted by Preston while playing in goal for Windsor & Eton just before the War. He became a Sergeant Pilot in the RAF and his duties meant that he only played two Wartime games for Preston although he guested for several other clubs. Released by Preston, Ken returned to Berkshire to play in Reading's first four League games after the War. By coincidence, he let in two goals in each of these appearances, but Reading were scoring 21 times at the other end. Ken lost his place and was released at the end of the season to quit League football due to defective eyesight.

Reading Record: Lge 4

GULLIVER Joffre '**Jeff**'
b. Troedyrhiw 2.8.1915 d. Reading 1.8. 1999
Ht 5ft 9 Wt 12st 8 (49-50)
Career: Southend U. August 1934; Bangor C; Leeds U. March 1938; READING June 1939; Liverpool (Wartime guest); Swindon August 1951; Didcot manager, READING youth team manager 1954

A former Welsh junior international, Jeff failed to break into League football with either Southend or Leeds, while his move to Reading saw his debut further delayed by the War. Although he toured with Liverpool during the hostilities, Jeff's first League outing, at the age of 31, eventually came in Reading's initital game after the War. Like many players who suffered a similar break in their career, he soon made up for lost time.

Over the next four seasons he was a regular at left back, missing only a handful of games and notching up a 104 match consecutive run during that time while his stylish play attracted the attention of several big clubs. The Reading programme of the day noted that Jeff *'made up for his lack of inches with exceptional speed, sureness of tackle and sound kicking'*. As the years began to catch up with him he lost his first team place during 1950-51 and moved to Swindon at the age of 36. Jeff stayed in Reading, working as a sales rep for hairdressing goods, and lived a few hundred yards from Elm Park.

Reading Record: Lge 161, FAC 11, Wartime 12, Total 184
League Career Total: 172

GUNNING Henry 'Harry'
b. Leigh on Sea 8.2.1932
Ht 5ft 9 Wt 11st (57-58)
Career: Gravesend & Northfleet; West Ham U. June 1952; Crystal Palace May 1954; READING (£300) 6 May 1957; Guildford C. July 1958

Harry was capable of playing on either wing, but only made one League appearance for the Hammers during his two years with them. He was far more successful with Palace, but in 1957 Harry moved to Reading where he started on the left but soon switched to his more favoured right wing position. He scored in his first game at number seven but although Reading were then unbeaten during his next six games, Harry lost his first team place when Jimmy Wheeler was switched to the right. After that his first team chances were limited and at the end of the season he moved to Guildford.

Reading Record: Lge 12/1, SPFC 1/1, Total 13/2
League Career Total: 77/5

GURNEY Andrew Robert
b. Bristol 25.1.1974
Ht 5ft 10 Wt 12st 2 (98-99)
Career: Yate T; Kingsmead; St Valier; Bristol R. from youth July 1992; Weymouth (loan) July 1997; Torquay U. July 1997; READING (£100,000) 15 January 1999; Swindon T summer 2001

A tenacious defender with a strong attacking streak, Andy began with his home town club, helping them reach the 1995 Division Two play-offs. Two years later Andy moved to Torquay where he continued to display an eye for goal, ending with 14 goals in 74 games, and, again, he made the play-offs with them. His move to Reading was not an immediate success as he was used in midfield more than defence but Andy eventually won a regular place and started to get the fans on his side with some committed displays at right back, combined with surging runs down the wing. Reduced first team chances in 2000-01 saw Andy ask for a transfer and, despite two great performances in the play-off semis, he was released at the end of that season.

Reading Record: Lge 55(12)/3, FAC 5(1), LC 5, AMC 3(1), Play-offs 2, Total 70(14)/3
League Career Total: 219(20)/22 +

ANDY'S CLAIM TO FAME - Andy tasted defeat on each of his debuts for his first three clubs. Strangely, his League debut was for Bristol Rovers in their 2-0 defeat at Reading's Elm Park, while his Reading debut was against Rovers, who won 6-0 at the Madejski Stadium.

HABBIN Richard Leonard
b. Cambridge 6.1.1949
Ht 5ft 9 Wt 10st 6 (69-70)
Career: Cambridge U; READING (trial) 14 April 1969 then permanent; Rotherham U. (£10,000) 29 January 1975; Doncaster R. September 1977; Maltby Miner's Welfare manager 2000

Born next to the Abbey Stadium, Dick joined Reading on trial the day Jack Mansell took over as Reading manager and his unorthodox style of centre forward play would become a vital part of the new manager's strategy. Although Dick's introduction to the first team began with a defeat, Reading were then unbeaten for his next 15 games as the club went to the top of the table with a hatful of goals. Reading finished 1969-70 as the League's top scorers and although Dick scored nine times in 24 starts he was more a creator with most of the moves revolving around him. After topping Reading's League scorers the following season, Dick moved into midfield creating many goals, especially for Les Chappell who regularly headed in Dick's nearpost corners. In 1974 Dick went on the transfer list but, despite regaining his scoring touch, the Tribunal set fee of £35,000 was reduced four times until he moved to Rotherham for just £10,000.

He immediately helped them to promotion and, in the process, made a total of 48 League appearances that season but a knee injury while with Doncaster prematurely ended his career.

Reading Record: Lge 204(15)/42, FAC 14/3, LC 14/4, Watney Cup 1/1, Total 233(15)/50
League Career Total: 340(23)/73

HADDOW Alexander
b. Fleet 8.1.1982
Ht 5ft 8 Wt 11st 2 (99-00)
Career: Arsenal assoc. schoolboy; READING YTS 1998; Barnet (loan) July 2000; Rochdale (trial) February 2001, Kidderminster H. (trial) April 2001; Carlisle U summer 2001.

An injury while an associate schoolboy with Arsenal led to Alex being released and after a trial he joined Reading as a youth trainee. After reaching the final trial for England's U16s, Alex later scored for an FA XI against the SW Counties side in February 1999, and this progress culminated in him joining the first team squad. In August 1999 he made his first team debut in midfield in the League Cup-tie at Peterborough and four days later he got his first League game. A year later Reading turned down a £75,000 offer from Barnet for the promising youngster but Alex was eventually released at the end of 2000-01.

Reading Record: Lge 1(2), LC 1, Total 2(2)

HADLAND Phillip Jonathon
b. Warrington 20.10.1980
Ht 5ft 10 Wt 10st 7 (98-99)
Career: READING YTS 1997 then professional; Aldershot T. (loan) December 1999; York C. (trial) August 2000; Rochdale 7 August 2000; Leyton O. summer 2001

A lightning fast left winger, Phil was snapped up by Reading after he had spells with Liverpool and Blackburn as a schoolboy. He made excellent progress in the youth sides and was rewarded with a first team appearance against Barnsley in the League Cup in September 1998. Phil was still 17 at the time and, in playing, became the first player born in the 80's to make it to Reading's first team. Although he made no more first team appearances, Phil played for an FA Youth Select XI in March 1999.

Reading Record: LC 1
League Career Total: 12(20)/2

HALKYARD Cecil

b. Rochdale 17.4.1902 d. 1989
Ht 5ft 9 Wt 11st 6 (30-31)
Career: Accrington Stan; Rochdale 1925; Connahs Quay 1928; READING June 1930; Rhyl A. summer 1931; Colwyn Bay; Charlton A. 1932; Barrow 1934

Cecil has the remarkable record of having played in seven League seasons over an 11 year period yet he only managed 25 appearances during that spell. Four seasons at Rochdale produced 15 League starts before Cecil dropped out of the League with Connahs Quay. This Welsh club was a regular source of players for Reading at that time and so he moved to Elm Park in 1930. After a club record 8-1 reverse at Burnley, six changes were made including bringing in Cecil at left half and a winning start saw him keep his place for eight games. A run of three consecutive defeats saw more team changes but this time Cecil was a victim, and his Reading League career was over. After more non-League football Cecil tried his luck with Charlton and Barrow but only managed one game with each of them.

Reading Record: Lge 8
League Career Total: 25

HALL Kenneth Dennis
b. Southwell 24.12.1930
Ht 5ft 8 Wt 11st 4 (54-55)
Career: Portsmouth from jnrs September 1948; READING (free) 27 August 1954; Bournemouth July 1955

Dennis was a product of Portsmouth's youth scheme and in both of his first two seasons as a professional with them they won the League championship. Not surprisingly, he found it difficult to get a regular game with such a well established and successful first team and after lengthy negotiations, Reading persuaded Pompey to let the player join them. The well built right back went virtually straight into Reading's first team but had to wait until his tenth game for his first win bonus. He lost his first team place after a Cup draw against Colchester and eventually Dennis was released at the end of the season. He joined Bournemouth but never added to his League total.

Reading Record: Lge 13, FAC 1, Total 14
League Career Total: 23

HALL William Furness
b. Walton le Dale 6.2.1926 d. 1986
Ht 5ft 9 Wt 11st (53-54)
Career: Preston N.E. from jnrs 1948; Blackpool July 1949; READING (£750) 13 July 1953; Worcester C. August 1954

Although on the short side for a goalie, Willie played all his career, prior to joining Reading, in the First Division. After a handful of games for Preston, George moved to Blackpool where he was understudy to George Farm whose form was such that Willie had to wait three years before getting a chance in the League. His move to Reading in 1953 saw him go straight into their first team, but he lost his place in October and after one season he joined Worcester City.

Reading Record: Lge 16
League Career Total: 26

HAMMOND Nicholas David
b. Hornchurch 7.9.1967
Ht 6ft Wt 11st 13 (96-97)
Career: Ford U; Swindon T. (trial); Arsenal from apprentice July 1985; Bristol R. (loan) August 1986; Peterborough U. (loan); Aberdeen (loan) 1987; Swindon T. (free) July 1987; Plymouth A. (£40,000) August 1995; READING (loan) 12 December 1995, permanent (£40,000) 13 February 1996, coach April 2000, youth academy director October 2000

Nicky's League career was hampered by a series of injuries that resulted in him just failing to reach a century of League appearances in a 15 year period. After establishing himself at Swindon, a broken leg in 1989 slowed his progress and after 92 first team starts he moved to Plymouth, but within four months he had moved on to Reading. Here Nicky displayed his fine goalkeeping talents and helped steady Reading's nervy defence but injury problems were never far away. A bout of chicken pox was followed by a recurrence of a back problem that was to keep him out of the game for almost two years. A cartilage injury sustained while obtaining his FA coaching badge in July 1998 all but ended his career, and in April 2000 he announced his retirement, not having played in the first team for 18 months. When fit, he was a brilliant keeper and Nicky will always be remembered for his display against Cardiff in a 1998 FA Cup replay that saw him save three shots in the penalty shoot-out. Fortunately, Nicky had established himself as part of Reading's coaching staff and he was appointed head of Reading's Youth Academy, a just reward for a player who had always worked in the community with all his clubs.

Reading Record: Lge 25, FAC 5, LC 3, Total 33
League Career Total: 97(2)

HANNEY Edward Terence
b. Reading 19.1.1889 d. Reading
Ht 5ft 10 Wt 12st 10 (21-22)
Career: Royal Berks Regiment; Wokingham T, READING July 1910 amateur, professional 1913; Manchester C. (£1,250) 26 November 1913; Brentford (Wartime guest); Coventry C. (£2,500) November 1919; READING August 1921; Northfleet summer 1922; Stuttgart coach

One of the great players of Reading's Southern League days, Ted was a tough but skilful centre half who, according to Brigham's cigarette cards *'can use his hands'*! He quickly gained amateur international honours, being capped against Belgium and Norway before his greatest honour. Ted played in all of Great Britain's games in the 1912 Olympics up to the semi-finals, when he sustained an injury that forced him to watch his teammates win the gold medal. Soon after he turned professional and captained the Southern League v the Irish League and played for the South v the North before Reading sold him to Manchester City for a big fee. After the War Ted moved to Coventry but returned to Reading to end his playing career. Back at Elm Park, Ted captained the club and was a great talker on the pitch, only missing one game all season and after a short spell with Northfleet he spent four happy years coaching in Stuttgart. He then ran a pub in Reading but continued to take an interest in local football and ran coaching sessions at Elm Park during the Second World War, as well as being the Berks & Bucks FA coach.

Reading Record: Lge 41/1, FAC 11, SL 82/10, Total 134/11
League Career Total: 141/2

HARBRIDGE Charles William
b. Tipton 15.7.1891 d. Ash 1.10.1980
Ht 5ft 11 Wt 11st 8 (20-21)
Career: Civil Service Strollers; Corinthians; Reading Aeronautic School; READING amateur summer 1918; Charlton A. June 1921; Civil Service

A typical amateur career saw Charles playing for Corinthians, the top amateur side in the country, before joining Reading while serving at the local RAF base. A skilful, defensive left half, he was nicknamed 'Ginger' and won four England amateur caps and played for Great Britain in the 1920 Olympics in Antwerp which caused him to miss the start of Reading's first League season. He was only used spasmodically in the League up to February 1921 when he won a regular place to the end of the season, but turned down Reading's offer to turn pro and left the club.

Reading Record: Lge 19, FAC 1, SL 34/1, Total 54/1
League Career: 25

HARGREAVES John 'Jack'
b. Rotherham 1.5.1915 d. Bristol 22.12.1978
Career: Sheffield jnrs; Leeds U. August 1934; Bristol C. August 1946; READING May 1947; Yeovil summer 1948

Another player who lost his best years to the War, Jack made his debut for Leeds in 1935-36 and was beginning to establish himself on their left wing during the last season before hostilities began. When the League restarted, Jack was with Bristol City but joined Reading late in the first post-War season. Although he was signed well after the transfer deadline, he was able to play in the last two games of the season as neither Reading or their opponents were involved in matches affecting promotion or re-election. He started 1947-48 in the first team but he spent more time in the reserves than the League side, helping Reading win the Combination Cup before moving to Yeovil.

Reading Record: Lge 15/1
League Career Total: 86/20

HARLEY Richard John
b. March 22.4.1949
Ht 5ft 10 Wt 10st 6 (71-72)
Career: Cambridge U; Stevenage T; READING (£1,350) 29 September 1969; Aldershot July 1973; Wokingham T. July 1975; Hartlepool September 1976; Wokingham T. 1976

John was one of several players picked up by Jack Mansell from non-League football and was initially a left winger with a ferocious, swerving left foot shot. In March 1971 an injury crisis saw John used as a central defender and it soon became apparent that this was his best position. He read the game well, possessed a strong tackle and the extra time available in this position enabled him to distribute the ball accurately. His form attracted the attention of several First Division clubs but when Charlie Hurley took charge at Elm Park, John's first team opportunities were reduced and he left Reading. During his stay, John took a keen interest in coaching, helping out the club plus several local sides, including Reading's newly formed Supporters' Club team.

Reading Record: Lge 64(10)/6, FAC 7, LC 1(1), Total 72(11)/6
League Career Total: 84(22)/7

HARMAN Peter Robert
b. Guildford 11.10.1950
Ht 5ft 11 Wt 11st 2 (71-72)
Career: Bournemouth from apprentice August 1968; READING (trial) August 1971, permanent 8 October 1971; Bath C. summer 1973

Having made just one first team appearance for Bournemouth, coincidentally against Reading, Peter had a two month trial at Elm Park and was Jack Mansell's last signing before he was sacked a week later. Caretaker manager, Jimmy Wallbanks, saw the strong, old fashioned style centre forward as just what Reading's struggling side needed and was proved right when Peter scored on his debut against Hartlepool. He provided a much needed physical presence and was soon nicknamed 'Elbows' by the fans for reasons that would get him into trouble with today's stricter referees! Peter scored on his FA Cup debut and then hit a hat trick as Reading beat Blyth Spartans to meet Arsenal in the next round. Unfortunately, Peter's goal touch deserted him in 1972-73 and with his nine first team appearances failing to produce a goal, he was released at the end of that season.

Reading Record: Lge 34(2)/9, FAC 4/4, LC 2(1), Total 40(3)/13
League Career Total: 35(2)/9

HARPER James Alan John
b. Chelmsford 8.11.1980
Ht 5ft 10 Wt 11st 2 (2000-01)
Career: Arsenal from assoc. schoolboy 1 July 1999; Cardiff C. (loan) December 2000: READING (£400,000) 28 February 2001

Reading had tracked James' career with Arsenal for some time and when it became clear that the Gunners were willing to let him move on Alan Pardew had no hesitation in paying a big fee for the youngster. James had been at Highbury since he was 10 but, apart from a loan spell with Cardiff, he had only 19 reserve appearances to his credit. However, he rewarded his new manager's faith by scoring on his debut in a vital promotion clash against Rotherham. He also developed a long throw which created both Reading goals in the play-off final. A pacey, skilful player, James looks set to be a fixture in Reading's midfield for years to come.

Reading Record: Lge 9(3)/1, Play-offs 1(1), Total 10(4)/1 +
League Career Total: 12(3)/1 +

HARRIS George Alfred
b. Woking 10.6.1940
Ht 5ft 9 Wt 11st 3 (68-69)
Career: Tottenham H. amateur May 1957; Woking April 1961; Chelsea April 1961; Newport Co. July 1961; Watford (£1,500) April 1962; READING (£4,500) 18 July 1966; Cambridge U. (£2,000) 17 October 1969; Hillingdon Bor. July 1972; Wokingham T. player coach then player manager June 1974; Maidenhead U. manager June 1975

With a career average of a goal in fewer than every three games, George was one of the most prolific wingers in the lower divisions throughout the Sixties, and so it is remarkable that he never commanded anything more than token transfer fees. A promising start at Newport saw him move to Watford where he was a regular scorer and there was some concern when he was sold to Reading in 1966. That concern was justified as George broke Reading's 25 year goalscoring record for a winger as he hit 25 in his first season and was voted Player of the Year. George possessed plenty of pace and a powerful shot but what was remarkable was his heading ability - despite his height he could outjump much taller opponents with perfect timing as he flew in from the wing to meet Alan Scarrott's inch perfect crosses. He actually exceeded his total for all competitions the following season with a 26 goal haul, but managed 'only' 11 in 1968-69. The arrival of Jack Mansell saw George regarded as surplus to requirements and he was allowed to join Cambridge United. A hat trick on his debut helped him to finish top scorer as they won the Southern League and was a member of their team that entered the League the following season.

Reading Record: Lge 134(2)/56, FAC 11/4, LC 9/5, Total 154(2)/65
League Career Total: 360(5)/130

HARRISON Peter

b. Grantham 25.10.1927
Ht 5ft 9 Wt 10st 12 (57-58)
Career: Peterborough U. amateur; Notts Co. amateur; Leeds U. January 1949; Bournemouth August 1952; READING (player exchange + £150) 5 June 1957; Southport (free) 29 June 1959

Peter began his League career with Leeds and made 65 appearances, scoring nine times, before moving to Bournemouth after three years. There he became a fixture on their left wing and some fine performances against Reading inspired his move to Elm Park in 1957. A regular during his first season, Peter played on either flank and helped Reading to the final of the Southern Floodlit Cup.

The signing of George McLuckie, plus the form of Jimmy Wheeler, meant that his chances were greatly reduced the following season so, at the age of almost 32, Peter moved to Southport where he was a first team regular for another three seasons.

Reading Record: Lge 40/5, FAC 5, SPFC 7/1, Total 52/6
League Career Total: 402/70

HARSTON Edward

b. Monk Bretton 27.2.1907 d. ?
Ht 5ft 7 Wt 11st 2 (31-32)
Career: Cudworth Village; Sheffield Wed; Barnsley 1930; READING June 1931; Bristol C. summer 1934; Mansfield T. October 1935; Liverpool (£2,500) June 1937; Ramsgate T.

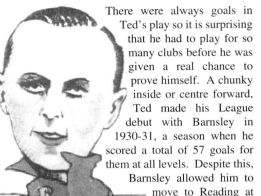

There were always goals in Ted's play so it is surprising that he had to play for so many clubs before he was given a real chance to prove himself. A chunky inside or centre forward, Ted made his League debut with Barnsley in 1930-31, a season when he scored a total of 57 goals for them at all levels. Despite this, Barnsley allowed him to move to Reading at the end of that season, but although Ted scored in his first two League games he lost his place. First team chances were few until he scored six goals against Charlton reserves on Good Friday 1933 when he was given a seven match first team run to the end of the season that saw Ted average a goal a game. Still Reading did not get the message and let him move to Bristol City in 1934. Ted topped City's scorers in his first season but they let him move to Mansfield in October 1935. Ted made certain that Mansfield could not miss his goalscoring skills by scoring a hat trick within seven minutes of his debut, the first of six hat tricks in a year. 26 goals from his 29 games that season paled into insignificance in 1936-37. In 41 Third Division North games Ted hit an amazing 55 goals, the third highest total in League history that included seven against Hartlepool.

Not surprisingly, Ted was attracting a lot of attention and a big money transfer took him to Liverpool where he scored on his debut. Sadly, after five games and three goals, he suffered a serious leg injury that ended his League career.

Reading Record: Lge 18/11, FAC 1, Total 19/11
League Career Total: 133/116

TED'S CLAIM TO FAME - As well as giving him the third highest season's total in the League, Ted's goal haul in 1936-37 was also the highest proportion that any one player has contributed to his team's total, being 55 out of Mansfield's 91 that season.

HARTENBERGER Uwe

b. Leuterecken 1.2.1968
Ht 6ft 1 Wt 13st (93-94)
Career: FC Kalserlauten; Hassia Bingen; TSG Pfeddersheim; SV Edenkoben; Bayer Uedingen 1992; READING (£100,000) 30 September 1993; S V Waldhov Mannheim summer 1995; VJL Osnabruck October 1999

Uwe moved to Reading through the German contacts manager Mark McGhee had built up while playing for Hamburg. The big German came with a reputation for goalscoring, having netted 75 goals in 100 German League games, and he got his English career off to a flying start by coming off the bench to score an equalizer at Swansea the day after joining Reading. He quickly became a favourite with the fans, being a pacey, strong striker, with a distinctive 'airplane' goal celebration, but McGhee and then the Quinn/Gooding partnership found it difficult to get Uwe to play to team plans. Consequently he was used mainly as a substitute, significantly only playing the full 90 minutes in two of his 29 first team games and in 1995 he was freed to return to Germany.

Reading Record: Lge 8(16)/4, FAC (2), AMC 3/1, Total 11(18)/5

HATCHER Clifford H

b. Currie Dando 27.6.1925
Ht 5ft 11 Wt 11st 12 (48-49)
Career: READING amateur June 1946, part-time May 1948

A promising young goalie, Cliff was signed as cover for more experienced keepers after impressing in a Reading friendly against the Army. Although his League career was restricted to a couple of games in his three years at Elm Park, on each occasion he was called on he acquitted himself well and Cliff had the satisfaction of keeping a clean sheet in his one game at Elm Park.

Reading Record: Lge 2

HAYHURST Albert

b. Birdwell 17.9.1905 d. Reading 8.11.1991
Ht 6ft Wt 12st 6 (38-39)
Career: Barnsley (trial); Frickley Colliery; Luton T. 1932; READING (free) 23 June 1933; Southampton (Wartime guest)

Having been missed by his local League club, Barnsley, Albert only played one League game for Luton but impressed Reading in reserve fixtures between the two sides which resulted in his move to Elm Park. Luton had converted Albert from a right back to a centre half and it was in this position that he commanded Reading's defence.

He only missed seven games over the next five seasons and although he was a consistently high performer, he gave an exceptional display against Arsenal in the 1935 FA Cup-tie during which he marked Ted Drake out of the game. In December 1937, Albert reverted to right back and it was in this position that he helped Reading win the 1938 Southern Section Cup. A year later he lost his place and was released in 1939. As well as being a fine footballer, Albert also played county cricket, making seven appearances for Warwickshire as a medium fast bowler in 1934.

Reading Record: Lge 219/10, FAC 18/2, SSC 10, Total 247/12
League Career Total: 220/10

HAZELL Robert Joseph

b. Kingston, Jamaica, 14.6.1959
Ht 6ft 2 Wt 14st 6 (86-87)
Career: Wolverhampton W. from apprentice May 1977; QPR (£240,000) September 1979; Leicester C. (£100,000) September 1983; Wolverhampton W. (loan) September 1986; Luton T. (trial); READING (trial) 31 October 1986; Port Vale December 1986

A giant but skilful central defender, Bob made his debut for Wolves in December 1977, and within two years he was the subject of a big money move when Tommy Docherty signed him for QPR. There he won England U21 and B caps to add to the youth cap won with Wolves. Bob played in the 1982 FA Cup final and replay against Spurs before a less successful move to Leicester in 1983. By October 1986 Bob was looking for a club and so he joined Reading on trial as a possible replacement for the injured Martin Hicks. His spell at Elm Park could not have got off to a worse start when, after just 29 minutes against Barnsley, he became the first Reading player to be sent off on his debut, and he was released after a five match spell.

Reading Record: Lge 4/1, FMC 1, Total 5/1
League Career Total: 259(7)/13

HEAD David George

b. Midsomer Norton 11.8.1940
Ht 5ft 9 Wt 11st 7 (60-61)
Career: Swindon from jnrs August 1958; Arsenal March 1959; READING (free) July 1960; Bristol R. July 1961; Trowbridge manager 1962

The son of manager Bert Head, centre forward David failed to make any appearances at his father's two clubs so his League debut came with Reading. After five goalless games leading the attack he lost his place and although he was occasionally tried in other positions none were a success.

David's Reading career ended after one season and his 12 first team games failed to produce a goal (of which only two were victories). He never added to his League career, but in 1962 he followed in his father's footsteps when he became Trowbridge's manager at the age of only 23.

Reading Record: Lge 12

HEAD Steven J
b. Reading 22.8.1966
Ht 5ft 10 Wt 11st (86-87)
Career: READING youth team then non contract 1985; Miramar (New Zealand), Southampton Academy coach 2000

Steve captained Reading Schools and played for Berkshire before performing regularly for Reading's youth and reserve teams and came on as sub at Bournemouth in the Freight Rover Trophy, without being offered a contract. In 1986 the determined midfielder took the brave decision to give up his job in local government and pay his own way. With the aid of sponsorship he raised enough money to try to get the contract he so wanted. Although Steve got on the bench at Derby and came on as sub in a Full Members Cup game there was much regret around Elm Park when his gamble failed to come off and he was released by the club in April 1987.

Reading Record: FMC (2)

HEALE Gary John
b. Canvey Island 15.7.1958
Ht 5ft 11 Wt 11st 7 (80-81)
Career: Southend U. assoc. schoolboy; Canvey Island; Luton T. August 1977; Exeter C. (loan) December 1979; READING (£40,000) 23 August 1979; Sparta Rotterdam (£11,000) August 1982; Tacoma (USA Indoor League) 1983; FC Sparta coach

A centre forward who relied on his skills rather than strength, Gary found it difficult to break into Luton's Second Division side, despite scoring on his debut in September 1977. Two years later he had only seven games with them to his credit but it took a club record fee to bring him to Reading. Although not a prolific scorer, Gary proved a valuable addition and hardly missed a game until he suffered a ligament injury in a League Cup-tie in August 1980, ironically against Luton. Gary was back the following January but a year later his career was in doubt again when he left the club to be with his wife in America. Reading retained his registration and although Gary returned for pre-season training in the summer of 1982 he was eventually sold to Sparta Rotterdam. There he rediscovered his desire for the game and helped them get into European competition.

Reading Record: Lge 68(8)/20, FAC 5/3, LC 7/4, FLGC 3, Total 83(8)/27
League Career Total: 78(9)/21

HELLIWELL Sidney
b. Sheffield 30.1.1904 d. Sheffield 11.1939
Ht 5ft 9 1/2 Wt 11st 9 (26-27)
Career: Wycliffe; Sheffield Wed; READING (free) May 1926; Tottenham H. (£1,000) May 1927; Walsall summer 1929; Hednesford T; Halifax T. August 1933

Although he had not played for their first team, Sheffield Wednesday originally wanted a fee for Sid but eventually they allowed him to join Reading on a 'free'. Sid was a centre half but he only played one League game for Reading in that position with his other four games being as a makeshift centre forward. He made quite a good job of leading the attack, scoring twice, including the winner against Manchester City on his debut, and getting 21 goals for the reserves. This form earned him selection in the London Combination side in a representative game against the London League. In May 1927 he moved to Spurs but it was not until Sid moved on to Walsall that he at last got regular first team football.

Reading Record: Lge 5/2
League Career Total: 112/10

HENDERSON Darius Alexis
b. Doncaster 7.9.1981
Ht 6ft 1 Wt 13st 9 (99-00)
Career: Leeds U. assoc. schoolboy; READING YTS July 1998, professional 11 December 1999

Darius made a little bit of history when he signed professional terms in front of the crowd before Reading's FA Cup-tie against Plymouth, as he was the first player to progress through the club's youth academy to become a full professional. It says much for the club's confidence in the young striker that they signed him on a four year contract even though he had just suffered a serious knee injury. This delayed his League debut for three months, when he came on as a late substitute at Burnley, but great things are expected of this old fashioned centre forward who has a physical presence beyond his years.

Reading Record: Lge 2(8), LC 1, AMC (1), Total 3(9) +

HENDERSON Raymond
b. Ashington 31.3.1937
Ht 5ft 8 Wt 10st 10 (68-69)
Career: Willington Quay; Howden B C; Ashington; Middlesbrough May 1957; Hull C. (£3,000) June 1961; READING (free) 10 October 1968
See also 'The Managers'

Ray followed a typical path for players in the North East, playing for schools, boys clubs and non-League sides before turning professional with Middlesbrough. After a handful of League games he joined Hull as Cliff Britton's first signing and was converted from a goalscoring inside forward to a deep lying winger. At Hull, Ray made almost 250 first team appearances, helping them win the Third Division title in 1965-66 and, after qualifying as an FA coach, he became their assistant coach in 1967. After seven successful years with Hull, Ray was allowed to join Reading as player coach to Roy Bentley, but after a short run in the first team he concentrated on his coaching duties. When Roy Bentley was sacked in February 1969, Ray became caretaker manager for two months until Jack Mansell was appointed.

Reading Record: Lge 5, FAC 4(1)/1, Total 9(1)/1
League Career Total: 240(3)/59

HENDERSON James **Stewart**

b. Bridge of Allan 3.5.1956
Ht 5ft 6 Wt 10st 11 (73-74)
Career: Chelsea from apprentice July 1964; Brighton July 1965; READING (free) 2 June 1973, director of Centre of Excellence May 1983; Southampton youth development officer July 1991

Stewart owes his success to a school teacher who suggested that he switch from centre half to right back because of his lack of inches. Shortly after this change Stewart won three Scottish Schools caps and was signed as an apprentice by Chelsea. It took a move to Brighton for Stewart to make his League debut and in 1969-70 he was their Player of the Year. After over 200 first team appearances he was signed by Charlie Hurley and for 18 months was Reading's first choice right back. Then, in February 1975, an injury crisis saw Stewart pushed into a midfield role. Amazingly, for a player who had only scored one goal in over 250 League games, Stewart scored twice in the first 17 minutes at Bradford City. He stayed in midfield for the rest of that season but from then on he was mainly used at full back again.

In May 1977 Stewart was made club coach, but after a two season absence he was recalled to the first team for the first game of 1979-80. It was not a happy return as Stewart scored an own goal - the first goal that Reading had conceded in a League record 1,103 minutes. Stewart carried on playing intermittently until May 1983 when he finally retired and became Reading's first Director of their Centre of Excellence. In 1971 Stewart joined Ian Branfoot at Southampton as their Youth Development Officer.

Reading Record: Lge 159(7)/6, FAC 7, LC 13, Total 179(7)/6
League Career: 357(7)/7

HENLEY Leslie Donald

b. Lambeth 26.9.1922 d. 1996
Ht 5ft 9 W 11st 8 (49-50)
Career: Nunhead; Arsenal amateur September 1940; Margate; Arsenal professional 1941; READING (£250) December 1946; Bohemians FC coach/manager 1953; Wimbledon manager June 1955

A successful schoolboy career saw Les win three England Schools caps in 1936-37 and eventually he joined Arsenal shortly after the War broke out. For part of the hostilities he was PT instructor in the Royal Berks Regiment and played a few impressive games for Reading. After the War, Les could not force his way into Arsenal's first team, apart from one FA Cup game, so he was allowed to join Reading for 'a fairly reasonable fee'. Playing at inside forward or half back, Les was a vital part of the free scoring Reading side for seven seasons. Although he was a creator of chances rather than a scorer, Les still hit double figures in his last two full seasons and in 1951-52 he scored the first League goal of the season when he netted after just 30 seconds, at Port Vale. After Reading, Les embarked on a successful management career. An FA qualified coach, Les spent 17 years in charge at Wimbledon where they won three Isthmian League titles, the Amateur Cup, promotion to the Southern League Premier Division at the first attempt plus the Southern League Cup, and is generally credited with setting the club on its rise to prominence.

Reading Record: Lge 181/29, FAC 17/3, Wartime 7/6, Total 205/38

LES'S CLAIM TO FAME - In January 1943 Les scored a hat trick for Arsenal that gave them a 5-4 win over Reading. But it was the Reading manager who had to provide the hat after he had bet Arsenal manager, George Allison, a hat and three fresh eggs on the result of the game.

HEPPLE Robert

b. Mickley 1897 d. ?
Ht 5ft 7 1/2 Wt 11st 6 (21-22)
Career: Bradford C. 1920; READING May 1921; Mickley summer 1922; Ashington 1923

A right winger who provided chances for others with his crosses rather than a goalscorer, Robert made his League debut with Bradford City in 1920-21 before joining Reading for the following season. Robert played in Reading's first 17 games of that season but not only did he fail to score, the team were goalless in 10 of those matches so he lost his place and was released in the summer.

Reading Record: Lge 19, FAC 1, Total 20
League Career Total: 32/1

HETZKE Stephen Edward Richard

b. Marlborough 3.6.1955
Ht 6ft 3 Wt 11st 10 (73-74)
Career: Newbury T; Hungerford U; READING apprentice June 1971, professional 4 June 1973; Vancouver Whitecaps (loan) summer 1976; Blackpool (£12,500) July 1982; Sunderland March 1986; Chester C. June 1987; Colchester U. March 1988; Chesham U. 1989

A series of fine displays at the centre of Reading's reserve defence saw Steve play at Darlington in December 1971 at the age of just 16 years 193 days and so become Reading's youngest ever League player. Steve gradually established himself over the following seasons but Reading's strength at the centre of defence meant that he always played fewer than half the games each campaign up to 1978-79. In that season Steve was at last a first team regular as the team won the Fourth Division championship, but not in his usual centre half role. Steve was used as a striker and scored many vital goals, including the winner against Halifax that clinched promotion. From then on Steve was a fixture in the first team, as a central defender, winning a Mecca Loyalty award in 1981 and captaining the club in 1981-82. In 1982 he eventually left Reading, moving to Blackpool for a tribunal fixed fee, and was their Player of the Year in 1983 before winning promotion with them the following year. After three more clubs, a knee injury ended Steve's League career, but in 1999 he returned to Reading to assess the club's successful application for Youth Academy status on behalf of the FA.

Reading Record: Lge 254(7)/23, FAC 8(3)/1, LC 28/5, FLGC 3/3, Total 293(10)/32
League Career Total: 466(9)/43

STEVE'S CLAIM TO FAME - During the summer of 1976 Steve played for Vancouver Whitecaps and was awarded the Man of the Match trophy when he marked Portuguese legend, Eusebio, out of the game.

HICKS Martin

b. Stratford on Avon 27.2.1957
Ht 6ft 2 Wt 13st 6 (85-86)
Career: Stratford T. 1974; Walsall (trial); Wolverhampton W. (trial); Worcester C. (trial); READING (trial) October 1976; Charlton A. February 1977; READING (£3,000) 13 February 1978; Birmingham C. (free) August 1991; Newbury T. player coach July 1993; Worcester C.

Reading very nearly missed out on the player who was to set their appearance record and play a major role in some of the club's greatest achievements. Martin was spotted by Reading's former appearance record holder, centre half Dick Spiers, who recommended the giant centre half to Reading. Although he scored on his reserve debut, Martin was released by Charlie Hurley. Shortly after, he joined Charlton but a year later, with Maurice Evans now in charge at Elm Park, Martin was at last signed by Reading. For the next 13 seasons, Martin was the club's first choice centre half and only two broken jaws and a serious ankle injury kept him out of the side. During his spell with Reading the club won the Fourth Division championship in his first full season of 1978-79, promotion to the Third Division in 1983-84, the Third Division title two years later and the Simod Cup in 1988. In addition he was ever-present as the club set two League records - 11 consecutive League games without conceding a goal, in 1979, and the 13 match winning start to 1985-86. As well as being a dominant defender who was rarely beaten in the air, Martin weighed in with many vital goals and was an inspirational captain.

Financial restraints led to him being given a free transfer in 1991 and he immediately helped Birmingham to promotion in his first season with them. In 1993 he returned to non-League football and has since been a regular in the England over 35's side that plays in the Pele Cup, having once marked the great man himself.

Reading Record: Lge 499(1)/23, FAC 39/1, LC 38/2, FLGC 8, FMC 6, AMC 11(1), Total 601(2)/26
League Career Total: 556(4)/24

HIGGINBOTHAM Henry 'Harry'

b. Sydney, Australia 27.7.1897 d. ?
Ht 5ft 11 Wt 12st 7 (24-25)
Career: South Shields 1919; Luton T. 1920; Clapton O. (£1,000) 1923; Nelson 1924; READING May 1924

Capable of playing anywhere in the forward line, the right footed Harry had his best spell with Luton where he twice got into double figures with League goals. Spells with Clapton Orient and Nelson did not work out, so Harry moved to Reading in an attempt to regain his goal touch. Here he was used mainly at inside right and although he scored three times, the trio coming at Elm Park, Harry was released at the end of 1924-25 having been diagnosed as suffering from sleeping sickness.

Reading Record: Lge 24/3, FAC 1, Total 25/3
League Career Total: 135/30

HIGH David Henry

b. Reading 22.4.1941
Ht 5ft 8 Wt 11st 1 (59-60)
Career: READING groundstaff April 1956, professional 24 February 1958

A successful youth career saw David captain Reading Youth to victory in the 1958 Neuminster Centenary Tournament in Germany and then play alongside Bobby Moore as England Youth beat Wales 8-1 at Elm Park. David made his League debut at 18 and his first games were at wing half, but in October 1961 he came back into the side at left back. He kept his place for a year, topping the Reading Chronicle's merit ratings for 1962-63 but, unfortunately, David's career was hampered by illness and, just when he was set to join Bristol Rovers during the summer of 1964, he was forced to give up the game through ill health.

Reading Record: Lge 72/2, FAC 3, LC 2, Total 77/2

HILLIGAN Samuel

b. Glasgow c. 1902 d. ?
Ht 5ft 9 Wt 11st 8 (26-27)
Career: St Miren; Bo'ness; READING (£100) August 1926

One of many signings from Bo'ness by Reading manager, Andrew Wylie, Sam was brought in as cover for goalie Joe Duckworth and so he was never likely to get many first team starts. As it was he got just one game, at South Shields, when Joe was rested to protect him for the following week's FA Cup semi-final against Cardiff. Sam's only League game ended in a 3-0 reverse and he was released at the end of that season.

Reading Record: Lge 1

HINSHELWOOD Walter Alexander Alan

b. Battersea 27.10.1929
Ht 5ft 6 Wt 10st 11 (52-53)
Career: Fulham from jnrs October 1946; Chelsea (player exchange) January 1951; Fulham May 1951; READING (player exchange) 5 December 1952; Bristol C. (£5,500) 15 February 1956; Millwall June 1960; Newport Co. November 1961; Canadian football

Wally spent six years with Fulham in a stay that was interrupted by a four month spell at Chelsea and National Service that saw him play for the Army on several occasions. With first team chances restricted, Wally came to Reading in an exchange deal that saw Gordon Brice move to Craven Cottage. Although he scored on his Elm Park debut, Wally was not on the winning side in his first 10 Reading games and actually asked to be dropped. Fortunately, Reading persevered with the nippy winger and a move to inside forward saw Wally score 17 times the following season. He continued to be used on the wing or inside forward in equal parts and in March 1955 he played for the first Third Division South side that played the Northern select team at Elm Park. In 1956 Wally moved to Bristol City where he was also a first team regular for four season and while there his son, Paul, was born and like his older brother, Reading born Martin, both went on to play for Crystal Palace.

Reading Record: Lge 135/31, FAC 7, SPFC 1/1, Total 143/32
League Career Total: 336/50

HIRON Raymond Michael Charles

b. Gosport 22.7.1943
Ht 6ft 1 1/2 Wt 11st 10 (75-76)
Career: Brocklehurst; Gosport Colts; Fareham T; Portsmouth 30 April 1964; READING (free) July 1975; Fareham T. (free) July 1978; Waterlooville

A successful schools career was carried on into youth football when Ray scored 268 goals in three seasons for Gosport Colts, including nine on his debut and 16 in another game. After scoring 39 times in 25 games for Fareham, the lanky striker was snapped up by Portsmouth, where the goals continued as Ray was top scorer in four seasons and ended up with 110 in the League to his credit. Given a free transfer as a reward for his loyal service, Ray moved to Reading where he was made captain and led the club to promotion from the Fourth Division in his first season. His experience and steady play alongside the flamboyant Robin Friday, plus his skill in the air, made a vital contribution to the success of that season. Neither Ray nor the club had much success the following season when he was used in a more withdrawn role and he went part-time in 1977-78, during which period he had a spell in the centre of Reading's defence.

Reading Record: Lge 88(4)/14, FAC 6, LC 8, Total 102(4)/14
League Career Total: 411(11)/124

RAY'S CLAIM TO FAME - While at Portsmouth Ray was nicknamed 'Charlie' after someone thought Ray's skinny frame looked like a similarly named skeleton in the Fratton Park medical room!

HISLOP Neil Shaka
b. Westminster 22.2.1969
Ht 6ft 4 Wt 12st 2 (96-97)
Career: Baltimore Blast; READING (trial) July 1992, permanent 9 September 1992; Newcastle U. (£1.575 m.) 10 August 1995; West Ham U. (free) 1998

Although born in London, Shaka and his family moved to Trinidad when he was two. There he played in the same school cricket team as Brian Lara and was non playing sub for Trinidad & Tobago's World Youth Cup squad that included Dwight Yorke. Shaka then moved to Washington to study robotics and it was there that the lofty goalie was recommended to Reading manager, Mark McGhee, after a brilliant display in an indoor game against Aston Villa. After a short trial, Shaka was soon in Reading's first team and his form was such that McGhee sold first choice keeper, Steve Francis, at the end of 1992-93. From then on Shaka was ever-present as Reading first won the Division Two title and then missed out on a Premiership place in the play-off final. Shaka's form was nothing short of sensational, his height enabling him to claim the highest of crosses while he was a brilliantly agile shotstopper. He was the fans' Player of the Year and won a PFA Divisional award in 1994-95, but Reading's failure to get promoted after finishing second in Division One meant that Shaka was the target of several top clubs. Eventually Kevin Keegan paid a Reading record to take Shaka to Newcastle, where he was forced to share the first team shirt with Parvel Smicek despite keeping 11 clean sheets and only conceding 20 goals in 27 games.

Shaka turned down the chance to play for Trinidad on several occasions in the hope that he would get a chance for England. While he won U21 (as an overage player) and B honours for England, Shaka's reluctance to play for Trinidad cost him his place on a set of sporting phone cards that the West Indian island were producing! Eventually Shaka relented and made his Trinidadian debut against Jamaica in 1998-99. A Bosman move to West Ham saw Shaka get the regular Premiership place his talents deserved and he has established himself as one of the country's top keepers.

Reading Record: Lge 104, FAC 3, LC 10, AMC 6, Play-offs 3, Total 126
League Career Total: 250 +

HITCHCOCK Alan Peter
b. Easthampstead 5.10.1949
Ht 5ft 9 Wt 10st 8 (68-69)
Career: READING apprentice 25 July 1966, professional 7 October 1967: Dallas Tornados (trial) November 1969

A local player, Alan progressed through the youth and reserves to make his League debut at home to Barnsley in January 1969 at left back. The following season Alan found it increasingly difficult to get into the first team and in February 1970 his contract was cancelled by mutual consent.

Reading Record: Lge 4

HODGES Lee Leslie
b. Epping 4.9.1974
Ht 6ft Wt 12st 1 (99-00)
Career: Tottenham H. from trainee February 1992; Plymouth Arg. (loan) February 1993; Wycombe W. (loan) December 1993; Barnet (free) May 1994; READING (£100,000) 29 July 1997; Plymouth Arg.(trial); Luton T. (trial) 2001

Lee played alongside the likes of Fowler, Campbell and Caskey when England won the 1993 UEFA Youth Cup, but his four appearances for Spurs were as substitute so his League starts came during loan spells. In 1994 Lee joined Barnet and the young striker was regularly amongst the goals for three seasons, so, when his manager moved to Reading, Lee became one of Terry Bullivant's first signings in a joint deal with Linvoy Primus. At first he struggled against Division One defences but a move to the left side of midfield saw Lee developing into a fine prospect with a knack of scoring vital goals until he was put out of the game for 18 months by a bad foul in a match versus Manchester City. Significantly, Lee's injury was the turning point of that season as Reading lost 13 of their remaining 14 games without him and were relegated. Gradually Lee regained his old form during 1999-00 and was a regular the following season until he lost his place to Jimmy McIntyre, and was released in May 2001.

Reading Record: Lge 58(21)/10, FAC 7(1)/1, LC 7(3), AMC (2), Total 72(27)/11
League Career Total: 160(39)/38 +

HODGES Leonard Herbert
b. Bristol 17.2.1920 d. 1959
Ht 5ft 7 Wt 10st (51-52)
Career: Portway; Kingswood Aero; Soundwell; Bristol R. August 1946; Swansea T. August 1950; READING (£250) 1 August 1951; Chippenham T. July 1953

A slightly built inside left, Len served in the RAF during the War and was 26 when he eventually signed for Bristol Rovers.

There he enjoyed a reasonably successful time with them, scoring 20 goals in 118 League games. Once he moved away from his home town, Len's first team chances reduced dramatically, first at Swansea and then at Reading. At least with Reading he had the satisfaction of helping the reserves win their division of the Combination in his first season. Although a short first team run in 1952-53 gave Len another two goals he was released at the end of the season.

Reading Record: Lge 6/2
League Career Total: 126/22

HODGKISS Thomas
b. Sheffield c.1904 d. ?
Ht 5ft 9 Wt 11st (30-31)
Career: Wincobank CFS; Sheffield Wed. 1924; READING (£1,000) June 1930

In almost six years at Sheffield Wednesday, Tommy only made two League appearances and so he moved to Reading in 1930 in order to get regular first team football. He achieved this for the first two months at Elm Park, but then Tommy lost his place and was only used intermittently as Reading fought a fruitless battle against relegation. 1931-32 saw Tommy establish himself as the regular right back, although he did play a couple of games on the left, scoring at Watford. Released at the end of that season, Tommy quit the League game.

Reading Record: Lge 49/1
League Career Total: 51/1

HOLLIS Kenneth **Michael**
b. Loughborough 14.11.1949
Ht 5ft 10 Wt 11st 5 (76-77)
Career: Leicester C. from apprentice November 1966; Barrow July 1969; Chester July 1972; Stockport Co. July 1973; READING (£4,000) 11 March 1976; Shepshed Charterhouse summer 1977; Rhyl 1978

Mick had a varied career before settling down as one of the lower Leagues' more consistent scorers. A half back when he moved from Leicester to Barrow, he was converted to a right back and then to a forward in January 1971. His goals were not enough to save Barrow from falling out of the League in 1971-72 even though Mick was their top scorer. Having played in Barrow's last League game, Mick was actually transferred to Chester by the Football League who held his registration after Barrow's exit from the League. After a successful season at Chester he was, surprisingly, given a 'free' and moved to Stockport where he topped their scorers for each of his three seasons with them and was their Player of the Year in 1974-75.

In March 1976 he joined Reading to boost their promotion bid and although he only scored once in the run in, Third Division status was achieved. Mick was troubled with a knee injury for much of his stay at Reading and he moved to Shepshed Charterhouse at the end of 1976-77 and helped them to the semis of the FA Vase.

Reading Record: Lge 18(7)/6, FAC 1, Total 19(7)/6
League Career Total: 246(19)/60

HOLMES Henry James **'Harry'**
b. Reading 4th qtr 1901 d. 22.1.1975
Ht 5ft 9 Wt 12st 4 (20-21)
Career: READING amateur 1919, professional September 1920

Harry was a true 'Biscuitman' since he worked for Huntley & Palmers while playing for Reading as an amateur. He was a speedy player, as one would expect from someone who was a sprint champion, and excelled at all sports, especially cricket, hockey and snooker, all of which he played at the highest local level. But football was Harry's main sport and on 5 September 1920, he made a dream debut at left half, scoring a spectacular diving header against Newport in what was Reading's first League win at Elm Park. The club immediately signed him as a professional but after another three games Harry suffered a knee injury and his playing career was over.

Reading: League 4/1

HOLMES James
b. St Helens 27.12.1908 d. 1971
Ht 6ft Wt 12st 4 (38-39)
Career: Sutton Commercial; Sutton Parish; Liverpool amateur; Wigan Bor; Prescot Cables; Chesterfield 1930; Sheffield U. 1931; West Ham U. June 1936; READING June 1937

Jim played for a number of North West clubs before finally getting his chance in the League with Chesterfield where his form attracted Sheffield United. There Jim became a regular at the centre of their defence, but he had the disappointment of missing out on their 1936 Cup Final appearance through injury. Shortly after that he had a season at West Ham before moving to Reading in 1937. Initially Jim was used at left half before switching back to centre half and was made captain for 1938-39. One of his first duties was to collect the Southern Section Cup, the final of which was held over from the previous season. The War saw the end of Jim's career although he was a regular for Reading during the first season of Wartime football.

Jim was a popular player at Reading and was described in the club's pen pictures as a *'whole hearted 90 minute player who is a fearless tackler and fine ball distributor. Although looks are deceptive in his case, always moves at great speed.'*

Reading Record: Lge 70/5, FAC 3, SSC 6, Wartime 37, Total 116
League Career Total: 233/6

HOLSGROVE Paul
b. Telford 26.8.1969
Ht 6ft 1 Wt 11st 10 (95-96)
Career: Aldershot from trainee February 1987; Wimbledon (loan); West Bromwich Alb. (loan); Wokingham T. (free) summer 1990; Luton T. (£25,000) January 1991; Heracles (Holland) November 1991; Millwall (free) August 1992; READING (free) 10 August 1994; Grimsby T. (loan) October 1997; Crewe Alex. November 1977; Stoke C. (trial) January 1998; Brighton (trial); Hibernian July 1998; Doncaster R. 2000; Darlington 2000; Slough T. September 2000

The son of Wolves and Sheffield Wednesday defender, John Holsgrove, Paul had a varied career in attempts to break into the League but it was only when he joined his sixth League club, Reading, that he got regular first team football. Even then the elegant midfielder's run was interrupted when he became one of two Reading players to break their leg in a game against Bristol City. Back in the first team by January he scored the winner in Reading's shock win at Middlesbrough but missed out on the run in to the play-offs. The following season he was also used in a sweeper role but after a loan spell with Grimsby, Paul was released so he could join Crewe and continue his nomadic soccer career, coming on as sub in Darlington's unsuccessful play-off final in May 2000.

Reading Record: Lge 63(7)/6, FAC 5, LC 9(2)/1, Total 77(9)/7
League Career Total: 89(30)/8

HOLZMAN Mark Robin
b. Bracknell 21.2.1973
Ht 5ft 7 Wt 10st 7 (93-94)
Career: READING from YTS May 1991; Newbury T. summer 1994; Slough T; Windsor & Eton 2000

Brothers Gary, Stephen and Mark Holzman all played for Reading's youth teams but only midfielder Mark was taken on as a full professional. He had attended the same school that produced Reading stars, Steve Wood and Gary Peters, and joined Reading's Centre of Excellence, going on to represent Berkshire U19s at the age of 16 and help Reading win the Allied Counties Cup in 1987.

Mark was given his debut in the first game of 1991-92, against Hull, and played in all but one game up to the end of November, wearing seven different shirts, until a horrific challenge in an FA Cup replay against Slough left him with a broken and dislocated ankle. Not surprisingly, this kept him out for a year but he heralded his return with an assured performance at Manchester City in another Cup-tie. Although he went on to make 20 first team appearances during the rest of that campaign, Mark was not a part of the 1993-94 Division Two championship period, and was released at the end of that season.

Reading Record: Lge 23(9)/1, FAC 4, LC 2, AMC 5, Total 34(9)/1

HONEY Daniel
b. Ascot 2.4.1973
Ht 6ft 2 Wt 13st (91-92)
Career: Reeves Rngrs; READING YTS 1989, professional May 1991; Newbury T. May 1993; Slough T.

Danny graduated through a two year YTS contract to be voted Reading's Young Player of the Year and sign as a first year professional in 1991. The young goalie made his first team debut in the FA Cup replay against Slough in November 1991, but, although he was named Man of the Match, Reading decided that they needed a more experienced keeper and brought in Jim Leighton on loan. A year later, Danny was loaned to Newbury Town, a club he subsequently joined permanently in May 1993, and he can count himself unlucky in never having added to his first team record.

Reading Record: FA Cup 1

HOOD Melvyn Arthur
b. Reading 5.10.1939
Ht 5ft 7 Wt 10st 6 (57-58)
Career: READING amateur 1 September 1955, professional 8 October 1956

When Melvyn made his debut against Norwich in September 1956, he became the first 16 year old to play for Reading in the League. That game saw him begin a run of seven games on the left wing but after a couple of heavy defeats, Reading decided to revert to experience and Melvyn lost his place. Melvyn only made another three appearances the following season and moved into non-League football from 1958.

Reading Record: Lge 10, SPFC 1, Total 11

HOPKINS Jeffery

b. Swansea 14.4.1964
Ht 6ft Wt 12st 12 (92-93)
Career: Fulham from apprentice September 1981; Wokingham T. (loan); Crystal Palace (£240,000) August 1988; Plymouth Arg. (loan) October 1991; Bristol R. (free) March 1992; READING (free) 13 July 1992; Notts Co. (trial); Barry T. (trial); Selangor (Malaysia) summer 1997; Gippsland Falcons (Melbourne) player coach 1998; Eastern Spirit coach 2000

Although born in Wales, Jeff was brought up in the Reading area and played on the right wing for Reading U15 Schools in 1978-79 but by the time he joined Fulham he had moved to right back. During his 250 plus appearances for Fulham, Jeff was converted to centre half and was seen as the driving force behind their team, winning the first of his 14 Welsh caps at 19. A big money move to Palace saw Jeff captain them to promotion to the First Division in his first season but injury then hampered his career and caused him to miss out on their FA Cup final appearances in 1990. After a short spell with Bristol Rovers, Jeff moved to Reading, initially on a short contract to prove his fitness, but this was soon made permanent. He was a regular member of Reading's Division Two title winning side and although Jeff was used less frequently during 1994-95 he still played an important part in that season's successes and came on as sub in the play-off final. Jeff continued to be a valuable and popular squad member for the next two seasons although an achilles injury kept him out for six months in 1995-96. Released at the end of the following season, Jeff moved to Selangor, where he helped them win the Malaysian Cup.

Reading Record: Lge 127(4)/3, FAC 6(1), LC 8(1), AMC 6, Play-offs (2), Total 147(8)/3
League Career Total: 422(12)/9

JEFF'S CLAIM TO FAME - Jeff has an ardent fan in his former Palace colleague, Ian Wright, who included a glowing tribute to Jeff in his autobiography, describing him as *one of the most dedicated and underrated players I have ever met* and saying *I've never met another player who could match Jeff for honesty, courage and commitment*. None of the fans of the clubs Jeff played for would disagree with Mr Wright on that.

HORLER George Henry

b. Coleford 10.2.1895 d. Reading 16.3.1967
Ht 5ft 11 1/2 Wt 13st (21-22)
Career: Coleford; Frome T; READING 1913; West Ham U. (£250) June 1924; Fulham summer 1927; Aldershot 1928

Despite being a powerful full back, George was described in the press as *one of nature's gentleman* and this appears to have applied to his life both on and off the pitch.

Signed as an 18 year old from Frome Town, George had to wait until he had completed his War service in Mesopotamia before breaking into Reading's first team. A regular at left back during Reading's first League season, George played in the club's first ever League game, but was used less frequently the following season when he played on both flanks. On leaving Reading, George spent five years with West Ham although he only got into double figures twice for appearances, playing 47 League games for them. George never moved away from Reading where he ran a soft drinks company as well as the tea bars at Elm Park, and was a leading light in the local pigeon racing scene, winning many titles and becoming a national judge.

Reading Record: Lge 53, FAC 5, SL 36, Total 94
League Career Total: 108

GEORGE'S CLAIM TO FAME - George had a fine voice and was in great demand for church and masonic functions and it was during one of these that he became the first person to sing 'Bless This House' in Reading.

HORRIX Dean Victor

b. Taplow 21.11.1961 d. Tadley 11.3.1990
Ht 5ft 11 Wt 11st 10 (83-84)
Career: Millwall from apprentice April 1979; Gillingham March 1983; READING (£10,000) August 1983; Cardiff C. (loan) February 1987; Millwall (£75,000) 6 March 1988; Bristol C. (£50,000) 1 March 1990

The son of an ABA champion boxer, Dean played in the same Slough Schools team as Steve Richardson before joining Millwall where he enjoyed a successful youth career. Having won their Young Player of the Year award, Dean progressed to the first team, scoring on his League debut and topping Millwall's scorers in 1981-82 when he was voted the club's Player of the Year. A short, unhappy, and goalless spell at Gillingham followed before he joined Reading just before the start of what was to be a golden era for the club. Dean proved an immediate hit at Elm Park where he formed a deadly partnership with Trevor Senior. While Senior was the League's top scorer in 1983-84, Reading players and fans recognized Dean's help as well as marvelling at his own spectacular goalscoring contribution. Dean played football with a smile on his face and was always looking to go for the spectacular - volleys, powerful long range shots or outrageous swerves didn't always come off, but when they did the results were memorable. In 1984-85 Dean had his best scoring season with 19 League goals and the following season he played in 41 games of the club's runaway Third Division championship. He was less regular in the Second Division sides and in March 1988 he faced a difficult decision - stay with Reading and play at Wembley in the Simod Cup or return to Millwall and help them to the First Division.

Dean decided on Millwall, but not before his final goal for Reading in the penalty shoot-out helped take them to Wembley. Although he only played a handful of games at the Den, he did achieve his ambition to play in the top flight. In March 1990, Dean moved to Bristol City in a move that looked certain to be good for both him and his new club. Sadly, ten days later tragedy struck when he was a passenger in a car that crashed and the 28 year old Dean was killed outright. A well supported benefit game was staged at Millwall for Dean's family but he was mourned by football fans at all his clubs.

Reading Record: Lge 135(23)/35, FAC 9/4, LC 10(2)/1, AMC 5, FMC 7/3, Total 166(25)/43
League Career Total: 224(43)/58

DEAN'S CLAIM TO FAME - Dean was a member of the Millwall squad that won the 1979 FA Youth Cup. Remarkably every one of that side made it into Millwall's first team and no fewer than five of them, including Dean, had two spells at the Den.

HOUGHTON Raymond James
b. Glasgow 9.1.1962
Ht 5ft 7 Wt 10st 10 (98-99)
Career: West Ham U. from amateur July 1979; Fulham (free) July 1982; Oxford U. (£147,000) September 1985; Liverpool (£825,000) October 1987; Aston Villa (£900,000) July 1992; Crystal Palace (£300,000) March 1995; READING (free) player coach 15 July 1997; Stevenage Bor. 1999; Crystal Palace coach August 2000

In an 18 year career Ray won all the major honours available and played 73 times for Eire. His family moved to London when he was 10 and after one substitute appearance for West Ham, Ray developed into a driving, inspirational midfielder with Fulham. It was under Maurice Evans at Oxford that he won his first cap and his first club honour, scoring in the 1986 League Cup final. A big fee took him to Liverpool and he repaid them with a trophy in each of his first three seasons at Anfield - the Championships in 1988 and 1990 plus the FA Cup in between. Moves to Villa and then Palace further enhanced his reputation, as did his spectacular winner against Italy in the 1994 World Cup finals. Keen to develop his coaching career, Ray joined Terry Bullivant at Reading as player coach in 1997 but while his experience and guile where there for all to see, he could not help Reading avoid the drop from Division One. Initially, Reading's new manager, Tommy Burns, was ready to release Ray but he was subsequently retained to push his League total to over 570 games. Another three international caps plus a goal in the World Cup play-off against Belgium were added before finally finishing his League career at the end of 1998-99.

Reading Record: Lge 33(10)/1, FAC 2(2), LC 7(2), Total 42(14)/1
League Career Total: 544(32)/68

HOULDSWORTH Frederick Charlton
b. Caversham 29.5.1911 d. 1994
Ht 5ft 9 Wt 11st 4 (38-39)
Career: Swindon T. 1934; Stoke C. 1935; Ipswich T; READING May 1938; Southampton (Wartime guest); Thorneycroft A. November 1945

Fred was spotted playing in goal for the Army by Swindon where he made his League debut in 1934 before quickly being snapped up by Stoke. From there he moved on to Ipswich during their non-League days and then joined Reading as cover for the popular Percy Whittaker. Apart from a couple of games over Christmas, Fred had to wait until April for a run in the first team, but his call up for the War came in July 1939 and so ended any chance of establishing himself with his home town club.

Reading Record: Lge 8, FAC 1, SSC 1, Wartime 6, Total 16
League Career Total: 39

HOWIE Scott
b. Glasgow 4.1.1972
Ht 6ft 3 Wt 13st 7 (98-99)
Career: Ferguslie; Clyde January 1992; Norwich C. (£300,000) August 1993; Motherwell (£30,000) October 1994; Coventry C. (loan); READING (£30,000) 26 March 1998; Bristol R. summer 2001

Initially a centre half, Scott became a goalie at secondary school and came to prominence with Clyde, helping them win the Scottish Second Division championship in his first full season. After 60 first team games, Norwich paid a big fee for the young keeper but Scott only made two League appearances before returning to Scotland. Again Scott's form attracted attention, this time earning him a call up to train with the Scotland squad on several occasions prior to the 1998 World Cup. In March 1998 he was one of 'the magnificent seven' who were signed for Reading by Tommy Burns on transfer deadline day. He held down the first team spot until a traumatic spell culminated in him being substituted at half time at Wycombe. Despite this setback, and the signing of Phil Whitehead, Scott got his first team place back and won the fans support again with a series of brilliant saves. A great shot stopper with tremendous reactions, Scott had to play second fiddle to Phil Whitehead during 2000-01 and with his first team chances restricted to the Associate Members Cup he was released in June 2001.

Reading Record: Lge 84(1), FAC 4, LC 6, AMC 7, Total 101(1)
League Career Total: 85(2)

HUDSON Raymond James
b. Slough 21.11.1937
Ht 5ft 9 Wt 10st 12 (59-60)
Career: READING groundstaff August 1953, professional 30 November 1954

In almost seven years with Reading, first on the groundstaff and then as a professional, Ray only played in two of those seasons with a total of just 11 League appearances. A right back, Ray made his debut at Brentford on Boxing Day 1955 and was given a blue and white decorated cake presented to Reading by Brentford on the day.   He made another two appearances that season but then had to wait until 1959 when he had two four match runs, but another season of reserve football followed and Ray was released by Reading at the end of 1959-60.

Reading Record: Lge 11

HULME John
b. Mobberley 6.2.1945
Ht 6ft 0 1/2 Wt 12st 1 (72-73)
Career: Bolton W. from apprentice February 1962; Notts Co. (loan) March 1972; READING (£7,000) 13 July 1972, player coach March 1974; Bury (£6,600) 1 July 1974; Chaux-de-Fonds (Switzerland) player manager

John developed into a solid central defender with Bolton and could score vital goals, usually with powerful headers from free kicks and corners. In 1970-71 he was their Player of the Year as he shared the captaincy with Charlie Hurley and when it became clear that Bolton were willing to release John, Hurley, by then manager of Reading, was quick to sign on his former defensive partner. Immediately installed as club captain, John was an inspiration in the Reading defence that set club defensive records of 38 and then 37 goals conceded in his first two seasons.   He won a PFA Divisional award in 1973-74, the first season they were presented, and was appointed club coach in March 1974. Unfortunately, John's wife found it difficult to settle in the South and the club was forced to allow the popular defender to return to Lancashire.

Reading Record: Lge 86(1), FAC 7, LC 6, Total 99(1)
League Career Total: 366(3)/12

JOHN'S CLAIM TO FAME - Non-playing captains are not unusual in some sports but are unheard of in football, except at Chester on 27 April 1974. That last game of the season was to be John's last for Reading and saw him captain Reading as substitute. Apart from tossing the coin before the kick off, he played no further part in the game.

HUMPHREY John
b. Paddington 31.1.1961
Ht 5ft 10 Wt 11st 4 (91-92)
Career: Wolverhampton W. from apprentice February 1979; Charlton A. (£60,000) July 1985; Crystal Palace (£400,000) August 1990; READING (loan) 9 December 1993; Charlton A. (free) July 1995; Gillingham August 1996; Brighton January 1997

A fine attacking right back, John made over 150 appearances for Wolves before moving to Charlton where he became a favourite of the fans, winning their Player of the Year award on three occasions. He helped Charlton to the First Division in his first season and played a vital role in their annual battle to stay in the top flight. In 1990 John moved to Crystal Palace without changing grounds as Palace were Charlton's landlords at Selhurst Park, and he again enjoyed immediate success by helping them win the 1991 Full Members Cup. Loaned to Reading in December 1993, John had the misfortune to be the victim of a ridiculous sending - off on his debut at Burnley but, despite the FA asking the referee to review the decision, the official refused to correct his error. Even so, John was able to complete a unique double, making eight appearances for Reading and 32 for Palace as both clubs won their divisions' championships that season.

Reading Record: Lge 8, AMC 1, Total 9
League Career Total: 563(7)/8

HUNT Robert Rex
b. Colchester 1.10.1942
Ht 5ft 10 Wt 11st 12 (73-74)
Career: Colchester U. November 1959; Northampton T. (£18,000) March 1964; Millwall September 1966; Ipswich T. November 1967; Charlton A. (£12,000) September 1970; Northampton T. (loan) November 1972; READING (£5,000) 5 January 1973; Maidstone U. July 1974; Bury T.

A widely travelled and regular goalscorer in the lower divisions, Bobby was the youngest and most successful of three brothers to play for Colchester. Twice the top scorer, Bobby holds their club record with 38 goals in 1961-62 when United won promotion to the Third Division.   Northampton had to break Colchester's transfer record to acquire his goalscoring talent, and another promotion in 1964-65. This was followed by moves to Millwall and Ipswich where Bobby got his chance to play in the First Division, having helped the Suffolk club win the Second Division title in his first season with them. Bobby was with Charlton when he made his final League move, joining Reading six years after the club had originally tried to sign him during the days of Roy Bentley.

Although Bobby scored on his Reading debut, his time at Elm Park was hindered by a series of niggling injuries and so he suffered his poorest goal return of his career before joining non-League Maidstone in 1974.

Reading Record: Lge 15(1)/3, FAC 2, Total 17(1)/3
League Career Total: 302(13)/125

HUNTER Barry Victor
b. Coleraine 18.11.1968
Ht 6ft 4 Wt 13st 2 (99-00)
Career: Coleraine; Newcastle U. November 1987; Coleraine summer 1988; Crusaders; Wrexham (£50,000) August 1993; READING (£400,000) 8 July 1996; Southend U. (loan) February 1999; Rushden & D.(laon) summer 2001

After failing to make the grade with Newcastle, Barry built up a strong reputation in Northern Ireland football but his career was hampered by two broken legs. He returned to League football after being spotted by Wrexham while playing in a pre-season tournament in the Isle of Man. Having been capped at youth and B level, Barry's powerful play at the centre of Wrexham's defence earned him the first of 13 caps for Northern Ireland against Latvia in 1995. In 1996 Barry joined Reading as a replacement for Adie Williams, having opened his League goalscoring account at Elm Park two years earlier. Barry settled in quickly and looked a great asset when, in March 1995 he sustained a serious knee injury that kept him out of the game for almost two years. Although it understandably took Barry some time to regain his form with Reading, he was back in the Northern Ireland side by April 1999 after just one substitute appearance for Reading. A month later he played in Ireland's first ever victory over Eire. Despite being no longer first choice towards the end of the play-off season, when called on Barry was never 'The Weakest Link', despite being the first footballer to audition for the popular quiz!

Reading Record: Lge 76(7)/4, FAC 3(1)/1, LC 5/1, AMC 5, Play-offs 1(1), Total 90(9)/6 +
League Career Total: 169(10)/10 +

BARRY'S CLAIM TO FAME - It's no wonder that Barry was capped by Northern Ireland - his father, Vic, played in goal twice for them while his uncle, Allan Hunter won 50 caps and another relative, William McFaull played six times for Northern Ireland.

HUNTER John
b. Stenhousemuir 11.4.1905 d. ?
Ht 5ft 7 1/2 Wt 11st 7 (29-30)
Career: Falkirk; READING (£800) July 1928; Guildford C.

Unimaginatively nicknamed 'Jock' at Elm Park, John was a prolific goalscorer with Falkirk where he scored over 100 goals in five seasons, a feat that saw him play in all matches during a Scotland XI tour of Canada in 1927-28. At Reading, Jock was a typical Scottish inside forward who was an eye catching player even though his lack of pace meant that goals were harder to come by in English football. Ever-present in his first Reading season, John's first team chances decreased over the next two campaigns and he was put on the transfer list at the end of 1930-31. Initially he quit football to run a business in Guildford, but he later joined the local club who were managed by Andrew Wylie, the manager who signed him for Reading.

Reading Record: Lge 88/7, FAC 6, Total 94/7

HURLEY Albert Victor
b. Tiverton 2nd qtr 1901 d. ?
Ht 5ft 9 Wt 11st 6 (20-21)
Career: Oxford C; Keeble College; Oxford University; Dulwich Ham; READING 1921; Yorkshire Amateurs; Corinthians

A former RAF pilot, Albert was a footballing vicar who won an Oxford 'blue' and was spotted by Reading when he played against them in a friendly for the University. He played two games as an amateur on Reading's left wing while he was living in the town, and after that Canon Hurley concentrated on his ecclesiastical career. He still found time to represent Oxford in the first University Air Race in 1921.

Reading Record: Lge 2

HURLOCK Terence Alan
b. Hackey 22.9.1958
Ht 5ft 9 Wt 13st 2 (86-87)
Career: West Ham U. from apprentice; Leytonstone & Ilford; Brentford (£10,000) August 1980; READING (£87,500) February 1986; Millwall (£95,000) February 1987; Glasgow Rngrs (£400,000) August 1990; Southampton (£400,000) September 1991; Millwall March 1994; Fulham July 1994

After leaving West Ham, Terry spent three seasons with Leytonstone & Ilford winning the Isthmian League and the London Senior Cup before making his League debut with Brentford. Terry proved an inspiration at Griffin Park where he captained the side from his second season and led them out for the first Wembley Freight Rover Trophy final in 1985. A year later Ian Branfoot paid a record fee for both clubs, to bring Terry to Reading as the impetus to clinch the Third Division title. This tough tackling midfielder achieved, along with a PFA Divisional award for his displays at Brentford, but he never quite recaptured his form with Reading and after a year Terry was sold to Millwall.

This proved a great move for Terry, winning both the Second Division title and then the Player of the Year in his first season in the top division. He also won three England B caps and was close to a full cap when his form earned him a move to Glasgow Rangers where, in his first season, Rangers did the League and Skol Cup double. After two goals in 35 appearances for Rangers, Terry returned to England and was signed by Ian Branfoot on two more occasions - for Southampton and Fulham, where a broken leg in 1995 ended his career.

Reading Record: Lge 29, FAC 1, LC 3, FMC 2, Total 35
League Career Total: 451(3)/27

HUTTON Joseph
b. Dundee 18.11.1927
Ht 5ft 3 1/2 Weight 10st (50-51)
Career: Albion R; Leytonstone; READING amateur March 1949, professional 19 October 1950; Ayr U. (£1,250) 25 September 1951; Stoke C. December 1993; Gillingham July 1957; Millwall August 1958; Poole T. summer 1959

As an Albion Rovers player, Joe played for Leytonstone and for Reading as an amateur while completing his National Service. He had played eight games as an amateur for Reading but, having played twice more the week after he signed professional, Joe never featured in the first team again. He was a scheming inside forward but Reading thought that his lack of inches - he is the shortest player to play for the club - counted against him and he returned to Scotland. His form at Ayr prompted Stoke to sign him and he scored on his debut but only made 37 League appearances in three seasons.

Reading Record: Lge 8
League Career Total: 102/22

IGOE Samuel Gary
b. Spelthorne 30.9.1975
Ht 5ft 6 Wt 10st (99-00)
Career: Portsmouth from trainee September 1994; READING (£100,000) 23 March 2000

Sammy progressed through Portsmouth's youth ranks and attracted the attention of Premiership clubs with a series of bright, incisive displays on the right side of their midfield. He was unable to maintain that form consistently during his almost 180 first team appearances, but even so when he joined Reading, who signed him just 15 minutes before the 2000 transfer deadline, they were thought to have got a bargain. Although never sure of a starting place in 2000-01 Sammy added a different dimension to Reading's play as well as scoring some vital goals.

Reading Record: Lge 18(19)/6, FAC 2, LC 2, Play-offs 3, Total 25(19)/6 +
League Career Total: 118(79)/17+

INGLIS William John
b. Hebburn on Tyne 4.9.1899 d. Sale 20.1.1968
Ht 5ft 11 1/2 Wt 12st 10 (28-29)
Career: Derby Co. June 1921; Hebburn Collier; Brentford May 1922; READING June 1925; Exeter C. (£200)May 1930; Stockport Co. August 1931; Watford July 1932; Dartford August 1933; Cray W. August 1934

Having spent three seasons at Brentford where he played 80 League games at centre half, Bill joined Reading. Although he was unable to displace Alf Messer his form forced him into the first team at wing half. Bill was a dour but dependable, strongly built player and he made the right half position his own as Reading won the Third Division South title and then reached the FA Cup semi-final in 1927. The signings of Sid Chandler and Jack Johnstone in 1928 greatly reduced Bill's first team chances and in 1930 he was released to join Exeter.

Reading Record: Lge 120/1, FAC 16, Total 136/1
League Career Total: 262/3

IRWIN George William
b. Smethwick 7.1.1891 d. ?
Ht 6ft Wt 12st 6 (21-22)
Career: West Bromwich Alb. August 1919; Crystal Palace June 1921; READING June 1923; Southend U. trainer summer 1924; Sheffield Wed. trainer 1925; Crystal Palace trainer 1937, manager July 1939, scout May 1947; Darlington manager April 1950

A youth international goalie, George got his chance in the League when he moved to Crystal Palace in 1921 but his best season came with Reading when he played 37 first team games in 1923-24. Although he lost his place after letting in 17 goals in his first six starts George was soon back in the first team but the signing of Joe Duckworth at the end of that season spelt the end of his League career as a player. George then began a long coaching career that saw him help Sheffield Wednesday win the Cup in 1935, before becoming the first former player to manage Crystal Palace. He was in charge of Palace when they lost 10-2 at Reading in 1946 and later retired from management when his club, Darlington, had to apply for re-election in 1952.

Reading Record: Lge 36, FAC 1, Total 37
League Career Total: 53

JACKSON Darren William
b. Keynsham 24.9.1971
Ht 6ft 1 Wt 12st 1 (92-93)
Career: Bristol C. assoc. schoolboy; Bristol R. assoc. schoolboy; Oxford U. from YTS May 1990; READING (loan) 3 February 1993

Reading missed out on signing Darren when they failed to follow up on the offer of a trial after he had impressed during a schools game at Elm Park in 1986-87. Instead he joined Oxford, making his League debut in 1989-90, but he was allowed to spend a month on loan at Reading in 1993. Despite missing a penalty in an Autoglass Trophy shoot-out at Exeter, Darren impressed during his spell at Reading where his classy displays at left back saw them unbeaten in his five match League run. Reading were interested in keeping Darren longer, even permanently, but Oxford recalled him for their first team. Unfortunately, his first game back with United saw him rupture an achilles tendon that was to end his promising League career.

Reading Record: Lge 5, AMC 1, Total 6
League Career Total: 16(3)

JACKSON Tom F
b. c.1900 d. ?
Ht 5ft 7 Wt 11st 2 (20-21)
Career: Aberdeen University; New College; Oxford University; READING 1919

Although he had already played for them in the Southern League, Tom reminded Reading of his capabilities when he scored twice for his University against them in a friendly. He must have thought he was destined for a long career with Reading when, on Easter Saturday 1921, he scored twice on his debut as Reading beat Merthyr 2-0 at Elm Park. Strangely, he only got one more chance a couple of weeks later and the inside left's career was over almost as soon as it had begun, although he later scored the winner in the 1921 'Varsity game.

Reading Record: Lge 2/2 SL 2, Total 4/2

JAMES George Charles
b. Oldbury 14.2.1899 d. West Bromwich 12.12.1976
Ht 5ft 10 Wt 12st (30-31)
Career: Chances Glass Works; Daimler Repair Works; Bilston U; West Bromwich Alb. 1921; READING May 1929; Watford (player exchange) February 1930

Originally a wing half, George was converted to a very effective centre forward at West Brom where, in 1924-25, he finished their top scorer with 24 goals in 29 League games. This form earned him an international trial but as his scoring rate decreased, so did his first team chances and he moved to Reading. A talkative player, on and off the pitch, by the end of November George was Reading's top scorer but lost his place after a goalless spell. Even so it was something of a surprise when they exchanged him for Watford's Frank McPherson in February 1930.

Initially Reading seemed to have got the better of the deal as McPherson hit eight goals in 11 games while George failed to score for Watford. That soon changed as George hit 49 goals over the following two seasons before retiring at 34.

Reading Record: Lge 19/7, FAC 1, Total 20/7
League Career Total: 226/116

GEORGE'S CLAIM TO FAME - In December 1924, George scored four times against Nottingham Forest with the first coming after just five seconds, and thus recording West Brom's fastest ever goal.

JAMES Martin Charles
b. Slough 18.2.1953
Ht 6ft 2 Wt 12st 2 (71-72)
Career: Chelsea amateur; READING from amateur 17 August 1971

After a year at Reading as an amateur while also training to be an accountant, Martin made his League debut four days after signing professionally and immediately added much needed stability and aerial power to Reading's defence. Martin had a no nonsense style of defending and his willingness to transfer the ball from the danger area to the streets surrounding Elm Park earned him a cult status amongst Reading fans that is still fondly recalled to this day. The signing of more experienced defenders led to Martin being released at the end of 1971-72 and he subsequently emigrated to South Africa.

Reading Record: Lge 21, FAC 1, Total 22

JENKINS Glyn
b. Llandaff c.1915
Ht 5ft 10 Wt 11st 11 (36-37)
Career: Llandaff C; READING amateur June 1936 then professional

After a series of fine displays in the Welsh League, Glyn turned down the chance to sign for Derby before joining Reading, initially as an amateur. He was so impressive in a pre-season friendly that he was signed as a professional at half time. The young right back made good progress in the reserves but Glyn's only first team appearances came in the Southern Section Cup playing in the first round tie in 1936-37, and again the following season when Reading went on to win the competition. Unfortunately, Glyn suffered a bad injury and was forced to retire from football in January 1939 but he stayed in Reading where he progressed to the rank of inspector in the police.

Reading Record: SSC 2

JENKINS Thomas Ernest

b. Bethnal Green 2.12.1947
Ht 5ft 10 Wt 10st 10 (69-70)
Career: Leyton O. January 1966; West Ham U. December 1967; Margate February 1968; READING (£1,500) July 1969; Southampton (£60,000) 8 December 1969; Swindon T. November 1972; Seattle Sounders March 1976; Pittsburgh Spirit 1981, Phoenix Inferno; Washington State Soccer Programme director; Seattle Storm manager 1981

Few players have had a more meteoric rise to the top than Tom who went from Southern League football to the First Division in seven months. Twice rejected by League clubs, Tom was plucked from non-League obscurity by Reading for a £500 fee that increased by £1,000 after 10 League games. This was an amount Reading were pleased to pay as Tom was already a fixture on the wing by then. Capable of playing on either flank where his skill and trickery made him an instant favourite with the fans, Tom was soon attracting the attention of First Division scouts. When a host of them turned up to watch him at Tranmere he responded with a stunning hat trick. From then on it was only a matter of which club would buy him - it turned out to be Southampton with a fee that broke both clubs' transfer records. Tom spent three years at the Dell, making 96 appearances including four in European games, before moving to Swindon as a replacement for Don Rodgers. Although Reading tried to get Tom back on loan in 1976 he eventually carved out a career in the States as a player, coach and administrator.

Reading Record: Lge 21/5, FAC 1, LC 2, Total 24/5
League Career Total: 195(11)/13

JENNINGS Samuel

b. Cinderhill 18.12.1898 d. Battle 26.8.1944
Ht 5ft 11 Wt 11st 6 (23-24)
Career: Coldstream Guards; WW1 guest for Tottenham H. & Notts Co; Basford U; Norwich C. May 1919; Middlesbrough (£2,500) April 1920; READING (loan) June 1921; West Ham U. (£1,000) June 1924; Brighton March 1925; Nottingham For. May 1928; Port Vale June 1929; Stockport Co. September 1931; Burnley January 1931; Wisbech T. coach; Olympique Marseilles coach May 1932; Scarborough September 1934; player coach in Switzerland; Glentoran coach June 1936; Rochdale manager October 1937 to May 1938,

A goalscoring inside left, Sam cost Middlesbrough a big fee but they loaned him to Reading where he developed into a fine player topping their goalscorers in all three seasons. He was, however, often in trouble with referees for swearing and was once reprimanded by the board for it. The length of his loan period confused West Ham who tried to sign him and it was only when the Hammers tried to register him with the League that the true situation became apparent.

Eventually, West Ham agreed terms with Middlesbrough and the deal went ahead, but not until the Hammers had been fined for making an illegal approach. Although Sam only stayed a few months with West Ham, he carried on scoring regularly, particularly for Brighton, Nottingham Forest and Port Vale. After he retired as a player, Sam coached in France, Switzerland and Ireland before managing Rochdale, until ill health forced his retirement.

Reading Record: Lge 110/46, FAC 3, Total 113/46
League Career Total: 349/173

JOHNSON George Alfred

b. Newcastle 20.7.1905 d. Reading 26.5.1985
Ht 5ft 9 Wt 11st 10 (32-33)
Career: Ashington Welfare; Ashington October 1914; Sheffield Wed. July 1929; READING (£90) June 1932; Watford May 1937; Krooger coach; Gauda coach; Chelsea scout; Oxford C. groundsman/coach December 1949

A free scoring centre forward with Ashington, George scored 65 League goals in five seasons with them where he was regularly their top scorer and this earned him a move to League champions Sheffield Wednesday. Although he scored on his debut for Wednesday the rest of George's appearances for them were in their reserves, helping them win the Central League in 1930-31, so in 1932 he was transferred to Reading. George had to wait until December to make his first Reading League appearance and he marked it in sensational style, scoring a hat trick against Northampton. Strangely after such a start, he played just two more games at centre forward before being converted to right half, but in hindsight this was a clever move as George became a fixture in Reading's defence for the next four years. He captained the club many times and was, according to the Reading programme, 'a very determined tackler'. At the age of 32 George was released by Reading and joined Watford where he had a season back in the goals, scoring eight times in 22 games.

After the War, George coached in Holland and in 1946 his Krooger FC of Zandaam, beat Reading 5-2 in a friendly. When George's soccer wanderings were over he returned to Reading where he lived for the rest of his life.

Reading Record: Lge 161/8, FAC 15, SSC 3, Total 179/8
League Career Total: 351/82

JOHNSTON James C
b. Aberdeen 12.4.1923
Ht 5ft 9 Wt 10st 10 (50-51)
Career: Peterhead; Aberdeen; Leicester C. April 1947; READING (£2,750) 15 May 1950; Swindon T. (£1,500) 16 March 1953

Jimmy developed a reputation with Aberdeen as a tireless, tough tackling left half and his career in England did nothing to diminish this view. He was a first team regular for Leicester in 1948-49 and was their twelfth man for their 1949 FA Cup final appearance. Despite this, Jimmy failed to make the first team the following campaign, and moved to Reading in 1950 where he missed just five games in almost three seasons. Just before the 1953 transfer deadline, Jimmy moved to Swindon and helped them keep clear of the re-election zone, staying with them for another two seasons before retiring from League football.

Reading Record: Lge 120, FAC 10, Total 130
League Career Total: 230

JOHNSTONE John Charles
b. Fergonhall 4.1896 d. Erdington 1952
Ht 5ft 9 1/2 Wt 11st 4 (28-29)
Career: Dundee Harp; Dundee; Aston Villa 1921; READING (£400) July 1928

After moving from Scotland, 'Jock' spent six seasons with Aston Villa where he played 115 first team games, mainly at right half. He left Villa at the end of 1926-27 and appears to have spent a season out of the game, in fact Villa's history records him as having retired! Perhaps he wished he had retired because, having signed for Reading in July 1928, Jack played in their first six games from which they gained just one point. Those six games at left half signalled the end of Jack's League career as he was not retained by Reading at the end of that season.

Reading Record: Lge 6
League Career Total: 111/1

JOHNSTONE William
b. Markinch 18.5.1900 d. ?
Ht 5ft 10 Wt 12st 7 (29-30)
Career: Rosyth Jnrs; Dundee U; Kings Park; Clyde; READING October 1926; Arsenal (player exchange) May 1929; Oldham A. (£2,130) January 1931; Clyde July 1933

Bill was a prolific scorer with Clyde where he netted 120 times in four seasons and was their top scorer during their 1925-26 promotion season. His move to Reading saw him used in all of the three inside forward positions but centre forward seemed to be the best position for Bill's bustling style. This was born out when he hit his best League total of 18 goals, in 1928-29, from that position. However, Bill seemed to save his best performances for the Cup as he scored nine in Reading's run to the semi-final in 1927. Two years later he followed up his two goals that beat Spurs, with that which knocked out runaway League leaders Wednesday, in what is regarded as the club's greatest victory. At the end of that season Bill was exchanged for Arsenal's Charlie Barley and he scored four times in nine First Division games before moving on to Oldham.

Reading Record: Lge 78/33, FAC 13/12, Total 91/45
League Career Total: 155/65

JONES Abraham
b. West Brom 4.1899 d. ?
Ht 5ft 7 Wt 11st 4 (21-21)
Career: West Bromwich Sandwell; Birmingham 1919; READING August 1921; Brighton summer 1922; Merthyr T. summer 1923

Despite scoring twice on his debut for Birmingham, Abe only made two more first team appearances for them, and after a season in their reserves he joined Reading in 1921 making his debut in a friendly as 'A N Other'. Used in all three inside forward positions, Abe scored five times in a season that saw the club average less than a goal a game and fail to score in 21 of their 43 first team matches. He sometimes tended to over elaborate and a move to Brighton the following season only produced one more League goal for Abe, but he came back to haunt his previous club when he scored four against Reading's reserves. His father, also Abe, had played for West Brom and Middlesbrough.

Reading Record: Lge 23/5
League Career Total: 49/14

JONES David
b. Aberdare 7.1.1932
Ht 5ft 9 Wt 10st 5 (58-59)
Career: Harwell; Dover T; Brentford December 1951; READING (free) 1 July 1953; Aldershot (free) July 1961; Dartford 1968

When he was a youngster, David's family moved to Kent from where he was evacuated to Berkshire during the War and during that time he played for Harwell. On returning to Kent, David signed for Brentford but National Service prevented him from progressing, so he joined Reading in 1953 where he was coached by former War international goalie, George Marks. Within three months of joining Reading he was making his League debut and although David faced a challenge from Dave Meeson, in 1956-57 he was the club's number one keeper up until 1960. His acrobatic displays brought him to the attention of the Welsh selectors who named David as one of their initial 40 for the 1958 World Cup in Sweden although he never made the final 22. Meeson eventually replaced David in September 1960, and at the end of that season he moved to Aldershot where he played for another five seasons. He returned to Elm Park, and in the Nineties he could be seen assisting groundsman, Gordon Neate, in replacing divots at half time.

Reading Record: Lge 215, FAC 10, SPFC 9, Total 234
League Career Total: 402

JONES Frederick George
b. Gelligaer 11.1.1938
Ht 5ft 6 Wt 10st 12 (63-64)
Career: Hereford U; Arsenal (player plus £5,000) January 1958; Brighton September 1958; Swindon T. December 1960; Grimsby T. July 1961; READING (£2,900) 1 July 1963; Hereford U. (£1,500) summer 1964; Cheltenham T.

Freddy caught Arsenal's eye while playing on the wing at Hereford but, despite commanding a hefty fee for a non-League player, he only stayed eight months at Highbury before moving on to Brighton. There he was virtually ever-present and won two Welsh U23 caps, then had spells with Swindon and Grimsby before joining Reading in 1963. His speed earned him a long run in the first team, being used on both wings but, following a pay dispute, Freddy left Reading and returned to Hereford.

Reading Record: Lge 30/5, FAC 1, LC 1, Total 32/5
League Career Total: 175/29

JONES Keith Aubrey
b. Dulwich 14.10.1965
Ht 5ft 8 Wt 11st 2 (00-01)
Career: Chelsea from apprentice August 1983; Brentford (£40,000) September 1987; Southend U. (£175,000) October 1991; Charlton A. (£150,000) September 1994; READING (free) 3 July 2000

Capped at schools and youth levels, Keith made his debut for Chelsea at 17 and a year later was Robinson's Young Player of the Month. The hard working, midfield playmaker then began a career based around the capital, making his name at Brentford as club captain and being voted into the PFA Divisional team of 1990-91. Later, six years at Charlton saw him twice help them to promotion to the Premiership before joining Reading on a well deserved 'free'. A pre-season injury delayed his career with them and he took a while to produce his real form, being used more in away games where his defensive skills and experience were always an asset.

Reading Career: Lge 18(5), FAC 3/1, AMC 1, Play-offs 1, Total 23(5)/1 +
League Career Total: 458(34)/37 +

JONES Linden
b. New Tredegar 5.3.1961
Ht 5ft 6 Wt 11st 2 (88-89)
Career: Cardiff C. from apprentice February 1979; Newport Co. (player exchange) September 1983; READING (£30,000) July 1987; Newport AFC manager July 1992; Merthyr Tyd. manager; Inter Cardiff manager; Swansea C. community officer; Ebbw Vale

Selected at centre forward for the Welsh YMCA side, Linden was converted to a defender at Cardiff where he won three U21 caps and was a key member of their 1982-83 Fourth Division promotion side. In 1983 he moved to Newport in a player exchange involving five players, including Karl Elsey and Nigel Vaughan. Linden was twice selected for the full Welsh squad but had to withdraw each time. He was in the County team that lost, to give Reading the record 13 consecutive winning League start in 1985-86. He often partnered his brother, Peter, as Newport's full backs, but the club's worsening financial position forced Linden's sale to Reading in 1987. Linden started the season at right back but in December the tough tackling player was switched into midfield and scored twice on his debut in this role at QPR as Reading started their run to the Simod Cup final. From then on Linden had spells in either role, scoring several goals with his heading ability that belied his height. Released by Reading at the end of 1991-92, Linden subsequently played for or managed several South Wales clubs.

Reading Record: Lge 147(5)/8, FAC 15/3, LC 17(1)/1, FMC 5/2, Total 184(6)/14
League Career Total: 430(8)/16

JONES Thomas

b. Aldershot 7.10.1964
Ht 5ft 10 Wt 11st 7 (96-97)
Career: Chelsea apprentice; Woking; Farnborough; Weymouth; Aberdeen (£30,000) 1987; Swindon T. September 1988; READING (player exchange) 9 July 1992; Oxford U. (loan) December 1993; Woking 11 July 1996; Swindon T. coach; Swindon Supermarine summer 2000

After several years in non-League football, Tom was involved in one of Britain's longest moves when he went from Weymouth to Aberdeen, making his debut in the Dons 1-0 win at Rangers. After 31 appearances in Scotland, Tom moved to Swindon but he requested a transfer because their long ball tactics did not fit his skilful midfield play. The change of style introduced by Ossie Ardilles suited Tom and he helped them win a First Division place via the play-offs in 1990, only to be relegated due to financial irregularities. Two years later he was exchanged for Reading's Craig Maskell and was a part of the squad that won Division Two, then made the play-off final in 1995. Unfortunately, Tom's Reading career was hampered by two broken legs but when fit he proved a cultured and intelligent performer at either left back or in midfield. Tom was a member of the team that won the 1995 Berks & Bucks Senior Cup before being released at the end of the following season, although shortly after he was involved in a friendly between Reading and Swindon, as referee. He maintained his refereeing career while continuing to play non-League football, coming on as sub at Wembley as Woking won the 1997 FA Trophy.

Reading Record: Lge 63(16)/2, FAC 5, LC 7, AMC 1, Total 76(16)/2
League Career Total: 225(22)/14

JORDON John 'Jimmy'

b. Glasgow 25.2.1944
Ht 5ft 9 1/2 Wt 11st (48-49)
Career: Celtic; READING October 1948; Brentford (£3,750) September 1949

A nippy outside right, Jimmy went straight into Reading's first team after joining the club from Celtic, in place of the injured Freddy Fisher. With Fisher back in the first team, Jimmy was relegated to the reserves and although he scored nine times for the second team he never made a League appearance after Christmas. After less than a year at Elm Park he moved on to Brentford but failed to make their League side.

Reading Record: Lge 3

JOSEPH Francis

b. Paddington 6.3.1960
Ht 5ft 10 Wt 12st (87-88)
Career: Wealdstone; Willesden; Hillingdon Bor. July 1979; Wimbledon (£3,000) November 1980; Brentford July 1982; Wimbledon (loan) March 1987; READING (£20,000) July 1987; Bristol R. (loan) January 1988; Aldershot (loan) March 1988; HJK Helsinki summer 1988; Sheffield U. (free) July 1988; Gillingham March 1989; Crewe Alex. December 1989; Fulham August 1990; Racing Ghent (Belgium) 1991; Barnet October 1991; Slough T. (trial) November 1991; Wokingham T; Leatherhead August 1992; Dulwich Ham. October 1992; Chertsey T. July 1993; Wealdstone youth coach 2000

One of many players to come to prominence at Hillingdon Borough, Francis played alongside Paul Canoville before moving to Wimbledon. In his first full season the lively striker topped their scorers and was Player of the Year. A move to Brentford saw Francis enjoy his best spell, being top goalscorer in his first two seasons with them, and he recorded 44 goals in 103 League starts for them. A broken leg hampered his stay with Brentford and he never achieved the same success again, playing for another nine League clubs after leaving Brentford but only adding another 11 League goals in that spell. At Reading he rarely featured after September and, after a couple of loan spells, he joined Sheffield United where he scored on his debut - at Reading.

Reading Record: Lge 5(6)/2, LC 1, FMC (1), Total 6(7)/2
League Career Total: 193(49)/69

JOSLYN Roger Douglas William

b. Colchester 7.5.1950
Ht 5ft 10 Wt 11st 2 (80-81)
Career: Leeds U. (trial); Colchester U. from amateur May 1968; Aldershot (£8,000) October 1970; Watford (player exchange) November 1974; READING (£40,000) 5 November 1979

Roger made his League debut for Colchester at 17 and had over 100 first team games to his credit before he moved to Aldershot. A fixture in their midfield, Roger was twice Player of the Year, and in 1973 he scored the goal that clinched the Shots first promotion - on his 23rd birthday. More success followed when he moved to Watford where his dynamic style drove them to successive promotions plus a League Cup semi. Maurice Evans had been trying to bring Roger to Reading for three seasons and eventually succeeded in 1979. Starting in midfield, Roger was soon converted to right back at Reading where his tigerish tackling proved an asset but he later returned to the midfield. At the start of 1981-82, he began to be troubled by an arthritic hip which soon started to affect his mobility, and by January 1982 it forced the retirement of a man who was a model professional throughout his career.

Reading Record: Lge 67(1)/1, FAC 5, LC 4, FLGC (1), Total 76(2)/1
League Career Total: 523(12)/39

JUDGE Alan Graham

b. Kingsbury 14.5.1960
Ht 5ft 11 Wt 11st (83-84)
Career: Luton T. from apprentice January 1978; READING (loan) August 1982 & February 1983, permanent summer 1983; Oxford U. (£10,000) 22 December 1984; Lincoln C. (loan) November 1985; Cardiff C. (loan) October 1987; Hereford U. July 1991; Bromsgrove; Kettering summer 1995; Banbury U. 1999

Having won an international tournament keeping goal for the British Catholic Schools U18s, Alan progressed through Luton's youth system to make 11 first team appearances for them. Two loan spells to Reading in 1982-83 saw Alan make 33 appearances before moving to Elm Park permanently in the summer, winning promotion to the Third Division in the following season. Having lost his place to Gary Westwood he was sold to Oxford United, again winning promotion in his first season as they won the Second Division title, then in 1986 he kept a clean sheet at Wembley as United won the League Cup. Later, after 105 League games for Lincoln, Alan started a successful non-League career that included victory in the 1995 Bob Lord Trophy with Bromsgrove.

Reading Record: Lge 77, FAC 3, LC 4, FLGC 3, Total 87
League Career Total: 283

JURYEFF Ian Martin

b. Gosport 24.11.1962
Ht 5ft 11 Wt 12st (84-85)
Career: Southampton from apprentice November 1980; Markfurs (loan) March 1984, Mansfield T. (loan) March 1984; READING (loan) November 1984; Leyton O. (£10,000) February 1985; Ipswich T. (loan) February 1989; Halifax (£40,000) August 1989; Hereford U. (£40,000) December 1989; Halifax (£50,000) September 1990; Darlington (free) August 1992; Scunthorpe U. (free) August 1993; Farnborough February 1995; Weston Super Mare

Ian was a burly but skilful striker who played and scored for a number of, mainly, lower league clubs after failing to make more than two substitute appearances for his local club, Southampton. During his loan spell at Reading he quickly formed a successful partnership with Trevor Senior but was allowed to return to Southampton. In 1985, Ian moved to Orient where he enjoyed his longest and most successful run with 45 goals in 111 League appearances that included promotion from the Fourth Division in 1988-89. A series of moves ended when Ian graduated with a sports science degree and became Southampton's Community Development Officer.

Reading Record: Lge 7/2, FAC 3/2, Total 10/4
League Career Total: 303(25)/95

KANE Alexander

b. Aberdeen 22.1.1899 d. ?
Ht 5ft 11 Wt 13st (22-23)
Career: Hearts; READING (loan) summer 1922; Portsmouth May 1923; West Ham U. 1925

Loaned to Reading by Hearts, where he was valued at £1,250, Sandy was ever-present in Reading's goal during 1922-23. He repeated that feat in the following two seasons with Portsmouth as they first won the Third Division South title, and then finished fourth in the Second. His form earned him a move to West Ham, but Sandy's run ended there as he only played twice in his two year spell with them.

Reading Record: Lge 42, FAC 1, Total 43
League Career Total: 140

KEARNEY Michael Joseph

b. Glasgow 18.2.1953
Ht 6ft Wt 12st (80-81)
Career: Possil YM; Peterhill; St Peter; Shrewsbury December 1953; Chester (£8,000) March 1977; READING (£10,000) 28 January 1978; Chester (£50,000) July 1980; READING (£50,000) 13 October 1980; Marlow 1983; Basingstoke T. July 1984; Marlow; Chertsey; Reading T.

Having started with the same club that produced Kenny Dalglish and Robert Fleck, Mike was signed for Shrewsbury by Maurice Evans. Although he scored twice on his League debut, Mike was switched from centre forward to centre half and helped them to get promoted to the Third Division before moving to Chester. He stayed there less than a year but won the Debenhams Cup for FA Cup giantkillers, then moved on to rejoin Maurice Evans at Reading as a forward. Again success followed as Reading won the Fourth Division title in his first full season at the club but, having topped the club's scorers in 1979-80, Mike became unsettled and was sold to Chester for their record fee. Almost immediately, Mike realized that his future lay with Reading and three months later he returned to Elm Park. Mike was not an out and out scorer but was an intelligent and skilful forward and, on his return to Reading he was used in a deeper role as well as the occasional game in the defence. In December 1982 Mike broke a bone in his foot and this injury eventually forced his retirement from League football. In 1990 he returned to Elm Park to run the club's social club with his wife, and when Reading moved to the Madejski Stadium, Mike became Promotions Manager.

Reading Record: Lge 135(10)/36, FAC 9(1)/6, LC 10/1, FLGC 3/2, Total 157(11)/45
League Career Total: 324(17)/82

MIKE'S CLAIM TO FAME - All of Mike's five transfers to League clubs involved manager Maurice Evans who bought him three times and sold him twice.

KEARNS Oliver Anthony
b. Banbury 12.6.1956
Ht 6ft Wt 12st (80-81)
Career: Banbury U; READING (trial) February 1977, professional July 1977; Oxford U. August 1981; Walsall August 1982; Hereford U. June 1983; Wrexham December 1987; Kettering T; Rushden T; Worcester C; Rushden & Diamonds; Racing Club Warwick

One of many strikers discovered by Maurice Evans, Ollie was spotted at Banbury United and quickly made an impact with Reading, scoring on his full debut at Rotherham in May 1977. Despite missing the first three months through injury, Ollie still topped Reading's goalscorers in his first full season and was the second highest in 1978-79 when the club won the Fourth Division title. Despite his success, Ollie's awkward looking style did not win over all the Reading fans, while he was unhappy when he lost his place. He rejected the club's terms in 1980 and moved to Oxford, then on to Walsall where he teamed up with his older brother, Mick, the Eire international goalie.

Reading Record: Lge 75(11)/40, FAC 6(1)/2, LC 4(2)/1, Total 85(14)/43
League Career Total: 317(41)/127

KEELEY John Henry
b. Plaistow 27.7.1961
Ht 6ft 1 Wt 14st 2 (91-92)
Career: Southend U. from apprentice July 1979; Chelmsford C. 1984; Brighton August 1986; Oldham A. (£240,000) August 1990; Oxford U. (loan) November 1991; READING (loan) February 1992; Chester C. (loan) August 1992; Colchester U.(free) July 1993; Chelmsford C; Stockport C. March 1993; Peterborough U. January 1995, Bognor Regis T. 2000

A powerful keeper, John resurrected his career at Brighton where he was ever-present in their 1987-88 Third Division promotion season. His displays earned him a big money move to Oldham but he had failed to make their first team when he joined Reading on loan, taking over from another on loan keeper, Jim Leighton. John gave a series of consistent displays for Reading but he never got a run in Oldham's first team and left them having made just two appearances in three seasons.

Reading Record: Lge 6
League Career Total: 257

JOHN'S CLAIM TO FAME - His two appearances for them may have cost Oldham £120,000 each but John hardly enjoyed his stay in Lancashire. By the time he came to Reading his move to Oldham had produced no first team appearances, three different hand injuries, a sending off, broken ribs, two burglaries and a vandalised car while his team mates nicknamed him 'Lucky'!

KEETLEY Charles Frederick
b Derby 10.3.1906 d. 1979
Ht 5ft 9 1/2 Wt 12st (35-36)
Career: Alvaston & Boulton; Leeds U.1927; Bradford C. September 1934; READING June 1935

A prolific goalscoring inside left with Leeds, Charlie hit 108 goals in 160 games over seven seasons but a move to Bradford failed to see him maintain this rate. On joining Reading he scored twice in his first six games before injury restricted his appearances for the rest of the season. Released at the end of the season, Charlie retired from League football.

Reading Record: Lge 9/3, SSC 1, Total 10/3
League Career Total: 191/115

KELLY Patrick
b. Kircaldy 26.4.1978
Ht 6ft Wt 11st 7 (97-98)
Career: Celtic; Newcastle U. August 1997; READING (loan) 26 March 1998; Livingstone summer 1999

Paddy had been with Tommy Burns at Celtic and Newcastle and so when he became manager of Reading, Tommy made the classy Scottish Youth international defender one of his first signings, albeit on loan. They cut it close though - Paddy was still in Newcastle at 2.30 pm when he was told of Reading's interest and flew down to beat the 5 pm deadline by minutes. Burns regarded him as the best player in United's reserves but was unable to make the move permanent in the summer because Paddy wanted to move back to Scotland.

Reading Record: Lge 3

KEMP Raymond William
b. Bristol 18.1.1922 d. 1989
Ht 5ft 10 Wt 11st 7 (49-50)
Career: Grays A; READING amateur September 1949; Hendon

When Reading suffered an injury crisis with both regular keepers out over Christmas 1949, they were lucky to be able to call on Ray, an experienced amateur goalie.

He had won a string of representative honours playing for the Athenian and Corinthian League sides and London and performed ably in the three League games in which he appeared.

Reading Record: Lge 3

KEMPTON Arthur Richard
b. Rye, West Thurrock 1893 d. ?
Ht 5ft 10 Wt 12st 12 (21-22)
Career: Hastings St Leonards; Tuffnell Park; Arsenal; READING May 1921

Arthur had first come to Reading's attention when he played at Elm Park for the RAF at the end of the First World War. He joined Arsenal but, not having made any League appearances for them he finally joined Reading in 1921 as cover for goalie Syd Crawford. In November and December Arthur got two runs in Reading's goal but failed to impress enough to replace the popular Crawford and he was released at the end of his only season at Elm Park.

Reading Record: Lge 9, FAC 1, Total 10

KENNEDY Frederick 'Frank'
b. Bury 1902 d. Failsworth 11.1992
Ht 5ft 7 Wt 11st 2 (29-30)
Career: Rossendale U; Manchester U 1923; Everton 1924; Middlesbrough May 1927; READING (£500) May 1929; Oldham A. (£200) October 1930; Rossendale U; Northwich V; Racing Club de Paris; Blackburn R. 1933; Racing Club de Paris; Stockport C. 1937

A tricky inside forward, Frank made his League debut with Manchester United during 1923-24 before spending three seasons at Everton. Frank then moved on to Middlesbrough, where he became their penalty taker, and then on to Reading in 1929. Starting at inside right, Frank lost his place to Bill Baggett and was later tried on the left but despite finishing joint top scorer he was released and began a nomadic soccer career.

Reading Record: Lge 23/8, FAC 1, Total 24/8
League Career Total: 138/37

FRANK'S CLAIM TO FAME - Frank held the Royal Humane Society Certificate which was presented to him after he saved a woman from drowning.

KENNEDY James
b. Burradon 20.2.1897 d. 1988
Ht 5ft 8 1/2 Wt 11st 7 (25-26)
Career: Bedlington; Portsmouth 1921; READING (£100) July 1925

A lightning fast right winger, James won many honours as a sprinter during the War and while with Bedlington in the North Eastern League he combined football with a successful professional sprinting career. His four seasons at Portsmouth only produced 22 League appearances and then it wasn't until April 1926 that James got a run in Reading's first team. Although he didn't score he must have done something right because his six games produced 20 goals as Reading clinched the Third Division South title after a tight run in. Unfortunately, that wasn't enough to earn him another season at Elm Park and James' League career was over.

Reading Record: Lge 6
League Career Total: 28

KERR Andrew
b. Falkirk c. 1900 d. ?
Ht 5ft 8 1/2 Wt 11st 8 (25-26)
Career: Ardrossan Winton R; Luton T. 1923; READING May 1925; QPR March 1926

Andrew was spotted by Luton while playing in Scottish junior football and the lively centre forward got off to a flying start, scoring 20 goals in his first League season. A leaner period followed and so he moved to Reading in 1925 where he only managed three games, despite scoring on his debut and topping the reserves' goalscorers with 17.

Reading Record: Lge 3/1, FAC 1, Total 4/1
League Career Total: 73/26

KERR Dylan
b. Valetta, Malta 14.1.1967
Ht 5ft 9 Wt 11st 4 (96-97)
Career: Doncaster R; Sheffield Wed. from YTS August 1984; Arcadia Shepherds (South Africa); Leeds U. (free) February 1989; Doncaster R. (loan) August 1991; Blackpool (loan) December 1991; READING (£75,000) 15 July 1993; Crystal Palace (trial); Swansea C.(trial); Carlisle U. (trial) September 1996; Kilmarnock October 1996; Slough T. October 2000; Hamilton Acc. February 2001; Exeter C. summer 2001

An immensely popular player at all his clubs, Dylan was an attacking left back with a powerful long range shot that produced some spectacular goals. He built his reputation at Leeds where he was understudy to Tony Dorigo before moving to Reading where he missed just one game in their Division Two championship season, being voted Player of the Year and winning a PFA Divisional award. Dylan was a member of the side that won the 1995 Berks & Bucks Senior Cup but he suffered a bad injury on New Year's Day 1996 and fears over his fitness lead to him being released in the summer.

After several trials he joined Kilmarnock where he won the Scottish Cup in his first season, but injuries again plagued Dylan and he left Killie in June 2000. His move to Slough hit the headlines as each game involved a 900 mile round trip from his Troon home. It says much of Dylan's personality that, while recovering from injury, he would join Reading's fans at away games and led the cheering while he continued his membership of the Supporters' Club long after he left the club.

Reading Record: Lge 84(5)/5, FAC 2, LC 8(1), AMC 3(1), Total 97(7)/5
League Career Total: 109(13)/7

DYLAN'S CLAIM TO FAME - When Dylan scored his first Reading goal, at Plymouth in March 1994, he is thought to be the first player to use the now familiar celebration by covering his head with his shirt

KERR Peter
b. Paisley 25.9.1943
Ht 5ft 10 Wt 11st 7 (63-64)
Career: Third Lanark; READING (free) 20 May 1963; Port Elizabeth summer 1965; Guildford C. 1967; READING (trial) December 1967; Port Elizabeth January 1968; Cape Town C.

Following the collapse of Third Lanark, Peter joined Reading, along with David Grant, after a three year spell with the Scottish club. A marine engineer by trade, Peter went straight into Reading's first team, playing in all three inside forward positions, but in 1964-65 he had a run at left half. At the end of that season he was allowed to leave Reading so he could emigrate to South Africa where he joined Port Elizabeth, scoring a hat trick for them as they won the South African FA Cup. Peter came back to England in 1967 and had a trial with Reading again but soon returned to South Africa.

Reading Record: Lge 41/7, FAC 6/1, LC 3/1, Total 50/9

PETER'S CLAIM TO FAME - Peter was once responsible for putting the BBC off the air. He scored Reading's equalizer against First Division giants, Burnley, in a 1965 FA Cup-tie at Elm Park and the crowd noise was so loud as Reading pressed for the winner that the BBC had to abandon their live coverage for a while.

KING Andrew John
b. Thatcham 30.3.1970
Ht 6ft Wt 11st 7 (88-89)
Career: READING from YTS April 1988; S K Torhout summer 1989; Thatcham T; Fleet T.

Andy was recommended to Reading by club director and reporter, Brian Roach, and was signed professional after the club's youth team reached the fifth round of the FA Youth Cup in 1988. The young forward made his one League appearance five months later at Wigan, when he came on for the last 25 minutes in place of Steve Moran. At the end of that season he left for a spell in Belgium football and scored eight goals in his first nine games there.

Reading Record: Lge (1)

KING Barry
b. Chesterfield 30.3.1935
Ht 5ft 7 Wt 10st 6 (57-58)
Career: Norton Woodseats; Chelsea November 1957; READING 15 March 1958; Chelsea 28 June 1958: Cambridge C.

After a short spell at Chelsea, where he never got further than their reserves, Barry moved to Reading. Within a month he was making his debut at QPR on Reading's right wing, but was back in the reserves after four games and shortly after he left the club to go back to Chelsea, then non-League football.

Reading Record: Lge 3, SPFC 1, Total 4

KINSELL Thomas Henry 'Harry'
b. Cannock 3.5.21 d. 13.8.2000
Ht 5ft 11 1/2 Wt 13st 2 (50-51)
Career: West Bromwich Alb. from jnrs June 1938; Wartime guest for Grimsby, Mansfield, Middlesbrough, Southport & Blackpool; Bolton W. (£12,000) June 1949; READING (£3,500) 24 May 1950; West Ham U. (£5,000) 5 January 1951; Bedford T. July 1955

After trials for England Schools and winning an England U17 cap, Harry went on to gain several Wartime honours including three Wartime caps for England as well as helping Blackpool to the Football League North championship. After the War his forceful play at left back earned a club record transfer to Bolton, but Harry failed to settle and moved on to Reading a year later. An injury sustained early in a game against Brighton disrupted his career despite the fact that Reading went on to win 7-0 - a record for 10 men. Having failed to make the impact hoped for, despite his speedy, overlapping play, Harry moved to West Ham early in 1951 and saw a return to form making over 100 League appearances, many as captain.

Reading Record: Lge 12
League Career Total: 213/2

HARRY'S CLAIM TO FAME - Some contemporary reports stated that Harry was sent off on his England debut, against Wales. Although he was involved in 'a scuffle' he certainly was not dismissed and, despite the fact that this would have made Harry the first England player to be sent off, he was always at great pains to correct this sleight against his record.

KIRKMAN Gerald
b. Bolton 2nd qtr 1912
Ht 5ft 10 Wt 10st 9 (38-39)
Career: Bolton YMCA; Bolton W. from amateur 1933; READING 30 April 1936; New Brighton May 1938

Gerry made just one League appearance during his five years with Bolton but his move to Reading only saw him double that figure in two years at Elm Park. As well as his one League match, in a home defeat against Walsall in September 1936, Gerry also played in the first round of the Southern Section Cup - a competition Reading went on to win. Both of those games were at left half, and in 1938 Gerry moved to New Brighton where his career was ended by the War.

Reading Record: Lge 1, SSC 1, Total 2
League Career Total: 4

KIRKUP Brian Alexander
b. Ashington 16.4.1932
Ht 5ft 9 Wt 11st (56-57)
Career: Bedford T; READING 15 August 1955; Northampton T. July 1958; Aldershot November 1959; Dover July 1962

Brian's family moved south when he was nine and he was recommended to Reading by the brother of the club's trainer, Jimmy Wallbanks, signing initially on a two month trial after he completed his National Service.

The young centre forward was in the first team within a month and scored twice on his home debut, ending the season with 16 goals in 38 League games. First team games and goals were harder to come by after that and even though he topped the reserves' goalscorers in 1957-58, Brian moved to Northampton at the end of that season. He retired from League football when he claimed that, *'the linesmen began overtaking him'*!

Reading Record: Lge 55/19, FAC 2, SPFC 5, Total 62/19
League Career Total: 140/41

KIRKWOOD Ian
b. Edinburgh 29.11.1932
Ht 5ft 6 Wt 10st 12 (54-55)
Career: Wokingham T; READING from amateur 30 March 1953; East Fife; Arbroath; Montrose

After his release from the RAF, Ian joined Reading as a professional, having already made his League debut as an amateur a few weeks earlier. He had to wait 18 months before his next first team games and by that time he had moved from the left wing to inside forward. Despite topping the reserves scorers with 18 goals in 1954-55, Ian's first team chances were limited so he returned to Scotland to continue his career.

Reading Record: Lge 5/1

KIRKWOOD John Flemming
b. Falkirk 27.2.32
Ht 5ft 10 1/2 Wt 10st 12 (49-50)
Career: Blairhall Colliery; READING (£100) 16 December 1949; Dartford July 1955; Worcester C; Dartford 1962; Dover 1963

A blond, brave goalie who was understudy to George Marks, Joe McBride and then Willie Hall, John's first team chances were understandably limited but he never let Reading down when called upon. After five and a half years he moved to non-League football and in 1958-59 he recovered from a serious stomach injury to help Worcester City knock Liverpool out of the FA Cup.

Reading Record: Lge 31, FAC 1, Total 32

KNIGHT Brian Thomas Arthur
b. High Wycombe 14.11.1946
Ht 5ft 7 Wt 10st 8 (65-66)
Career: READING amateur June 1962, apprentice 1 July 1963, professional 14 November 1965; Crawley T. summer 1966; Guernsey; Wallingford T.

An industrious left winger/midfielder, Brian was a regular member of the Reading side that won the Football Combination Division Two title in 1965-66 but failed to make an impression in the first team. He did have the rather unusual experience of scoring his only goal in his final League game, during a 3-0 win over York in December 1965. After his spell with Reading, Brian ran a hotel in Guernsey for a time and played for the Guernsey side that won the 1978 Muratti Cup.

Reading Record: Lge 4/1

KNIGHT Keith
b. Cheltenham 16.2.1969
Ht 5ft 8 Wt 11st (90-91)
Career: Cheltenham T; READING (£7,000) 9 September 1988; Gloucester C (£5,000) October 1990; Veendam (Holland); Trowbridge; Cheltenham T; Worcester C. 2000

Keith won six U18 England Schools caps plus an U19 appearance, scoring four goals before joining Cheltenham in favour of playing rugby union for Moseley. After just 11 first team games for Cheltenham, Reading bought the young right winger for his potential, but he went virtually straight into the League side and scored on his debut. Only a troublesome hamstring injury restricted Keith's appearances that season but he failed to maintain his form and was tried at full back before going back to non-League football. He eventually returned to Cheltenham and helped them gain League status in 1998-99.

Reading Record: Lge 39(4)/8, FAC 7(1), LC 3, AMC 3/2, Total 52(5)/10

KNIGHT Peter Robert
b. Ilford 26.12.1937
Ht 5ft 8 Wt 10st 12 (64-65)
Career: Southend U. June 1958; Nottingham For. August 1959; Oxford U. July 1960; READING (£3,500) 6 November 1964; Guildford C. summer 1966

Capable of playing on either wing, Peter helped Oxford win the Southern League title in 1960-61 and then took them into the League a year later. After his transfer to Reading he started on the right wing but a switch to the left did not help him retain his first team place. Most of 1965-66 was spent in the reserves, even though, at just £3,500, he was the most expensive player at Elm Park for most of that season. Peter did play a major part in the club's Football Combination promotion that season and followed it up with another success the next, when his new club, Guildford City, won the Southern League Cup in 1967.

Reading Record: Lge 26/3, FAC 3, LC 3, Total 32/3
League Career Total: 124/15

KNOX William
b. Old Cumnock 2.5.1904 d. ?
Ht 5ft 8 Wt 10st 6 (27-28)
Career: Kilbrachan A; Dundee; St Mirren; Third Lanark; READING (free) June 1927; Norwich C. 1929; Carlisle U 1930

A fast and clever right winger, Bill came from a footballing family - his uncle, Peter Ellis, was a Scottish international while his cousin played for Burnley and his father for Everton. He joined Reading after an extensive career in Scotland but, apart from a three match run in November 1927, Bill's only other League appearance was in the last game of that season.

Reading Record: Lge 4
League Career Total: 7

KROMHEER Elroy Patrick
b. Amsterdam 15.1.1970
Ht 6ft 4 Wt 12st 11 (98-99)
Career: Volendam; Motherwell July 1992; Volendam January 1994; FC Zwolle; READING (£150,000) 7 August 1998; FC Nuremberg 1999

A giant Dutch central defender, Elroy was occasionally mistaken for Dennis Bergkamp although, it must be said, never on the pitch! He had played for the Dutch U21s alongside the likes of Overmars and Van Hooijdonk but in 1992 Elroy faced a tough decision. He was in line for selection for the Barcelona Olympics at Judo but withdrew in the hope he could play for the U21s in the football competition. Unfortunately, Elroy missed out completely on the Olympics when Holland failed to qualify. Elroy played 14 games for Motherwell during an 18 month spell in Scotland but returned to Volendam and he reached the Dutch Cup final with them. After impressing Tommy Burns in a pre-season friendly, Elroy moved to Reading and went straight into their first team. Although dominant in the air, Elroy was less mobile on the ground and after a long spell out of the first team his contract was cancelled by mutual agreement.

Reading Record: Lge 11, LC 1, Total 12

LACEY William
b. Tynemouth 17.11.1931 d. Reading 5.1988
Ht 5ft 10 Wt 13st (60-61)
Career: Sheffield U. amateur; Middlesbrough May 1952; Aldershot (£600) March 1953; READING (£500) 24 July 1959, asst. trainer 1 July 1963

Bill was a powerful centre forward who, as an ex-trawlerman, was nicknamed 'Sailor'.

Having failed to make Boro's first team, Bill began his League career with Aldershot and, after an early dispute with their board, he became a popular player who scored over 70 goals for them and was club captain for a time. Bill became equally popular at Reading, scoring regularly and creating chances for others with his physical strength and clever play. Unfortunately, Bill was taken ill in October 1962 and was diagnosed as having a heart problem. Although this led to his playing retirement, Bill became Reading's assistant trainer and then assistant manager up to 1965 when he worked at the Reading Co-op until his premature death at only 56.

Reading Record: Lge 90/40, FAC 6/4, LC 2/2, Total 98/46
League Career Total: 300/99

LAMBERT Christopher **James**
b. Henley 14.9.1973
Ht 5ft 7 Wt 10st 4 (96-97)
Career: READING from amateur 3 July 1992; Walsall (loan) October 1998; Checkendon March 1999; Watford (trial) April 1999; Oxford U. September 1999; Port Vale (trial) 2000; Slough T. August 2000

On his day James could be a sensational player with great dribbling skills and vision but lacked consistency in parts of his career. He burst onto the scene in October 1992 and a brilliant display in a televised game for Reading against Birmingham led immediately to a three day training session with Arsene Wenger's AS Monaco, and then a trial at Kenny Dalglish's Blackburn. More an old fashioned left winger than a midfielder, it wasn't until 1995-96 that James made more starts than substitute appearances and, apart from 1997-98, he was never a first team regular. On form he could score some spectacular goals and one against Huddersfield in November 1995 earned him a place in the Football League squad that played the Italian Serie B, while another televised game saw him beat the entire Nottingham Forest defence to score a wonderful goal. When Tommy Burns took over he made it clear that James was not part of his plans and his contract was eventually paid up in March 1999.

Reading Record: Lge 77(48)/16, FAC 9(2)/1, LC 8(3)/1, AMC 2(3)/1, Total 96(56)/19
League Career Total: 89(55)/18

JAMES' CLAIM TO FAME - In October 1999 James scored the Manor Ground's fastest ever goal when he netted for Oxford against Colchester after only 17 seconds.

LAMBLE John
b. Reading 10.11.1948
Ht 5ft 8 Wt 10st 12 (67-68)
Career: READING apprentice 7 August 1966, professional 17 November 1966; Guildford C. summer 1968; Cork Hibs

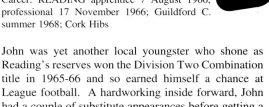

John was yet another local youngster who shone as Reading's reserves won the Division Two Combination title in 1965-66 and so earned himself a chance at League football. A hardworking inside forward, John had a couple of substitute appearances before getting a three match run in the first team during February 1968. Unfortunately for John, he did not do enough to impress manager Roy Bentley and was given a free at the end of the season.

Reading Record: Lge 3(2), FAC (1), Total 3(3)

LANE (LOHN) **William** Henry Charles
b. Tottenham 23.10.1904 d. Chelmsford 10.11.1985
Ht: 5ft 9 1/2 Wt 11st 2 (28-29)
Career: London City Mission; Gnome A; Park Avondale; Barnet; Northfleet; Tottenham H. from amateur May 1924; Leicester C. November 1926; READING (£490) May 1928; Brentford (player exchange) June 1929; Watford (£1,000) May 1932; Bristol C. (£200) January 1936; Clapton O. July 1937; Gravesend summer 1938; Brentford asst. manager; Wartime guest for Watford, Reading & Brighton; Guildford C. manager 1946; Brighton manager April 1950; Gravesend manager December 1961; Arsenal scout 1963; QPR scout 1968; Brighton scout 1970

Billy's League career took a few seasons before he became one of the most feared goalscorers in the Third Division and by the time he joined Reading he had scored just nine goals in 30 games spread over five seasons. His form at Elm Park did nothing to suggest a change was imminent, even though he scored on his debut, and with his six games producing five defeats he was exchanged for Brentford's Ted Douglas. For the next five seasons Billy could not stop scoring, netting 141 League goals for first Brentford, then Watford. During the War, Billy once turned out for Reading when the team was a man short at Watford. After the War he embarked on a long managerial career where he impressed his teetotal, Christian beliefs on his players with strict discipline and stringent punishments. Billy spent 11 years in charge at Brighton, resigning in May 1961 because of the abolition of the maximum wage which he described as the most retrograde step in football's history.

Reading Record: Lge 6/2, Wartime 1, Total 7/2
League Career Total: 298/170

BILLY'S CLAIM TO FAME - Billy is one of several players who claim to have scored the League's fastest hat trick - his trio coming in three minutes for Watford against Clapton Orient in December 1933.

LAWRENCE David

b. Poole 15.5.1933
Ht 5ft 10 Wt 11st (57-58)
Career: Poole T. amateur March 1953; Bristol R. June 1956;
READING (free)12 June 1957; Poole T.   August 1959;
Trowbridge T. May 1961

A robust tackling full back, David made all his appearances for Bristol Rovers at left back yet when he moved to Reading all but one of his 28 games were on the right. During his first season at Elm Park, David was ever-present from the end of August until Christmas but from then on he was kept out of the right back spot by Eddie McLaren and went into non-League football before commencing a career in the police.

Reading: Lge 23, FAC 2, SPFC 3, Total 28
League Career Total: 28

LAWSON Herbert Thomas

b. Sunderland 1st qtr 1913
Ht 5ft 7 Wt 11st 2 (35-36)
Career: READING (trial) July 1934, permanent August 1934;
Bournemouth (player exchange) November 1934; Barrow 1935; Frickley Colliery 1937

A strong running centre forward, Herbert made his League debut with Reading when Frank Newton was out injured and scored in his second game, an away win at Northampton.   No more League chances followed and within three months he was on his way as part of the deal that saw Tommy Tait move from Bournemouth.

Reading Record: Lge 2/1, SSC 1, Total 3/1
League Career Total: 29/10

LAYTON William Herbert

b. Shirley 13.1.1915 d. Colchester 2.1984
Ht 5ft 10 1/2 Wt 10st 9 (38-39)
Career: Shirley T; READING March 1937; Bradford PA (£6,000) February 1947; Colchester U. August 1949; Harwich & Parkstone 1951

Spotted playing in the Midlands, Bill had a terrific left foot shot and was likened to the legendary Charles Buchan when he joined Reading. Once he got in the first team Bill made the inside left shirt his own for 1937-38 and was part of the team that won the Southern Section Cup in 1938.   Bill spent more time in the reserves next season but six goals against Clapton Orient reserves earned him a recall. Like many, the War robbed him of some of his best years, but he helped Reading win the London War Cup in 1941, while his performances for the RAF brought him a place as reserve for England in 1945.

During the War Bill had switched to left half and his form back in the League was such that Bradford paid Reading a club record for his services in 1947.   In 1949 Bill moved to Colchester and they won the Southern League Cup in his first season and were then elected into the League. This meant that United then had to pay a fee to Bradford a year after his transfer as the Yorkshire club had retained Bill's League registration.

Reading Record: Lge 51/17, FAC 4/1, SSC 5/1, Wartime 171/35, Total 231/54
League Career Total: 105/22

LEACH Brian Ernest

b. Reading 20.7.1932
Ht 5ft 9 Wt 10st 10 (51-52)
Career: Coley Boys Club; READING groundstaff 7 February 1950, professional 15 November 1950; Headington U. July 1957; Tunbridge Wells 1958; Clacton T. 1959; Henley T.; Mapledurham

Spotted by Gilbert Glidden and coached by another Reading favourite, Tony MacPhee, Brian began his career as a forward but developed into a fine left half. At one stage he almost joined Burnley but stayed at Reading for seven years, scoring his only goal in his final season when he had moved back to inside left. Brian left Reading in 1957 and played for several non-League clubs, including Clacton with whom he won the Southern League Division One title in 1959-60.

Reading Record: Lge 108/1, FAC 7, SPFC 3, Total 118/1

LEE David John

b. Kingswood 26.11.1969
Ht 6ft 3 Wt 13st 12 (91-92)
Career: Chelsea from trainee July 1988; READING (loan) 30 January 1992; Plymouth Arg. (loan) March 1992; Portsmouth (loan) August 1994; Sheffield U. (loan) December 1997; Bristol C. (trial) December 1998; Bristol R (free) December 1998; Crystal Palace October 1999; Colchester U; Exeter C. February 2000; Gillingham April 2000; Parramatta Power (Australia) 2000

During his 10 years at Chelsea, David was used mainly as a stand-in at centre half or midfield but in November 1995 he played so well at sweeper that Ruud Gullit had to move to midfield. He helped Chelsea win the Second Division title in 1988-89, the 1998 League Cup and he won 10 U21 caps plus a youth cap. While at Chelsea, David was loaned out four times and the first was to Reading. In a sensational spell he began by scoring for both sides at Peterborough. In all he scored five goals for Reading in as many games, despite playing at centre half, and his play inspired a local reporter to describe him as *'the nearest thing to Superman'*. In 1998 David moved to Bristol Rovers, the club he had supported as a boy, but stayed there under a year.

Reading Record: Lge 5/5
League Career Total: 155(35)/18

LEGG Andrew

b. Neath 28.7.1966
Ht 5ft 8 Wt 10st 7 (97-98)
Career: Briton Ferry; Swansea C. August 1988; Notts Co. (£275,000) July 1993; Birmingham C February 1996; Ipswich T. (loan) November 1997; READING (£75,000) 20 February 1998; Peterborough U.(loan) October 1998; Cardiff C.(free) 16 December 1998

Andy developed into a versatile player with Swansea who could play in any position on the left side of the pitch. With them he won the Welsh Cup in 1989 and 1991 and during the subsequent Cup Winners Cup campaign, Andy scored against AS Monaco. A big money move to Notts County was less successful but he played his part in their 1995 Anglo Italian Cup triumph, before moving on to Birmingham. Again Andy was unable to command a regular first team place but worse was to follow when he joined Reading. Although he performed consistently at left back for Reading, Andy's arrival coincided with the club's loss of form that lead to a change of manager and relegation. Andy's record for Reading saw him lose 11 of his 12 League games, score an unlucky own goal and get sent off. It soon became clear that he did not feature in Tommy Burns' plans and, along with several others, Andy found himself isolated by his new manager until he joined Cardiff. There, Andy's fortunes changed as Cardiff won the Division Three title and he gained his fifth Welsh cap.

Reading Record: Lge 12, LC 1, Total 13
League Career Total: 393(32)/51 +

ANDY'S CLAIM TO FAME - Andy possesses one of the longest throws in football and he was the 'World Record holder' with a throw of 44.54 metres that earned him an entry into the 1995 Guinness Book of Records.

LEIGHTON James

b. Johnstone 24.7.1958
Ht 6ft 1 Wt 11st 9 (91-92)
Career: Dalry Thistle; Aberdeen 1976; Derondale (loan) 1977; Manchester U. 1988; Arsenal (loan) March 1991; READING (loan) November 1991; Dundee (£200,000) February 1992; Sheffield U. (loan) 1993; Hibernians summer 1993; Aberdeen August 1997; Scotland goalkeeping coach

One of the most honoured goalkeepers in Scottish football, Jim won two championships, four Cups, a League Cup, the 1983 European Cup Winners Cup and the Super Cup with Aberdeen. His move to Manchester United saw him maintain his reputation as one of the top keepers until he was blamed for United's 3-3 draw in the 1990 FA Cup final and lost his place. By November 1991 he was their third choice keeper until his former Aberdeen team mate, Mark McGhee, brought him to Reading on loan. His fine performances, that included six clean sheets in 11 games, earned him a transfer to Dundee. Jim regained his place as Scotland's number one keeper and he ended his international career with 91 caps, having represented his country in four World Cups, and was honoured with an MBE in the 1998 New Year's lists. Unfortunately, his illustrious career, that saw him play 839 club games, came to a sad end when he broke his jaw two minutes into his last game - Aberdeen's Scottish Cup Final in May 2000.

Reading Record: Lge 8, FAC 3, Total 11
League Career Total: 81

LEMON Paul Andrew

b. Middlesbrough 3.6.1966
Ht 5ft 10 Wt 11st 11 (89-90)
Career: Sunderland from apprentice May 1984; Carlisle U.(loan) December 1984; Walsall (loan) November 1989; READING (loan) December 1989; Chesterfield September 1990

A former schools international, Paul spent over six years with Sunderland during which time he made more than 100 League appearances and was also loaned out three times. The last of these spells was at Reading where he played on the right wing with a view to a permanent move but the clubs couldn't agree a fee. Strangely, a year earlier, the clubs had agreed a fee, but Paul was put off by house prices in the South on that occasion.

Reading Record: Lge 3
League Career Total: 178(21)/24

LENARDUZZI Robert Italo

b. Vancouver 1.5.1955
Ht 5ft 11 Wt 11st 7 (73-74)
Career: Vancouver Spartans; READING apprentice November 1970, professional 14 May 1973; Vancouver Whitecaps (£1,500) April 1976; Vancouver 49ers 1987; Canada national coach

Bob was spotted while Reading manager, Jack Mansell, was coaching in Canada, and despite work permit problems he played regularly for the youth and reserve teams. Mature beyond his years, Bob was selected to play for Canada at 17 and although injury delayed his international debut for a year he still became Canada's youngest, and Reading's first post War international. A natural left footer , Bob was comfortable wherever he played and was voted best full back in the Fourth Division in 1974-75. He was destined for a long and successful career with Reading but became homesick and was allowed to return to Canada in April 1976.

He became a legend in his home country, playing 47 times for Canada, often alongside his brothers Danny and Sam, and appeared in the 1984 World Cup finals. With Vancouver Whitecaps, Bob made a record 312 NASL appearances that included their first and last game in this League, and played in all 11 positions, being voted the North American Player of the Year in 1978. Bob became player-coach of Vancouver 49ers in 1987 and in his first season guided them to the Canadian championship. He later became manager-coach of the national side. Bob is so popular in Vancouver that he was once asked to run for parliament!

Reading Record: Lge 63(4)/2, FAC 2, LC 1 (1), Total 66(5)/2

BOB'S CLAIM TO FAME - When Bob's Canada played USA in World Cup qualifiers in 1976, the home game was the first World Cup game to be played on plastic while the away leg was the first to be played indoors. But it was Bob's Canadian debut that hit the British headlines - after he had played in the friendly against Poland, the 18 year old was contacted by Sir Alf Ramsey for background on England's upcoming World Cup opponents.

LEWIS Alan Trevor

b. Oxford 19.8.1954
Ht 5ft 8 Wt 10st 12 (79-80)
Career: Derby Co. from apprentice May 1972; Peterborough U.(loan); Brighton (loan) January 1975, permanent (£7,000) March 1975; Sheffield W. (loan); READING (free) 17 July 1977; Witney T. July 1982

Although he only made two first team appearances for Derby, Alan achieved success with England Youth with whom he won the World Youth Cup in 1972 and 1973. After a loan spell at Peterborough, where he helped them win the Fourth Division title in 1973-74, he followed Brian Clough to Brighton. Two years later Alan moved to Reading but, having established himself at left back, he was then converted to an impressive left sided midfielder and it was in this position that he played an influential role in Reading's 1978-79 Fourth Division championship. After that he was a less regular first teamer and in his final season with Reading he reverted to left back.

Reading Record: Lge 145(4)/5, FAC 9/1, LC 13/1, FLGC 2, Total 169(4)/7
League Career Total: 160(4)/6

LEWIS John 'Jack'

b. Walsall 26.8.1919
Ht 5ft 11 Wt 12st 4 (51-52)
Career: West Bromwich Alb. amateur; Crystal Palace July 1938; Bournemouth (£7,500) November 1949; READING (£1,500) 13 July 1951; Kettering T. summer 1953; Worcester C. coach 1954 to December 1962

Jack made just one League appearance for Palace before War broke out but was a regular in their first team after the hostilities, playing in their 10-2 defeat at Reading, until he joined Bournemouth. Having scored just once in 45 games, a move to Reading saw a dramatic change for Jack. With seven games to go of the 1951-52 season, he had equalled Arthur Grimsdell's 30 year record for League goals by a half back. Jack then hit a barren spell until Reading were awarded a penalty in the second half of their final game. Jack had already scored eight spot kicks that season and rumour has it that he told the goalie, his former team mate from Bournemouth, exactly where he was going to hit the kick. It did the keeper no good and Jack's 15th goal gave him the record and a bottle of champagne from a delighted fan. Strangely, the goals dried up again and Jack had to wait until the last game of the next season before he scored again, hitting two penalties in what was his last League match. Jack went on to run a pub in the Birmingham area and in 1986 he hosted a celebration stop for Reading fans after the club clinched promotion at Darlington.

Reading Record: Lge 74/17, FAC 7, Total 81/17
League Career Total: 243/23

LEWORTHY David John

b. Portsmouth 22.10.1962
Ht 5ft 8. Wt 12st 7 (89-90)
Career: Portsmouth from apprentice September 1980; Fareham T summer 1982; Tottenham H. (£51,000) August 1984; Oxford U.(£165,000) December 1985; Shrewsbury (loan) October 1987; READING (free) July 1989; Colchester U. (loan) March 1991; Farnborough January 1992; Dover; Rushden & Diamonds 1996; Kingstonians 1997; Havant & Waterlooville summer 2000

A prolific non-League goalscorer, David cost Spurs a Southern League record fee, but apart from a win in the London Five a Side tournament he had little success with them. Even so Spurs were able to treble their fee when David moved to Oxford where he again proved more successful indoors by winning the Guinness Sixes Cup. After 25 starts in four years, David joined Reading but still could not command a regular first team place, even though he scored 24 goals in 26 reserve games in his first season. Eventually he returned to non-League football, where he set a record for a fee paid between two Southern League clubs when he moved to Dover. He won several non-League representative honours plus FA Trophy winners medals with Kingstonian in 1999 and 2000.

Reading Record: Lge 23(21)/7, FAC (2), LC 2(1), AMC 2(3)/1, Total 27(27)/8
League Career Total: 62(37)/21

LIDDLE James Sigsworth

b. Felling 7.1912 d. Basingstoke 7.10.1994
Ht 5ft 7 1/2 Wt 10st 6 (35-36)
Career: West Stanley; Middlesbrough; READING (£50) April 1932; Crystal Palace June 1937

Jimmy was more direct than most Thirties wingers and this brought him a regular flow of goals with Reading. He scored a hat trick on his League debut for the club against Bournemouth in October 1932, but lost his place, which proved typical for Jimmy who rarely got a run in the first team. Despite this he ended with 41 goals from 76 games on Reading's right wing before retiring after a short spell with Crystal Palace.

Reading Record: Lge 67/35, FAC 9/6, SSC 3, Total 79/41
League Career Total: 80/36

LINDSAY Thomas

b. Paisley 11.3.1903 d. Leyland 25.1.1979
Ht 5ft 6 1/2 Wt 11st 4 (27-28)
Career: Ardeer Thistle; Kilmarnock September 1924; Alloa A. June 1926; READING July 1927; Wigan Bor. December 1931; Rochdale June 1929; Watford September 1930; New Brighton July 1931; Southport November 1931; Chester December 1931; Prescott Cables February 1932; Wrexham July 1933; Leyton Motors April 1934

'Jock' was a goalscoring left winger who attracted Reading's attention after he hit 20 goals for Alloa in 1926-27. He was a terrier of a player whose crosses were described as ' a model of accuracy' but, apart from a 10 match run around Christmas that produced three goals for him, Jock was mainly a reserve player at Reading. This trend continued for most of his career and he rarely spent more than a year at any of his future clubs.

Reading Record: Lge 11/3, FAC 2, Total 13/3
League Career Total: 56/7

LISBIE Kevin Anthony

b. Hackney 17.10.1978
Ht 5ft 8 Wt 10st 12 (99-00)
Career: Charlton A. from apprentice May 1996; Gillingham (loan) March 1999; READING (loan) 26 November 1999; QPR (loan) December 2000)

A quick, ball playing former youth international striker, Kevin was used mainly as substitute at Charlton but a promising loan spell at Gillingham that produced four goals in four starts ended when he ruptured his knee ligaments. Out for eight months, Kevin was loaned to Reading to regain match fitness, but after a couple of games he suffered a recurrence of the injury. Fortunately, he recovered to play at the start of Charlton's 2000-01 Premiership campaign.

Reading Record: Lge 1(1)
League Career Total: 16(56)/6 +

LITTLEHALES Harold

b. Burslem 26 August 1901 d. Wrexham 24.5.1989
Ht 5ft 7 1/2 Wt 11st (32-33)
Career: Goldenhill W; Rudyard; Port Vale; READING August 1921; Tranmere R. summer 1923; Wrexham 1932

Capable of playing in any forward position, Harold impressed Reading during a pre-season friendly and made his League debut at centre forward but was also tried on the right wing. He scored one goal but his other five games failed to produce any for the club, and at the end of the season he moved to Tranmere. Harold spent nine seasons with them, scoring over 50 goals in 170 plus first team games.

Reading Record: Lge 6/1
League Career Total: 174/50

LIVINGSTONE William Rennison

b. Greenock 8.2.1929
Ht 6ft 1 1/2 Wt 13st 8 (53-54)
Career: Ardeer Rec; READING (£500) 9 April 1949; Chelsea (£2,000) June 1955; Brentford July 1959

Reading signed Bill from Scottish junior football in the face of fierce competition from several other clubs. He came as a defender but his first games in the League were at centre forward, scoring on his debut. His career was interrupted by his National Service when he represented the RAF several times, then, back in Reading, Bill suffered a further setback when he missed most of 1952-53 through a serious illness. He recovered to become the club's regular right back for much of the next season, and in 1955 Bill moved to Chelsea to rejoin Ted Drake, the manager who had signed him for Reading. After retiring from football, Bill had a spell running Reading's ten-pin bowling centre during the craze for that sport in the Sixties.

Reading Record: Lge 49/2, FAC 3, Total 52/2
League Career Total: 88/2

LOCKHEAD Matthew
b. Beith 1885 d. ?
Ht 5ft 9 Wt 11st 6 (21-22)
Career: Bath C; Swindon T; READING May 1921

When Matt eventually made his League debut, at centre half for Reading at Northampton in September 1921, he was 36 and only eight other players have ever made their League debut at an older age. Initially released at the end of that season, Matt rejoined Reading in November 1922 and added a cup appearance and another five League games, but he was never on the winning side and his seven games included three defeats by Northampton.

Reading Record: Lge 6, FAC 1, Total 7

LOFTY James Kenneth
b. Farnham Royal 5.12.1945
Ht 5ft 9 Wt 10st 9 (63-64)
Career: READING amateur January 1962, professional 1 May 1963; Birmingham C. July 1964

Jim came through the youth ranks at Reading and played for England Youth but, although he played the first game of 1963-64 on the left wing, he only got one more chance in the League. Released in 1964, he joined Birmingham but failed to add to his League total.

Reading Record: Lge 2

LONG Trevor George
b. Smethick 1.7.1931
Ht 5ft 8 Wt 10st 8 (55-56)
Career: Mitchell & Butlers; Wolverhampton W. December 1950; Gillingham July 1952; READING 6 July 1955; Yeovil July 1956

After starting his career as a wing half, Trevor was converted to a right winger, with an eye for goal by the time he came to Reading. He made his League debut with Gillingham but enjoyed his best scoring spell at Reading where he scored five goals in September 1955. Shortly after Trevor lost his place and never added to his goal count at Elm Park.

Reading Record: Lge 12/5, FAC 1, Total 13/5
League Career Total: 79/20

LOVELL Stuart Andrew
b. Sydney 9.1.1972
Ht 5ft 10 Wt 11st (96-97)
Career: Wokingham T; READING YTS 1988, professional 13 July 1990; Hibernian summer 1998; Livingston summer 2001

Despite being born on the other side of the world, Stuart was always regarded as a local hero by Reading fans. Brought up in the town, Stuart was attached to the club's Centre of Excellence from 11, after he had scored a record 57 goals for Reading Primary Schools. As an apprentice he cleaned Trevor Senior's boots but still had time to be voted Young Player of the Year in 1989-90, before scoring the winner on his Elm Park debut, against Fulham in December 1990. The likeable, hard working striker quickly built up a rapport with the Reading fans who picked up on his club nickname and the chant of 'Archie, Archie' was one of the features of Elm Park through the Nineties. Unable to command a regular place, Stuart almost joined Wycombe in March 1993, but a burst of six goals saw the start of a formidable partnership with Jimmy Quinn. Between them they scored 62 goals, 22 from Stuart, as Reading won the Division Two title the following season. Stuart was top scorer as Reading made it to the play-off finals, but the season ended on a sad note when Stuart missed a penalty in the final that would have put Reading 3-0 up before half time in the game, only to eventually lose 4-3. Although the miss haunted Stuart for some time, his popularity with the Reading fans never waned and their vocal demand for 'Archie' when the next penalty was awarded was a memorable moment.

Often used in a deeper role, Stuart was a less frequent scorer but he increased his cult status when he netted two injury time goals against arch-rivals, Wolves, in a 2-1 win that secured Division One football in 1996-97. A knee ligament injury kept him out for much of the next season but he played in the final game at Elm Park, which also proved to be his last for Reading. Stuart moved to Hibs and helped them regain their Premier League place in his first season while he made his debut for Australia, v Kuwait, in October 2000. Off the pitch, Stuart played in a rock band and wrote a column in the local press but will always be remembered as one of Reading's most popular players.

Reading Record: Lge 177(50)/58, FAC 7(9)/2, LC 13/5, AMC 4 (3), Play-offs 3/2, Total 204(62)/67

McBRIDE John

b. Kilsyth 31.12.1923
Ht 5ft 10 1/2 Wt 12st 2 (49-50)
Career: Third Lanark; READING (£500) 15 March 1948; Shrewsbury T. (£850) 16 January 1953; Kidderminster H. July 1957; National Sporting Club of Cairo coach 1961

Three representative games for the Army during 1947-48 led to John being spotted by Ted Drake who signed him from Third Lanark upon the goalie's release from the Army. John went straight into Reading's first team but faced a constant battle with George Marks for the keeper's jersey from then on. This competition between two fine goalkeepers meant that Reading enjoyed a high standard between the posts during that spell. A feature of John's game was his powerful punched clearances and his habit of spitting on his hands when about to face action.

Reading Record: Lge 100 FAC 6, Total 106
League Career Total: 178

McCAIG Alexander Reid

b. Larbert 18.10.1895 d. ?
Ht 5ft 7 Wt 11st 10 (22-23)
Career: Lambert Central; Stenhousemuir; Falkirk; Alloa A; Stenhousemuir; Coventry C; READING (£50) June 1922; Cowdenbeath summer 1923; Stenhousemuir; St Bernard's; Stenhousemuir

Reading had tried to sign Alex from Stenhousemuir in 1920, eventually getting the inside forward from Coventry two years later. 'A veritable demon' he started his only season at Elm Park as centre forward but played the majority of his Reading first team games at inside left during two spells, in December and April. Reading's need for more goals resulted in Alex being released at the end of 1922-23 so he returned to Scotland, where he completed four separate spells with Stenhousemuir.

Reading Record: Lge 16/2
League Career Total: 26/4

McCALL Anthony Edward

b. Bucklebury 15.1.1936
Ht 5ft 5 Wt 9st 11 (53-54)
Career: READING groundstaff September 1952, professional 9 May 1953; Headington U. summer 1957

A local youngster, Tony was a nippy winger who made his League debut for Reading in the last match of 1955/56 at Coventry. With Bobby Campbell and Jimmy Wheeler occupying the wing spots at Elm Park, Tony's first team chances were restricted so he moved to Headington United.

Reading Record: Lge 8/1

McCANCE Darren

b. Consett 13.9.1973
Ht 6ft 0 Wt 10st 12 (92-93)
Career: READING from YTS July 1992; Newbury T. March 1994; Abingdon T. 1995

Darren progressed through Reading's youth teams to make his League debut in the centre of the defence at Mansfield in February 1993. A loan spell with Newbury proved disastrous as Darren sustained a broken leg and he made just one more first team appearance after that. He was released, but, proving he held no grudges against Newbury, Darren joined the Berkshire non-League club on a permanent basis.

Reading Record: Lge 1 AMC 1, Total 2

DARREN'S CLAIM TO FAME - In March 1992 Darren was a member of the Reading team that won the town's annual Shrove Tuesday Pancake Race!

McCARTHY Kenneth

b. Merthyr Tydfil 2nd qtr 1918
Ht 5ft 8 1/2 Wt 10st 8 (38/39)
Career: Chester; Wolverhampton W. 1938; Bangor C; READING 24 August 1938, Aberaman, Barry T.

Having made one League appearance with Chester, Ken joined Reading after a short spell at Wolves. He found first team chances equally difficult to come by at Reading and it wasn't until the end of 1938/39 that Ken was given a short run in the League when he was tried in both inside forward positions. Although that was the end of his League career, Ken played a handful of games for Reading during the first two War seasons.

Reading Record: Lge 3 SSC 1, Wartime 4, Total 8
League Career Total: 4

McCARTNEY Richard

b. c.1940
Ht 5ft 9 Wt 11st (58-59)
Career: READING groundstaff 1953; West Brom Alb. 1954, READING (trial) July 1958, permanent September 1958

For the 1958-59 season Dick was the centre forward for Reading's reserve side and finished second highest scorer in that season in his second spell with the club. He had just signed after a two month trial when his one first team chance came, playing in Reading's Southern Professional Floodlit Cup defeat at Crystal Palace.

Reading Record: SPFC 1

McCONNELL William Henry

b. Corbolis 2.9.1901 d. Slough 1974
Ht 5ft 10 Wt 12st 3 (27-28)
Career: Slough YMCA; Slough T; Arsenal (trial); Charlton A.(trial); READING May 1924

One of Reading's greatest players, Billy's family moved to Slough from Ireland when he was four and by 16 he was in Slough's first team, helping them win the Berks & Bucks Cup. After joining Reading, Billy was virtually ever-present at left back during the club's golden era in the mid-Twenties, when they won the Third Division South title and then reached the FA Cup semi-finals. His form for Reading won him a number of representative honours including playing for the Football League and in a game for the Professionals of the South against their amateur equivalents, which was used to try out the eventual change to the off side law. Billy was also selected for 10 consecutive Irish internationals but injury and club requirements restricted him to eight caps. Even so, Billy was to be the most capped Reading player for the next 60 years.

A finely built player who 'used his physical strength to the limit', Billy was sent off during Reading's stormy FA Cup-tie against Manchester United in 1927 but three months later he scored his only goal for the club - against the Second Division champions elect, Middlesbrough. Unfortunately, in scoring that goal Billy sustained an ankle injury that was to eventually end his playing career and trouble him for the rest of his life. He recovered from the initial injury, but he suffered a recurrence at Barnsley a year later and never played again. Billy remained in Reading, running a local pub while qualifying as a League linesman. During the War he refereed several games at Elm Park, as well as playing cricket for Berkshire and later ran a newsagents in Slough.

Reading Record: Lge 142/1, FAC 20, Total 162/1

McCROHAN Frederick Alan T

b. Reading 11.6.1921 d. Reading 12.1990
Ht 5ft 7 Wt 10st 10 (45-46)
Career: READING amateur 1945

Alan was a popular local player who helped out Reading during the final season of War-time football. He was a regular on the club's left wing between October 1945 and January 1946, scoring three times as well as playing in Reading's two FA Cup-ties against Aldershot during the only season that the competition was staged on a home and away basis. Although Alan never got a professional contract with Reading he did work at Elm Park, providing clerical assistance to Fred May, the club secretary. Some 12 years after his Reading appearances, Alan scored a hat trick for Reading Railways as they reached the semis of the British Rail (Western) Cup.

Reading Record: Wartime 16/3, FAC 2, Total 18/3

McCROHAN Roy

b. Reading 22.9.1930
Ht 5ft 10 1/2 Wt 10st 10 (50/51)
Career: READING from jnrs 17 January 1949; Norwich C. (player exchange) 5 July 1951; Colchester U. September 1962; Bristol R.(£400) August 1964; Crawley T. player-coach summer 1966; Fulham coach July 1968; Aldershot trainer-coach; Ipswich T. coach; Luton T coach 1972

National Service interrupted Roy's professional career at Reading and, although he played for the RAF during that time, he only made four League appearances before being exchanged for Norwich's Les Owens. At Norwich, Roy developed into a hard working, versatile player with a distinctive long striding style that earned him 426 first team appearances, mainly at wing half. He helped them win promotion to the Second Division in 1960, the League Cup in 1962, and to a dramatic FA Cup run to the semis in 1959. Roy also played for the Third Division South side against the North in October 1957. After his playing career was over he became a successful coach and was tipped as a possible successor to Charlie Hurley as Reading manager before eventually emigrating to the States to coach youngsters in Florida.

Reading Record: Lge 4/1
League Career Total: 474/27

MacDONALD David Hugh

b. Dublin 2.1.1971
Ht 5ft 11 Wt 11st 7 (92-93)
Career: Tottenham H. from YTS August 1988; Gillingham (loan) September 1990; Bradford C.(loan) August 1992; READING (loan) 6 March 1993; Peterborough U.(free) August 1993; Barnet (free) March 1994

Capped at every level by Eire except full international, David was highly thought of at Spurs and although he only made two League appearances during his five years with them, he regularly captained their reserves. David had three successful loan spells and while at Reading he proved himself to be a reliable, hard tackling right back with good distribution. Shortly after returning to Spurs, they decided to release him and he joined Peterborough.

Reading Record: Lge 11
League Career Total: 144 (11)

McDONALD Murdoch 'Matt'
b. 1.7.1901 Redding, Stirlingshire d. 12.1954
Ht 5ft 7 Wt 11st 0 (29-30)
Career: Glasgow Rngrs; Bo'ness; READING (£100) August 1926; Brighton (£500) March 1930; Cowdenbeath; Bo'ness

Initially signed by Reading as an inside left, Matt had only made four first team appearances in almost six months when he was called on to replace right winger, Ted Porter, who had broken his leg. Matt proved an immediate success, ending the season with eight goals from his new position but was rarely used on the wing after that first season. Matt was in and out of the first team from then on, usually playing as an inside forward where he was, according to the club pen pictures, *'a tenacious player with unbounded pluck and enthusiasm'* But, perhaps because he was hankering after his early success on the wing, it was also commented that he *'tended to drift out of position'*. His first team appearances gradually reduced and he eventually moved to Brighton, along with McDougall and Webster. Sadly, Matt died of blood poisoning following an accident at work just weeks after getting married.

Reading Record: Lge 65/13, FAC 11/3, Total 76/16
League Career Total: 75/14

McDONALD Terence James
b. London 12.11.1938
Ht 5ft 7 Wt 10st 4 (65-66)
Career: West Ham U. from jnrs April 1956; Leyton O. July 1959; READING 18 May 1965; Wimbledon (free) July 1966

After failing to make West Ham's first team, despite being capped at England Youth level, Terry established himself at Leyton Orient. There he helped them gain promotion in 1962 and then played in their only season in the First Division. After six years at Brisbane Road, the crew-cut left winger moved to Reading but a suspension following a sending off at Bournemouth in October 1965 cost him his place.

His form in Reading's high flying reserves eventually earned him a brief recall but he was released at the end of the season.

Reading Record: Lge 13/2, LC 5/1, Total 18/3
League Career Total: 165/25

McGANN James L.
b. Wilmslow c.1909 d. ?
Ht 5ft 10 Wt 11st 0 (35-36)
Career: Wilmslow; Stockport Co. 1929; READING June 1934; Scarborough

Jimmy spent five years with Stockport but after only playing twice in his first three seasons, he then played 52 league games in the next two, conceding only 58 goals and was on the losing side just five times. After his move to Reading, his goalkeeping average took rather a dive as he let in 31 goals in 14 League games. This may have been partly due to his strange catching style of one hand to the side and one behind the ball.

Reading Record: Lge 14, FAC 2, Total 16
League Career Total: 68

McGARRY Arthur Martin
b. Burslem 3rd qtr 1898 d. ?
Ht 5ft 9 1/2 Wt 11st 11 (21-22)
Career: Port Vale; READING July 1921; Rochdale summer 1923

After the First World War, Arthur joined his local club, Port Vale, playing in 30 of their games in 1919-20 but he rarely got a game the following season. Arthur then joined Reading on the recommendation of a former player and played in the majority of their games over the next two seasons, all of his appearances being as a defensive left half. In 1923 he joined Rochdale where he scored his only League goal.

Reading Record: Lge 60, FAC 1, Total 61
League Career Total: 135/1

McGHEE Mark Edward
b. Glasgow 25.2.1957
Ht 5ft 10 Wt 12st (92-93)
Career: Cumbernauld Bor; Stirling jnrs; Bristol C. apprentice 1973; Morton 1975; Newcastle U. (£150,000) December 1977; Aberdeen (£80,000); S V Hamburg (£285,000) May 1984; Celtic (£200,000) November 1985; Newcastle U.(£200,000) August 1989; Brage Sweden summer 1991; READING player manager May 1991
See also 'The Managers' section

After an unsuccessful spell with Bristol City, Mark came to the fore with Morton where he scored 37 goals in 64 games, including four in front of Newcastle's scout. His move to Newcastle was not a great success, although he did win an U21 cap, so he moved to Alex Ferguson's Aberdeen. In a golden five year spell Mark scored 63 goals in 164 games as he helped the Dons win two Scottish championships and the Cup three times as well as the European Cup Winners Cup in 1983. Mark was also capped four times by Scotland, scoring against England in 1984 and was the Scottish PFA Player of the Year in 1982. A short spell in Germany was followed by more Scottish success, this time with Celtic where he added two more championship and two cup wins to his tally. In 1989 Mark returned to Newcastle and although his spell was blighted by injuries he managed to score five goals against Reading in four cup games in his first season. Mark was looking to move into management and in May 1991 he was appointed Reading's player manager at the recommendation of Alex Ferguson. Although beginning to slow down slightly, Mark maintained his excellent all-round, if unorthodox, striking play, and his good ball control made him difficult to dispossess. In his first season, Mark started half of Reading's games but, as he concentrated more on his managerial role, his first team appearances reduced in number, and he announced his retirement as a player at the end of the 1994 Division Two championship season, although he had not made any first team appearances for a year.

Reading Record: Lge 32(13)/7, FAC 1, LC 1(1), AMC 2, Total 36(14)/7
League Career Total: 116 (24)/36

McGHEE Thomas Edward
b. Manchester 10.5.1929
Ht 5ft 8 Wt 11st 4 (58-59)
Career: Wealdstone; Portsmouth May 1954: READING (£2,500) 9 July 1959; Poole T. July 1960; Fareham T. 1967

Tommy won England Amateur International honours while at Wealdstone and was in the England squad for the first British Amateur International Championship. During his National Service, Tommy played for the Royal Navy and appeared at Elm Park against the RAF in March 1954. Shortly after, full back Tommy joined Portsmouth where he played 136 First Division games and won an England B cap. Following Pompey's relegation in 1958-59, he was allowed to join Reading but his debut coincided with a poor start and he lost his place in September. Apart from one game in December, he never played for Reading again, his eight games producing just one point. A move to Poole proved much more fruitful as Tommy set a, then, club record with 285 Southern League appearances and helped them to two promotions.

Reading Record: Lge 8
League Career Total: 144

McGOUGH Joseph
b. South Shields 27.10.1909
Ht 5ft 8 Wt 10st 4 (35-36)
Career: Middle Dock; READING (£10) January 1932; Chester (£500) May 1938; Southport

Spotted playing in the North Eastern League, Joe was a hard working inside right with an eye for goal who became one of Reading's most popular players during the Thirties. When he came to Elm Park Joe only weighed 9st 2 so the club 'prescribed' him a bottle of Guinness a day to increase his strength and, although he was always slightly built, the medicine obviously worked. The club programme described Joe as a *'forager with ball control and a real 90 minute player'* but after being almost ever-present in 1933-34 and 1934-35 he no longer became a regular in the first team. In 1938 Joe moved to Chester and stayed in that area, scouting for Reading after the War and remaining in contact with the club for the rest of his life.

Reading Record: Lge 142/50, FAC 12/3, SSC 5/1, Total 159/54
League Career Total: 176/55

McHALE John 'Sam'
b. Odiham 7.5.1954
Ht 6ft 3 Wt 13st 7 (73-74)
Career: Alton T; READING amateur April 1974

A centre half, 'Sam' came to Reading's notice after a fine performance for a leading Hampshire amateur side, All Blacks, in a local cup final staged at Elm Park. He combined his career as an engineer with playing for Alton on Saturdays and for Reading's reserves in mid-week, but in February 1975 an injury crisis saw Sam get his one chance in the first team. Although he lacked finesse, Sam stuck to his task well and played an effective part in the 1-0 win over Brentford.

Reading Record: Lge 1

McILVENNY John Anthony
b. Hinkley 2.3.1930
Ht 5ft 7 Wt 10st 4 (59-60)
Career: Stafford Rngrs January 1949; Hinkley T; West Bromwich Alb. October 1949; Cheltenham summer 1951; Bristol R. July 1952; READING (£2,300) 6 June 1959

A tricky right winger, John made his League debut with Bristol Rovers for whom he made 80 Second Division appearances in a seven year spell. A move to Reading saw him establish himself on the right wing, playing as a creator of chances for others rather than a prolific scorer himself. At the end of 1960-61 John retired and ran a pub near Basingstoke.

Reading Record: Lge 77/4, FAC 8/2, LC 1, SPFC 1, Total 87/6
League Career Total: 157/15

McINTYRE James

b. Alexandria 24.5.1972
Ht 5ft 11 Wt 12st 0 (98-99)
Career: Duntchter BC; Bristol C. October 1991; Exeter C. (loan) February 1993; Airdrie September 1993; Kilmarnock March 1996; READING (£420,000) 26 March 1998; Dundee U. summer 2001

After a relatively unproductive spell with Bristol City, Jimmy returned to Scotland and helped Airdrie reach the Scottish FA Cup final in 1995 before moving to Kilmarnock. There he went one better, winning the Cup in 1997, having scored the goal that put them in the final. On the 1998 English transfer deadline day Jimmy was training with Kilmarnock at 10.30 a.m. but by 5 pm he was in Reading, having become the most expensive of Tommy Burns' seven signings that day. His first goal for his new club was the first to be netted at the North End of Reading's Madejski Stadium, but generally Jimmy was used to bring others into play rather than as a goalscoring forward. His lack of goals disappointed the Reading fans but Jimmy won them over after he looked more comfortable when new manager, Alan Pardew, used him on the left side of midfield. It was from there that he made a significant contribution to the club's play-off season but he was released in June 2001, a victim of cutbacks following the club's failure to gain promotion.

Reading Record: Lge 68(27)/14, FAC 2(2)/1, LC 2(2), AMC 4(1)/1, Play-offs 3, Total 79(32)/16
League Career Record: 81(30)/17 +

McKECHNIE James

b. c.1899 d. ?
Ht 5ft 7 Wt 12st 2 (23-24)
Career: Luton T. 1920; Mid Rhondda; Manchester C.(trial); Partick Thistle; READING (trial) September 1923

James' career reveals several attempts to break into League football but all he had to show was one game for Luton and another, three years later, for Reading. His one game for Reading was on their right wing at Swansea but a 5-1 defeat signalled the end of his trial.

Reading Record: Lge 1
League Career Total: 2

McKEEVER Mark Anthony

b. Derry 16.11.1978
Ht 5ft 9 Wt 11st 8 (98-99)
Career: Norwich C; Peterborough YTS; Sheffield Wed.(£500,000) April 1997; Bristol R.(loan) December 1998; READING (loan) 8 March 1999; Bristol R. (loan) February 2001

A brilliant youth career saw Mark first play for Northern Ireland at U17 level, but he subsequently elected to represent the Republic. He came over to England to join Norwich but followed the Canaries' youth coach when he moved to Peterborough. Mark made his League debut at 17 and did enough in three first team games to inspire Sheffield Wednesday to pay £500,000, plus more after certain appearances. In December 1998 Mark was loaned to Bristol Rovers and played a vital role in their 6-0 destruction of Reading a month later. His loan spell at Reading had an equally sensational outcome - he scored in his first two games and created the other three goals in those games. Although Mark still lacked the strength to always last the full 90 minutes, his spell at Reading earned him a call up to the full Eire squad and within days of his return to Wednesday, he at last made his Premiership debut.

Reading Record: Lge 6(1)/ 2
League Career Total: 22(12)/2 +

McKENNA Thomas

b. Paisley 11.11.1919
Ht 5ft 8 Wt 12st (47-48)
Career: St Mirren 1943; READING (free) June 1946; Grimsby T. June 1948; Chelmsford C. July 1950

Reading beat Celtic and Birmingham for Tommy's services after he had spent the previous two seasons as St Mirren's captain. Capable of playing in either wing half position, Tommy was on the right when Reading achieved their record win, 10-2 over Crystal Palace in September 1946. Despite being 'always at his best when the game is fiercest', Tommy could not hold a regular first team place at Elm Park and was released after two seasons.

Reading Record: Lge 28/1, FAC 3, Total 31/1
League Career Total: 78/3

MACKIE John

b. London 5.7.1976
Ht 6ft 1 Wt 13st (00-01)
Career: Crawley T; Sutton U summer 1999; READING (free) October 1999

It proved second time lucky at Reading for John who had impressed reserve team boss, Alan Pardew, while on trial in March 1998 but this interest had not been followed up by Tommy Burns. Once Pardew became Reading's manager, one of his first signings was that of John, who was regarded as one of the best young defenders outside the League. The plan was for John to give up his fruit and veg stall near Highbury, train with Reading, but to continue to play for Sutton, since Reading did not operate a reserve side that season.

Unfortunately, John almost immediately sustained a knee injury that kept him out until the start of the next season. Having impressed in pre-season friendlies, John was soon part of the first team squad and had a promising nine match run at the end of 2000.

Reading Record: Lge 7(3), FAC 3, LC 1(1), AMC (1), Total 11(5) +

McLAREN Andrew

b. Glasgow 5.6.1973
Ht 5ft 10 Wt 11st 6 (98-99)
Career: Rangers BC; Dundee U. June 1989; Barnsley (trial) March 1999; READING (£100,000) 25 March 1999; Livingston (loan) November 1999; Kilmarnock summer 2000

While with Dundee United, Andy developed into a creative winger and made 212 first team appearances, scoring 18 goals. In 1994 he won a Scottish Cup winners medal and his form earned him four U21 caps. On transfer deadline day, Reading beat Barnsley to sign him, but Andy never really settled in the South and, having failed to make the first team so far that season, he was loaned to Livingston seven months later. During this spell it became apparent that Andy's personal problems were more serious and on returning to Reading in January 2000, he requested that his contract be terminated. After leaving Reading it was discovered that he had tested positive for drugs and was suspended by the FA, a ban that was lifted in the summer of 2000. He then made a spectacular return with Kilmarnock, scoring twice against Rangers on his first game back and was voted the Scottish Premier League's Player of the Month.

Reading Record: Lge 9/1

McLAREN Edward

b. Dundee 8.9.1929
Ht 5ft 10 Wt 11st 8 (53-54)
Career: Dunkeld Jnrs; Blackpool June 1946; READING 29 September 1952; Guildford C. July 1959

Having made no first team appearances with Blackpool, Eddie joined Reading following his release from National Service. He played regularly as a defensive wing half until January 1956 when he was switched to right back and immediately made the position his own. A strong but classy defender, Eddie failed to score at half back so it was a surprise that he netted three times from right back in days when full backs had few attacking responsibilities.

Reading Record: Lge 184/2, FAC 13, SPFC 10/1, Total 207/3

McLEAN Peter Young

b. Lochgelly 27.11.1923
Ht 5ft 10 1/2 Wt 10st 3 (50-51)
Career: Lochgelly Violet; Bo'ness; READING (£400) 17 January 1949; Exeter C. August 1953; Bath C. June 1954

A slim wing half in the Scottish tradition, Peter spent four and a half years with Reading but was only a first team regular in 1950-51 when he played 35 games. For the rest of his spell at Elm Park he had to rely on short runs in place of Les Henley and then Jack Lewis. Towards the end of 1952-53, Peter was given a chance at inside left but, although he scored three times in those nine games he was released at the end of that season.

Reading Record: Lge 70/6, FAC 5/1, Total 75/7
League Career Total: 85/6

McLUCKIE George Robertson

b. Falkirk 19.9.1931
Ht 5ft 9 Wt 11st 8 (58-59)
Career: Lochore Welfare; Blackburn R. August 1952; Ipswich May 1953; READING (£2,000) 12 June 1958; Poole March 1961

The son of Scottish international, Jimmy McLuckie, George began his career with Blackburn but made his name with Alf Ramsey's Ipswich as they made their way to the top. Playing on the wing, he scored 24 times in 141 League games and helped them into the Second Division before joining Reading. George was the club's first choice left winger for his first two seasons, his thoughtful play providing a contrast for the more direct, goalscoring style of Jimmy Wheeler on the other flank. In his final season, George only made 14 League appearances and he joined Poole towards the end of 1960-61.

Reading Record: Lge 85/8, FAC 5, LC 1, SPFC 1, Total 92/8
League Career Total: 246/34

McMAHON Desmond

b. Reading 22.3.1956
Ht 5ft 8 Wt 11st (82-83)
Career: Hungerford T; READING trial then non-contract 1982; Wycombe W; Thatcham player, asst. manager and manager

Des played for many of the top local sides in the Reading area before getting his chance, in his mid twenties, to play for his local League side. After a trial Des joined Reading on a non-contract basis while still playing for Wokingham when not required by Reading.

He made two appearances in the Football League Trophy but as the two League appearances for the busy midfielder were as substitute, Des's games provided him with a total of just 60 minutes League football.

Reading Record: Lge (2), FLT 2, Total 2(2)

McMAHON Hugh J
b. Grangetown 24.9.1909 d. Cleveland 10.1986
Ht 5ft 7 1/2 Wt 11st 2 (34-35)
Career: Mexborough T; Sheffield Wed. (trial); Cowdenbeath; Blackpool 1930; Stoke C; READING (trial) August 1932; Mexborough T; Southend U. 1933; READING June 1934; QPR May 1936; Sunderland (£3,000) November 1937; Hartlepools U. 1946; Rotherham U. summer 1947

After a hesitant start to his League career that saw Hugh making only one appearance before he was 24, he managed to keep playing until he was nearly 40. His League debut came in his first spell with Reading and was made at left half, but by the time Hugh returned to Elm Park he had been converted by Southend to a left winger. It was in the number 11 shirt that Hugh made his spasmodic appearances for Reading before moving to QPR where his form earned him a move to big spenders, Sunderland. Hugh's career continued after the War, eventually ending with Rotherham where he achieved his best appearance and goal totals - 8 in 59 games.

Reading Record: Lge 11/2, FAC 2, SSC 1, Total 14/2
League Career Total: 157/24

McNEILL John Law
b. Inverkeithing c.1906 d. ?
Ht 5ft 11 1/2 Wt 12st 7 (29-30)
Career: Bo'ness; Musselburg Bruntonians; Hearts; Portsmouth December 1928; READING (£500) January 1930; Third Lanark 1931; Guildford C; Inverness Caledonian; Plymouth Arg. August 1934; Clapton O. summer 1939; Plymouth Arg. (Wartime guest); Merthyr manager; Torquay U. Manager June 1947; Bury manager March 1950

Having played all his career at centre forward, John played just six games in Reading's attack before being converted to a solid centre half and club captain. His injury near the end of 1930-31 was a major factor in Reading's failure to avoid relegation from the Second Division, but the appointment of Joe Smith as manager saw John lose his first team place and he quit League football for a while. His career was resurrected at Plymouth where he stayed for five years and after the War he embarked on a managerial career.

Reading Record: Lge 39/5, FAC 3, Total 42/5
League Career Total: 189/22

MacPHEE Magnus George 'Tony'
b. Edinburgh 30.4.1914 d. 1960
Ht 6ft 0 Wt 12st 2 (38-39)
Career: Wellington Rngrs; Edina; Hearts; Belfast Celtic; Workington; Bradford PA. October 1936; Coventry C.(£2,750) 1937; READING (£2,950) 16 May 1938, coach 1950; Walsall manager 1 August 1951

No player scored more goals for Reading than 'Tony' who, initially, made his name with Bradford PA where his form encouraged Coventry to pay a record fee for him. A hat trick at Elm Park in a reserve game persuaded Reading to sign him. Contemporary reports accused him of over elaborating at first but he still scored 31 goals in his first Reading season, including four against Bristol City in the final of the Southern Section Cup. The War interrupted Tony's League career but not his goals. An organ maker by trade, he worked in the local aircraft industry and so was able to play for Reading throughout the hostilities. During this period, Tony scored 217 goals in 226 games - a total beaten by only four other players, while in 1940-41 he scored an amazing 45 goals in just 30 games and captained Reading as they won that season's London Cup. Tony was Reading's top scorer in each of the three seasons after the War but retired in 1949 to concentrate on coaching the youth team. Two years later, Tony was appointed manager of Walsall but his team struggled and he left after six months to run a pub in Basingstoke. Sadly, Tony's health declined and he died at the age of only 45.

Reading Record: Lge 132/90, FAC 14/9, SSC 5/5, Wartime 226/217, Total 377/321
League Career Total: 174/ 113

McPHERSON Francis Comber
b. Barrow 14.5.1901 d. Daveyhulme 5.3.1953
Ht 5ft 8 Wt 11st 7 (30-31)
Career: Barrow Shipbuilders; Partick Thistle April 1919; Chesterfield Municipal October 1919; Barrow February 1921; Manchester U. May 1923; Manchester Central July 1928; Watford (£850) September 1928; READING (player exchange + £1,200)) February 1930; Watford (£100) July 1933; Barrow March 1937

A widely travelled centre forward, Frank began his League career with his home town club then had five years with Manchester United where he played 159 League games, scoring 45 goals. Remarkably, Frank then drifted out of League football until he joined Watford where he averaged a goal a game for 15 months, scoring 22 of Watford's first 28 goals of 1929-30. Then Reading offered George James plus £1500 for his services. After a bright start at Reading, the goals dried up and Frank was switched to the left wing where he could use his speed to good effect. Although Frank scored regularly from the wing he failed to command a regular place and in 1933 he returned to Watford.

Reading Record: Lge 79/28, FAC 8/3, Total 87/31
League Career Total: 388/145

FRANK'S CLAIM TO FAME - During his time with Manchester United, Frank developed a liking for visits to Leicester, scoring hat tricks on three consecutive visits to Filbert Street.

McPHERSON Keith Anthony
b. Greenwich 11.9.1963
Ht 5ft 10 Wt 11st 6 (90-91)
Career: West Ham U. from apprentice September 1981; Cambridge U.(loan) September 1985; Northampton T. (£15,000) January 1986; READING (£100,000) 24 August 1990; Brighton (free) 19.3.1999; Slough T. August 2000

Keith won the FA Youth Cup with West Ham in 1981 but he only made one League appearance for them in four years. That changed when he moved to Northampton where he was a king pin at the centre of their defence and won a PFA Divisional award as they won the Fourth Division title in 1987. Although not a prolific scorer, Keith scored twice on his visits to Elm Park and this must have helped in his move to Reading. Keith quickly repaid his fee, that included Darren Wood and Stuart Beavon, missing just four games in his first three seasons and being made club captain in 1991. Although not a regular in either the Division Two championship season of 1993-94 or the following play-off season, Keith made a vital contribution to both.

In December 1995 he suffered a pelvic injury that kept him out for eight months, but Keith showed great determination to win back his place. Despite his lack of height for a centre half, Keith was rarely beaten in the air, while his speed made him a difficult opponent and he continued to show these strengths when he moved to Brighton where he was soon appointed captain.

Reading Record: Lge 264(7)/8, FAC 12(1), LC 21(1), AMC 7(1), Play-offs 3, Total 307(10)/8
League Career Total: 491(9)/18 + 00-01

MADDEN David John
b. Stepney 6.1.1963
Ht 6ft Wt 13st (87-88)
Career: Southampton from apprentice January 1981; Bournemouth (loan) January 1983; Arsenal August 1983; Charlton A. June 1984; Los Angeles Razors; READING after trial November 1987; Crystal Palace August 1988; Birmingham C. (loan) January 1990; Maidstone U. June 1990

A skilful midfielder, Dave had a varied career in which he played for eight different League clubs and, although he made under 80 League appearances in total, he still managed to play in an FA Cup final when he came on as sub for Palace against Manchester United in 1990. After a couple of games for Arsenal and 20 for Charlton, Dave played indoor football in America before paying his own fare to accept a trial with Reading. He had a short run in the middle of that season, scoring one goal which, by coincidence, was in exactly the same net at Selhurst Park that he had scored his only other League goal with Charlton three years earlier. It was no surprise, then, that he moved to Palace at the end of the season, helping them to promotion to the First Division as their penalty taker as well as making that Wembley appearance.

Reading Record: Lge 7(2)/1, FAC 1, FMC 2(1), Total 10(3)/1
League Career Total: 67(11)/8

MAIDMENT Ian Michael
b. Newbury 9.8.47
Ht 5ft 7 Wt 10st 7 (66-67)
Career: READING from apprentice 10 August 1965; Trowbridge T

Ian's first season as a professional at Reading saw him play a major role in the reserves winning the Combination's Second Division title and it was as a result of this that he got his first team chance. A nippy left winger, Ian played in seven of the last nine games of 1965-66 but that proved to be the total of his League career and his contract was cancelled in November 1966.

Reading Record: Lge 7

MANSELL Ronald **Barrington**

b. Petersfield 8.3.32
Ht 5ft 10 Wt 11st (57-58)
Career: Portsmouth from jnrs August 1949; READING (free) 11 February 1954; Bournemouth June 1957

Barry only made 16 First Division appearances in more than four years with Portsmouth, although he was honoured by the Army and the FA. He took the opportunity to move to Reading in order to get first team football. He was virtually ever-present for the next two years, playing mainly in one of the full back positions, but also being used occasionally as a half back or even on the wing. Having lost his place through injury in January 1956, Barry failed to win it back and was allowed to join Bournemouth at the end of the following season.

Reading Record: Lge 84, FAC 9/1, SPFC 1, Total 94/1
League Career Total: 100/1

MAPSON John

b. Birkenhead 2.5.1917 d. Salisbury 8.1999
Ht 6ft Wt 12st 7 (34-35)
Career: Westrop R; Highworth; Swindon amateur; READING amateur December 1934, professional April 1935; Guildford C.(loan) January 1935; Sunderland (£2,500) 10 March 1936; READING Wartime guest; Guildford C. 1952

Reading spotted Johnny playing as an amateur for Swindon's reserves and the Wiltshire club tried to claim that he had been poached when Reading offered him professional terms, initially as assistant groundsman. He was loaned out to Guildford but was recalled when the club's two senior keepers were injured, and saved a penalty on his debut, against Newport in February 1936. After just one more game he was snapped up by Sunderland after the tragic death of their goalie, Jimmy Thorpe. Johnny played in their last six games as Sunderland won the Championship and the following year he became the youngest Cup Final goalie when he got a winners medal the day before his 20th birthday. Despite only playing two League games for Reading many of their older fans regard Johnny as the club's best ever keeper, their claim being supported by his 188 Wartime games, a record for a Reading guest player.

A cool, if unorthodox, keeper with a long kick, he was capped by England against Wales in April 1941 and was selected for the away match as well but chose to help Reading win the London War Cup final instead. Johnny also played against South Africa as well as the FA, before returning to Sunderland after the War, playing on until 1952.

Reading Record: Lge 2, Wartime 188, Total 190
League Career Total: 347

MARKS William **George**

b. Figheldean 9.4.1915 d 21.1.1998
Ht 5-11 1/2 Wt 10-11 (50-51)
Career: Salisbury Corinthians; Arsenal from amateur May 1936; Margate (loan); Blackburn R.(£5,000) August 1946; Bristol C. August 1948; READING (player exchange)15 October 1948; Bulford U. 1955

George managed just two League games in goal for Arsenal before the War interrupted his career. However, during 109 Wartime games George won the League Cup in 1941 plus the League Cup South two years later and established himself as England's first choice keeper, winning eight caps until injured. George was a safe, very precise and brave goalie who, after the War, became the most expensive goalie in the world when he was sold to Blackburn. He was with Bristol City when Reading exchanged him for Vic Barney, and so George returned to the club he had guested for at the end of the War. He was Reading's first choice keeper until December 1950 when he suffered a serious thigh injury in a friendly against Rotherham that kept him in a plaster from head to foot for five months. Having regained his first team place, George had to share it with John McBride and spent much of his time as Reading's first goalkeeping coach. In 1955 he was reinstated as an amateur and joined Bulford United.

Reading Record: Lge 118, FAC 8, Wartime 12, Total 138
League Career Total; 196

MARLOW Leonard Frederick

b. Putney 30.4.1899 d. Huddersfield 1975
Ht 5ft 10 1/2 Wt 12st (23-24)
Career: Wimbledon; Old Kingstonians; Huddersfield T; READING June 1923; Ebbw Vale; Grays T; Thames Mills

An inside forward who played just one League game in his two years at Huddersfield, Len moved to Reading during the 1923 close season. He started the season at inside left but failed to make an impact there or at centre forward and Len never featured in the first team after December.

Reading Record; Lge 5
League Career Total: 6

MARSDEN Ben

b. Hanley 2nd qtr 1898 d. ?
Ht 5ft 9 Wt 12st 6 (25-26)
Career: Port Vale; QPR late 1920; READING July 1925

Ben was Rangers' first choice right back for over four years, making 132 first team appearances for them before moving to Reading. Unfortunately for Ben, he was up against two of Reading's greatest full backs, Bert Eggo and Billy McConnell, and consequently he only made one first team appearance in each full back position before leaving Elm Park at the end of that season.

Reading Record: Lge 2
League Career Total: 128/6

MARSHALL Robert

b. Ayrshire c.1899 d. ?
Ht 5ft 9 Wt 12st (23-24)
Career: Dalry Thistle; West Ham U. (trial); Kilmarnock; READING June 1923

Like Ben Marsden, Rob found Reading's regular full back pairing, in his case Eggo and Len Grant, a virtually impenetrable barrier and so he only made one first team appearance before returning to Scotland.

Reading Record: Lge 1

MARSHALL William Edwin

b. Birmingham 1.10.1898 d. Grimsby 14.11.1966
Ht 5ft 7 Wt 11st 0 (32-33)
Career: Rotax Works; Chesterfield; Grimsby T. summer 1923; READING (£150) July 1932; Boston U. summer 1933

A regular on Chesterfield's left wing, Billy achieved his success with Grimsby where he helped them rise from the Third Division North to the First during his eight years with them. He was ever-present in Grimsby's 1925-26 championship season that was part of a run of 132 consecutive appearances. Grimsby's relegation back to the Second Division heralded Billy's sale to Reading where he had a couple of runs in the first team, but he was put on the transfer list at the end of the season and sold to Boston for a small fee.

Reading Record: Lge 19/4, FAC 1, Total 20/4
League Career Total: 426/74

MARTIN James Caird

b. Dundee 27.5.1938
Ht 5ft 10 Wt 11st 7 (63-64)
Career: Evenwood T; Blackpool December 1961; READING (free) 29 May 1962; Yiewsley July 1964

Jimmy did not make his League debut until he joined Reading and took a while to find his scoring touch which resulted him being out of the first team for almost a year. In September 1963 Jimmy made a scoring return to the League side but, just when the pacey centre forward was beginning to make his mark, he suffered a broken leg in a collision with Watford's Pat Jennings and his League career was over.

Reading Record: Lge 22/6, FAC 2, Total 24/6

MARTIN James Colin

b. Stoke 2.12.1898 d. Stoke 27.6.1969
Ht 5ft 9 Wt 11st 10 (24-25)
Career: Stoke St Peters; Stoke 1919; Aberdare A. summer 1921; Wolverhampton W; READING (£250) July 1924; Aberdare A. (£100) August 1925; Bristol C. summer 1926; Blackpool; Southend U; Halifax T; Congleton T

After a spell with his home town club, Stoke City, Jimmy began scoring regularly with Aberdare and this earned him a move to Wolves. Although he averaged a goal every two games, Jimmy was allowed to join Reading a few months later but this move was not a success. Despite playing most of his games at centre forward he only scored three times in 21 games and his last six appearances saw the club suffer a then record goalless run. This was just a blip in Jimmy's career and a return to Aberdare restored his goal touch that continued throughout the Twenties with another four League clubs.

Reading Record: Lge 18/2, FAC 2/1, Total 20/3
League Career Total: 226/85

MASKELL Craig Dell

b. Aldershot 10.4.1968
Ht 5ft 10 Wt 11st 7 (90-91)
Career: Southampton from apprentice April 1986; Swindon (loan) April 1987; Huddersfield (£50,000) May 1988; READING (£250,000) 7 August 1990; Swindon T. player exchange 9 July 1992; Southampton (£250,000) February 1994; Bristol C.(loan) January 1995; Brighton (£40,000) March 1996; Happy Valley (Hong Kong) (free) December 1997; Leyton O. March 1998; Hampton & Richmond September 1999

Possibly the only footballer to have the same middle name as the ground on which he made his full debut (!), Craig had earlier made a scoring start for Southampton when he came on as sub at Spurs. This wasn't enough to earn Craig a regular place and he was sold to Huddersfield where he immediately set the club's post-War scoring record. Craig had averaged a goal every other game for Huddersfield when Reading equalled their record fee to sign him.

His spell at Elm Park was fraught with problems; not only did Craig ask for a transfer during an unsettled period but the strain of paying the fee, plus a League fine for its late payment, contributed to bringing Reading to the verge of bankruptcy. Despite this, Craig topped Reading's scorers in 1991-92 but at the end of that season he moved to Swindon in exchange for Tom Jones. He continued his nomadic career, even returning to Southampton, and later played for Orient in their 1999 play-off final.

Reading Record: Lge 60(12)/26, FAC 5(1), LC 2, AMC 1, Total 68(13)/26
League Career Total: 284 (42)/116

MASON Arthur

b. Cornsay Colliery 7.1895 d. ?
Ht 5ft 10 Wt 12st 1 (25-26)
Career: Cornsay Colliery; Craghead U; West Stanley; READING August 1925; Norwich C. summer 1927; Hartlepools U. summer 1929; Crook T; Annfield Plain; Thorne Colliery

Arthur was signed by Reading as cover for Billy McConnell which meant that his first team chances were always going to be limited but he did get a run at left back towards the end of the club's Third Division South championship season. He enjoyed few more chances with his other two League clubs, and his 33 League games were spread over seven seasons.

Reading Record: Lge 6
League Career Total: 33

MATTHEWS Mark

b. Reading 17.9.1961
Ht 5ft 6 Wt 9st (82-83)
Career: READING non contract 1981; Wokingham T.

During the torrid relegation season of 1982-83, Reading manager Maurice Evans was forced by financial constraints to call on several local players and Mark was one such youngster. A bricklayer by trade and a nippy forward, Mark never let the club down and although he only made five League starts for the club his career was spread over three seasons. Mark's honest endeavour was appreciated by the fans and his spectacular volleyed goal against Bradford in January 1983 was one of the few bright spots of that season.

Reading Record: Lge 5(3)/1, FLT 1, Total 6(3)/1

MAUGHAN Wesley James

b. Sholing 17.2.1939
Ht 5ft 9 Wt 10st 11 (61-62)
Career: Cowes; Southampton from amateur May 1957; READING (£4,000) 28 February 1962; Chelmsford C. July 1963; Cambridge U. 1965; Margate (loan) January 1968; Chelmsford C. 1968; Bexley U. summer 1969; Basingstoke T. November 1972; Fleet January 1973; Bexley U. reserve coach August 1974

A member of Southampton's successful youth team of the mid fifties, Wes was a hardworking, stylish inside forward who scored regularly for the Saint's youth and reserve teams. He made his League debut at Elm Park in February 1959 but, unable to break into Southampton's League team regularly, Wes moved to Reading three years after that debut. Initially, his form was disappointing and he was subsequently discovered to have defective eyesight which led Reading to make an unsuccessful attempt to get some of the transfer fee back. With contact lenses fitted, Wes started to show some of the skills expected but was still unable to get a first team run. As well as being a footballer, Wes played trombone in the Salvation Army.

Reading Record: Lge 16/3, FAC 1, LC 1, Total 18/3

WES'S CLAIM TO FAME - His two goals at Old Trafford helped the Saints become the first team to beat Manchester United in the FA Youth Cup, ending a 42 match unbeaten run in the competition.

MAUTONE Steven

b. Myrtleford 10.8.1970
Ht 6ft 1 Wt 12st 0 (96-97)
Career: South Melbourne; Gippsland Falcons; Como; Canberra Cosmos; West Ham U. (£60,000) March 1996; Crewe Alex. (loan) September 1996; READING (loan) 19 February 1997, permanent (£250,000) 28 March 1997; Wolverhampton W. August 1999; Crystal Palace non contract 2000; Gillingham March 2000; Barry T. summer 2000; Slough T. summer 2000

As well as representing Australia at U17 and touring England with their Olympic squad in 1991, Steve also had a year with Serie A club, Como, as a result of his Italian family. After playing in goal for Australia v Malaysia in 1995, Steve sent a video of his performances to an English agent and was subsequently signed by West Ham. He made just one Premiership appearance but was spotted by Reading in a friendly against South Korea and they signed him after a month on loan. Steve soon impressed with a series of fine displays, including his knack of stopping penalties, and he looked set for a long career in Reading's goal. Unfortunately, he suffered a freak injury while warming up for the game at Port Vale in November 1997 that was to result in four knee operations and keep him out of action for 18 months.

Steve never regained his first team place at Reading and had spells with Wolves and Crystal Palace before becoming part of Gillingham's 1999-00 play-off winning squad and gaining a recall to the Aussie squad.

Reading Record: Lge 29, LC 5, 34
League Career Total: 36

MAVIN Frederick James

b. Newcastle 1885 d. Bradford 5.1957
Ht 5ft 10 Wt 12st 2 (14-15)
Career: Tods Nook; Benwell Adelaide; Newcastle U. Swifts; New Brompton July 1905; Fulham summer 1909; Bradford P.A. December 1913; Fulham (WWI guest); READING 1919; Bournemouth summer 1921; Exeter C. manager January 1923; Crystal Palace manager November 1927 to October 1930; Gillingham manager January 1932 to May 1937

Fred made his name as a centre half with New Brompton and then Fulham where he captained the club. He also developed a knack for scoring from set pieces, netting 29 goals in 140 League games for Fulham - a club record for a defender that stood for 70 years. After the War he joined Reading and in September 1920 he scored the club's first League penalty. Despite being in his mid-thirties, Fred turned in a series of fine displays during Reading's first League season but a move to Bournemouth saw injury end his playing career. He then enjoyed a 15 year managerial career that saw him discover a young Cliff Bastin while he was in charge at Exeter.

Reading Record: Lge 26/3, FAC 3/1, SL 27/1, Total 56/5
League Career Total: 179/33

MAYBURY Alan

b Dublin 8.8.1978
Ht 5ft 11 Wt 11st 7 (98-99)
Career: St Kevin's BC; Leeds U. August 1995; READING (loan) 25 March 1999; Crewe Alex. (loan) October 2000

Despite being capped by the Republic of Ireland at youth, B, U21 and at full international level, Alan had only made 13 starts in nearly four years at Leeds, although he had won the FA Youth Cup in 1997 with them. He had missed most of 1998-99 with a shin injury and so he jumped at the chance to go on loan to Reading for the season's run in. Unfortunately, he was sent off on his debut in a home defeat by Manchester City that ended Reading's outside play-off chances and his spell only saw him on the winning side once. However, his own displays at both wing back and midfield were good enough to earn him a further U21 cap and a second full cap while at Reading.

Reading Record: Lge 8
League Career Total: 24(3) +

MEADS Thomas

b. Grassmoor 2.11.1900 d. Chesterfield 30.1.1983
Ht 5ft 8 Wt 11st 12 (28-29)
Career: Grassmore Ivanhoe; Clay Cross T; Matlock T; Stockport Co. 1923; Huddersfield T. March 1927; READING October 1928; Tottenham H. (£2,750) May 1929; Bournemouth; Notts Co. August 1935

Originally a centre forward, Tommy was converted to a fine half back after he moved to Stockport although he never lost his scoring touch. A move to League champions, Huddersfield, saw him make 40 First Division appearance as they twice finished as runners-up but the signing of Dai Evans, coincidentally from Reading, saw Tommy lose his place and he subsequently moved into Evans' old shirt at Elm Park. Tommy scored on his home debut and was a regular to the end of the season when he was sold to Spurs, giving them good service in nearly 200 first team games.

Reading Record: Lge 31/4, FAC 3, Total 34/4
League Career Total: 390/35

MEAKER Michael John

b. Greenford 18.8.1971
Ht 5ft 11 Wt 11st 5 (95-96)
Career: Hayes Boys; QPR from trainee February 1990; Plymouth Arg. (loan) November 1991; READING (£550,000) 19 July 1995; Gillingham (trial) July 1998; Crystal Palace (trial) July 1998; Bristol R.(free) 7 August 1998; Swindon T. (loan) March 2000; Plymouth Arg. February 2001

Although born in Middlesex, Michael won a Welsh B cap and two at U21 level, via his Welsh mother, while he was with QPR. He was in and out of the first team at Loftus Road and eventually moved to Reading as part of the deal that took Simon Osborn in the opposite direction. Capable of brilliant displays on either wing or frustrating fans and managers in equal amounts, Michael's inconsistency meant that he never held down a regular first team place. He did not score his first goal until the last match of his second season but on his day Michael could be a sparkling match winner. He proved this when he destroyed Reading with a scintillating display and a goal, shortly after moving to Bristol Rovers.

Reading Record: Lge 46(21)/2, FAC (3), LC 3/1, Total 49(24)/3
League Career Total: 101(48)/6 +

MICHAEL'S CLAIM TO FAME - On 4 April 1998 Michael became the last Reading player to score a League goal at Elm Park.

MEESON David John

b. Oxford 6.7.1934 d. 1991
Ht 6ft 1 Wt 13st 5 (54-55)
Career: Oxford C; Wolverhampton W. February 1952; READING (£600) 9 August 1954; Coventry C.(£3,000) September 1962; Wisbech July 1965; Cheltenham T. August 1956, Oxford U. director

Like his father, Arthur, Dave kept goal for Oxford City before turning professional with Wolves. A move to Reading was soon followed by his League debut and after fine displays against Manchester United in the Cup, Dave was reserve for England B v Italy in January 1955. Over the next seven seasons, he battled with Dave Jones for the goalie's jersey but the arrival of the up and coming Arthur Wilkie and Mike Dixon allowed Reading to sell Dave to Coventry. After helping them to the 1963-64 Third Division title, Dave moved to non-League football, reaching the Southern League Cup final with Cheltenham in 1969, before having a spell as a director of Oxford United.

Reading Record: Lge 156, FAC 18, LC 2, SPFC 5, Total 181
League Career Total: 180

MELDRUM Colin

b. Glasgow 26.11.1941
Ht 5ft 11 Wt 12st 4 (63-64)
Career: Arsenal from jnrs December 1958; Watford December 1960; READING (£1,300) 4 April 1963; Cambridge U.(£2,000) 17 October 1969; Hillingdon Bor. player manager July 1971 to October 1972; York C. coach November 1973; Workington player coach November 1974; Stafford Rngrs manager September 1975 to May 1976; Workington manager February to May 1977; Scarborough asst. manager 1979; Frickley A. asst. manager 1980; Barnet coach 1981; York C. asst. manager 1982; Hull C. chief scout 1983; Swansea C. asst. manager 1984; coaching in Saudi Arabia 1986; Wealdstone manager February 1987; Wokingham manager November 1987

After making his League debut with Watford, Colin became Roy Bentley's first, and arguably best, signing for Reading. For the next six seasons he was the first choice left back at Elm Park and was the club's first Player of the Year when he finished top of the Reading Chronicle's merit table in 1963-64. A tough, inspirational player, Colin often captained Reading and was also used at centre half for a spell as well as a few games at centre forward during 1968-69. The arrival of Jack Mansell, signalled the end of Colin's Reading career and, after spells with Cambridge United and Hillingdon, he began a long managerial career without any great success, although he did guide Stafford Rangers to the final of the 1976 FA Trophy. On the other hand he was in charge at Workington in 1977 when they finally lost their League status.

Reading Record: Lge 265(1)/8, FAC 21, LC 17/1, Total 303(1)/9
League Career Total: 334(4)/9

COLIN'S CLAIM TO FAME - On 15 August 1970, Colin headed a late equalizer against Lincoln and so scored Cambridge United's first League goal.

MELLORS Richard Dugdale

b. Mansfield 17.3.1905 d. ?
Ht 5ft 11 Wt 12st (31-32)
Career: Mansfield Woodhouse; Chesterfield; Mansfield T; Sheffield Wed. December 1925; READING (£150) July 1931; Bournemouth (free) summer 1934; Queen of the South 1938

Dick only made 14 League appearances during his five years with Sheffield Wednesday, who were one of the strongest sides in the country at that time, but helped them to win the Central League in 1928-29. A solid keeper in both style and physique, Dick was, nonetheless one of the quickest players in the League and was rumoured to have once won the Powderhall Sprint.

His move to Reading saw him a regular in the first team for the next two years until the arrival of Percy Whittaker cost him his place.

Reading Record: Lge 85, FAC 7, Total 92
League Career Total: 216

DICK'S CLAIM TO FAME - After Reading's FA Cup-tie at Millwall in January 1933 was abandoned due to fog, the team returned to the dressing room but noticed that Dick wasn't with them. A search was launched and Dick was eventually found, still guarding his goal, totally unaware that the game had been called off!

MELLOWS Michael Anthony
b. Epsom 14.11.1947
Ht 5ft 10 Wt 11st 6 (73-74)
Career: Sutton U; READING (amateur) summer 1970; Winchester C. summer 1971; Wycombe W; Portsmouth September 1973; Waterlooville player coach 1978

A former schoolboy, youth and amateur international, Micky scored 91 goals in over 200 games for Sutton including their goal in the 1969 Amateur Cup final. His season with Reading saw his appearances restricted by a number of games for the British side that tried to qualify for the 1972 Olympics. A powerful left winger who made 16 amateur international appearances, Micky remains the last amateur to play for Reading. He left Reading at the end of 1970-71 to concentrate on a physical education course while helping Wycombe win the Isthmian League. Two years later Micky was persuaded to sign professionally for Portsmouth where he spent five successful seasons and was their Player of the Year in 1974-75.

Reading Record: Lge 14(2)/2
League Career Total: 188(9)/18

MEREDITH Jack
b. Grimsby 12.9.1899 d Grimsby 1970
Ht 5ft 6 1/2 Wt 10st (29.30)
Career: Scunthorpe U; Blackpool summer 1923; Chelsea (£4,500) summer 1928; READING (£500) 16 October 1930

Virtually ever-present with Blackpool, Jack made 200 first team appearances for them, scoring 30 goals before moving to Chelsea. He was not able to command a regular place with Chelsea and so he was sold to Reading but the move proved to be a disaster for both club and player. Jack's first four games for Reading on their right wing failed to produce any goals for the club and although his fifth game produced goals and a win, his first team career was over within a month of his transfer.

Reading were so disappointed in Jack's form that Chelsea were asked to waive the balance of his fee.

Reading Record: Lge 5
League Career Total: 218/33

MESSER Alfred Thomas
b. Deptford 8.3.1900 d. Reading 28.7.1947
Ht 6ft Wt 12st (23-24)
Career: Sutton T; Mansfield T; Nottingham For. (£250); READING (£250) June 1923; Tottenham H. (£2,000) 17 July 1930; Bournemouth player coach May 1934; Thorneycroft A. coach August 1937; Oxford C. coach.

In his day, Alf was widely regarded as the best uncapped player in the League and he is undoubtedly one of Reading's all time greats. From his League debut in December 1923 to his transfer to Spurs in July 1930, Alf missed just six games, being ever-present at centre half in Reading's Third Division South championship win and during two other seasons. He was club captain from 1928 and despite his tough, uncompromising play, he was described as 'a gentleman both on and off the pitch'. Alf was a very powerful header of the ball and only a poor team display in Reading's FA Cup semi-final against Cardiff, when he was watched by the England selectors, denied him the England cap he deserved. His sale to Spurs earned Reading a big fee but it was the final nail in the club's hopes of staying in the Second Division, especially as his Spurs debut saw them beat Reading 7-0. A subsequent move as player coach at Bournemouth saw Alf's playing career ended by an injury after just 10 games for them.

Reading Record: Lge 271/18, FAC 24/1, Total 295/19
League Career Total: 331/20

MIHAILOV 'Bobby' Borislav Biserov

b. Sophia, Bulgaria 12.2.1963
Ht 6ft Wt 12st 10 (96-97)
Career: Levski Sophia; Beleneses (Portugal); Mulhouse (France); Botev Plovdiv; READING (£300,000) 19 September 1995; Levski Sophia technical director

Bobby followed his father, Biser, by also playing in goal for Levski Sophia where he achieved almost endless success, winning the League four times and the cup five times. He established himself as Bulgaria's number one keeper after making his international debut in 1983 but really came to prominence during the 1994 World Cup when he was voted second best keeper in the tournament as they reached the semi-finals in USA. A year later a club record fee brought Bobby to Reading where he quickly displayed his pedigree with some spectacular continental style displays. In theory, Bobby should have been one of the very best keepers in the League but international calls and a series of niggling injuries prevented Reading from seeing his best. While with Reading, Bobby played in all three of Bulgaria's Euro '96 games and became the first Bulgarian to win 100 caps. In February 1997 he suffered a cruciate injury to his knee while making a brave save against Bolton, and a month later the club paid up his contract so that he could return to Bulgaria.

Reading Record: Lge 24, FAC 2, LC 2, Total 28

BOBBY'S CLAIM TO FAME - While Reading and the rest of the world were admiring Bobby's goalkeeping skills during the 1994 World Cup, the British press were more interested in his hair piece and subsequently nicknamed him 'Wiggy'. Just as well they never realized that one of his business interests in Bulgaria was a rug factory!

MILLARD Robert 'Ray'

b. South Shields 2.6.1927
Ht 5ft 7 Wt 11st 4 (49-50)
Career: Middlesbrough; Blyth Spartans; READING (£100) 22 June 1949; Walsall (£750) June 1950; Crystal Palace August 1955

A ball playing inside forward, Ray failed to make the grade at Middlesbrough but was given another chance at Reading. Despite his undoubted talents his career never really got going but he did make two League app-earances, both at Elm Park. The second of these was at home to Tommy Lawton's Notts County in the game that attracted Reading's record League attendance of 29,092. Therefore Ray's two games produced an average attendance of over 22,000 - surely no Reading player can claim a higher average.

Reading Record: Lge 2
League Career Total: 12/1

MOODY Paul

b. Waterlooville 13.6.1967
Ht 6ft 3 Wt 14st (92-93)
Career: Challenger FC; Fareham T. October 1986; Waterlooville (£4,000); Southampton (£50,000) July 1991; READING (loan) 9 December 1992; Oxford U.(£60,000) February 1994; Fulham (£200,000) July 1997; Millwall (£150,000) June 1999

A prolific goalscorer in his non-League days, Paul, cost Waterlooville their record fee but repaid them by topping their scorers for two seasons before earning them their record incoming fee when he became Ian Branfoot's first signing for Southampton. Although the perfect build for a centre forward, Paul did not get many chances in the First Division and was loaned to Reading where he used his height to good effect but was only rewarded with one goal. A move to Oxford saw him top their goalscorers in his first two seasons before Paul moved on to Fulham. A broken leg in September 1998 denied him a major role in their runaway Division Two championship and he was sold to Millwall who he helped to the play-offs in 1999-00, scoring a hat trick against Reading on the way. The following season he won another Division Two winners medal as the Lions pipped Reading to automatic promotion.

Reading Record: Lge 5/1, AMC 1, Total 6/1
League Career Total: 184(67)/93 +

PAUL'S CLAIM TO FAME - Paul came on as sub for Fulham's last game of 1998-99 and scored a hat trick in 13 minutes in what was to be his last game for the club. Not that that was anything new for Paul - three years earlier he had come off the bench to become the first Oxford sub to score a hat trick, and that only took him 12 minutes.

MOORE Andrew D

b. Wantage 2.10.1964
Ht 6ft Wt 12st (81-82)
Career: READING apprentice 1980; Henley T.

A product of Reading's youth programme, Andy got his only chance at League football when an injury crisis saw him named as sub for the home game against Doncaster in February 1982. An injury to Mark White after only 20 minutes saw the versatile 17 year old take over in midfield and although he acquitted himself well, Andy never got another taste of League football.

Reading Record: Lge (1)

MORAN Stephen James

b. Croydon 10.1.1961
Ht 5ft 8 Wt 10st 11 (87-88)
Career: Sarisbury Sparks; Price's College; Southampton August 1979; Leicester C. (£300,000) September 1986; READING (£250,000) November 1987; Exeter C.(free) August 1991; Hull C. August 1993, then youth coach

Steve is one of the select band of footballers to score with their first touch in the League, when he came on as sub for Southampton against Manchester City in January 1980. The following season he scored 18 times and in 1982 he was voted the PFA Young Player of the Year as well as winning two U21 caps. Unfortunately, Steve's progress was slowed by a back injury that kept him out for nine months and this was followed by a less successful spell at Leicester. In 1987 Ian Branfoot broke Reading's transfer record to sign the striker he had helped develop while he was youth coach at Southampton. Again the move did not really work out for, although Steve displayed undoubted class, he never produced the goals for which he was bought and he only reached double figures in one of his three and a half seasons at Reading.

Reading Record: Lge 91(25)/30, FAC 10(4)/3, LC 6/2, AMC 7/3, Total 114(29)/38
League Career Total: 360(53)/154

STEVE'S CLAIM TO FAME - Steve cost Southampton an unusual signing on fee. When Lawrie McMenemy went to watch him play, he bet the teenager a pair of boots that he wouldn't score a hat trick - Steve won his boots and a professional contract.

MORELINE David John

b. Stepney 2.12.1950
Ht 5ft 9 Wt 10st 8 (80-81)
Career: Fulham from apprentice January 1968; READING (£3,000) 3 June 1974

Left back Dave had been on Charlie Hurley's wanted list for 18 months after he had impressed the Reading manager in a League Cup-tie against Reading. Dave had been a classy player at Fulham and continued in style at Reading, helping them win promotion to the Third Division in 1975-76. After Maurice Evans took over at Reading, he switched Dave to the centre of defence to great effect but a serious knee injury sustained in an FA Cup-tie at Wealdstone kept him out for 18 months. Despite having his knee reconstructed with muscle from his hamstring, Dave defied the odds to come back and hardly miss a game in 1979-80. Unfortunately, he suffered further injury problems the following season and was forced to retire, becoming a postman.

Reading Record: Lge 166, FAC 10, LC 16, Total 192
League Career Total: 229(7)

MORGAN Stuart Edward

b. Swansea 23.9.1949
Ht 5ft 11 Wt 12st 7 (70-71)
Career: Waen Wan BC; West Ham U. from jnrs March 1967; Torquay U.(loan) February 1969; READING (£9,000) 6 November 1969; Colchester U.(free) August 1972; Bournemouth (£3,500) March 1975; Weymouth June 1977 then manager November 1978; Bournemouth asst. manager November 1983; Torquay U. manager September 1985; Weymouth manager June 1987; Brentford coach; Dorchester T. manager October 1993; Clift R. manager 1999; West Ham U. scout 2000

As a youngster Stuart was a promising amateur boxer, fighting eight times for his country and winning the Welsh Amateur Light Heavyweight title at 17. He turned down a further international appearance to have a trial for West Ham that eventually led to a professional contract. Although his only League experience was a 14 match loan spell with Torquay, Reading paid a record fee for a defender to bring the tough centre half to Elm Park. Unfortunately, Stuart was blighted with injuries almost as soon as he joined Reading, breaking his leg in his third game and then a year later suffering a serious knee injury that required several operations. When Stuart was fit he proved a formidable opponent, even by the hard tackling standards of the early seventies and yet, as is often is the case, he was a gentleman off the pitch. His style often attracted the attention of referees and his return to Elm Park after leaving Reading was marred by his dismissal. After his playing career ended, Stuart managed a number of clubs in the South West, winning the Alliance League Cup with Weymouth in 1982 but he only avoided his Torquay side only avoided being the first to suffer automatic relegation from the League in 1986-87, thanks to an injury time goal.

Reading Record: Lge 42(4)/1, FAC 6, Watney Cup 1, Total 49(4)/1
League Career Total: 215(7)/16

STUART'S CLAIM TO FAME - A week before he joined Reading, Stuart became the first West Ham player to be sent off since the War when he reverted to his boxing skills and was dismissed with Arsenal's Ray Kennedy during a London Challenge Cup match.

MORLEY Trevor William

b. Nottingham 20.3.1961
Ht 5ft 11 Wt 12st (96-97)
Career: Derby Co. amateur; Corby T. August 1979; Nuneaton Bor.(£7,700) January 1981; Northampton T.(£30,000) June 1985; Manchester C.(£175,000) January 1988; West Ham U. (£500,000) December 1989; Brann Bergen (Norway) summer 1995; READING (free) 1 August 1995; Sogndal (Norway) summer 1998; Bergen Sparta (Norway) manager 2000

A prolific goal-scoring record in non-League football earned Trevor a Southern League Midland Division winner's medal with Nuneaton in 1981-82 plus six England semi pro caps, before he followed his father, Bill, 12 seasons with Forest, into full time professional football. A Fourth Division title win in 1986-87 with Northampton plus a PFA Divisional award were rewarded with a move to Manchester City and then on to West Ham. With the Hammers, Trevor repeated the promotion and PFA award double, this time for the Second Division in 1990-91 and built up a great rapport with their fans. Rewarded this time with a free transfer, Trevor was snapped up by his old striking partner, Jimmy Quinn, and joined Reading. Although he had bad luck with injuries at Reading, suffering a broken skull, a knee cyst and cruciate damage he still became a popular player with the fans. They appreciated his skill, bravery and cunning use of his strength that produced goals for his teammates, and, in 1996-97, for himself as he topped Reading's scorers with 22 goals that won him the Player of the Year award. As well as spectacular goals and powerful headers, Trevor was an expert penalty taker and in January 1997 he became only the sixth player to head in a penalty after Huddersfield's former Reading keeper, Steve Francis, had blocked his spot kick. At the end of 1997-98 Trevor retired from League football at the age of 37.

Reading Record: Lge 67(10)/31, FAC 9/5, LC 5/2, Total 81(10)/38
League Career Total: 402(32)/145

TREVOR'S CLAIM TO FAME - Top TV writer, Tony Grounds is an ardent West Ham fan and in his 1999 BBC 2 series *Gone to the Dogs*, the main character was named Jim Morley as a tribute to Trevor.

MORRIS Alan
b. Swansea 6.4.1941
Ht 5ft 7 Wt 10st (63-64)
Career: Swansea T. from jnrs June 1958; READING (£4,500) 13 August 1963

A speedy right winger, Alan had only made 12 league appearances in his five seasons with his home town club, Swansea, before he joined Reading. After a run at the start of the season, Alan was mainly restricted to the reserves and it was in such a game in April 1964 that he sustained a serious knee injury that ended his playing career. His footballing days over, Alan returned to Swansea where he ran a small engineering firm.

Reading Record: Lge 12, FAC 2, LC 2, Total 14
League Career Total: 24/1

MORRIS Percy
b. Abergavenny 1911
Ht 5ft 8 1/2 Wt 10st 6 (33-34)
Career: Ebbw Vale, Luton (trial); READING (trial) March 1933

Percy joined Reading on a professional contract with his Ebbw Vale teammate, Pallow, who signed as an amateur. Between them, they managed just one first team game when Percy played at left back in Reading's first ever game in the Southern Section Cup, at QPR in February 1934.

Reading Record: SSC 1

MORROW Stephen Joseph
b. Belfast 2.7.1970
Ht 6ft Wt 12st 2 (92-93)
Career: Bangor; Arsenal from trainee May 1988; READING (loan) 16 January 1991; Watford (loan) August 1991; READING (loan) 30 October 1991; Barnet (loan) March 1992; QPR (£500,000) March 1997; Peterborough U. (loan) March 2001

Capped at all levels for Northern Ireland before he had made his League debut, Stephen had represented the Irish League at 15 and then helped Arsenal win the 1988 FA Youth Cup. Normally a midfielder at that stage of his career, Steve made his League debut at left back while on loan at Reading in a stormy game against Exeter that saw three players sent off. After a hesitant start, he quickly settled into League football and won the Player of the Month award before returning to Arsenal. Nine months later, Steve had another month on loan at Reading, making three more league appearances, before eventually establishing himself in Arsenal's first team. He hit the headlines when he broke his arm in the post-match celebrations after scoring the winner in the 1993 League Cup Final, but recovered in time to play in Arsenal's win in the following year's Cup Winners Cup final. A move to QPR in 1997 did not harm his international career and by the end of 1999-00 he had won 39 caps, often as captain.

Reading Record: Lge 13
League Career Total: 155(31)/3 +

MOYSE Ronald
b Portsmouth 2.4.1920 d. 1992
ht 5ft 8 1/2 Wt 12st 7 (50-51)
Career: Portsmouth (trial); READING October 1946

During the War, Ron was a PT instructor in the Army and played for the Egyptian Command against Palestine and Yugoslavia. After his demob, he joined Reading as a part-time professional but he was soon making his League debut. Initially Ron was used at half back but his speed and powerful, two footed kicking resulted in him becoming a fine right back, a position he dominated during the early fifties. As well as using his speed during the game, it appears that Ron used it at the final whistle as he was always the first player to bath and change after the game.

Reading Record: Lge 189, FAC 12, Total 201

MULLEN James
b. Oxford 16.3.1947
Ht 5ft 7 Wt 10st 7 (66-67)
Career: Oxford C; READING amateur July 1965, professional 21 November 1966; Charlton A.(£7,000) 20 November 1967; Rotherham U. February 1969; Blackburn R. August 1974; Bury June 1976; Rochdale (loan) March 1977

A fast player who was capable of performing on either wing, Jimmy was the nephew of the Wolves and England winger of the same name. After just eight appearances at Reading, Jimmy was surprisingly sold to Charlton but it took another move to Rotherham for him to establish himself, making 177 League appearances for them, scoring 24 goals.

Reading Record: Lge 8/1
League Career Total: 203(11)/26

MURPHY Michael
b. Reading 15.4.1939
Ht 5ft 10 Wt 11st 2 (57-58)
Career: Thorneycroft A; READING amateur 1958; Thorneycroft A; Redhill

A former Reading schoolboy, Mike worked in the local Inland Revenue office and was plucked from the Hampshire League side as cover for Reading's two professional goalies. He got his one game when Dave Jones was suspended and Dave Meeson was injured for the last game of 1957-58, against Brentford.

Reading Record: Lge 1

MURPHY Michael James
b. Slough 5.5.1977
Ht 5ft 11 Wt 11st 9 (94-95)
Career: Slough T; READING from assoc. schoolboy 6 October 1994; TPV Tampere (Finland) summer 1996; Rips (Finland) September 1996; Slough T. (trial) November 1996

An associate schoolboy with Reading since he was 14, Mick gave up his A level studies to sign for Reading and nine days later made his League debut, coming on as sub for Uwe Hartenberger after only 16 minutes, against Bristol City. Originally a left winger, Mick was converted to a striker and was top scorer in the youth team when he signed pro. Although he never got another first team game, Mick was a key member in the side that won the 1995 Berks & Bucks senior Cup and it was the foul on him that led to the penalty that won the final.

Reading: Lge (1)

MURPHY Nicholas Michael
b. West Bromwich 25.12.1946
Ht 5ft 11 Wt 11st 4 (70-71)
Career: Manchester U. from apprentice February 1966; READING (free) 2 July 1970

Nick was developed at Manchester United under the watchful eye of his father, assistant manager Jimmy Murphy, but the young midfielder only managed one substitute appearance for the first team. Despite this, Reading beat off fierce competition from several clubs to sign him and within weeks Nick was making his debut - against United in the Watney Cup. Although he had obvious skills, Nick did not make any impact on the first team in either midfield or defence and was released at the end of that season.

Reading Record: Lge 3(1), Watney Cup (1), Total 3(2)

MURRAY George William
b. Denny c.1900 d. ?
Ht 5ft 7 Wt 11st (22-23)
Career: Dunipace; READING July 1920; Exeter C. summer 1923; Stenhousemuir 1927

George was snapped up by Reading while he was waiting to hear the outcome of a trial with Glasgow Rangers. He had to wait two seasons to make his League debut and although he only made three League appearances that season he displayed his versatility by playing in both wing half positions and on the right wing. Each of George's appearances ended in defeat for Reading but, despite becoming the first Reading player to be sent off in the League, in a 4-0 defeat at Exeter, he joined the West Country club.

He was signed by his former Reading colleague, Fred Mavin but a serious injury in 1924 ended George's League career.

Reading Record: Lge 3
League Career Total: 23/1

GEORGE'S CLAIM TO FAME - George married a local girl while at Exeter and despite his comparatively short League career, he was remembered 70 years later when his relatives sponsored the matchball for the Exeter v Reading game in October 1993.

MURRAY James

b. Edinburgh 4.2.1933
Ht 5ft 8 Wt 11st 4 (54-55)
Career: Merchiston Thistle; Newtongrange Star; Hearts September 1950; READING (loan) February 1954; Falkirk 1961; Clyde 1962 to 1964; Falkirk asst. manager summer 1967

After a playing for Scotland at schoolboy level, Jimmy joined Hearts, but when his National Service saw him stationed with the RAF in Berkshire, the Scottish club allowed him to play for Reading. As well as winning a number of honours in the RAF, Jimmy played in the League between April and September 1954. On his return to Hearts Jimmy developed into a fine player, combining a hard shot, with outstanding heading, and with lively and intelligent play that saw him capped four times for Scotland in 1958. He also helped Hearts to a golden era at the end of the Fifties when they won the Championship twice plus the League Cup.

Reading Record: Lge 7/3

MURRAY John

b. Newcastle 2.3.1948
Ht 5ft 8 1/2 Wt 11st (76-77)
Career: Newcastle U.(trial);Wolverhampton W.(trial); Middlesbrough (trial); Burnley from jnrs March 1965; Blackpool (£15,000) March 1971; Bury (player exchange) February 1971; READING (£4,000) 13 August 1974; Brentford (£3,000) 8 February 1978; Dartford July 1978; Newbury player manager 1978; Wallingford player manager 1981; Northampton youth coach 1986

Despite only making 22 League appearances for Burnley, John's performances were good enough to get a place on the bench for the England U23s. A transfer to Blackpool did not work out, but his move to Bury got off to a flying start as John scored on his debut in a 5-1 win over Reading which resulted in the Berkshire club putting their entire playing staff up for sale.

John continued to score regularly at Gigg Lane but after 37 League goals in 117 starts, and promotion to the Third Division in 1973-74, he was sold to Reading after a pre-season bust up with Bury's manager. His Reading career got off to a scoring start but despite some spectacular goals from his powerful shooting, John's form was erratic and he was transfe- listed at the end of 1974-75. John rose to this challenge and although the chunky winger was never totally consistent, he proved a regular scorer and his 15 goals in the following season played a vital part in getting Reading out of the Fourth Division. He lost his first team place in September 1977 but 'Minty' will always be remembered for possessing one of the most powerful shots seen at Elm Park.

Reading Record: Lge 123(8)/44, FAC 5/1, LC 13(1)/4, Total 141(9)/49
League Career Total: 267(25)/89

JOHN'S CLAIM TO FAME - Easter Monday 1973 was a mixed day for John. Having scored a hat trick for Bury against Doncaster, his celebrations were able to start early when he was later sent off!

MURTY Graeme Stuart

b Saltburn 13.11.1974
Ht 5ft 10 Wt 11st 2 (98-99)
Career: Middlesbrough assoc. schoolboy; York C. from trainee March 1993; READING (£700,000) 10 July 1998

Graeme developed at York where he played in the side that knocked Manchester United out of the League Cup and scored in their win over Everton in the same competition. Most of his 130 plus appearances for York were on the wing but he was also used as a wing back. His move to Reading saw him sustain a pre-season injury that was to keep him out until February 1999, but when Graeme did play he impressed in the wing back position. A bad foul at Luton meant that he missed another six months and further injuries saw him restricted to 40 League starts in his first three seasons with Reading.

Reading Record: Lge 40(9)/1 FAC 4(1), AMC 2(2) Play-offs 1, Total 47(12)/1 +
League Career Total: 146(20)/8 +

NEATE Gordon

b. Reading 14.3.1941
Ht 5ft 10 Wt 12st (60-61)
Career: READING groundstaff April 1956, professional 17 March 1958

One of the most popular personalities ever to play for Reading, Gordon played for Reading Schools at various levels but he could never have imagined that when he joined his home town club at 15 he would still be with them at 60.

The ideal physique for a defender, Gordon could play in either full back role or at centre half, but injuries and the form of team mates meant that he only made 106 first team appearances in seven seasons. In 1963-64 Gordon appeared to have established himself as the club's right back but a knee injury sustained at Walsall put his career under threat. He fought his way back into the first team but a year after the initial injury his knee gave way again and Gordon was forced to retire in 1966, but not before helping the reserves to promotion. Within a few months of leaving Elm Park as a player, Gordon was back as groundsman, a position he still holds, although now at the Madejski Stadium. Gordon, or 'Fred' as he is also known thanks to Maurice Evans likening him to Fred Karno's Army in his early days, built up a reputation for a keen sense of humour that has kept hundreds of Reading players amused over the years, as well as receiving Canon Loyalty and League Long Service awards. It was fitting that one of the last games played at Elm Park should be a testimonial for Gordon.

Reading Record: Lge 99/2, FAC 5, LC 2, SPFC 1, Total 107/2

GORDON'S CLAIM TO FAME - In 1972 a competition was held to find the footballer with the hardest shot. To the embarrassment of Reading's players, Gordon beat them with an effort timed at 72 mph.

NELSON Dennis

b. Edinburgh 25.2.1950
Ht 5ft 8 Wt 11st 8 (77-78)
Career: Hibernian; Dunfermline summer 1972; Crewe Alex. July 1972; READING (£10,000) 10 March 1975; Crewe Alex. (free) May 1978; Altrincham

An all-action inside forward, Dennis played one game for Hibs before helping Dunfermline gain promotion to the Scottish First Division in his first season. He became a popular player with Crewe and was their top scorer when Charlie Hurley signed him to boost Reading's Fourth Division promotion chances. Dennis did this, scoring on his debut and helping the club into the Third Division. He was a tough, all action player who manager Hurley described, with some justification, as being 'as hard as nails' but never a prolific scorer, Dennis was rarely amongst the goals at Reading. He also found it difficult to settle in the South and in 1978 he was allowed to return to Crewe.

Reading Record: Lge 53(6)/6, FAC 3, LC 3(2)/1, Total 59(8)/7
League Career Total: 215(22)/39

NEWMAN Richard Adrian

b. Guildford 5.8.1970
Ht 5ft 10 Wt 12st 6 (99-00)
Career: Crystal Palace from jnrs January 1988; Maidstone U.(loan) February 1992; Millwall (£500,000) July 1995; READING (loan) 17 March 2000, (free) 27 July 2000

A hard working midfielder, Ricky spent seven years on the fringes of Palace's first team before a big money move to Millwall gave him regular first team football. Ricky played mainly in the centre of midfield for the Londoners, and he appeared in their 1999 Auto Windscreen final at Wembley. The following season first team chances were fewer and it became apparent that he no longer featured in Millwall's plans so he was allowed to join Reading on loan before earning a permanent move. This teamed him up with Reading manager Alan Pardew and he rewarded his old Palace team mate with some steady performances and a thunderous winner at Notts County. The following season Ricky was used mainly at full back but was still one of the club's most consistent performers until a cruciate injury put him out of the run-in.

Reading Record: Lge 41(5)/1, FAC 3/1, LC 1, AMC 1, Total 46(5)/2 +
League Career Total: 237(17)/10 +

NEWTON Frank

b. Romiley 12.11.1902 d. Romiley Autumn 1977
Ht 5ft 9 1/2 Wt 12st 10 (29-30)
Career: Ashton National; Ponypridd; Stockport Co. 1928; Fulham (£575) summer 1931; READING (£650) 19 September 1933; Fulham (£400) 5 October 1934

After running away to sea as a boy, Frank then joined the Army where he won representative honours at football, hockey, rugby and boxing. Out of the Army, Frank eventually signed for Stockport and played alongside future Reading manager, Joe Smith. His prolific scoring skills saw him bag 87 goals in only 94 games, a ratio he maintained when he moved to Fulham. In his first season with Fulham, Frank, who was nicknamed 'Bonzo', scored 43 League goals that remains their club record to this day, while the following season he netted in nine consecutive matches. Reading had tried to sign Frank as a replacement for Jack Palethorpe but they could not believe their luck when Fulham agreed to sell him six months later. The Fulham board could not believe it either, and they sacked their manager, former Reading player James McIntyre for agreeing the sale, despite the fact that Frank requested the move to Reading as his wife wanted to move to the country.

'*A brilliant leader who can shoot first time*', the goals continued to flow at Reading but a knee injury in January 1934 kept him out for 10 games and probably cost Reading promotion. A year after his controversial transfer, Frank returned to Fulham but soon after he suffered a badly broken leg in a friendly match that forced the retirement of one of the best goalscorers the Third Division had seen. As well as his footballing talents, Frank played the trombone and appeared on stage at Reading's Royal County Theatre.

Reading Record: Lge 32/29, FAC 2/2, Total 34/31
League Career Total: 209/193

NIBLETT Victor
b. Ash Vale 9.12.1924
Ht 6ft Wt 11st 11 (49-50)
Career: Battle A; READING from jnrs July 1947; West Ham U. June 1950; Gillingham August 1951; READING scout mid '60s

Vic captained the Reading Schools side that reached the seventh round of the 1939 English Schools Trophy and was twice reserve for England U15 schools, but came to Reading's attention when he attended a War-time training session at Elm Park. He was unlucky that as he developed into a fine centre half, his first team career was blocked by the exceptional form of Gordon Brice, and so, in 1950 he moved to West Ham. It took another move, to Gillingham, for Vic to get regular first team football and he settled in Kent, where, as well as being a fixture in the Gills' defence, he and his wife graduated to gold medal standard at ballroom dancing.

Reading Record; Lge 6, FAC 4, Wartime 47, Total 57
League Career Total: 160

VIC'S CLAIM TO FAME - Although he missed out on a schoolboy cap, Vic got his England call-up when he played in the very first Air Training Corps international, against Scotland at Clyde.

NICHOLS Mark
b. Hillingdon 30.5.1977
Ht 5ft 10 Wt 10st 4 (99-00)
Career: Chelsea from trainee July 1995; READING (loan) 30 December 1999; Grimsby T. (loan) February 2000; Colchester U. (loan) October 2000; Torquay U. summer 2001

A highly rated, quicksilver striker, Mark's appearances for Chelsea were restricted, mainly to substitute appearances due to their glut of international strikers.

Loaned to Reading at Christmas 1999, Mark scored a sensational goal on his debut at Gillingham that was Reading's first of the new Millennium. Although Mark lacked a little of the strength necessary for Division Two, his talent was obvious and he scored another stunning goal, at Bristol Rovers, before returning to Stamford Bridge.

Reading Record: Lge 4(1)/1 AMC 2/2, Total 6(1)/3
League Career Total: 24(27)/4 +

MARK'S CLAIM TO FAME - Mark's loan move to Reading was the last transfer to be completed in the old Millennium

---

NICOLI Attolia
b. Switzerland 1922
Ht 5ft 7 Wt 10st 2 (38-39)
Career: READING (trial) March 1939

Attolia was a Swiss schoolboy who was attending a local Reading school 'to learn English language and customs' when his skills came to the attention of Reading. Also a fine rugby player, he was offered a trial and proved exceptionally fast, beating the club's quickest professional, Sam Doran, in a training sprint. After just one reserve game he played his only first team match, against Crystal Palace in the Southern Section Cup. Attolia gave a promising display on the right wing but the impending hostilities in Europe prevented Reading from following up their interest.

Reading Record: SSC 1

NIMMO James
b. Longridge c.1905 d. ?
Ht 5ft 8 Wt 11st 4 (29-30)
Career: Broxburn U; READING (trial) August 1927, permanent October 1927

Signed from Edinburgh junior football, James spent three seasons with Reading but rarely got a chance at a run in the Second Division during that time. Although always regarded as a left half, James' best spell in the first team was at left back at the start of 1930 but he was released at the end of that season.

Reading Record: Lge 24

NIXON Eric Walter

b. Manchester 4.10.1962
Ht 6ft 4 Wt 15st 7 (94-95)
Career: Curzon Ashton; Manchester C.(£1,000);
Wolverhampton W.(loan) August 1986; Bradford C.(loan)
November 1986; Southampton (loan) December 1986; Carlisle
U.(loan) January 1987; Tranmere R.(loan) then permanent
(£60,000) March 1988; READING (loan) 9 January 1996;
Blackpool (loan) February 1996; Bradford C.(loan) March
1996; Stockport Co.(£100,000) August 1997; Wigan A.(loan)
August 1998 then permanent (free) March 1999; Stockport Co
summer 1999

A giant goalkeeper, Eric made 44 League appearances
in 1986, 39 of which were while on loan to four different
clubs. A move to Tranmere saw Eric build up a great
reputation, keeping over 100 clean sheets and playing in
a remarkable 11 play-off games. Eric lost his place in
1995-96 and was signed on loan to Reading one minute
before the deadline, so he could play in their League
Cup quarter-final at Leeds - that one game for Reading
was his first since Tranmere's 3-1 play-off defeat, by
Reading, eight months earlier.

Reading Record: LC 1
League Career Total: 516

NOGAN Lee Martin

b. Cardiff 21.5.1969
Ht 5ft 10 Wt 11st (96-97)
Career: Luton T.(trial); Port Talbot Yth; Oxford U. from
trainee March 1987; Brentford (loan) March 1987; Southend
U.(loan) September 1987; Watford (£300,000) December
1991; Southend U.(loan) March 1994; READING (£250,000)
12 January 1995; Notts Co. (loan) February 1997; Grimsby
(£170,000) 24 July 1997; Darlington; Luton T. (loan)
November 2000; York C. (loan) February 2001

Spotted by Maurice Evans for Oxford United while
playing for Port Talbot in a friendly against Oxford
University, Lee is the older brother of fellow striker
Kurt. Although he developed into a vital player with
Oxford, they were forced to sell him to raise cash
following the death of Robert Maxwell. At Watford
Lee's initial form earned him a full Welsh cap, against
Austria in 1992, to add to his U21 and B caps, but Lee
felt his form suffered when he was moved to play on the
wing. Eventually he became Jimmy Quinn and Mick
Gooding's first signing when they equalled Reading's
transfer fee. After a slow start, Lee hit great form in the
run-in to the play-offs and scored a brilliant opener in
the final at Wembley. This earned the pacey striker a
second Welsh cap, against Moldova, but after that Lee
only displayed his exciting play in patches and was
eventually sold to Grimsby in 1997.

In his first season he helped them win the Auto
Windscreens Shield and two years later he was back at
Wembley when he suffered another play-off defeat, this
time with Darlington.

Reading Record: Lge 71(20)/26, FAC 2, LC 5(1)/1,
Play-offs 3/2, Total 81(21)/29
League Career Total: 374(60)/88 +

NORTH Ernest Joseph

b. Burton on Trent 23.9.1895 d Havant 24.8.1955
Ht 5ft 9 Wt 11st 2 (22-23)
Career: Atlas & North; Sheffield U; Arsenal from amateur
December 1919; READING May 1922; Gillingham summer
1923; Norwich C. summer 1924; Watford summer 1926;
Northfleet U. player coach

Joe played for the Tank Corps during the First World
War and won the Military Medal for bravery before
joining Arsenal when League football restarted. He
played a handful of games for the Gunners over three
seasons, appearing at either inside or centre forward.
His move to Reading was less successful as his three
games leading the attack and one on the right wing
failed to produce a goal, but Joe rediscovered his
scoring touch with subsequent spells at Gillingham and
then Norwich. Joe could also played first class cricket,
having been on the playing staff at Lords, and later
became a Minor Counties umpire.

Reading Record: Lge 4
League Career Total: 128/36

NORTON Ralph

b. Aylesham 11.10.1942
Ht 5ft 7 Wt 10st 6 (64-65)
Career: READING groundstaff 23 August 1958, professional
12 October 1959; Bournemouth July 1966; Poole T. July 1968;
Cheltenham T. 1969

Having prog-
ressed through
R e a d i n g ' s
youth system,
Ralph made
his League de-
but a year after
signing pro-
f e s s i o n a l .
Most of his
appearances
were at inside
forward.

Yet towards the end of his Reading career, Ralph moved back to wing half and, despite his versatility, he only played in more than half of the League games twice in six seasons. On 21 August 1965, Ralph wrote himself into Reading's record book when he became the club's first substitute, coming on for Peter Shreeves.

Reading Record: Lge 99(1)/9, FAC 8/1, LC 6/1, Total 113(1)/11
League Career Total: 143(5)/13

NUTTON Michael William
b. St John's Wood 3.10.1959
Ht 6ft Wt 12st 4 (82/83)
Career: Chelsea from apprentice October 1977; READING (loan) 3 February 1983; Millwall March 1983; Erith & Belvedere

A classy central defender developed by Chelsea, Micky made over 80 first team appearances for the London club during his five years as a professional with them. Towards the end of his Chelsea career, Micky was loaned to Reading who were struggling against relegation. He helped to shore up the defence and his six games coincided with Reading's longest unbeaten run of a disappointing season. Unfortunately for Reading, Micky joined their relegation rivals, Millwall, as soon as his loan period was over and he helped the Lions stay up at Reading's expense.

Reading Record: Lge 6
League Career Total: 164(3)/4

OAKLEY James Ernest
b. Tynemouth 10.11.1901 d. Northumberland 7.1972
Ht 5ft 6 1/2 Wt 11st 4 (30-31)
Career: Blyth Spartans; Sunderland 1922; READING (£875) July 1930; Northampton T. (£350) June 1931; Kettering T.

Although never a regular in Sunderland's First Division side, James spent nine seasons with them, playing 84 times before moving to Reading . The move south and Reading's dire form hardly helped James settle down, and he was in and out of the left back role until a broken ankle at Christmas signalled the end of his first team chances at Reading.

Reading Record: Lge 9
League Career Total: 127

ODELL Robert Edward

b. Isle of Wight 10.12.1934
Ht 6ft 1 Wt 11st 12 (52-53)
Career: Newport (IoW); READING amateur 5 September 1951, professional 5 July 1952; Headington U.

Spotted playing for Newport, Bobby signed as a professional for Reading after impressing in their youth team that won the Hampshire League Second Division title and its cup competition. His National Service interrupted his career and Bobby was dogged by injuries after he returned to the club so he only made two League appearances, both at centre half, in February 1954.

Reading Record: Lge 2

O'NEILL Michael Andrew Martin
b. Portadown 5.7.1969
Ht 5ft 11 Wt 11st 10 (97-98)
Career: Coleraine; Newcastle U.(£80,000) October 1987; Dundee U. (£35,000) August 1989; Hibernian August 1993; Coventry C.(£500,000) July 1996; Aberdeen (loan) January 1998; READING (loan) March 1998; Wigan A.(free) September 1998; St Johnstone August 2000

Capped at six levels for Northern Ireland and a full international at 18, Michael made a sensational start at Newcastle when he scored 13 first team goals in his first 21 games and was voted their Player of the Year. He couldn't maintain this form but spells with Dundee United and then Hibs, where he played in the 1995 Scottish Cup final, persuaded Coventry to bring him to the Premier League. Michael was a tricky, speedy winger but his spell at Coventry hardly got started due to a series of injuries, so he was loaned out to Aberdeen and then Reading. Despite his lack of match fitness he showed some nice touches and scored in the relegation battle against Stoke, a goal that was the first for Tommy Burns as Reading manager. Michael's two months at Elm Park were quite eventful as it saw three different managers, relegation from Division One, and the last League game at Elm Park. Early in the following season he joined Wigan and scored the winner in the semi-finals as they went on to win the Auto Windscreens Shield at Wembley and reach the play-offs.

Reading Record: Lge 9/1
League Career Total: 113(15)/18

ORDISH Cyril Stanley
b. Heanor 23.5.1915
Ht 5ft 10 1/2 Wt 11st 8 (37-38)
Career: Blackwell; Chesterfield 1931; Wolverhampton W. summer 1936; READING February 1938

Having made just one League appearance in four years with Chesterfield, and then one in each of his two seasons at Wolves, Cyril had better fortune at Reading. The stylish left back went straight into the first team and was described in the club programme as *'a nice type of young player'*. The signing of Jimmy Fullwood in the summer meant that Cyril had to switch to the right and, as his opportunities became more restricted he left the club at the end of 1938-39.

Reading Record: Lge 21, SSC 2, Total 23
League Career Total: 24

OSBORN Simon Edward
b. Croydon 19.1.1972
Ht 5ft 10 Wt 11st 4 (96-97)
Career: Crystal Palace from trainee January 1990; READING (£90,000) 17 August 1994; QPR (player exchange + £500,000) 7 July 1995; Wolverhampton W. (£1 million) December 1995, Tranmere R. (free) March 2001; Port Vale (loan) summer 2001

Simon made his debut for Palace at 17 and, although he suffered a series of injuries, he was very popular with their fans. He was equally popular when he moved to Reading where his long passing and shooting were a major influence on the club's bid for Premiership football. Despite his undoubted attacking skills, Simon also did his fair share of defensive work, and it was a last ditch tackle in his own penalty area at Christmas that injured his knee and kept him out for three months. His return to the first team sparked Reading's run to the play-off finals, but when the club missed out at Wembley it was clear that they would not be able to hold on to the classy midfield general. It took a deal worth a club record £1.1 million to take Simon to QPR but six months later he rejoined Mark McGhee at Wolves where again his career was hampered by injuries.

Reading Record: Lge 31(1)/5, LC 4, Play-offs 3, Total 38(1)/5
League Career Total: 244(23)/23 +

O'SULLIVAN Cyril John
b. Lewisham 22.2.1920
Ht 6ft Wt 12st 9 (47-48)
Career: Crown Villa; READING September 1946; Headington U summer 1948

Cyril played for the RAF's Indian Command side during the War, and was playing in goal for a local club when he wrote to Reading for a trial. Although he let in five on his League debut, Cyril soon established himself as the club's first choice keeper for the much of that season. Cyril started the next season in the first team but there was much more competition and, following the signing of John McBride, he moved back to the non-League game.

Reading Record: Lge 36, FAC 5, Total 41

O'SULLIVAN Peter Anthony
b. Colwyn Bay 4.3.1951
Ht 5ft 6 Wt 10st (82-83)
Career: Manchester U. apprentice; Brighton (free) April 1970; San Diego Sockers (£50,000) May 1980; Fulham June 1981; Charlton A.(loan) October 1982; READING (loan) November 1982; Hong Kong; Aldershot July 1983; Maidstone U. February 1984; Crawley T. summer 1984; Worthing; Newhaven T; Peacehaven & Telscombe manager

Originally a left winger, Peter was converted to midfield by Brighton and won three full Welsh caps to add to his schoolboy and U23 honours. After over 450 appearances for Brighton in a spell that saw them rise from the Fourth to the First Division, Peter moved to Fulham and promptly helped them to win promotion to the Second Division. He was loaned to Reading to add experience to the side struggling near the foot of the Third Division but while Peter helped the Royals avoid defeat in six of his nine League games, they only produced one victory. However, Peter's only goal for Reading was part of the best win of the season - a 5-3 Football League Trophy win over First Division runners up, Watford.

Reading Record: Lge 9, FLT 1/1, Total 10/1
League Career Total: 504(5)/40

OSWALD Robert Ray Broome
b. Bo'ness 20.12.1910
Ht 5ft 7 Wt 10st 7 (29-30)
Career: Hearts; Bo'ness; READING (£400) June 1928; Sheffield U. June 1930; Southend U. summer 1934

A free scoring left winger, Bert scored 44 goals in two seasons at Hearts before moving to Bo'ness. Bert then followed Bo'ness' former manager, Andrew Wylie, to Reading and, if the records are correct, this was his third club before he was 18. At Reading he missed just one game in two seasons and scored regularly in the Second Division. A neat player, Bert attracted the attention of several clubs, eventually joining Sheffield United at the end of 1929-30.

Reading Record: Lge 82/15, FAC 3/1, Total 85/16
League Career Total: 311/59

OWEN William
b. Northwich 17.9.1906 d. Newport 26.3.1981
Ht 5ft 5 Wt 9st 11 (35-36)
Career: Macclesfield; Manchester U. 1934; READING 14 January 1936; Exeter C. December 1936; Newport C. May 1937

Billy made 17 League appearances in two seasons with Manchester United before joining Reading for a big fee. He made his debut at home to QPR in the game that saw Reading lose after 55 undefeated League games at Elm Park. Despite this setback, Billy kept his place on the left wing to the end of the season even though Reading disputed the fee due to United, but the League ordered Reading to pay the full amount. He was used less frequently at the start of 1936-37, and after a transfer request he moved to Exeter. Another move, to Newport, proved a statisticians' and fans' nightmare since County already had a forward called Billy Owen.

Reading Record: Lge 23/2
League Career Total: 100/11

OWENS Thomas Leslie
b. Sunderland 17.10.1919 d. Hellesdon 28.3.1974
Ht 5ft 11 Wt 13st 3 (51-52)
Career: Hylton Colliery Jnrs; Ditchburn Social Club; Washington Chemical Works; Sunderland (trial); Charlton A.(£100) September 1937; Doncaster R.(£1,000) February 1939; Wartime guest for Charlton A & Coventry C; Southport December 1947; Hartlepools U. July 1949; Norwich C. March 1950; READING (player exchange) 5 July 1951; Brighton (£1,000) June 1952; Dartford July 1953; Hellesden manager

After failing to be taken on by Sunderland, despite scoring in his trial match, Les signed for Charlton and played in front of their record crowd, when 75,031 were at the Valley for their 1938 FA Cup-tie against Villa.

A move to Doncaster was interrupted by the War, but he was still with them for the first half of Rovers' runaway Third Division North championship. Four moves later the dashing inside forward came to Reading in exchange for Roy McCrohan who moved to Norwich. Again Les was part of a record breaking side as Reading hit 112 goals that season, but the success of the forward line meant that Les only got the occasional start, coming in when Les Henley and then Ron Blackman were injured. As well as the four first team goals in his one season at Reading, Les also topped the reserve scorers with 22 goals as they won the Combination title. Les's career was eventually ended by a broken leg.

Reading Record: Lge 8/4
League Career Total: 157/55

OXBERRY John 'Jack'
b. Sunderland 4.4.1901 d. ?
Ht 5ft 8 Wt 11st 6 (32-33)
Career: Bolden Colliery; South Shields 1919; Blackpool (£3,500) 1928; READING (£300) July 1932; Aldershot 1935; Gillingham trainer September 1937; READING asst. trainer/coach 16 May 1938; Chelsea trainer June 1953

An inside left with an eye for goals, Jack's move to Blackpool came after his best season with South Shields when he scored 21 goals in 29 games. He was part of the team that won the Second Division title in 1929-30 but was allowed to join Reading two years later. In his first season, Jack played in every one of Reading's 49 first team games, and in 1934-35, Jack played eight games at centre forward, scoring six goals in that spell. The arrival of Tommy Tait heralded the end of his Reading career so Jack moved to Aldershot where he began studying massage, and in 1938 he returned to Elm Park as assistant trainer/coach. During the War Jack often acted as trainer for FA teams and he even came out of retirement to play at West Ham in a London League match three weeks after his 41st birthday. When Reading manager, Ted Drake, moved to Chelsea he asked Jack to join him and together they guided Chelsea to the League Championship in 1954-55.

Reading Record: Lge 87/24, FAC 9/3, SSC 1, Wartime 1, Total 98/27
League Career Total: 345/111

PAINTER Andrew
b. Henley 1.12.1958
Ht 5ft 10 Wt 10st 7 (77-78)
Career: Henley T; Chelsea (trial); READING amateur October 1974, apprentice August 1975, professional December 1976; Maidenhead U. summer 1978

Andy wrote to Reading for a trial while scoring 42 goals as Henley Town's centre forward but, although he was successful, he played most of his early games in the back four of Reading's youth team. On signing as an apprentice, Andy moved into midfield and formed a devastating goalscoring partnership with Jerry Williams. While Jerry got the majority of the goals, Andy scored hat tricks in three consecutive youth team games. Andy looked to have everything necessary for a promising career and in November 1976 he was named as sub for Reading's FA Cup-tie against Wealdstone. He came on for the last seven minutes but was guilty of a glaring miss, and this appeared to affect his form and he never played for the first team again.

Reading Record; FAC (1)

PALETHORPE Christopher Glynne

b Maidenhead 6.11.1942
Ht 5ft 7 Wt 10st (61-62)
Career: READING amateur August 1958, professional 9 November 1959; Aldershot June 1963; Gravesend August 1965

A nephew of Thirties centre forward, Jack Palethorpe, Chris was an outside right who played for Berks & Bucks in the FA Youth championship and for the National Association of Boys Clubs while a junior with Reading. Chris was a speedy player who made his debut in August 1958 at Newport but, although he showed a handy goalscoring knack in his first two seasons, he could never be sure of his first team place. His best spell came at the start of 1961-62 when Chris scored a hat trick at QPR as Reading headed the division early on.

Reading Record: Lge 55/10, FAC 1, LC 1, Total 57/10
League Career Total: 111/14

PALETHORPE John Thomas 'Jack'

b. Leicester 23.11.1909 d. Slough 5.1984
Ht 5ft 10 Wt 11st (31-32)
Career: Crystal Palace amateur; Maidenhead U; READING part-time 12 May 1930, full time February 1931; Stoke C.(£2,500) 15 March 1933; Preston NE 1934; Sheffield Wed. December 1935; Aston Villa November 1936; Crystal Palace 1936; Chelmsford C. summer 1938; Shorts Sports 1939

As a free scoring centre forward, Jack scored a record 65 goals in 39 games for Maidenhead before joining Reading. Jack scored at will for the reserves, but although he was also successful in both of his League games, the directors, who picked the team in those days, claimed he was too young for the first team.

Many fans believed that Jack could have saved Reading from relegation that season and they appear to have been proved right when he got his chance. By March 1933 Jack had scored 54 goals in 57 League games when Stoke signed him to help their promotion bid which he did, scoring twice on his debut. A year later he almost returned to Reading but went to Preston instead, where he repeated his promotion winning feat, scoring the goal that returned Preston to the First Division with seven minutes to go in the deciding match. Jack's consecutive promotions earned him the nickname 'SOS' and he lived up to it when, six months after joining Sheffield Wednesday, he scored in four of their 1935 FA Cup rounds, including a goal after just two minutes of the final. Jack ended his peacetime playing career with Chelmsford where he scored 31 times in 36 Southern League games, and helped them knock Darlington and Southampton out of the Cup.

As well as his goalscoring skills, Jack was a great asset to all his teams as his happy temperament always improved team spirit wherever he was.

Reading Record: Lge 57/54, FAC 7, Total 64/54
League Career Total: 175/107

PARKER William

b. Liverpool 15.8.1925
Ht 5ft 7 1/2 Wt 11st 2 (50-51)
Career: Runcorn; READING (free) 30 May 1950; Swindon T. (£1,000) February 1953; Exeter C. July 1953

Bill was recommended to Reading by former player, Bill Ratcliffe, and soon made his League debut on the left wing. He never got a game in the year of 1951, and did not appear in the first team until April 1952, by which time he had moved to inside left. The following season was both his best and his last for Reading - Bill scoring six goals in 14 games, including four in the first five matches of the season. While Bill was with Reading, his brother, Sam, was playing for Accrington and Crewe.

Reading Record: Lge 32/6, FAC 2, Total 34/6
League Career Total: 60/8

PARKINSON Philip John

b. Chorley 1.12.1967
Ht 6ft Wt 12st 12 (93-94)
Career: Southampton from apprentice•December 1985; Bury
(£12,000) March 1988; READING (£37,500) 10 July 1992

Although he played in the same Southampton youth team as Alan Shearer and Matt Le Tissier, Phil had to return to his native Lancashire to make his League debut, with Bury. During his time there, Bury twice missed out on promotion to the Second Division in the play-offs and in 1992 Phil's former teammate, Craig Maskell, recommended him to Reading. By coincidence Phil joined Reading on the day that Craig was sold to Swindon to fund his purchase. A tough tackling midfielder, Phil developed at Reading to become one of the club's most popular players. Initially, his powerful tackling earned him the nickname 'Psycho', becoming 'Parky', and eventually, in the Press at least, 'Captain Marvel'. Throughout the difficult years at the end of the last century, Phil was the one player that could be relied upon and, even if he was not the most skilful player at the club, Reading inevitably played better and with more passion when Phil was in the team. Not surprisingly, Phil walked away with the fans' Player of the Year awards in 1998 and 1999.

Made club captain, Phil's charge across the pitch towards the fans before the start of each game became the Madejski Stadium's first ritual. Although there have been no signs of his influence on the pitch diminishing, Phil has already been earmarked a place in Reading's coaching staff when he hangs up his boots.

Reading Record: 300(23)/18, FAC 21/1, LC 24(1)/2, AMC 8(2), Play-offs 3, Total 356(26)/21 +
League Career Total: 433(35)/23 +

PARSONS Frank Ronald

b. Amersham 29.10.1947
Ht 6ft Wt 12st (73-74)
Career: Crystal Palace from jnrs July 1965; Cardiff C. August 1970; Fulham January 1974; READING (trial) April 1974, part-time September 1974; Staines T. May 1975; Slough T

In his nine years as a professional before he joined Reading, Frank had only played 21 League games and his one game in goal for Reading was his first League appearance for three years. At that time he was running a car showroom and only training a couple of days a week. With Reading slipping down the Fourth Division, it was hardly surprising that Frank's last League game should end in a 3-1 defeat. Frank carried on playing non-League football and in 1983 he had the novel experience of scoring Slough's winner in an FA Cup-tie against Hampton.

Reading Record: Lge 1
League Career Total: 22

PATERSON James

b. Stirling 1907 d. ?
Ht 5ft 8 Wt 10st (36-37)
Career: Causewayhead; Camelon Jnrs; Everton January 1921; St Johnstone 1927; Cowdenbeath summer 1930; Leicester C. May 1932, READING (£350) 3 July 1935; Clapton O. June 1938

Despite his slight build, Jim was a brave player and this, allied to his speed, made his a regular scorer at inside left throughout his career. He averaged over a goal every other game, scoring 53 in 74 matches for Cowdenbeath, form that saw Jim top their scorers in both his seasons with them, and earn him three Scottish caps in 1931. A big fee took him to Leicester and, three years later he moved to Reading. Again, the goals flowed until March 1937 when Jim hit a dry spell and he lost his place after 17 goalless games.

Reading Record: Lge 72/23, FAC 7/3, SSC 3, Total 82/26
League Career Total: 125/40

JIM'S CLAIM TO FAME: Jim was one of three unrelated Patersons who all played for Leicester as well as Scotland. He also scored City's first goal against foreign opposition when he netted v Rapid Vienna in a 1933 friendly.

PATTISON John William **Phillip**

b. Portsmouth 23.2 1925 d 1993
Ht 5ft 9 Wt 11st (45-46)
Career: Portsmouth CS; READING (amateur) June 1945, professional July 1945; Grimsby T. (Wartime guest); Canterbury C

Phil started playing for Reading as a Wartime guest and was often Matt Busby's replacement at right half when the Scot was playing representative games. He was rewarded with a contract at the end of the War and played two League games in April 1947 before being released.

Reading Record: Lge 2, FAC 2, Wartime 26, Total 30

PAYNE Lee John

b. Luton 12.12.1966
Ht 5ft 11 Wt 11st (89-90)
Career: Barnet; Newcastle U. (£100,000) September 1988; READING (£60,000) March 1989; Veendam (£70,000) August 1990

A flying winger, Lee played under Barry Fry during Barnet's Vauxhall Conference days before spending six months with Newcastle, where he made his debut in the derby game against Middlesbrough, and was voted Man of the Match. Lee had even quicker success when he moved to Reading, scoring within a minute of his home debut against Northampton. Although he scored a wonder goal in the pre-season friendly versus Oxford, running the length of the pitch and through the visitors' defence before firing home, Lee could not command a regular place that season. A change of manager finally ended Lee's hopes of regaining it and he was sold to Belgium side Veendam.

Reading Record: Lge 25(2)/3, FAC 6, LC 3, AMC 1, Total 35(2)/3
League Career Total: 31(3)/3

PENFORD Dennis Henry

b. Reading 31.8.1931
Ht 5ft 11 Wt 12st 1 (58-59)
Career: READING amateur 1949, professional 13 May 1952; Torquay U. (£500) 13 June 1959

Many players appear to start their careers in a forward position and gradually move back through the years, but Dennis did the opposite. Signed as a right back by Reading, he played in this position when he represented the RAF against the Navy at Elm Park in 1954. After more than 50 first team games at the back Dennis was switched to right half in 1955 and played a similar number of matches from there.

Having spent 1957-58 in the reserves, Dennis was then tried at centre forward, scoring three goals in five games before he was allowed to join Torquay. Dennis settled in Devon, helping in their backroom after his playing career was over, and he later set up a youth league in the area.

Reading Record: Lge 101/7, FAC 8, SPFC 3, Total 112/7
League Career Total: 178/7

PENNY Hubert G

b. Reading c.1886 d. Reading 20.12.61
Ht 5ft 10 Wt 12st 4 (22-23)
Career: British Workers' Institute; READING amateur August 1910, professional September 1922

Although he only played one League game for Reading, Bert was one of the club's longest serving employees. After signing for Reading in the same week that Florence Nightingale died, Bert played in every position for the reserves and was 'an excellent utility man at all times'. Much of his Elm Park career was on the groundstaff and he did not make his first team debut until January 1923 when he was centre half at Exeter. Bert stayed with Reading, initially as assistant trainer. Later he became trainer, groundsman and head turnstile operator, but carried on turning out occasionally for the reserves until he was nearly 40. In 1927 he was trainer for England for their amateur international against Wales that was played at Elm Park. Sadly, Bert died within months of finally retiring after almost 52 years at Elm Park.

Reading Record: Lge 1

PETERS Gary David

b. Carlshalton 3.8.1954
Ht 5ft 11 Wt 11st 12 (77-78)
Career: Aldershot apprentice; Guildford C. July 1972; READING from (loan) (£1,000) 23 May 1975; Fulham (£40,000) August 1979; Wimbledon July 1982; Aldershot July 1984; READING February 1985; Fulham non contract August 1988 asst. manager August 1989; Cambridge U. asst. manager; Preston NE asst. manager 1992, manager 1994, Centre of Excellence manager February 1998

Gary seems to have the magic touch as far as promotion is concerned, with six to his credit to date. Having joined Reading at a bargain fee, his debut season saw Reading's first promotion for 55 years and in 1978-79 Gary won a Fourth Division champions medal plus a PFA award as the division's best right back. After over 170 first team games for Reading, Gary spent three seasons with Fulham that saw them move up to the Second Division, a feat he repeated at Wimbledon when they won the Third Division title in 1982-83.

After a short spell with Aldershot, Gary returned to Reading in 1985 with a view to assisting the reserves. However, it was clear that he had lost none of the skill and passion that made him the club's best post-War right back, and within a month Gary was in the first team.

Still playing mainly at full back, he was also used as an emergency centre forward and, after Martin Hicks was injured, Gary took over as centre half and captain in the run-in for Reading's 1985-86 Third Division championship season. Although Gary's first team appearances slowly reduced in number, he remained a valuable squad member, never letting the team down, while his personality ensured that morale was always at a high. One of Gary's last appearances for Reading came at Wembley when he came on as a sentimental but well deserved substitute near the end of the 1988 Simod Cup victory. Gary then began learning the managerial trade and in 1995-96 he guided Preston to the Division Three title, but resigned a year later to run their Centre of Excellence.

Reading: Lge 243(13)/11, FAC 14(1), LC 19(2)/1, AMC 1, FMC (1), Total 277(17)/12
League Career Total: 407(24)/23

PETERS Peter
b. c.1925
Ht 5ft 10 Wt 12st (45-46)
Career: READING amateur 1945

A young goalie, Peter was called on by Reading to play in the second leg of the FA Cup at Aldershot in November 1945. 3-0 up from the game at Elm Park, Peter let in seven as Reading crashed out on aggregate, but he did better in his two other War games as both ended in 3-2 victories and he continued to play for the reserves for two more seasons.

Reading Record: FAC 1, Wartime 2, Total 3

PETTS John William Frederick James
b. Edmonton 2.10.1938
Ht 5ft 8 Wt 10st 7 (63-64)
Career: Arsenal from groundstaff May 1956; READING (£5,000) 10 October 1962; Bristol R. (trial) June 1965 then (£5,000) 3 September 1965; Bath C. player manager June 1970; Trowbridge T. November 1971, manager March 1972; Northampton T. trainer-coach July 1973, manager January 1977; Northampton Spencer manager March 1983 to February 1988

Johnny spent six seasons at Highbury, winning seven England Youth caps and scoring a lot of goals for Arsenal's reserves at inside right. However, his only first team games came as a more defensive wing half when Tommy Docherty was not available, so he was released to Reading. He was Harry Johnston's last signing but within a month of Roy Bentley's first game in charge at Reading, Johnny could no longer be sure of a first team place. Having played in the first 17 games after joining Reading, he then took over two years to double that figure as fans debated the merits of the skilful, attacking half back. After Reading, Johnny joined Bristol Rovers and then began a managerial career while his son, Paul, took up the playing mantle with Bristol Rovers and Shrewsbury.

Reading Record: Lge 34, FAC 1, LC 1, Total 36
League Career Total: 154(4)/3

PHILLIPS Gary Christopher
b. St Albans 20.9.1961
Ht 6ft Wt 13st 10 (88-89)
Career: Brighton non contract; West Bromwich Alb; Barnet; Brentford December 1984; READING (£15,000) August 1988; Millwall (loan) summer 1989; Hereford U.(loan) September 1989; Barnet (£12,500) December 1989; Windsor & Eton; Aylesbury U. player coach March 1996; Aldershot T; Aylesbury 2000; Stevenage Bor. February 2001

It took Gary several attempts to break into League football and he had already been capped at semi pro level when his chance came with Brentford. Within months he was playing in goal at Wembley as Brentford lost to Wigan in the first Freight Rover Cup final, but after over 150 first team games Gary moved to Reading as cover for Steve Francis. He soon got his chance when Steve broke his arm and made 34 appearances during 1988-89, but only kept two clean sheets. This cost Reading an extra £7,500 after 10 games, but Brentford missed out on another payment as Gary ended one League game short of the required 25. He eventually completed a move to Barnet and later in his career proved something of a thorn in Reading's side when he twice helped Aylesbury beat the Royals in the Berks & Bucks Senior Cup final.

Reading Record: Lge 24, FAC 7, AMC 3, Total 34
League Career Total: 290

PICKERING William Harold

b. Birmingham 1.11.1901 d. Warley 2.1971
Ht 6ft Wt 12st (29-30)
Career: Latch & Batchelors; Merthyr T. 1925; Gillingham
summer 1926; Huddersfield T.(£1,000) November 1927;
READING (£500) June 1929; Colwyn Bay U. August 1930;
Bristol R.(£250) May 1931; Accrington Stan. June 1937;
Oswestry T. player manager summer 1938; Cradley Heath
October 1938

A series of fine displays at left back for Gillingham
caught the eye of Huddersfield, but Bill only made one
First Division appearance for them in 18 months. He
went straight into Reading's first team after his transfer
but he lost his place in November. He regained it a
month later but two hefty defeats heralded the end of
Bill's first team career at Elm Park. After a spell out of
the League, Bill joined Bristol Rovers where he made
215 League appearances.

Reading Record: Lge 20, FAC 1, Total 21
League Career Total: 319/1

PLATNAUER Nicholas Robert

b. Leicester 10.6.1961
Ht 5ft 11 Wt 12st 10 (96-97)
Career: Northampton T. amateur; Bedford T; Bristol R. from
trial July 1982; Coventry C.(£50,000) August 1983;
Birmingham C.(£50,000) December 1984; READING (loan)
30 January 1986; Cardiff C.(free) September 1986; Notts
Co.(£50,000) August 1989; Port Vale (loan) January 1991;
Leicester C.(free) July 1991; Scunthorpe U. March 1993;
Kettering T.(trial) July 1993; Mansfield T. August 1993;
Lincoln C.(loan) February 1994, (free) March 1994, reserve
coach January 1995; Bedworth U. August 1995; Hinckley U.
July 1997; Rothwell T. manager 2000

A widely traveled player who could perform well in
almost any position, Nicky began as a striker, helping
Bedford Town win the Southern League Cup in 1981,
and was their Player of the Year in the last season before
their demise. Nicky played most of his League career in
midfield or defence, his League debut coming at Bristol
Rovers, but he was with Birmingham when he was
loaned to Reading. Although running away with the
Third Division, Reading were in the middle of an injury
crisis plus a dip in form when Nicky arrived and,
although his debut saw a 6-0 defeat at Walsall, he helped
steady the midfield. After this, Nicky enjoyed his
longest spell with any club, playing in Europe with
Cardiff during his three years there. He also helped
Notts County to consecutive promotions and was still
playing well into his late thirties.

Reading Record: Lge 7, AMC 1, Total 8
League Career Total: 367(23)/24

POLSTON John David

b. Walthamstow 10.6.1968
Ht 5ft 11 Wt 11st 12 (99-00)
Career: Tottenham H. from apprentice 16 July 1985; Norwich
C.(£250,000) July 1990; READING (free) 6 July 1998

A former England Youth international, John was
developed at Spurs, but after 20 first team starts, some
alongside his brother, Andy, he was sold to Norwich.
There he gave great service to the Canaries at either full
back or centre half making over 260 first team
appearances, the last of which was for the final four
minutes of Elm Park's last League game. John then
joined Reading on a free but suffered a series of injuries
that restricted him to just four games in his first season.
Things were only slightly better in 1999-00, then a knee
injury kept him out for the next season and in March
2001 he was forced to retire. When he did play John
displayed all the class and skill his pedigree indicated.

Reading Record: Lge 16(2)/1, FAC 4, LC 1, AMC 1,
Total 22(2)/1
League Career Total: 233(24)/10

PORTER Ernest Wesley

b. Annfield Plain 1st qtr 1901 d. ?
Ht 5ft 7 Wt 10st 10 (26-27)
Career: Birtley & Ouston R; Sheffield U; Boston T; READING
(£250) June 1926; Norwich C. (£150) June 1927; Tunbridge
Wells Rngrs summer 1931

Ernie had a successful non-League career winning
major local competitions with both his clubs, but his
first chance of a professional career was hampered by an
ankle injury while he was at Sheffield United. After
scoring 28 goals from either wing in 49 games for
Boston, including victory over Lincoln in the
Lincolnshire Cup, Ernie moved to Reading. There was
fierce competition for the right wing spot that season but
Ernie played in just over a third of that season's games.
He dropped down a division to join Norwich where he
was a first team regular for four seasons, becoming their
100th League player.

Reading Record: Lge 15/3, FAC 3/1, Total 18/4
League Career Total: 145/33

PORTERFIELD John 'Ian'

b. Dunfermline 11.2.1946
Ht 5ft 11 Wt 12st 7 (76-77)
Career: Leeds U. (trial); Hearts (trial); Glasgow Rngrs (trial);
Raith R; Sunderland (£38,000) December 1967; READING
(loan) 1 November 1976; Sheffield Wed. July 1977
See also the 'The Managers' section.

By scoring the Sunderland goal that beat Leeds in the 1973 FA Cup Final, Ian wrote himself a place in football's folklore. He had been signed from Raith as a replacement for Jim Baxter but 18 months after his Wembley success, Ian fractured his skull in a car crash, and for a time it looked as if his playing days were over. Fortunately, he gradually recovered and was loaned to Reading, managed by his former Sunderland team mate, Charlie Hurley. Ian went straight into the first team, even though he had hardly played for a year. He never let Reading down, despite not playing on the winning side during his five match spell. The move could have become permanent but Reading were put off by Sunderland's £20,000 asking price and eventually Ian joined Sheffield Wednesday before starting a long and varied managerial career.

Reading: Lge 5
League Career Total: 326(15)/20

POTTER Graham Stephen
b. Solihull 20.5.1975
Ht 6ft 1 Wt 11st 12 (99-00)
Career: Birmingham C. from trainee July 1992; Wycombe W.(loan) September 1993; Stoke C.(£75,000) December 1993; Southampton (£250,000) July 1996; West Bromwich Alb. (£300,000) February 1997; Northampton T.(loan) October 1997; READING (loan) 2 December 1999; York C. July 2000

Although he was only 24 when he joined Reading on loan, Graham had already played for six League clubs and had appeared in all four divisions as well as being capped by England at youth and U21 level. He possessed a fine left foot and was capable of playing in any position down that flank, although he was best suited to a wingback role. Graham's loan spell at Reading provided a temporary solution to the club's shortage of left sided players before he moved back to West Brom.

Reading Record: Lge 4, AMC 1, Total 5
League Career Total: 141(29)5 +

POULTON Alonzo 'Jerry'
b. Wolverhampton 28.3.1890 d. Wolverhampton 1966
Ht 5ft 9 Wt 12st (22-23)
Career: Priestfield Alb; West Bromwich Alb; Worcester C.(loan); Merthyr T; Middlesbrough 1920; Bristol C.(£1,000) 1921; READING (£400) November 1922; Llanelli (£200) September 1923

A creative inside or centre forward, Jerry was not a regular goalscorer, but two goals and fine performances for Bristol City against them persuaded Reading to sign him. It took three months and a large fee for the 'famous forward' to join Reading, who announced *it is doubtful if any signature had given greater satisfaction*.

Certainly, the optimism proved well founded as Jerry scored three goals in his first five games, but then they dried up and he failed to add to his total in his remaining 20 games.

Reading Record: Lge 25/3, FAC 1, Total 26/3
League Career Total: 80/18

JERRY'S CLAIM TO FAME - A great joker, Jerry once went too far and annoyed the groundsman's horse so much that the animal would attack anything in a blue and white shirt. Consequently, the horse had to be locked away while the players trained on the pitch!

PRATT John Leslie
b. Atherstone 1.3.1943
Ht 6ft 1 Wt 13st (69-70)
Career: Hayes; Amersham; Wycombe W; READING 1 July 1969; Bath C. summer 1972

After turning down the chance to sign for Aston Villa in order to concentrate on his teaching career, John played for a number of non-League clubs before signing for Reading on a part-time basis. He had already turned out for the team, keeping goal for them in the Wycombe Hospital Cup against his own club, Wycombe, but his League career was delayed by a broken leg sustained during pre-season training. John was a steady, if unspectacular keeper, and, although he was always number two to Steve Death during his three seasons at Elm Park, he did manage 19 games in 1970-71 when injuries and a rare loss of form affected the little keeper.

Reading Record: Lge 29

PRICE Kenneth Gordon
b. Dudley 26.2.1954
Ht 5ft 10 Wt 11st 11 (84-85)
Career: Dudley T; Southend U. May 1976; Gillingham December 1976; READING (£10,000) 27 January 1983; Basingstoke T.

Despite going to a rugby only school, Ken impressed Leicester enough to offer him an apprenticeship, but he decided to stay on at school and play for Dudley. Eventually he was persuaded to sign for Southend, but only made one League appearance before moving to Gillingham. There, Ken developed a reputation as a tough, goal-getting striker, who topped the Gills scorers in his first full season. In 1981-82 he scored 24 goals and Reading tried to sign him in exchange for Gary Heale. Ken eventually joined Reading as a replacement for the injured Kerry Dixon but he could not keep Reading in the Third Division despite some committed displays.

Although the signing of Trevor Senior and Dean Horrix restricted Ken's chances, he got back into the first team in a deeper role for the last three months of Reading's promotion season but his final season was greatly hindered by a series of injuries.

Reading Record: Lge 40(3)/6, FAC 2/1, LC 1/1, AMC 1, Total 44(3)/8
League Career Total: 288(11)/84

PRICE Albert John **William**
b. Wellington 10.4.1917 d. 10.4.1995
Ht 5ft 10 11st 1 (48-49)
Career: Wrockwardine Wood; Huddersfield T. October 1937; READING October 1947; Hull C. (£3,750) January 1949; Bradford C. November 1949

Bill spent nine years with Huddersfield where he was a prolific goalscoring centre forward, and was the eighth highest Wartime goalscorer. He scored an amazing 190 goals in 202 Wartime matches, including a club record seven against Crewe in 1943, and a hat trick for the Football League against Northern Command a year earlier. Reading were thought to have a bargain when they signed Bill and George Green for a joint fee of £10,000 but, while Green scored on their joint debut, Bill had to wait five months for his first goal. By then he was no longer a first team regular, and although he topped the reserves scorers in 1948-49, Bill only made two first team appearances before being transferred to Hull in January 1949. After netting twice on his Hull debut, Bill moved on to Bradford where he regained his regular goalscoring touch.

Reading Record: Lge 15/2, FAC 2, Total 17/2
League Career Total: 128/58

PRIMUS Linvoy **Stephen**
b. Forest Gate 14.9.1973
Ht 6ft Wt 14st (99-00)
Career: Charlton A. from trainee August 1992; Barnet (free) July 1994; READING (£300,000) 28 July 1997; Portsmouth (free) August 2000

Although Linvoy only made four league appearances for Charlton, he got off to a flying start by being voted Man of the Match on his debut in a televised match against Birmingham. A move to Barnet saw Linvoy develop into one of the best central defenders in the lower divisions, being renowned for his pace and aerial ability and was twice voted Player of the Year.

The inevitable transfer came when new Reading manager, and former Barnet boss, Terry Bullivant, took Linvoy to Elm Park. Linvoy's form was soon attracting attention from Premiership clubs but he could not save Reading from relegation. Linvoy continued to turn out consistent performances for Reading, only missing games through injury, and a number of clubs were interested in the summer of 2000 when he became available on a 'Bosman', eventually joining Portsmouth.

Reading Record: Lge 94(1)/1, FAC 13/1, LC 9(1), AMC 4, Total 120(2)/2
League Career Total: 248(1)/8 +

PROUDLOVE Andrew George
b. Buxton 15.1.1955
Ht 5ft 10 Wt 11st (71-72)
Career: READING apprentice September 1970; Buxton T. May 1972; West Ham U. (trial) August 1974; Sheffield Wed. September 1975; Norwich C. February 1976; Hereford U. May 1977; Port Vale November 1978

For one month, in November 1971, Andy was Reading's youngest ever player when he played at Bridgewater in the FA Cup at 16 years 309 days and although Steve Hetzke soon took over that record, Andy remains the club's youngest Cup player. Left winger Andy went on to make a handful of League appearances but was not offered a professional contract. Over the next seven seasons, he played for four more League clubs without establishing himself at any of them.

Reading Record: Lge 4(1), FAC 1, Total 5(1)
League Career Total: 25(12)

QUINLAN Edward Maurice
b. Finsbury Park 15.8.1931
Ht 5ft 10 Wt 10st 1 (53-54)
Career: Great Yarmouth; Tottenham H. March 1952; READING (£850) 18 June 1953; Worcester C. June 1955; Dartford 1959

It took a substantial fee to bring Eddie to Reading where he made his League debut at the start of 1953-54, on the left wing. Eddie was unable to command a regular first team place until near the end of that season and strangely his three seasons at Elm Park followed the same format with 32 of his 51 League appearances coming in the March and April of each campaign.

Reading Record: Lge 51/11, FAC 2, SPFC 2, Total 55/11

QUINN James Martin

b. Belfast 18.11.1959
Ht 6ft Wt 11st 6 (96-97)
Career: Oswestry T; Swindon T.(£10,000) December 1981; Blackburn R.(£32,000) August 1984; Swindon T.(£50,000) December 1986; Leicester C. (£210,000) June 1988; Bradford C. March 1989; West Ham U. (£320,000) December 1989; Bournemouth (£40,000) August 1991, READING (£55,000) 27 July 1992; Peterborough U.(free) July 1997; Swindon T. player manager November 1998; Cirencester T summer 2000; Northwich Vic. September 2000; Highworth T. November 2000; Congleton; Hayes January 2001
See 'The Managers' for details of Jimmy's managerial career.

Having given up his job as a postman to sign for Swindon, Jimmy was soon delivering goals(!) for them and so began a career that was to establish him as one of the greatest goalscorers outside the top division. He made a scoring debut in the first of 46 games for Northern Ireland and was a member of their World Cup squad in Mexico. His goalscoring ability earned him a series of big money transfers but he rarely stayed more than a couple of years with any club, until Mark McGhee bought the 32 year old Jimmy for what proved to be one of Reading's all time bargains.

Jimmy topped Reading's scorers in his first season but that was nothing compared with his form in 1993-94. Forming a deadly partnership with Stuart Lovell, Jimmy scored 40 goals, won a Division Two Champions medal, a PFA Divisional award, an Adidas Golden Boot, and was Northern Ireland's Player of the Year. Midway through the following season, Jimmy was appointed joint player manager with Mick Gooding and his first team appearances gradually reduced as he concentrated on the managerial side. Even so, he scored the winner in the 1995 Berks & Bucks Senior Cup final and was top first team and reserve goalscorer in 1995-96. In addition he became Reading's most capped player with 17 international appearances that produced six goals, another club best.

Right up to his last season at Reading, Jimmy was coming on as a very effective substitute and not just as a striker - twice he came off the bench to play in goal and ended up on the winning side each time. At the end of 1996-97, the Quinn-Gooding managerial team was somewhat surprisingly released by Reading, but Jimmy proved he was still a potent striker, topping Peterborough's goalscorers and winning another PFA award at the age of 38, before moving to Swindon as manager. Even then he still played the occasional game and, on moving to Northwich, he netted twice on his Conference debut. Jimmy didn't always get the credit he deserved at Reading, particularly as a player. It was not just the quantity of Jimmy's goals that impressed but the quality - he displayed his full repertoire of acrobatic volleys, cheeky flicks, thunderous shots, towering headers and net busting penalties with several of his goals being candidates for the club's greatest ever strike.

Reading Record: Lge 149(33)/71, FAC 9/5, LC 12(4)/12, AMC 6(1)/5, Play-offs (2)/1, Total 176(40)/94
League Career Total: 475(103)/210

JIMMY'S CLAIM TO FAME - Jimmy is one of only three League players to have made more than 100 substitute appearances.

RANSON Raymond

b. St Helens 12.6.1960
Ht 5ft 9 Wt 11st 13 (93-94)
Career: Manchester C. from apprentice June 1977; Birmingham C. November 1984; Newcastle U. December 1988; Manchester C. January 1993; READING (free) August 1993; Whitton Alb. player-manager 1995

Ray made his debut for Manchester City reserves at 15 and progressed to make the right back spot his own, playing in the 1981 FA Cup final and replay as well as being capped for England at schools, youth and 10 times at U21. After over 200 first team appearances, Ray moved to Birmingham and then to Newcastle where he teamed up with Mark McGhee, who signed him for Reading after his second spell at Maine Road. Even at 33, Ray proved a class act and his experience helped Reading to the Division Two title, although injuries restricted his appearances. Eventually, an achilles injury eventually forced Ray to retire from League football in February 1995.

Reading Record: Lge 22(2), FAC 2, LC 3, AMC 1, Total 28(2)
League Career Total: 434(10)/2

RATCLIFFE Beaumont 'Bill'

b. Bolton on Dearne 24.4.1909
Ht 5ft 10 Wt 13st (46-47)
Career: Bolton Alb. 1928; Bradford P.A. amateur December 1930; Charlton A. (trial) September 1931; New Brighton October 1931; Le Havre summer 1935; Oldham A.(£500) June 1935; READING (Wartime guest); READING July 1946; Watford (£750) May 1948; Runcorn player-manager summer 1949

For the eight seasons prior to the War, Bill was a regular stopper centre half for, first New Brighton, and then Oldham, giving sterling service to both. During the War, Bill guested for Reading, including the win in the 1941 London War Cup, but he was taken prisoner of war in Italy and also injured his shoulder while serving in the RAF. Bill was 37 when League football recommenced, but he still had plenty to offer after he joined Reading. Despite suffering a cartilage injury in his first season, Bill recovered to play 28 first team games in 1947-48, making his last appearance one week after his 39th birthday, to be Reading's oldest post-War League player. Remarkably, Bill's League career was to continue for another season with Watford, and in August 1999 Bill was guest of honour at the official opening of the Madejski Stadium, the dapper 90 year being Reading's oldest living player.

Reading Record: Lge 32, FAC 1, Wartime 82, Total 115
League Career Total: 343/5

READ Albert

b. Ealing 1899 d. ?
Ht 5ft 9 Wt 12st (22-23)
Career: Tufnell Park; QPR May 1921; READING July 1922

A successful amateur career with Tufnell Park saw Albert win two England Amateur caps and play in the 1920 Amateur Cup Final. At the beginning of May 1921 he was selected for the full England team to play Belgium, but by the time the game was played he had joined QPR, which caused no end of confusion, some record books showing him as being capped with Rangers, while others record him as still a Tufnell Park player. Albert was an *unobtrusive yet effective right or centre back* whose ground passes were *astutely placed*. After joining Reading, Albert played in the first three games of the season before suffering a bad injury that subsequently forced him to retire at his peak.

Reading Record: Lge 3
League Career Total: 24

REAY George Turnbull

b. East Howden 2.1903 d. York 15.8.1962
Ht 5ft 10 1/2 Wt 12st (23-24)
Career: Percy Main; South Shields 1922; Blyth Spartans summer 1923; READING September 1923; Kettering T. July 1924; Raith R.(£700) December 1925; Bristol R. May 1928; Coventry C. July 1930; Burton T. June 1931; Rushden T. summer 1934; Kettering T. October 1934

A tall and fast inside forward, George was converted to a winger at Reading but he only played three first team games. George then spent four years with Kettering and Raith before returning to the League with Bristol Rovers.

Reading Record; Lge 3
League Career Total: 83/12

RECK Sean Mark

b. Oxford 5.5.1967
Ht 5ft 10 Wt 12st 7 (85-86)
Career: Oxford U. from apprentice April 1985; Newport Co. (loan) August 1985; READING (loan) March 1986; Wrexham July 1989

Sean featured twice in Reading's 1985-86 Third Division championship season while on loan to Newport and then Reading. Having played for County in Reading's record breaking 12th consecutive win at the start of the season, Sean came to Elm Park at Easter as midfield cover for the suspended Terry Hurlock. His one game came in a 3-0 defeat at Gillingham, although he was an unused substitute in two other games before returning to Oxford.

Reading Record: Lge 1
League Career Total: 68(7)/2

REEVE Frederick William

b. Clapton 1.5.1918 d. 1994
Ht 5ft 11 1/2 Wt 12st 5 (49-50)
Career: Ashford T; Leyton O; Crystal Palace 1937; Tottenham H; Rochdale 1938; Southend U. (Wartime guest); Grimsby T. 1946; READING 15 June 1948; Hastings U. summer 1950; Ashford T.

In a varied career that was hindered by the War years, Fred was always willing to move to get first team football. Even so, it was only in the two seasons either side of the War that left half Fred got to play in more than half of his clubs' first team games. He was released by Grimsby when they were relegated from the First Division and joined Reading, making 19 first team appearances in both his seasons at Elm Park.

Fred scored his only goal for Reading, a penalty against Torquay, in what was to be his penultimate League game.

Reading Record: Lge 34/1, FAC 4, Total 38/1
League Career Total: 108/4

REEVES Raymond Henry Ernest
b. Reading 12.8.1931
Ht 6ft Wt 13st (50-51)
Career: READING groundstaff 16 August 1947, professional 17 May 1949; Brentford July 1961; Dover 1962; Burton Alb; Rugby T.

During the Fifties most clubs seemed to have a player nicknamed 'Bomber' and at Reading it was Ray. A power-fully built full back, Ray earned his nickname by using his formid-able physique to good use, both in defence and with his thunderous shooting that brought him 32 goals, including a club record 22 penalties. He played twice for England in the 1948-49 Home Youth International tournament and was a member of the squad that took part in an international competition in Holland. Ray's strength also saw him used at centre half early in his career, but from March 1956 to the end of 1959-60 he made the left back position his own. Although defensively sound, Ray will always be remembered for his spectacular shooting - any free kick within 40 yards of the opposition's goal was within 'Bomber's' range, and one such goal, against Norwich in the Cup, is still talked about to this day. He also took penalties with such force that, even if a keeper got to the ball, it still usually ended up in the net. By 1961, Ray was no longer a regular in Reading's first team and he moved to Brentford, but injury cut his career there to just five games. Despite his awesome presence on the pitch, Ray was a soft spoken gentleman off it and lives in retirement in Reading.

Reading Record: Lge 284/29, FAC 22/2, SPFC 11/1, Total 317/32
League Career Total: 289/29

REID Sidney Edward
b. Belfast c.1908 d. ?
Ht 5ft 10 Wt 12st (36-37)
Career: Cliftonville Strollers; Belfast Distillery; Derby Co.(£1,150) 1931; READING June 1936

Although he only made 16 League appearances in his five seasons, Sid still won three caps with Northern Ireland, the first costing the Rams an extra £250 as an additional fee to Distillery. He also helped Derby win the Central League in 1935-36 but moved to Reading to get a regular first team place. This never materialized, and apart from three games at left back in October 1936, Sid spent his season at Reading in the reserves. That signalled the end of Sid's League career and he then concentrated on his sweet shops in Belfast.

Reading Record: Lge 2, SSC 1, Total 3
League Career Total: 18

REILLY Mark
b. Belshill 3.3.1969
Ht 5ft 8 Wt 10st 7 (98-99)
Career: Wishaw Jnrs; Motherwell August 1985; Kilmarnock July 1991; READING (free) 21 July 1998; Kilmarnock November 1998

Mark played over 240 games for Kilmarnock, scoring 10 goals, helping them win the Scottish Cup in 1997 and then qualify for Europe the following season. Rather than play in Europe, Scotland B international Mark joined Reading on a 'Bosman' and became the first player to make his debut for the club at the Madejski Stadium when he played in the opening game. This was the start of a run of eight matches for the tidy, if unspectacular, midfielder but Mark found it difficult to settle in the South and was allowed to return to Kilmarnock for a small fee.

Reading Record: Lge 4(2), LC 2, Total 6(2)

RICHARDSON Frank
b. Barking 29.1.1899 d. Wokingham 19.5.1987
Ht 5ft 9 Wt 11st (29-30)
Career: Barking; Plymouth Arg. summer 1921; Stoke (£2,000) March 1923; West Ham U. (£1,000) November 1923; Swindon summer 1924; READING February 1926; Swindon T. (£100) June 1930; Mansfield T. summer 1931; Guildford C. 1932

As a youngster Frank was a prolific goalscorer and this stayed with him throughout his career. He once scored 129 goals of his youth team's total of 156 in one season, and then followed this up with 70 for Barking in the first season after World War One.

After playing for London v Birmingham and representing the London League, Frank was sold to Plymouth along with two other Barking team mates. Frank scored a hat-trick on his League debut and ended his first season as the division's top scorer. A big fee took him to Stoke and then on to West Ham and Swindon where Reading saw him as the ideal replacement for the injured Hugh Davey.

It was Frank's signing that proved the catalyst for Reading's push for promotion - he scored on his debut to help Reading beat their closest rivals, Plymouth, and finished with a four goal burst as Reading beat Brentford to win the Third Division South title. The following season Frank was Reading's top scorer with 27 goals, nine of them coming in the Cup, and he was one of the first Reading players to have his own song, the Elm Park fans singing *'Rich, Rich, Richie, score another goal for me'* to the tune of *'Chick, Chick, Chicken'*. Although he remained a favourite of the fans with his shoot-on-sight style, Frank's first team chances were reduced, and in 1930 he moved back to Swindon. Frank never left Reading and thirty years later he was back at Elm Park, coaching the youth team for several years, including their run to the final of the Southern Floodlit Youth Cup. His last appearance at the ground he had graced was in May 1986, when he received a rousing reception on being introduced to the crowd as Reading were presented with their second Third Division trophy.

Reading Record: Lge 91/46, FAC 12/11, Total 103/57
League Career Total: 270/133

RICHARDSON John
b. Motherwell 11.11.1906 d. Uddington 1.1986
Ht 5ft 9 1/2 Wt 12st (29-30)
Career: Motherwell; Hamilton A; Northfleet; Tottenham H.1926; READING (£500) May 1929; Bournemouth summer 1934; Folkestone T.

After establishing himself as a dependable full back in Scotland, John moved south to join Spurs' nursery club, Northfleet, eventually making it to Tottenham's first team in 1926-27. Three years later he moved to Reading and with two Richardsons already at Elm Park he was immediately, but unimaginatively, known as 'Jock'. He gradually developed into the club's regular left back, although only in 1931-32 did he come close to playing in every game and he ended his Reading career playing on the right, before joining Bournemouth. Jock returned to Scotland when his playing days were over and after the War he was scouting for Reading in the Glasgow area.

Reading Record: Lge 128, FAC 8, Total 136
League Career Total: 174

RICHARDSON Lancelot Holliday
b. Crook 4th qtr 1899 d. Cordoba 22.2.1958
Ht 5ft 11 Wt 12st (29-30)
Career: Shildon Ath; South Shields 1923; Manchester U. 1926; READING May 1929; Bournemouth; Rowlands Gill

Lance began his professional career with South Shields and then made 40 first team appearances for Manchester United before joining Reading. He gave up the chance to work as a gaucho on his parents' Argentinean ranch, to move to Elm Park where he faced the difficult task of taking over from fans' favourite, Joe Duckworth. He was not helped in his quest to win the fans over by a widely publicized domestic dispute, while he had a habit of turning up for match days wearing spats, a stetson and carrying a rolled umbrella, which gave plenty of scope for fun. Despite this, Lance was first choice goalie for Reading's last two seasons in the Second Division, eventually losing his place to Dick Mellors in 1931, before finally moving to Argentina.

Reading Record: Lge 80, FAC 4, Total 84
League Career Total: 174

RICHARDSON Steven Earl

b. Farnham Common 11.2.1962
Ht 5ft 5 Wt 10st 3 (86-87)
Career: Slough T; Southampton from apprentice 1980; READING (free) July 1982; Newbury T.   May 1993; Basingstoke T. 1995; Finchampstead 2000

As a schoolboy, Steve qualified for the final of the All England 100 metres and his speed was a feature of his game throughout his career. He had already played for Slough and Berkshire at U15 and U19 level before joining Southampton. Although Steve played in their reserves that finished runners up in the 1980-81 Football Combination, the nearest he got to the first team was as an unused sub for a UEFA Cup-tie against Sporting Lisbon.   Things changed dramatically for Steve when he moved to Reading in 1982. For the next 10 seasons he was their regular left back and he was a major force in what was a roller coaster decade for Reading. A nippy, tenacious full back, Steve was one of the best defenders in the lower divisions and only an occasional lack of consistency in his distribution prevented him from playing at the highest level. As it was, Steve was Reading's Player of the Year in his first two seasons and won a PFA Award in 1984 as the club returned to the Third Division. He followed this up by winning a Third Division Championship medal in 1985-86 and turned in one of his best performances at Wembley in Reading's Simod Cup win. Steve's first team dominance ended at Christmas 1992, with over 450 first team appearances to his credit.

Reading Record: Lge 373(7)/3, FAC 32, LC 25(1), FMC 3, AMC 16, Total 449(8)/3

STEVE'S CLAIM TO FAME - Along with Lawrie Sanchez and Jerry Williams, Steve was 'loaned' to England in September 1983, so Bobby Robson could stage a full practice match before their vital European Championship qualifier v Denmark; all three played in the winning England reserve side.

RICKETT Horace Francis John

b. Orsett 3.1.1912 d. 1989
Ht 5ft 10 Wt 13st (46-47)
Career: Chelmsford C; Fulham (Wartime guest); Clapton O. February 1942; Chelmsford C; Fulham; READING June 1946; Tonbridge

When Horace played for Reading at Norwich in April 1947, he was 35 years 3 months old and as such was one of the oldest League debutants since the War. Horace celebrated by keeping a clean sheet and his place in goal to the end of the season, but competition amongst goalies was fierce at Elm Park. Consequently, Horace had more time to concentrate on his taxi driving and he was given a free at the end of 1946-47.

Reading Record: Lge 22, FAC 3, Total 25

HORACE'S CLAIM TO FAME - One of the most superstitious players in Reading's history, Horace always took the field with his lucky rabbit's foot in his shorts. Before one game, his team mates hid it for a joke, but Horace refused to leave the dressing room before it was found, and eventually, manager Ted Drake had to intervene to avoid Reading playing without a goalkeeper.

RIDLEY JOHN George

b. Burden Hill 19.1.1903 d. ?
Ht 5ft 8 Wt 11st 6 (33-34)
Career: Mickley; South Shields 1921; Aston Villa June 1927; READING (free) 26 June 1933; QPR summer 1934

A vastly experienced right back, John had made over 180 first team appearances with both South Shields and Manchester City, having made his League debut as an 18 year old. At Reading he turned in a series of solid performances and his first team run was not interrupted until he suffered a broken jaw in an FA Cup-tie against Oldham in January.   Amazingly, John insisted on returning to complete that game and only missed three matches before he was back in the team. Despite this bravery, John missed several more games and was released at the end of the season.

Reading Record: Lge 28, FAC 3, Total 31
League Career Total: 402/4

RIMMER John Woolfall 'Jack'

b. Southport 15..3.1910 d. Southport 3.3.1989
Ht 5ft 8 Wt 11st 3 (37-38)
Career: Birkdale South End; Southport amateur 1929; Bolton W. May 1930; Burnley February 1937; READING June 1937; Macclesfield T. summer 1938

Jack made his League debut as an amateur with Southport and won an England amateur cap before turning pro with Bolton. A strong outside left, Jack averaged 12 games a season during his seven years with Wanderers, but, after a short spell with Burnley failed to increase his League total, he moved to Reading. By September 1937 Jack had played eight games for Reading, scoring once, before losing his place to his former Bolton team mate, Willie Cook, and he was eventually released at the end of the season. After retiring from football, Jack won a number of trophies with his racing pigeons.

Reading Record: Lge 8/1
League Career Total: 107/23

RITCHIE Alexander Watson

b. Airdrie 2.4.1904 d. Mossend 13.7.1954
Ht 5ft 7 Wt 10st (30-31)
Career: Fauldhouse U; Airdrie September 1922; Armdale April 1923; St Bernards May 1923; Peebles R. August 1923; Raith R. December 1923; Dunfermline March 1926; Raith R. May 1926; Blackpool July 1927; READING March 1931; Watford (£150) July 1933; Bournemouth August 1934; Third Lanark June 1935; Albion R. September 1937; READING scout 1938; Third Lanark manager

After a nomadic career in Scotland, Alex spent 3 1/2 seasons at Blackpool before joining Reading as a replacement for the injured Frank Eaton. Initially an inside forward, Alex was turned into a free scoring right winger who averaged a very creditable goal every other game for Reading. He had a powerful shot and once, against Thames, struck an effort with such force that it hit both posts and the bar before going in. After his playing career was over Alex scouted for Reading in Scotland, and then was Third Lanark's manager when Reading played them in a 1951 Festival of Britain match.

Reading Record: Lge 72/36, FAC 3/1, Total 75/37
League Career Total: 153/55

RITCHIE George Wright

b. West Derby 3rd qtr 1889 d. Manchester 6.12.1960
Ht 5ft 8 Wt 11st (21-22)
Career: Norwich C; Brighton; READING July 1921; Northfleet summer 1922

A regular scorer in a short Southern League spell with Norwich, George made his debut for Brighton in their first League game before moving on to Reading. He scored Reading's opening goal of 1921-22 from inside left but lost his place in January and quit League football at the end of that season.

Reading Record: Lge 10/4
League Career Total: 13/4

RITCHIE Thomas

b. Bangor, Co. Down 10.7.1930
Ht 5ft 9 Wt 11st (52-53)
Career: Bangor C; Manchester U. December 1950; READING (£3,250) 4 February 1955; Dover; Dartford summer 1955; Grimsby T. August 1958; Barrow December 1958; Guildford C. 1959

Spotted playing in Irish football, Tom became a 'Busby Babe' but, despite topping their Central League scorers in 1951-52, he never made it to their first team. Tom went straight into Reading's first team, but after making 10 starts during the rest of 1952-53, he only made eight in the next two seasons. This was partly due to injuries which led to his transfer fee being reduced by £250. A hard working but unorthodox forward, Tom topped Reading's reserve goalscorers in 1953-54 but was only used as a stand-in when a first team forward was injured. Released during 1955, Tom flitted between League and non-League clubs until his retirement.

Reading Record: Lge 18/5
League Career Total: 35/11

ROACH Neville

b. Reading 29.9.1978
Ht 5ft 10 Wt 11st 1 (97-98)
Career: READING from YTS 10 May 1997; Kingstonian (loan) January 1998; Slough T.(loan) September 1998; Bury (trial) February 1999; Wycombe W.(trial) February 1999; Southend U. (£30,000) 26 March 1999; Kingstonians summer 2000; Eastern Spirit (Aus.) 2000; St Albans C. February 2001; Oldham A. March 2001; Torquay U. summer 2001

An ardent Reading supporter from a well known local footballing family, Neville turned down the chance to sign for Nottingham Forest in order to join his local club. Having scored 45 goals in all competitions during 1996-97, Neville was given his first team chance at the end of that season and was rewarded with a goal on his full debut. A full contract soon followed and Neville's Reading career looked assured, but changes of managers restricted his chances to substitute appearances. In November 1998 he appeared to have resurrected his career with some sparkling performances, despite playing on the wing instead of his favoured striker's role. Unfortunately for Neville, manager Tommy Burns regarded him as surplus to requirements and the pacey young forward was sold to Southend. In 2000, Neville was one of the League players to unsuccessfully apply to be allowed to play in the World Cup for the Cayman Islands.

Reading Record: Lge 5(11)/1, FAC (1), LC 1(4)/1, AMC (1), Total 6(17)/2
League Career Total: 18(15)/3 +

ROBERTS Brian James

b. Old Windsor 3.2.1967
Ht 5ft 10 Wt 12st (85-86)
Career: READING from YTS July 1985; Mikkelin (Finland); Palliogate (Finland); Wokingham T. 1988; Mount Maunganui (NZ)

Brian progressed through Reading's youth teams, where his consistent performances as a strong forward earned him a professional contract. He never got to start a League game, all his five appearances being as substitute, and Brian's only full 90 minutes came in the Freight Rover Trophy game at Bournemouth. Released in 1987, Brian played in Finland before emigrating to New Zealand and, although he was often touted as a potential Maltese international through his mother's birthplace, he eventually made his international debut as a naturalized New Zealander against Australia in May 1991.

Reading Record: Lge (5), AMC 1, Total 1(5)

ROBERTSON William S

b. Falkirk 20.4.1907 d. ?
Ht 5ft 8 1/2 Wt 12st (35-36)
Career: Third Lanark; Ayr U; Stoke C. 1929; Manchester U. March 1934; READING 14 January 1936

Having been virtually ever-present as Stoke won the Second Division title in 1932-33, Billy was transferred to Manchester United towards the end of the following season. A joint transfer with Billy Owen, for a fee that was later disputed, saw Billy join Reading, but as with his former United colleague, the move was not a success. Billy was a versatile player who was used mainly as a right back or centre half with his previous clubs, while Reading usually played him at right half until he was given a 'free' after two seasons.

Reading Record: Lge 24, SSC 4, Total 28
League Career Total: 187/4

ROBINS Mark Gordon

b. Ashton Under Lyne 22.12.1969
Ht 5ft 8 Wt 11st 11 (97-98)
Career: Manchester U. from apprentice December 1986; Norwich C.(£800,000) August 1992; Leicester C.(£1 m.) January 1995; FC Copenhagen (loan) 1996; READING (loan) 29 August 1997; Deportivo Orense (Portugal) January 1998; Palionis (Greece); Manchester C. (free) March 1999; Walsall; Rotherham U. summer 2000

One of the county's most promising young strikers, Mark won six U21 caps during his time with Manchester United. He also won an FA Cup winners' medal in 1990 and followed that with success in the European Cup Winners Cup and the Super Cup the following season.

A big money move to Norwich saw Mark continue to score regularly, having netted twice for City against Arsenal on his debut. Another big fee took him to Leicester as one of Mark McGhee's first signings, but the goals began to dry up and a change of manager saw him loaned out on a couple of occasions. Mark had a month with Reading, five months after winning the League Cup with City, in an attempt to turn round the club's poor start, but he lacked match fitness and failed to score in his five games, four of which were lost. He eventually regained his goalscoring touch with Rotherham and his goals helped them pip Reading to an automatic promotion spot in 2000-01.

Reading Record: Lge 5
League Career Total: 193(67)/73 +

ROBINSON David John

b. Newcastle 27.11.1969
Ht 6ft Wt 13st 2 (91-92)
Career: Newcastle U. from YTS June 1988; Peterborough U.(loan) February 1991; READING (non contract) March 1992; Blackpool July 1992; Bishop Auckland; Cambridge U. December 1995; Berwick Rangers June 1996; Whitley Bay

A big, aggressive striker who was good in the air, Dave's League appearances for his home town club, Newcastle, were restricted to coming on as substitute. He did score in the 1990 FA Cup replay against Reading, and so when Dave was released by United, they were quick to give him a chance. With Trevor Senior out injured, Dave lead the attack eight times but he failed to score in those games and was substituted five times.

Reading Record: Lge 8
League Career Total: 40(26)/8

ROBINSON Martin John

b. Ilford 17.7.1957
Ht 5ft 8 1/2 Wt 11st 5 (82-83)
Career: Tottenham H. from apprentice May 1975; Charlton A.(£15,000) February 1978; READING (loan) September 1982; Gillingham (£15,500) October 1984; Southend U. (£20,000) July 1987; Cambridge U.(free) June 1989

After failing to break into Spurs' first team on a regular basis, Martin moved to Charlton where he stayed for over six years. During that time he made over 250 first team appearances for them, scoring 67 goals. A contract dispute led to Martin being loaned to Reading and the pacey forward was used on the left side of the attack from where he scored a memorable solo effort against Orient.

On his return to the Valley, Martin agreed a new contract and so did not join Reading permanently.

Reading Record: Lge 6/2
League Career Total: 370(38)/101

MARTIN'S CLAIM TO FAME: At Charlton, Martin achieved a rare hat trick when he scored for them on his debuts in the League, the FA Cup and the League Cup.

ROBINSON Matthew Richard
b. Exeter 23.12.1974
Ht 5ft 11 Wt 11st 8 (99-00)
Career: Southampton from trainee July 1993; Portsmouth February 1998; READING (£150,000) January 2000

With first team chances limited at the Dell, Matt made the short but comparatively rare move to Portsmouth, where he quickly established himself at full back. The rivalry between the two clubs meant that Matt rarely got the credit his stylish play deserved at Fratton Park and when Reading's manager, Alan Pardew, refused to take 'no' for an answer from Pompey, they eventually allowed him to join Reading. Matt immediately solved the club's left back problem and he was voted Player of the Month within four weeks of joining Reading. 'Rooster' was also an instant hit with the fans who paid tribute to his all action attacking - but hairless - play by wearing bald wigs to one of Reading's home games.

Reading Record: Lge 48(3), FAC 2, LC 2, AMC 1, Play-offs 3, Total 56(3) +
League Career Total: 116(18)/1 +

ROBSHAW Henry **'Harry'** William
b. Edmonton 10.5.1927 d. 1990
Ht 5ft 10 Wt 12st 4 (52-53)
Career: Tottenham H. from jnrs November 1948; READING 4 February 1953; Tonbridge

Harry made just one League appearance in his four years with Spurs before signing for Reading. He played in every game to the end of that season, scoring once from his right half position, but Harry lost his place early into the next season and subsequently left Reading to join Tonbridge.

Reading Record: Lge 20/1
League Career Total: 21/1

ROBSON John **'Jack'** Cecil
b. Birtley 24.2.1906 d. Ashbourne 20.10.1966
Ht 5ft 10 Wt 12st 4 (27-28)
Career: Birtley; Hull C; READING (£25) August 1925; Derby Co. (£1,500) June 1928; Southend U. summer 1932; Chester; Rochdale summer 1933; Oldham A. summer 1934

After just one game for Hull, Jack was virtually ever-present for Reading during the club's golden period in the mid-Twenties. He played in all but the first game of Reading's Third Division South championship win in 1925-26 and then scored ten goals in the club's first season in the higher division. John was very fast and had a tremendous shot, but the Reading programme, never frightened to mince its words in those days, commented that he *'needs to learn when to part with the ball'*. In 1928 Reading parted with John but he carried on scoring regularly for another eight seasons.

Reading Record: Lge 108/22, FAC 14/3, Total 122/25
League Career Total: 236/55

ROBSON Mark Andrew
b. Newham 22.5.1969
Ht 5ft 7 Wt 10st 2 (96-97)
Career: Exeter C. from apprentice December 1986; Tottenham H.(£50,000) July 1987; READING (loan) 24 March 1988; Watford (loan) October 1989; Plymouth Arg. (loan) December 1989; Exeter C. (loan) January 1992; West Ham U. (free) August 1992; Charlton A. (£12,500) November 1993; Notts Co. (free) September 1997; Wycombe W. (loan) October 1999, Charlton A. Academy coach 2000, Aveley January 2001

A spectacular start to his career at Exeter saw Mark score seven times in 28 League games and just two months after his 18th birthday he was sold to Spurs. In five years with them Mark only made four first team starts for the White Hart Lane team, but played in another 20 League games during various loan spells. The first of these was with Reading where he belied his frail appearance by creating chances with his two footed skilful play. Mark was unable to save Reading from relegation but it was noticeable that they were unbeaten in the five games he started. Eventually leaving Spurs, in 1992, Mark continued to impress with his traditional wing play but later his career was hampered by injuries.

Reading Record: Lge 5(2)
League Career Total: 197(48)/29

MARK'S CLAIM TO FAME - Mark scored Notts County's winner v Leyton Orient on 28 March 1998, which ensured that club became the first to clinch promotion before the end of March.

ROBSON William

b. Southwick 26.3.1906 d. Oxford 11.8.1960
Ht 5ft 11 Wt 12st 6 (35-36)
Career: Hylton Colliery; Derby Co. 1927; West Ham U. 1933;
READING (£100) June 1934; Newbury T. coach; READING
assistant trainer August 1948

After making just 16 League appearances in seven
seasons with Derby and then West Ham, Bill became a
fixture in Reading's first team for almost four seasons.
A solid left back who was particularly good in the air,
Bill hardly missed a game from his Reading debut in
November 1934 until February 1938. From then on he
only played a couple more first team games and had the
rare distinction of scoring the only first team goal of his
career, at Northampton, in what was to be his final
League game. Given a free transfer in 1939, Bill
returned to Elm Park after the War as assistant trainer, a
position he held until the late fifties.

Reading Record: Lge 134/1, FAC 14, SSC 5, Total 153/1
League Career Total: 150/1

ROGERS Andrew

b. Charteris 1.12.1956
Ht 5ft 8 Wt 10st (85-86)
Career: Charteris T; Peterborough U. July 1976; Hampton
1978; Southampton February 1980; Plymouth Arg. (loan)
September 1981, permanent (£50,000) November 1981;
READING (£15,000) July 1985; Southend U.(£10,000)
January 1987; Farnborough T. July 1989

After making 29 appearances for Peterborough, Andy
returned to non-League football before his career was
resurrected at Southampton. A subsequent move to
Plymouth saw Andy become a regular on their left wing
and hit the headlines in 1984 when he scored directly
from a corner against Derby to put Argyle into the FA
Cup semi-finals. After 159 League starts, Andy moved
to Reading where he played a vital part in the runaway
Third Division title win, but he nearly never made it to
the end of the season. In February 1986, Andy fell
heavily after a collision with a Swansea defender and
only the prompt action of Reading physio, Glenn
Hunter, saved Andy's life after he swallowed his
tongue. Happily, Andy quickly recovered, but the
following season he was only on the fringe of the first
team and was sold to Southend the following January.
He moved on to Farnborough and in 1990-91 Andy
helped them win the Southern League Championship.

Reading Record: Lge 44/5, FAC 2, LC 4/1, AMC (1),
FMC 1, Total 51(1)/6
League Career Total: 268(18)/23

ROSE Harold Bernard

b. Reading 5.1900 d. 5.1990
Ht 5ft 8 Wt 11st 8 (20-21)
Career: Reading Liberal Club; Imperial FC; READING
February 1920; Bristol R. May 1921; Mid Rhondda U.
summer 1924

One of several local players tried by Reading during
their first League season, Harry was one of the few to go
on to play for another club. After three games at right
half earlier in the campaign, Harry ended 1920-21 at
centre half before moving on to Bristol Rovers for two
seasons.

Reading Record: Lge 4
League Career Total: 18

ROUGIER Anthony Leo

b. Tobago 17 July 1971
Ht 6ft Wt 14st (00-01)
Career: Trinity Prospect; Raith R. March 1995; Hibernian July
1997; Port Vale (£175,000) January 1999; READING
(£340,000) 10 August 2000

A strong, pacey striker, capable of playing on either
wing, Anthony had topped Port Vale's scorers in their
1999-00 relegation season but was sold to Reading two
days before the start of the following one. It proved an
eventful few days for Anthony who made his Reading
debut two days after signing, then flew out to score for
Trinidad and Tobago against Panama in their World
Cup qualifier. That was his 30th cap, many of which
had been won at right back, and in 2000 he captained the
'Socca Warriors' to the CONCACAF Gold Cup semis.
Back at Reading he earned a standing ovation after a
spectacular opening performance at the Madejski
Stadium but was then injured. His return to the first
team saw him score twice as a substitute as his late goals
beat Oxford. Unfortunately an ankle injury, international calls, and the form of Butler and Cureton
restricted Anthony to mainly substitute appearances.
He has established himself as a crowd favourite at
Reading despite his very unlucky own goal in the play-
off final.

Reading Record: Lge 14(17)/2, FAC 1(1), LC 1, AMC
2, Play-offs (2), 18(20)/2 +
League Career Total: 55(27)/10 +

ROWAN Barry

b. Willesden 24.4.1942
Ht 5ft 8 1/2 Wt 11st (70-71)
Career: Watford amateur; Brentford October 1960; Dover;
Millwall July 1960; Detroit November 1966; Middlesbrough
September 1968; Colchester U. November 1968; Durban U;
READING August 1969; Plymouth Arg. September 1969 and
April 1970; Exeter C. July 1970; Poole T. June 1973

One of soccer's nomads, Barry only really stayed for any length of time with Millwall and Exeter, while in 1968-69 alone he played in three different continents. Roy Bentley had tried to sign Barry for Reading in 1966 but it was Jack Mansell who gave him his chance, remembering the chunky right winger from his time in the States. Barry was given a one game trial by Mansell in a 4-3 reverse at Barnsley but was not offered a permanent contract.

Reading Record: Lge 1
League Career Total: 161(5)/28

ROWE Jonathan

b. Packmoor 1910
Ht 5ft 8 1/2 Wt 10st 10 (32-33)
Career: Manchester Central; READING June 1932; QPR May 1935; Port Vale July 1937

After three seasons with Manchester Central, Jonty made his League debut with Reading in his favoured left back position in December 1932. For the next two years he was Reading's first choice left back until he lost his place to Bill Robson, but a move to QPR saw Jonty recover a first team position.

Reading Record: Lge 77, FAC 5, SSC 1, Total 83
League Career Total: 201

RUSSELL Roger

b. Crowthorne c.1939 d. 2001
Ht 6ft 1 Wt 11st (59-60)
Career: READING groundstaff 3 January 1955, professional 5 January 1957

Roger spent seven years with Reading but, despite progressing through the youth and reserve teams, he only made one first team appearance in that time. That one game was against Chester, and Roger played a major role in securing what was Reading's first win in the new League Cup competition. Playing at centre half, Roger came out on top against Ron Davies, a player destined to become one of the best centre forwards of the Sixties. Reading's strength in depth at centre half meant that Roger was given a free transfer in 1962. He went to work at Broadmoor Mental Hospital where one of his duties was to escort the Kray twins to their mother's funeral.

Reading Record: LC 1

RYAN Thomas Stanley

b. Ascot 9.7.1952
Ht 6ft Wt 11st (70-71)
Career: Ascot U; READING apprentice 29 July 1968, professional 11 May 1970; Hillingdon Bor. July 1971; Hounslow 1980; Wokingham T. player coach

Destiny seemed to conspire against Tom at Reading. First a leg injury denied him an early first team chance, next the FA refused him permission to go on a club arranged coaching trip to Canada, and then he was picked to play in a prestigious friendly in Holland but the airline lost his kit! When Tom did get his first team chance it couldn't have gone worse for him. He was in fine form at centre half in the reserves but the first team were dropping down the League and Tom was included in a team low on confidence. The game ended in a 5-0 defeat at Swansea with Tom's opposing player, the deadly Dave Gwyther, getting a headed hat trick, and Tom was substituted. Although he never got to play another League game, he was able to display his class with Hillingdon Borough where he played in their first FA Cup win over a League club, reached the 1973 Southern League Cup final, and was ever-present in 1974-75 when they won promotion. He ended his career with Borough's second highest career total of 319 appearances and was awarded a testimonial against Chelsea.

Reading Record: Lge 1

SAAR Mass

b. Monrovia 6.2.1973
Ht 5ft 8 13st (98-99)
Career: Mighty Barrolle Sports Club 1988; AC Monaco 1990; Olympique Ales (loan); Hadjuk Split; READING (£158,000) 10 July 1998; Sydney Olympic 2000

A close friend of fellow Liberian international, George Weah, Mass was a regular in his national side and he often paid his own travelling expenses because of his country's financial plight. Having played under Arsene Wenger at Monaco, Mass then became a regular scorer in Croatia with 18 goals in 50 games for Hadjuk Split. On Wenger's recommendation, Reading signed the powerfully built left sided forward for 460,000 deutchmarks and that looked a bargain as Mass made a sensational debut in the opening game at the Madejski Stadium. Mass had an array of tricks and a direct approach but he flattered to deceive and a series of injuries led to a weight problem that meant he rarely lasted ninety minutes. He never started a game in 1999-00 and almost moved to Korea and the USA, but on each occasion the transfer fell through due to injury, and he was eventually released at the end of that season.

Reading Record: Lge 18(13)/3, FAC(2), LC 2, AMC (3), Total 20(18)/3

SAINSBURY Kim

b. Reading 21.9.1957
Ht 5ft 7 Wt 11st 4 (74-75)
Career: Rabson R; Newbury T; READING apprentice 12 August 1974; Wokingham T. October 1975

Kim was an all round sportsman, representing Berkshire Schools at rugby, cricket and football. He was a frequent scorer for Reading's youth and reserve sides but made his only first team appearance when he came on as substitute at half time in a brutal game against Hartlepool in February 1975. Kim was a strong and pacey forward but was not offered a professional contract on his 18th birthday, and he returned to establish a long career with a number of local clubs.

Reading Record: Lge (1)

SAINTY John Albert

b. Poplar 24..3.1946
Ht 5ft 10 Wt 12st 9 (67-68)
Career: Tottenham H. from apprentice July 1963; READING (£12,000) 18 August 1967; Bournemouth (£4,000) February 1970; Mansfield T. (loan) November 1971; Aldershot August 1974; Bournemouth coach; Norwich C. coach; Manchester C. coach 1980; Chester coach then manager November 1982; Burnley coach January 1984; Armthorpe Welfare manager 1986; Mossley manager 1987; Stockport Co. asst. manager 1990; Southampton asst. manager summer 1997

A prolific goalscorer with Spurs, John scored 31 goals in their reserves as they won the 1966-67 Combination title, plus an amazing 20 in just eight 'A' team games. Unable to break into Spurs' first team, John joined Reading on the eve of 1967-68 for a record equalling fee and scored twice on his debut. After averaging a goal a game for his first six games, John then found it more difficult to score despite his pace and strength. Sometimes used in a deeper position than his original striking role, John rarely featured after Jack Mansell took over at Reading and he was sold to Bournemouth. His final move as a player almost cost Aldershot relegation as they played him before his registration was confirmed and they were deducted a point which left them to rely on goal average to keep them up. After retiring as a player, John commenced a managerial and coaching career that has lasted over 25 years.

Reading Record: Lge 63(8)/19, FAC 3/1, LC 3/1, Total 69(8)/21
League Career Total: 203(18)/40

SAMS Alfred

b. Durham 1912 d. Adelaide 1990
Ht 5ft 5 Wt 11st 10 (38-39)
Career: Grantham T; Mansfield T. 1937; READING summer 1938; Accrington Stan. summer 1939; Grantham T.

Alf was a stocky inside left who played all his League games for Reading at the start of 1938-39 but failed to find the net and lost his place by November. At the end of that season, Alf moved to Accrington Stanley, but the War intervened and so he failed to add to the total accrued with Mansfield and Reading.

Reading Record: Lge 10
League Career Total: 21/2

SAMUEL David 'Dan' John

b. Swansea 1911
Ht 5ft 7 11st (33-34)
Career: Llanelly; Southend U. 1932; READING June 1933; QPR May 1935; Tunbridge Wells Rngrs; Barrow summer 1937

After a promising start to his League career, inside right Dan looked to further it at Reading. Unfortunately, he had to wait until the last three games of 1933-34 to make his Reading debut while, in the following season, he only got two starts. Remarkably, he scored in both of those last two games for Reading, including the club's first ever goal in the Southern Section Cup. A keen cricketer and pigeon fancier, Dan eventually got a regular game at Barrow where he made 78 appearances in the two seasons before the War.

Reading Record: Lge 4/1, SSC 1/1, Total 5/2
League Career Total: 99/19

SANCHEZ Lawrence Phillip

b. Lambeth 22.10.59
Ht 5ft 11 Wt 11st 7 (84-85)
Career: Maidenhead U; Southampton; Thatcham T; READING from non contract September 1978; Wimbledon (£25,000) December 1984; Swindon March 1994; Sligo R. player manager September 1995; Wimbledon reserve manager summer 1995, coach September 1997; Wycombe W. manager February 1999

After writing to the local paper as a nine year old asking if any clubs needed new players, Lawrie went on to represent Reading Schools at all levels and played twice for England U18 Schools. He graduated to Reading's League side while he was still at school, and he had to get his headmaster's permission to play in mid-week games. Playing for Reading clearly did not affect Lawrie's education as he left school with 13 'O' levels and four 'A's, and then went on to earn a B.Sc. in Business Studies. His first season as a professional saw him play a major part in the club's Fourth Division championship win and for the following four seasons Lawrie was a fixture on the left side of Reading's midfield.

An elegant and skilful player, Lawrie gradually added more steel to his play and, in his last full season at Elm Park, he was second highest scorer in Reading's promotion campaign. Eventually, Lawrie moved to Wimbledon, being signed by Dave Bassett who had marked Lawrie when he made his League debut against the Dons five years earlier. Lawrie played a key role in the South Londoners rise to the top flight but he will always be remembered for heading their winner in the 1988 FA Cup final against Liverpool. Lawrie qualified for three countries - England by birth, Ecuador through his father, but was capped three times by Northern Ireland, his mother's country of birth. Having made over 250 League appearances with both Reading and Wimbledon, Lawrie followed a short spell at Swindon by guiding Sligo Rovers into Europe as player manager. After becoming the youngest first team coach in the Premiership with Wimbledon, Lawrie became Wycombe's manager and immediately saved them from seemingly certain relegation. Two years later he hit the headlines again as Wycombe made it to the FA Cup semi-finals.

Reading Record: Lge 249(13)/28, FAC 14/1, LC 21(1), FLT 4(2)/2, AMC 1, Total 289(16)/31
League Career Total: 509(31)/61

LAWRIE'S CLAIM TO FAME - Lawrie was the first player to be sent off for a professional foul when he handled a goalbound shot in a Football League Trophy game against Oxford in August 1982. He did not wait long to show his goalkeeping skills legally, as in the next game Reading's goalkeeper was sent off - also for a professional foul - and Lawrie took over in goal.

SANDFORD LEE Robert
b. Basingstoke 22.4.1968
Ht 6ft 1 Wt 13st 4 (97-98)
Career: Portsmouth from apprentice December 1985; Stoke C. (£140,000) December 1989; Sheffield U. (£500,000) July 1996; READING (loan) 5 September 1997

While with Portsmouth, Lee turned down a £100,000 transfer to Reading in 1989, eventually moving to Stoke where he won the Autoglass Trophy in 1992 and the Second Division Championship the following year. A former Youth international, Lee moved on to Sheffield United after playing over 320 games for Stoke, either as a central defender of left back. Having lost his first team place, Lee spent an impressive month on loan at Reading but the move did not become permanent as Reading did not agree with United's £250,000 valuation.

The Royals were to regret this later in the season when, having fought his way back into their first team, Lee scored United's late winner to knock Reading out of the FA Cup. Later, Lee's studies were rewarded with a B.Sc. in Sport Science.

Reading Record: Lge 5
League Career Total: 463(17)/13 +

SAYLES George
b. Sheffield 1st qtr 1899 d. 7.1971
Ht 5ft 7 1/2 Wt 12st 2 (21-22)
Career: Cardiff C. 1919; READING June 1921; York C. 1927

Having played alongside his brother, Tommy, at Cardiff, George moved to Reading where he played 21 League games in both full back positions during his first three seasons. George stayed at Reading until 1927, when he moved to captain York prior to their election to the League. As well as football, George excelled at most sports, playing-off 6 at golf, and opening the batting for Berkshire, with whom he won the Minor Counties Championship in 1924 and 1928. Because of this, George was eminently qualified for his 40 year career as a groundsman for Sutton Seeds.

Reading Record: Lge 21

SCARROTT Alan Richard
b. Malmesbury 22.11.1944
Ht 5ft 10 Wt 10st 8 (66-67)
Career: Chippenham T; West Bromwich Alb. December 1961; Bristol R. June 1964; READING (£500) 20 April 1965; Hereford U. 1968; Cheltenham T. 1970; Gloucester C. January 1971; Ewyas Harold player manager August 1972

As one of the last of the old fashioned wingers to play for Reading, Alan made his League debut at Elm Park on the opening day of 1965-66. After a hesitant start, he developed into one of the best crossers in the lower divisions. His accuracy from out on the right wing or corners was outstanding and with two superb headers, in the form of George Harris and Pat Terry, it was not surprising that Alan was involved in almost two thirds of Reading's goals in 1966-67. As well as his crossing, Alan's style was memorable for the fact that he always gripped the cuffs of his sleeves while on the ball. Although he wasn't a prolific scorer himself, Alan scored one of Elm Park's most memorable efforts - chipping Scunthorpe's young Ray Clemence from way out on the touchline. But the changing role for wingers overtook Alan and his style was not suited to the 4-2-4 formation adopted by Reading, so he moved to Hereford to provide the crosses for another great header, John Charles.

Reading Record: Lge 90/7, FAC 5, LC 7, Total 102/7

SCOTT John

b. Crieff c.1898 d. ?
Ht 5ft 6 1/2 Wt 12st (22-23)
Career: Ayr U; READING October 1921

A free scoring centre forward in Scotland, John netted a hat trick on his Reading debut in a friendly against Oxford University. He followed that up with a scoring debut in the League but was soon converted to a right winger which reduced his chances. His Reading career lasted two season but, strangely, three of John's last four League goals came in games against Swansea.

Reading Record: Lge 54/8, FAC 2, Total 56/8

SCOTT Keith John

b. Westminster 9.6.1967
Ht 6ft 3 Wt 14st 2 (99-00)
Career: Leicester U; Lincoln C. March 1990; Wycombe W. (£30,000) March 1991; Swindon (£375,000) November 1993; Stoke C. (£300,000) December 1994; Norwich C. November 1995; Bournemouth (loan) February 1996; Watford (loan) February 1997; Wycombe W. (£55,000) March 1997; READING (£250,000) 24 March 1999; Colchester U. (loan) October 2000, permanent 20 March 2001; Dover A. summer 2001

A big, bustling centre forward, Keith played in all four divisions and the Conference but, despite some big money moves, he will always be remembered as a Wycombe player. With them, he scored 95 goals in 201 starts in all competitions, including a goal at Wembley in the 1991 FA Trophy final. In 1993 Keith helped Wycombe to a Conference and FA Trophy double and, after he had returned to Wycombe in 1997, it came as a great shock to their fans when Keith was sold to Reading on transfer deadline day two years later. He scored in his first two games for Reading, but he was now using his strength more to create chances for team mates although he was always a threat in the air. He also scored Reading's first 'golden goal' in an Associate Members Cup-tie at Barnet. A change in management saw Keith's first team chances reduce and he was allowed to leave the club.

Reading Record: Lge 20(15)/5, FAC 2(1), LC 2(1)/2, AMC 1(2)/1, Total 25(19)/8
League Career Total: 199(54)/61 +

SCOTT Robert William

b. Liverpool 22.2.1953
Ht 6ft 2 1/2 Wt 13st 5 (74-75)
Career: Wrexham from jnrs July 1971; READING (loan) 9 January 1975; Hartlepool July 1976; Rochdale July 1977; Crewe Alex. August 1979; Wrexham January 1986; Northwich Vic. 1986

Bobby was a solid and reliable centre half who, having failed to break into Wrexham's first team on a regular basis, was loaned to Reading for experience. He helped shore up the Royals' defence so that they only conceded two goals during his five match stay. Bobby refused an extended loan period at Elm Park and must have had a premonition of what was to come, as his own goal at Christmas 1977 gave Reading a 4-3 win over his club, Rochdale. Later, Bobby moved again, to Crewe, where he was made captain and missed just five games in as many seasons.

Reading Record: Lge 5
League Career Total: 368(6)/18

SEARS Douglas Reginald

b. Eton 5.1.1919 d. 1995
Ht 5ft 9 Wt 10st 12 (46-47)
Career: Datchet; Slough T; Grimsby T October 1943; Wartime guest for Portsmouth, Fulham & Chester; READING May 1946; Aldershot June 1947

At the age of only 12, Doug played for Windsor Schools U15 as they reached 6th round of the English Schools Trophy, and was then a member of the Slough team that won the Great Western Combination before the War. This brought him to the attention of Grimsby, but his professional contract never produced a League game so he returned south to join Reading. Doug played in the first League game after the War but was generally understudy to Maurice Edelston so he never got to play two first team games in a row at Reading. An inside forward with a good footballing brain, Doug was thought to be let down by his shooting, even though he scored 10 goals for the reserves, before moving to Aldershot. As well as his footballing skills, Doug was a fine batsman and played for Buckinghamshire in the Minor Counties Championship.

Reading Record: Lge 5
League Career Total: 51/13

SENIOR Trevor John

b. Dorchester 28.11.1961
Ht 6ft 1 1/2 Wt 12st 8 (84-85)
Career: Dorchester T. 1969; Bristol C. (trial) 1977; Portsmouth (£20,000) December 1981; Aldershot (loan) March 1983; READING (£35,000) July 1983; Watford (£325,000) July 1987; Middlesbrough (£200,000) March 1988; READING (£150,000) 10 October 1988; Woking (free) 3 July 1992; Weymouth August 1993; Basingstoke T; Dorchester T. November 1993; Farnborough December 1993; Weymouth player coach & manager May 1994; Farnborough T. May 1995; Dorchester T. commercial manager; Bridport T. manager 1998; Bashley coach 2000

Along with Ron Blackman, Trevor is rightly regarded as Reading's greatest goalscorer. Born in his grandmother's pub, Trevor is held in the same esteem at Dorchester, having been connected with that club from the age of seven. Originally a left winger, he was Dorchester's U14 player of the year at the age of nine, and later scored 59 goals in 78 Southern League games, topping their Southern League scorers twice. Trevor helped them to win their Southern League division in 1979-80, but after taking them to the second round of the FA Cup he moved to Portsmouth. First team chances were limited at Fratton Park but his two League goals came in a win over Reading. Seven goals in 10 loan games at Aldershot gave notice of Trevor's scoring potential and Reading snapped him up as a replacement for centre forward Kerry Dixon. Trevor's success at Reading can be gauged by the fact that the popular Dixon was never missed. Hat tricks in his first two games at Elm Park, his trio against Stockport coming in a club record four minutes, saw Trevor head the county's scorers throughout the season. He ended with a club record of 41 goals that season to become the first Reading player to be the League's top marksman, won a PFA Divisional award, an Adidas Golden Boot, a Rothman's Yearbook award, and promotion from the Fourth Division. Injury kept his total 'down' to 27 the following season, but these included a run of nine consecutive scoring games, another club record.

Despite offers of First Division football, Trevor remained loyal to Reading as they ran away with the Third Division title in 1985-86, but his regular scoring in the higher division at last attracted an offer that Reading couldn't refuse as a record fee took him to First Division Watford in 1987. It was a disaster for all concerned as Reading were relegated without their charismatic scorer, while he only managed one League goal for Watford. Within nine months Trevor was sold on to Middlesbrough where his goals helped them win promotion through the play-offs. Despite this, he never really settled in the North East and when it became clear that Trevor was available, Reading jumped at the chance to bring home their hero.

Trevor responded by topping their goalscorers for the next three seasons, but 1991-92 saw him feature less frequently in new manager Mark McGhee's line-ups, while a virus meant that this was the only one of his eight Reading seasons that he did not top the scorers. Released at the end of that season for economic reasons, Trevor subsequently played for a number of non-League clubs before going into management. He had a great left foot and was deadly in the air, allied to a formidable work rate and an uncanny knack to snap up half chances before most other players realized they even existed. All this made his 190 goals another Reading record. Add to this a scrupulously fair style of play and a rapport with fans, both on and off the pitch, and it is no wonder that Trevor remains one of the most popular Reading players in the club's history.

Reading Record: Lge 291(10)/153, FAC 32/18, LC 16(1)/14, FMC 1, AMC 11/5, Total 351(11)/190
League Career Total: 343(13)/165

TREVOR'S CLAIM TO FAME - As well as being Reading's top scorer, Trevor can also claim to be the club's best goalie! On four occasions, Trevor was used as stand-in keeper and he kept a clean sheet on each occasion. His last game for Reading saw him spend the second half in goal and, after his unorthodox style had inspired a come-back from 2-0 down to score a last minute winner, Trevor was chaired off the pitch by his adoring fans.

SEYMOUR Christopher David

b. Newbury 14.9.1971
Ht 5ft 11 Wt 11st (91-92)
Career: READING from YTS July 1990; Newbury T. summer 1992

A fair haired player, able to play in midfield or defence, Chris was signed professional after impressing as a youth player for Reading. Although never able to command a regular place, Reading made full use of Chris's versatility and in his first season his nine first team appearances saw him wear seven different numbered shirts. The arrival of Mark McGhee saw a reduction in Chris's chances and he was released at the end of his second season.

Reading Record: Lge 10(3), FAC (1), AMC 1, Total 11(4)

SHARPE Frederick Charles

b. Greenwich 11.11.1937
Ht 5ft 10 Wt 11st 10 (70-71)
Career: Tottenham H. from amateur May 1956; Norwich C. (£8,000) July 1963; READING (free) 10 July 1969

Several Army representative games and two League appearances were all Fred had to show for his nine years with Spurs but his transfer to Norwich saw him play over 100 league games for them. A move to Reading in the twilight of his career saw Fred bring experience and steadiness to the centre of their defence. He was a very brave player who, during a short spell after Christmas 1969, had stitches in a cut eye, dislocated his shoulder, broke his nose, and was involved in a car crash, but never missed a game - no wonder he was nicknamed 'Iron Man'. A superstitious player, Fred always liked to be last onto the pitch, but in 1970-71 his luck ran out as Reading were relegated and Fred was given a free at the end of the season.

Reading Record: Lge 64/1, FAC 5, LC 3, Total 72/1
League Career Total: 173(4)/2

SHEPPARD Simon

b. Clevedon 7.8.1973
Ht 6ft 4 Wt 14st 12 (94-95)
Career: Westown Harriers; Watford from YTS April 1991; Scarborough (loan) March 1994; READING (free) 9 September 1994; Chelsea (trial) summer 1996; Walsall (trial) summer 1996; Rotherham U. (trial) October 1996; Borehamwood T; Hemel Hempstead summer 1998; Harlow T.

A graduate from the FA School of Excellence, Simon won England Schools and Youth honours before becoming Graham Taylor's last signing during his first spell at Watford. A knee injury cost Simon his first team place in Watford's goal, but he played for England U20's in their Australian tour before joining Reading. In his first season he helped them win the Berks & Bucks Senior Cup but had to wait until Shaka Hislop was transferred to start his League career with Reading. Following Hislop, the fan's favourite, proved a tough task for Simon and the supporters' nervousness affected his play. Despite this, and being told that he would not be retained, Simon still continued to give brave performances when called on to fill in for his replacement, Boris Mikhailov, and remained committed to the club to the end of his contract.

Reading Record: Lge 18, LC 4, Total 22
League Career Total: 50

SHERWOOD Henry William 'Johnny'

b. Reading 3.9.1913 d. Reading 10.1985
Ht 5ft 9 Wt 12st 2 (38-39)
Career: READING amateur 1936; Maidenhead U; Islington Corinthians 1937; READING June 1938; Aldershot September 1947; Crystal Palace July 1949

Johnny's life story could, and should, warrant a book of its own. A member of a local family known as 'the Showbiz Sherwoods', his five brothers were a popular mime act. Johnny was a promising local youngster who played for Reading reserves before being selected for the crack amateur select side, Islington Corinthians, for a world tour. The 18 man squad played 96 games in 15 counties as they travelled through Europe, Asia and North America. Johnny was used as a right winger or centre forward and was the top scorer with 70 goals on the tour that saw him play before some huge crowds that included fans ranging from the King of Egypt to Hollywood stars. On his return, Johnny was signed by Reading, and he scored on his League debut although he was used as a wing half for most of his games.

He continued to play occasionally during the early years of the War and scored the opening goal of Reading's 1941 London War Cup triumph, but soon Johnny's War was to take a terrible downturn. In 1942 he was captured by the Japanese and forced to work on the notorious Burma railway of death, but his fitness saw him survive three and a half years before he was shipped to Japan. On the way, the ship was torpedoed and he spent three days in shark filled waters before being rescued by the enemy and taken to Nagasaki where he witnessed the dropping of the atom bomb. After the War, Johnny returned to Reading and even played in a couple of games, in February 1946, strangely against the two clubs he went on to play for after Reading - Aldershot and Palace. Although Johnny never got back into Reading's League side he finished top scorer for the reserves in 1946-47, as well as setting up the refreshment stalls at Elm Park. He stayed in Reading for the rest of his life and after his playing days were over he was a bookie and racing tipster.

Reading Record: Lge 9/1, Wartime 26/8, Total 35/9
League Career Total: 58/6

SHIPLEY George Michael

b. Newcastle 7.3.1959
Ht 5ft 8 Wt 10st 8 (76-77)
Career: St Mary's Boys Club; Southampton from apprentice March 1977; READING (loan) 22 March 1979; Blackpool (loan) October 1979; Lincoln C. (£38,000) January 1980; Luton T. (trial) May 1983; Charlton A. July 1985; Gillingham July 1987; Walsall (trial) June 1989; Lincoln C. August 1989; Maidstone U. scout 1990; Gillingham youth manger July 1991; Middlesbrough August 1991; Bradford C. asst. manager 1994

Reading took George on loan as a replacement for their injured midfielder, Richie Bowman, and he did a more than adequate job by playing in the last 12 matches of the 1978-79 Fourth Division championship season.

During that spell, the skilful youngster became the first player to score while on loan at Reading. More remarkable was the fact that Reading never conceded a goal while George was playing. Not surprisingly, Reading wanted to sign George permanently but he returned to the Dell before eventually moving to Lincoln where he made almost 250 first team appearances.

Reading Record: Lge 11(1)/1
League Career Total: 330(5)/52

SHIPMAN Thomas Eric Rollason

b. Langwith 4.8.1910 d. 1972
Ht 5ft 8 Wt 12st (37-38)
Career: Shirebrook; Birmingham; Blackpool summer 1933; READING summer 1937; Oldham summer 1938; Mossley

A two footed full back, Tommy made his League debut with Blackpool but after playing 26 games in his first season, he only managed 10 in the next three years. A move to Reading did little to improve Tommy's first team chances, playing just three times when the regular full backs were unavailable, although he impressed with his first time clearances. Tommy finally got regular first team football at Oldham until the War intervened.

Reading Record: Lge 2, SSC 1, Total 3
League Career Total: 78

SHIPPERLEY David John

b. Uxbridge 12.4.1952
Ht 6ft 3 Wt 14st (79-80)
Career: Charlton A. from apprentice April 1970; Plymouth Arg. (loan) February 1974; Gillingham May 1974; Charlton A. (£42,000) February 1978; READING (£50,000) 13 September 1979

A giant centre half who made over 150 appearances for both Gillingham and, during two spells, Charlton, Dave joined Reading for their record fee as a replacement for the injured Martin Hicks. He had been the Gills' Player of the Year on two occasions, but never got the chance to establish himself at Elm Park due to injury. Dave was reliable at the back and dominant in the air but a deep seated groin injury eventually resulted in his retirement in November 1981. His son, Neil, has carried on the family name with a number of clubs, occasionally being linked with Reading while Dave has established a career with the Metropolitan Police.

Reading Record: Lge 18(1), FAC 1, LC 3, Total 22(1)
League Career Total: 308(9)/25

SHREEVES Peter

b. Neath 30.11.1940
Ht 5ft 8 1/2 Wt 11st 7 (59-60)
Career: Finchley amateur; READING amateur 6 May 1958, professional January 1959; Chelmsford C. July 1966; Wimbledon July 1969; Stevenage T. 1971; Malden T; Charlton A. coach 1974; Tottenham H. youth manager 1974, coach manager June 1984; QPR coach August 1986, asst. manager December 1988; Watford coach; Tottenham H. manager July 1991 to May 1992; Wales asst. manager; Sheffield Wed. coach, 1996, caretaker manager March to May 2000 & February 2001, manager

Although brought up in London, Peter was born in Wales while his mother was an evacuee during the War. After making a scoring League debut for Reading early in 1959, Peter made such progress that he was selected for the Welsh U23 side within the year, but had the misfortune to break his leg days before the game and was never selected again. That injury kept him out of the first team and, not surprisingly, impaired his progress. Although the skilful, industrious inside forward was a consistent performer, Peter only played in more than half of Reading's first team games in one of his eight seasons as a professional. On 21 August 1965, Peter wrote himself into Reading's history when he became their first player to be substituted. On leaving Reading Peter began a non-League career that saw him win the Southern League championship with Chelmsford and the Southern League Cup with Wimbledon. Subsequently, Peter has had a long coaching and managerial career, particularly with Spurs, where he coached them to their 1981 FA Cup win.

Reading Record: Lge 112(1)/17, FAC 10/1, LC 9/1, SPFC 1, Total 132(1)/19

SILVESTER Peter Dennis
b. Wokingham 19.2.1948
Ht 5ft 11 Wt 11st 8 (68-69)
Career: West Ham U. (trial); Chelsea (trial); READING amateur September 1964, apprentice 25 November 1964, professional 19 February 1966; Norwich C. (£22,000) 12 September 1969; Colchester U. (loan) October 1973; Southend U. (£12,000) February 1974; READING (loan) 13 March 1975; Baltimore Comets (loan) summer 1975; Blackburn R. (loan) October 1976; Cambridge U. August 1977; Washington Diplomats (£7,500) 1978; San Diego; Maidstone U. August 1978

A tall, stylish centre forward with an eye for goal, Peter scored regularly for Reading's youth and reserve sides before netting the winner on his League debut, at Exeter, in April 1966. A month later he finished top scorer as the reserves won promotion in the Football Combination. Over the next two seasons Peter was eased into League football, sometimes being kept out of the first team by Roger Smee, his future brother-in-law, but there was no keeping him out in 1968-69. In his first start of that season, he scored four goals against Hartlepool and finished the season as Reading's top marksman and Player of the Year. It was now obvious that the likeable young striker had everything that was necessary to take him to the very top, and Reading soon accepted a record fee to sell him to Norwich. Peter took the step up in his stride, scoring regularly until January 1972 when he suffered a knee injury that kept him out for almost two years. He left Norwich with a creditable 37 goals in 99 League starts, but that injury was to trouble Peter for the rest of his career. But goals continued to flow, with Southend, although Peter's return to Reading, on loan, again saw him troubled with injury and he only managed one and a half games. Although Peter only played a few more League games, he enjoyed well deserved success during a spell in the States, where he was voted Player of the Year, and then with Maidstone until his knee could no longer stand up to regular football.

Reading Record: Lge 78(3)/27, FAC 4(1)/3, LC 3, Total 85(4)/30
League Career Total: 267(8)/98

SIMMS Ernest
b. Scotland c.1896 d. ?
Ht 5ft 9 Wt 13st (20-21)
Career: Clyde; Vale of Leven 1919; READING (trial) October 1920

A former Scottish Junior international, Ernie was one of nine centre forwards tried by Reading during their first League season. Ernie played in just one League game, a home win over Palace in October 1920, before being released weeks later after being involved in a fight with a team mate.

Reading Record: Lge 1

SIMPSON Dennis Ewart
b. Coventry 1.11.1919
Ht 5ft 10 Wt 11st (50-51)
Career: Coventry C from jnrs May 1939; READING (£3,750) 18 May 1950; Exeter C. May 1955

Reading beat Hull and Southend for Dennis' signature and it proved well worth the effort to bring the strong, pacey winger to Elm Park. Apart from a spell out injured at the end of 1952-53, Dennis was Reading's regular right winger for his first four seasons and his form earned him a game for England B against the British Olympic XI in 1952. Dennis' place came under threat during 1954-55 and he moved to Exeter before retiring and returning to Coventry.

Reading Record: Lge 172/32, FAC 17, Total 189/32
League Career Total: 269/41

SIMPSON Peter
b. Leith 13.11.1904 d. 3.1974
Ht 5ft 11 Wt 11st 7 (37-38)
Career: Leith Amateurs; St Bernards; Kettering T; Crystal Palace summer 1929; West Ham U. summer 1935; READING (player exchange) 11 November 1937

In his mid twenties when he began his League career, Peter made a sensational start with Palace, averaging over a goal a game in his first two seasons, including six against Exeter in October 1930. After 153 goals in 180 League games, the former shipping clerk moved to West Ham, but his goal rate reduced and 16 months later he moved to Reading, along with Len Young, in exchange for free scoring centre forward, Rod Williams. Peter modelled his style on Scottish international, Andy Wilson, but this did not appear to help him at Reading where he scored six times in 22 games before being released at the end of that season.

Reading Record: Lge 19/4, FAC 1, SSC 2/2, Total 22/6
League Career Total: 268/174

PETER'S CLAIM TO FAME - In 1930-31, Peter scored 46 League goals for Crystal Palace which is the highest total scored by any player for a London club in a season.

SMALLWOOD Frederick

b. Wrexham 19.9.1910
Ht 5ft 5 1/2 Wt 10st 2 (38-39)
Career: Llanerch Celts; Wrexham amateur September 1933; Chester from amateur October 1934; Macclesfield T. 1935; Southampton June 1936; READING (£500) June 1938; Wartime guest for Wrexham, Newcastle U, Sunderland & Hartlepools U.

Fred was a tricky left winger, fast in thought and movement, who had been capped by Wales at amateur level. Despite scoring on his League debut, with Wrexham in 1933-34, Fred had to wait until he moved to Southampton to get a professional contract and a regular League place. A move to Reading saw Fred score his first goal at Elm Park in the final of the previous season's Southern Section Cup which had been held over until September 1938. He also holds the unusual distinction of scoring all four Reading goals that were netted during Joe Cochrane's short managerial stay at Elm Park. Fred always carried a rabbit's foot with him on the pitch but his luck ran out when the War ended his League career. After the War, Fred pursued his other talent by forming a small dance band in the North East.

Reading Record: Lge 40/10, FAC 2, SSC 5/3, Wartime 36/14, Total 83/27
League Career Total: 90/21

SMEE Roger Guy

b. Reading 14.8.1948
Ht 5ft 11 Wt 11st 10 (67-68)
Career: Chelsea from apprentice March 1966; READING 28 January 1967; Chelmsford C. (loan) March 1970; Hillingdon Bor. August 1970; Hereford U. (£5,000) December 1970; KVG Ostend; READING 3 July 1973; Hillingdon Bor. July 1974

A short spell with Chelsea ended when Roger's contract was cancelled by mutual agreement so that he could join his home town team, Reading. Within weeks he had scored a stunning goal on his League debut and, keeping his place to the end of the season, his goals and form saw Reading lose just once as they almost sneaked a promotion place. His Reading career was scuppered when he broke his leg after just one minute of a 1967-68 pre-season friendly and by the time he had recovered, Roger was no longer a part of new manager Jack Mansell's plans. His form with Hillingdon produced a move to Hereford that generated the biggest fee between two Southern League clubs at that time. He returned to Reading, but his one season was blighted by injury and he only added another six starts and one goal to his League total.

Roger retired from football in 1976 to concentrate on his career as a quantity surveyor, having studied for his qualifications while recovering from his broken leg. By 1983, Roger was chairman of property company, The Rockfort Group, and he became the figurehead of the fight to save Reading from Robert Maxwell, and saved the club from Maxwell's merger plans with Oxford. He was Reading's chairman during the club's record breaking Third Division championship season and Simod Cup victory, as well as sowing the seeds for the move from Elm Park. The slump in the property market through 1990 led to Roger resigning as Reading's chairman in order to concentrate on his business, but there can be no doubt that without Roger Smee's intervention in 1983, Reading Football Club might not exist today.

Reading Record: Lge 55(4)/17, FAC 5, LC 2, Total 62(4)/17

ROGER'S CLAIM TO FAME - 18 years after winning the National Association of Boys Clubs 880 yard championship, Roger ran in the 1983 New York Marathon and raised £2,500 for Reading's youth development scheme.

SMILLIE Neil

b. Barnsley 19.7.1958
Ht 5ft 6 Wt 10st 7 (87-88)
Career: Crystal Palace from apprentice in October 1975; Brentford (loan) January 1977; Memphis Rogues (loan) April 1978; Brighton (player exchange) August 1982; Watford (£100,000) June 1985; READING (loan) 4 December 1986, (free) 26 March 1987; Brentford August 1988; Gillingham player asst. manager July 1993, caretaker manager February to June 1995; Wycombe W. coach August 1995, caretaker manager October 1996 and March 1998, manager April 1998; Fulham youth coach February 1999

The son of Barnsley and Lincoln winger, Ron Smillie, Neil played for the Chelmsford schools side that reached two successive English Schools Trophy finals. After establishing himself at Crystal Palace, Neil moved to Brighton and was a member of their 1983 FA Cup final team.

Loaned to Reading for a month from Watford, he then returned in March when the move was made permanent. Capable of playing on the left side of midfield or as a more traditional winger, Neil reserved his best performances for Reading's Simod Cup triumph. Having scored his first Reading goal in the semi-final, Neil turned on an inspired display at Wembley and was rewarded with the fourth goal on that memorable day. Surprisingly, Neil only played one more time for Reading before enjoying a successful five seasons with Brentford.

Reading Record: Lge 38(1), LC 3, Simod C 5(1)/2, Total 46(2)/2
League Career Total: 400(41)/33

NEIL'S CLAIM TO FAME - Neil hold's the unwanted record of twice playing in a Wembley cup final and being relegated in the same season - with Brighton in 1983 and Reading five years later.

SMITH Benjamin Peter
b. Chelmsford 23.11.1978
Ht 5ft 9 Wt 11st 9 (99-00)
Career: Arsenal; READING March 1997; Bath C. March 1998; Yeovil; Southend U. July 2001

Ben was snapped up by Reading when Arsenal did not offer him a contract after he had progressed through their youth system. A battling midfielder, he was soon given his chance when he came on as a half time substitute for the last game of 1996-97, at Manchester City. That was to be the total of his League career and after a year with Reading, Ben was released, although he got the chance to play at the Madejski Stadium when he appeared for Yeovil in a 1999 FA Cup-tie.

Reading Record: Lge (1)

SMITH Edward
b Sunderland 22.2.1902 d. Luton 1972
Ht 5ft 7 Wt 11st 12 (28-29)
Career: Thompsons Shipyard; Hartlepools U. July 1923; Newport Co. June 1925; Portsmouth February 1927; READING (£235) 22 June 1928; Luton T. (£250) June 1929; Preston N.E. June 1931; Bristol R. September 1931; Vauxhall Motors August 1932

An experienced left back, Ted had joined Portsmouth midway through 1926-27 and played 12 games as they won promotion to the First Division that season. He never played in the top flight and was allowed to join Reading for a season.

A poor start by Reading cost Ted his place after three games but he fought his way back by November 1928 and ended up playing 29 first team games that season.

Reading Record: Lge 26, FAC 3, Total 29
League Career Total: 187/2

SMITH Eric Victor
b. Reading 20..3.1928 d 4.4.1992
Ht 5ft 9 Wt 12st 2 (51-52)
Career: READING groundstaff October 1948, professional 23 April 1949; Yeovil June 1956

Another member of the Berks & Bucks team that won the 1946 FA County Youth Championship, to make his way into Reading's first team, Eric signed following his release from his National Service in the Army. Originally a centre half, he was used in every defensive position during his time at Elm Park, but he was at his best at left back and it was in this role that he made the most of his first team appearances. Eric was released at the end of 1955-56, his last appearance being in his own benefit match against an International Managers XI.

Reading Record: Lge 61/1, FAC 1, SPFC 1, Total 63/1

SMITH John 'Jack'
b. Fullwood c.1883 d. ?
Ht 5ft 9 Wt 12st 3 (10-11)
Career: Moorpark; Blackburn R. 1903; Portsmouth 1908; READING (£5) 23 August 1910
See 'The Managers' for details of Jack's managerial career.

The size of Jack's transfer fee is possibly explained by the fact that it is rumoured that he was signed for Reading while still recovering from a broken leg! Despite that he went on to captain Reading to the Southern League Division Two Championship in 1910-11 and was soon being described by Churchman's cigarette cards as having *'steadily improved and has few superiors'*. Jack was Reading's regular right back through the decade and into the club's first League season, only ceasing to be a regular first teamer when he became Reading's first player manager at Christmas 1920.

Reading Record: Lge 30, FAC 18, SL 172, Total 220

SMITH John H
b. Barnsley d. 11.1880 d. ?
Ht 5ft 8 Wt 11st (23-24)
Career: Wombwell; Huddersfield T; READING June 1923

A lightning fast right winger, John was capable of delivering accurate crosses at high speed as well as getting amongst the scorers. His entire League career was spent at Reading and he played a vital role in the club's 1925-26 Third Division Championship, finishing second highest scorer that season. Unfortunately John suffered a serious knee injury near the end of that season and was forced to retire just when he was being heralded as having a bright future. John stayed in Reading and worked in Simmonds Brewery.

Reading Record: Lge 102/17, FAC 9/2, Total 111/19

SMITH Mark Alexander
b. Bellshill 16.2.1964
Ht 5ft 9 Wt 10st 4 (90-91)
Career: Queens Park; Celtic; Dunfirmline A; Stoke C. (loan) February 1990; Nottingham For. March 1990; READING (loan) December 1990; Mansfield T. (loan) March 1991; Shrewsbury T. August 1991

A rightsided player who could play in either midfield or forward, Mark played three games on loan to Reading after Christmas 1990. All three games were won, but on each occasion Mark was substituted and replaced by Stuart Lovell. Reading wanted to extend his loan period but Mark was only interested in a permanent move and so returned to Forest.

Reading Record: Lge 3
League Career Total: 75(15)/4

SMITH Neil James
b Lambeth 30.9.1971
Ht 5ft 9 Wt 12st 12 (99-00)
Career: Tottenham H. from YTS July 1990; Gillingham (£40,000) October 1991; Fulham (£150,000) July 1997; READING (£100,000) 20 August 1999

Neil won the FA Youth Cup with Spurs in 1990 but never made their first team, his League debut coming with Gillingham. During almost 250 first team games for the Gills, Neil established himself as a committed and consistent midfielder and he was snapped up by Fulham in 1997. Despite some big money signings at Craven Cottage, Neil forced himself into the first team to play a vital role in their Division Two Championship season. Early into the next season, he moved to Reading but managerial changes saw him lose his place and in December 1999 he was almost sold to Notts County. Again, he showed his determination to force his way back into contention and Neil's long throw added another attacking option to Reading's arsenal.

He featured less frequently the following season and was told he could leave in June 2001.

Reading Record: 30(21)/2, FAC 1(1), LC 3(1), AMC 2(1), Total 36(24)/2 +
League Career Total: 296(41)/13 +

SMITH William Henry
b Plymouth 7.9.1926
Ht 5ft 11 Wt 11st 7 (47-48)
Career: Plymouth T amateur; Plymouth Arg. August 1945; READING August 1947; Northampton T. July 1948; Birmingham C. February 1950; Blackburn R. December 1952; Accrington Stan. July 1960

Like his brother, John, Bill began his career with Plymouth but was recommended to Reading by former Southampton and England player, Fred Titmuss, before he made it to Argyle's first team. Bill was a versatile player who was capable of playing in almost any position and was said to have the hardest shot at Elm Park. His three first team appearances were all in forward positions while Bill scored 10 times for the reserves as they reached the semi-finals of the Combination Cup. Although he rarely commanded a regular first team place with any of the four clubs he played for after Reading, he carried on playing in the League until his mid-thirties, his final game appearing in Accrington Stanley's last match before they resigned from the League.

Reading Record: Lge 3
League Career Total: 237/40

SPARKS Christopher James
b. Islington 22.5.1960
Ht 5ft 10 Wt 10st 8 (79-80)
Career: Crystal Palace from apprentice November 1977; READING (loan) September 1979

A promising young right back, Chris had won the FA Youth Cup with Crystal Palace in 1978 before joining Reading on loan. Despite promising displays for Reading, Palace manager Terry Venables made it clear that the youngster was only getting experience and was not for sale. Chris never made it to Palace's first team and his loan spell at Elm Park was to be the total of his League record.

Reading Record: Lge 3, LC 1, Total 4

SPENCE David McLachlan

b. Paisley c. 1895 d. ?
Ht 5ft 6 Wt 12st (27-28)
Career: St Mirren; READING July 1920; Walsall summer 1921; Oldham A. November 1927; Pontypridd July 1923

David joined Reading after serving as a young officer in the Black Watch during the First World War and made his debut in the club's first League game, at Newport, in August 1920. The right winger lost his first team place at the end of October but came back to play another seven times towards the end of the season before leaving the club for Walsall. David's League career ended with a short spell at Oldham as they lost their Second Division status.

Reading Record: Lge 20/1
League Career Total: 68/5

DAVID'S CLAIM TO FAME - At the time of signing for Reading, David was the reigning Scottish Amateur Golf Champion.

SPERRING Alistair

b Hayling Island 26.10.1963
Ht 6ft 2 Wt 13st 3 (84-85)
Career: Southampton from apprentice August 1983; Swindon T. (loan) August 1984; READING (trial) 28 December 1984; Bognor Regis T. summer 1985

As understudy to Peter Shilton at Southampton, Alistair's chances in the Saints' goal were limited to one first team appearance in the League Cup. In that game he was involved in a collision with Mark Wright that left the England defender with a broken nose and jaw. During his trial at Reading, he was also restricted to one appearance in a cup match, the Freight Rover Trophy game against Brentford in February 1985, before being released at the end of the season.

Reading Record: AMC 1

SPIERS Richard Alan Jesse

b. Benson 27.11.1937 d. 22.10.2000
Ht 6ft Wt 11st 4 (68-69)
Career: Cholsey U; READING from amateur 3 October 1955; Banbury June 1970; Witney T. manager April 1972; READING scout August 1976

One of Reading's greatest players, Dick was a one club man who regularly supported the team for whom he once set their appearance record. After a season as an amateur with Reading, Dick signed professional forms and gradually established himself as the club's first choice centre half.

This took five seasons, partly because of club strength at the centre of the defence and also because of his National Service. During this period, Dick played for the Army XI on a number of occasions, including marking a top form Brian Clough when he scored five times for the FA XI in October 1957. From Christmas 1960 to September 1966 Dick missed just six Reading games during which time he was remarkably consistent. Although slightly built for the bruising battles with physical Third Division centre forwards, Dick was deceptively strong and rarely beaten in the air. He regularly captained Reading and, while not a prolific scorer, scored on his last two Elm Park appearances - against Stockport and then in his testimonial match. After his playing days, Dick scouted for Reading and he recommended Martin Hicks to the club, not realizing that Hicks would now hold the Reading appearance record that Dick once held.

Reading Record: Lge 451(2)/3, FAC 27/1, LC 20, SPFC 5, Total 503(2)/4

SPRINGELL George William

b. Tilehurst 4th qtr 1902 d. ?
Ht 5ft 4 Wt 10st (23-24)
Career: Norcot R; Windsor & Eton; READING February 1923; Walsall summer 1927; Thames

A popular local footballer in the Reading area, George was a member of the all conquering Norcot School that won the Reading Senior League, Cup and Junior Cup in 1914-15. He had played on and off for Reading as an amateur for several years before signing professionally. The smallest player on Reading's books, George was a tricky player and his mazy runs down the left wing made him a great favourite with the Reading fans to whom he was known as 'Curly'.

Reading Record: Lge 75/2, FAC 3/1, Total 78/3
League Career Total: 108/3

STAKER John

b. Reading 24.12.1967
Ht 6ft Wt 12st 2 (85-86)
Career: READING from YTS 1985

A young central defender who joined Reading from school, John found his path to the first team blocked by the impressive pairing of Steve Wood and Martin Hicks so his first team appearances were limited to the Freight Rover Trophy. His debut came as a 72nd minute substitute for Hicks at Bournemouth in 1985-86 while his only start came six weeks later, against Orient, in a game that was postponed six times before John got his chance. Both games ended in heavy defeats and John was released at the end of the season.

Reading Record: AMC 1(1)

STAMP Neville

b. Reading 7.7.1981
Ht 5ft 10 Wt 10st 5 (99-00)
Career: READING from trainee; York C. September 2000

A versatile youngster he progressed through the Reading youth system to be rewarded with his League debut as a half time substitute in the last game of 1998-99. He played those 45 minutes at left back where he was able to combine his strength in the tackle with his skill from dead-ball situations. In October 1999 he was made a permanent member of the first team squad but a niggling injury prevented him from adding to his League total with Reading.

Reading Record: Lge (1)
League Career Total: 12 (2) +

STANT Philip John

b. Bolton 13.10.1962
Ht 6ft 1 Wt 12st 7 (82-83)
Career: Army; Camberley T; READING non contract 19 August 1982; Didcot; Hereford U. November 1986; Notts Co. (£175,000) July 1989; Blackpool (loan) September 1990; Lincoln C. (loan) November 1990; Huddersfield T. (loan) January 1991; Fulham (£60,000) February 1991; Mansfield T. (£50,000) August 1991; Cardiff C. (£100,000) December 1992; Mansfield T. (loan) August 1993; Bury (£90,000) January 1995; Northampton T. (loan) November 1996; Lincoln C. (£30,000) December 1996 player-asst. manager November 1998, manager; Brighton February 2001

Phil hit the national headlines in November 1982, when he made his League debut for Reading while still in the Army. He had served in the Falklands War earlier that year and had been spotted while playing for the British Army.

A bustling inside forward, Phil showed he had an eye for the goal when he scored in his first two League games for Reading, but Army commitments prevented him from playing regularly and a move to the SAS bomb disposal squad at Hereford ended Reading's interest in him. There, the local club offered him the professional contract he wanted and, having bought himself out of the Army, Phil scored a hat trick on his Hereford debut. From then on Phil scored goals for a number of clubs, winning a PFA Fourth Division award in 1991 while at Mansfield, plus a Third Division championship and Welsh Cup double with Cardiff two years later. With Lincoln he became their assistant manager while the club chairman took over the manager's role, before Phil later took full charge.

Reading Record: Lge 3(1)/2, FAC 1, Total 4(1)/2
League Career Total: 372(61)/170 +

STATHAM Brian

b. Salisbury, Zimbabwe 21.5.1969
Ht 5ft 8 Wt 11st (90-91)
Career: Tottenham H. from YTS August 1987; READING (loan) 19 March 1991; Bournemouth (loan) November 1991; Brentford (£70,000) January 1991; Gillingham (£10,000) August 1997; Woking (loan) 1998; Stevenage T. (loan) February 1999; Chesham U. summer 2000

Born in Zimbabwe while his father was serving in the RAF and named after the England Test bowler by his cricket mad dad, Brian began his playing career with Spurs. As well as 24 League appearances for them, he won three England U21 caps plus two at youth level and was named Spurs Young Player of the Year in his first pro season. A versatile player who could perform equally well at full back, centre half and midfield, Brian was used at right back during his loan spell with Reading. It was a turbulent time at Elm Park as Ian Porterfield was sacked during Brian's loan spell. A successful spell at Brentford was followed by three seasons with Gillingham although he never made their League side in his last two seasons.

Reading Record: Lge 8
League Career Total: 194(26)/1

BRIAN'S CLAIM TO FAME: Brian was sent off in his last game for Reading and his last match with Brentford. He was also sent off in his first away game for Gillingham and, as with his Reading dismissal, both were at Brentford!

STEVENSON Nigel Charles Ashley
b. Swansea 2.11.1958
Ht 6ft 2 Wt 12st 10 (85-86)
Career: Swansea C. from apprentice November 1976; Cardiff C. (loan) October 1985; READING (loan) March 1986; Cardiff C. (free) June 1987; Merthyr T. summer 1989; Yeovil (£5,000) December 1990; Haverfordwest Co. asst. manager

A strong no-nonsense centre half, Nigel was a member of the Swansea sides that rose from the Fourth to the First Division, and back to the Third. He also won the Welsh Cup twice and was capped at youth, U21, plus four times as a full international. His loan move to Reading was to replace the injured Martin Hicks as Reading looked to confirm their promotion to the Second Division. A year later Nigel joined Swansea's arch rivals, Cardiff, helping them to a Welsh Cup and promotion double in 1988.

Reading Record: Lge 3
League Career Total: 330(14)/17

STREETE Floyd Anthony
b. Jamaica 5.5.1959
Ht 5ft 11 Wt 14st (91-92)
Career: Rivet Sports; Cambridge U. July 1976; Utrect 1983; SC Cumbur; Derby Co. October 1984; Wolverhampton W. (£5,000) 1985; READING (free) July 1990; Leighton T. summer 1992; Aylesbury U. asst. manager 2000

Brought up in Aylesbury, Floyd played for Berks & Bucks Youth and was spotted by Cambridge United's manager, Ron Atkinson. 125 League games with them saw him win a Fourth Division champions medal in 1976-77 before playing in Holland for two years. The giant central defender had a baptism of fire in the Netherlands as he marked Marco van Basten on his debut. Floyd returned to England with Derby but re-established himself with Wolves and one of his first games for them saw him star as they ended Reading's 13 match winning sequence at the start of 1985-86. Successive championships in 1988 and 1989 plus a Sherpa Van triumph were won at Wolves before Floyd moved to Reading. His first season was a disaster with a knee injury restricting him to just four games, but the following year he was a regular at the centre of Reading's defence. It was a little surprising that he was given a free transfer at the end of that season, especially as he was *Match* magazine's top Third Division player of that season. At that point, Floyd quit League football to work in a Buckingham school for boys with behavioural difficulties.

Reading Record: Lge 38, FAC 5, AMC 3, Total 46
League Career Total: 341(16)/25

STUCKEY Bruce George
b. Torquay 19.2.1947
Ht 5ft 8 Wt 11st 6 (74-75)
Career: Exeter C. from apprentice February 1965; Sunderland (£9,000) November 1967; Torquay U. (£5,000) February 1971; READING (£10,000) 2 November 1973; Torquay U. (loan) January 1995; Bournemouth (loan) March 1976; Connecticut Bicentennial summer 1977; Barnstable; Brixham October 1979

A spectacular start to his League career saw Bruce move to Sunderland for Exeter's record fee but he failed to establish himself in the North East. He returned to his home town club where his father was a member of Torquay's Supporters' Club committee. By now, Bruce had progressed from an orthodox left winger to a midfielder and it was in this role that he was used when he joined Reading for a fee that was the largest between two Fourth Division clubs at that time. Bruce played in over half of Reading's 1975-76 Fourth Division promotion season, but was used less frequently during the following one, and was released at the end of that campaign. Bruce was a popular player off the pitch and occasionally entertained fans with his singing and guitar playing as well as forming a popular Devon Country and Western act with Torquay's Dick Edwards.

Reading Record: Lge 92(5)/7, FAC 5, LC 4, Total 101(5)/7
League Career Total: 232(27)/21

SUMMERFIELD Arthur 'Archie'
b. c.1924
Ht 5ft 9 Wt 11st (45-46)
Career: Battle A; Maidenhead U; READING amateur summer 1945, professional August 1946; Canterbury C. May 1947

A local amateur who played for Reading during the last season of the War, Archie had a good left foot and was used at inside forward or, occasionally, on the wing. He played in both legs of Reading's 1945-46 FA Cup-tie against Aldershot but, despite scoring in both games and playing regularly for the reserves, Archie was never offered a contract.

Reading Record: FAC 2/2, Wartime 10/2, Total 12/4

SUTTON David William
b. Tarleton 21.1.1957
Ht 5ft 11 Wt 11st (77-78)
Career: Liverpool amateur; Plymouth Arg. from apprentice July 1974; READING (loan) November 1977; Huddersfield T. (£15,000) March 1978; Bolton W. (£12,000) June 1985; Rochdale August 1988 caretaker manager; asst. manager then manager from February 1991 to November 1994; Chorley T. manager March 1995

Dave was on Liverpool's books from the age of 13 but when their Youth Development Officer moved to Plymouth, Dave followed. There he established himself at the centre of their defence but was allowed to join Reading on loan. Five clean sheets in nine games impressed Reading to try to sign Dave permanently but they failed to agree with Plymouth's valuation and eventually he joined Huddersfield. There, he played over 280 first team games as the Terriers moved from the Fourth to the Second, but a back injury kept him out for the whole of 1984-85. Despite this setback, Dave moved on to Bolton, playing in their promotion winning side and he captained them in the 1988 Sherpa Van Final. Another move, to Rochdale, saw injury end his playing career in 1989 but he went on to manage them.

Reading Record: Lge 9
League Career Total: 437(1)/17

SUTTON Stephen John

b. Hartington 16.4.1961
Ht 6ft 1 Wt 14st 11(95-96)
Career: Nottingham For. from apprentice April 1979; Mansfield T. (loan) March 1981; Derby Co. (loan) January 1985; Coventry C. (loan) February 1991; Luton T. (loan) November 1991; Derby Co. (£300,000) March 1992; READING (loan) January 1996; Birmingham C. August 1996; Grantham T 1999; Leeds U. coach

Originally Steve provided goalkeeping cover for Peter Shilton but he gradually emerged to make the first team place his own, gaining League Cup winners medals in 1989 and 1990 plus a Full Members' Cup triumph in 1989. At the age of almost 31, Steve cost Derby a big fee and was their club captain in 1995-96. A goalkeeping crisis at Elm Park saw Steve become Reading's seventh keeper of the season and he gave exceptional displays in his two games.

Reading Record: Lge 2
League Career Total: 304(1)

SWAIN Malcolm

b. Hornsey 2.2.1952
Ht 5ft 9 Wt 10st 6 (70-71)
Career: Ascot U; READING apprentice 29.7.1968, professional 4 February 1968; Ramsgate summer 1972; Hillingdon Bor. July 1973; Slough T. June 1974; Dulwich Ham. September 1976

An industrious midfielder, Malcolm's efforts in the reserves were rewarded with a professional contract and a debut as substitute against Manchester United in the Watney Cup, an appearance that saw him become the first Reading player to wear a number 13 shirt.

A League debut soon followed but this coincided with Reading's 1970-71 relegation season which might explain the unfair treatment he sometimes received. Despite never winning over the fans, Malcolm never shirked his responsibility but he lost his place in his second season and moved into non-League football.

Reading Record: Lge 37(4)/2, FAC (2), Watney Cup (1), Total 37(7)/2

SWALES Stephen Colin

b. Whitby 26.12.1973
Ht 5ft 8 Wt 10st 6 (96-97)
Career: Scarborough U. from apprentice August 1992; Millwall (loan) 1993; READING (£70,000) 13 July 1995; Hull C. (free) 7 December 1998; Halifax T. summer 2001

With Scarborough from 14, Steve made his League debut at 18 and had made over 60 first team appearances when Reading signed the promising young left back. Initially, he played mainly in the reserves and only made eight starts in his first two seasons at Elm Park, but then new manager, Terry Bullivant, selected him and made Steve virtually ever-present at left back. The signing of Andy Legg and the arrival of Tommy Burns spelt the end of Steve's first team chances with Reading and after trials with several clubs he joined Hull.

Reading Record: Lge 33(10)/1, FAC 6, LC 6(1), Total 45(11)/1
League Career Total: 141(24)/2 +

TAIT Michael Paul

b. Wallsend 30.9.1956
Ht 5ft 11 Wt 12st 5 (87-88)
Career: Oxford U. from apprentice October 1974; Carlisle U. (£65,000) February 1977; Hull C. (£150,000) September 1979; Portsmouth (£100,000) June 1980; READING (£50,000) 1 September 1987; Darlington (free) 3 August 1990; Hartlepool U. (free) July 1992; Gretna (free) summer 1994; Hartlepool U. (free) player manager September 1994; Blyth Spartans manager 1999; Darlington asst. manager February 2001

Mick began his career with Oxford as a centre forward and, although he was never a prolific scorer, he attracted several large fees. It was at Portsmouth where Mick enjoyed his best spell, helping them to the Third Division title in 1982-83 and making 240 League appearances, mostly in midfield, before joining Reading. Mick's fearsome strength of tackle was already legendary and his play at Elm Park did nothing to diminish his reputation. Known amongst some of the fans as 'Iron Mike', he built up a cult following and was used in the centre of defence as well as midfield.

Despite this, Mick's best display came in his original role of centre forward when, like the rest of the Reading team, he more than rose to the occasion as Reading beat Luton at Wembley in the 1988 Simod Cup final and scored the third goal. After

Reading, Mick carried on playing in the League until he was 39, having made almost 900 first team appearances, and had two years as Hartlepool manager where, by coincidence, his last signing was Peter Beardsley, the player who had replaced him at Carlisle 22 years earlier.

Reading Record: Lge 98(1)/10, FAC 16, LC 9/2, FMC 6/2, AMC 3/1, Total 132(1)/15
League Career Total: 731(30)/90

MICK'S CLAIM TO FAME - Mick's formidable tackling ability was not always appreciated by referees and so Mick set a couple of unwanted records. While with Oxford he was one of three of their players to be sent off against Plymouth while he later became the first player to be sent off with four different League clubs.

TAIT Thomas
b. Hetton le Hole 20.11.1908 d Barnton 22.4.1976
Ht 5ft 10 Wt 11st 7 (38-39)
Career: Sunderland; Hetton; Middlesbrough; Southport summer 1927; Manchester C. 1928; Bolton W. 1931; Luton T. summer 1931; Bournemouth summer 1934; READING (£1,000) 9 November 1934; Torquay U. (free) summer 1939; READING (Wartime guest)

A former schoolboy international, Tommy had played in all four divisions by the time he joined Reading. His best spell had been with Manchester City where he helped them to promotion in 1927-28 and then scored 28 goals in 31 First Division games two seasons later. £200 of his transfer fee was paid by Reading's Supporters' Club, and Tommy quickly repaid that by scoring a hat-trick on his debut, against local rivals Aldershot. Tommy was one of Reading's most popular players of all time and although he was a fiery, bustling forward, he was a deep thinker and was one of the first inside forwards to roam away from the centre to drag the centre half out of position.

He became the first Reading player to be sent off in an Elm Park League game when he took the date, Boxing Day, too literally. Tommy topped Reading's scorers in his first four seasons, consequently, there was uproar when it was announced that he would not be retained at the end of 1937-38, and angry supporters organised a petition to keep their favourite at Elm Park. Tommy had a better idea and scored five goals in the next two games to earn himself a new contract. Eventually, he left Reading in 1939 but although the War prevented him from extending his League career, he returned to Elm Park a year later as a Wartime guest.

Reading Record: Lge 144/79, FAC 15/14, SSC 9/10, Wartime 2, Total 170/103
League Career Total: 325/181

TAYLOR Alan F
b. Alfreton 7.3.1954 d. Reading 1981
Ht 5ft 10 Wt 11st 4 (74-75)
Career: Leicester C. apprentice; Alfreton T; Chelsea October 1972; READING (free) 29 April 1974; Rochester Lancers summer 1975; Worksop T. 1976

A tall, fair haired left winger, Alan was the son of a professional footballer, but although he scored a memorable winning header on his home debut for Reading, he did not hold down a regular first team spot in his season at Elm Park. Despite this, he was the club's penalty taker, having scored 10 out of 10 in a club competition to find the best spot kicker. After a spell in the States, a back injury ended Alan's professional career. He remained a popular local sportsman in Reading, taking part in skillmaster competitions and running for Reading Athletic Club, having once turned down the chance to run in the All England Schools trial at White City, to play for Leicester. Sadly, Alan was involved in a serious car crash in 1981 and died, aged only 37.

Reading Record: Lge 13(8)/4, LC 3(1)/2, Total 16(9)/6

TAYLOR Archibald
b. Glasgow 4.10.1918 d. 1976
Ht 5ft 10 1/2 Wt 11st 7 (46-47)
Career: Cambuslang; Burnley; READING 10 June 1939; Leyton O. (£600) August 1948

After making three League appearances for Burnley, Archie moved to Reading but had to wait seven years before he got to play in the League for them. The quiet and unassuming inside forward played in two of the abandoned 1939-40 season's game plus the occasional wartime game.

Despite being described in the Reading programme as *'one of the cleverest ball players in the South'*, Archie was only on the fringe of the first team playing just a handful of games after the War, all at inside left.

Reading Record: Lge 15/2, Wartime 22/4, Total 37/6
League Career Total: 64/4

TAYLOR Geoffrey Arthur
b. Henstead 22.1.1923
Ht 5ft 9 Wt 10st 8 (46-47)
Career: CNSOBU; Norwich C. August 1946; READING March 1947; Lincoln C. August 1947; Boston U. March 1948; Stad Rennais April 1948; Brighton August 1948; Stad Rennais December 1949; Bristol R. September 1951; managing in Switzerland December 1952; QPR November 1953

Few players can have had a more unusual career than left winger, Geoff. Although he played for six League clubs, he only managed a total of 10 League appearances in his eight year career that was interrupted by two spells in France and one as a manager in Switzerland. Not surprisingly in view of his overseas spells, Geoff was fluent in French and German. At Reading, a couple of goals for the reserves earned Geoff a game at Torquay in May 1947 but, as with his spells at Norwich and Lincoln, that was the total of his League career for the club.

Reading Record: Lge 1
League Career Total: 10

TAYLOR Leslie
b. North Shields 4.12.1956
Ht 5ft 8 Wt 11st 7 (87-88)
Career: Wallsend BC; Oxford U. from apprentice December 1974; Watford (£150,000) November 1980; READING (loan) October 1986 permanent (£20,000) 4 December 1986; Colchester U. (£20,000) January 1989; Oxford U. youth development officer

Having played alongside Mick Tait with Wallsend Boys Club, the two joined Oxford as apprentices with Les making his debut as an 18 year old. He quickly developed into one of the best young midfielders in the country, being voted the Sunday People's top Third Division player of 1977-78, and the following season Les was the youngest captain in the League. Les' move to Watford coincided with the best spell in their history and he captained them in Europe and in the 1984 FA Cup final. Having lost his first team place at Vicarage Road, Les joined Reading on his 30th birthday after a spell on loan, and his hardworking displays made him a first team regular for his first year.

Although he then lost his place, Les played in the Simod Cup matches, including the final, in place of cup-tied players.

Reading Record: Lge 69(6)/3, FAC 5/2, LC 8, FMC 4(1), AMC 2, Total 88(7)/5
League Career Total: 499(19)/32

TAYLOR Scott Dean
b. Portsmouth 28.11.1970
Ht 5ft 9 Wt 11st (96-97)
Career: READING apprentice 1987, professional 22 June 1989; Leicester C. (£500,000) 12 July 1995; Wolverhampton W. (free) summer 1999

Recommended to Reading by former player, Steve Wood, Scott was the club's Apprentice of the Year in 1987-88 when Reading's youth team reached the FA Youth Cup quarter-finals. Having made his League debut almost a year before signing professional, Scott became a first team regular. Tremendously fit, with good pace, Scott modelled himself on Bryan Robson and was used mainly on the right side of midfield but could also play at full back. In addition he was often called off the subs bench with devastating effect. A regular in Reading's 1993-94 Division Two championship season, Scott enjoyed his best spell the following year as Reading made it to the play-off final. Like several other Reading players, Scott's form attracted other clubs and he joined Leicester. There he made up for his play-off disappointment with Reading by winning through the following year, having dyed his hair blond for the Wembley final. He was successful at Wembley again when he helped Leicester win the 1997 League Cup final but from then on Scott's career was hit by a series of injuries. For a time it looked as if his League career might be over but Scott renewed his partnership with Mark McGhee and Colin Lee at Wolves to revive his career.

Reading Record: Lge 164(43)/24, FAC 11(2)/3, LC 7(5)/1, AMC 9(4)/1, Play-offs 3, Total 194(54)/29
League Career Total: 244(59)/33

TEARSE David James

b. Newcastle 7.8.1951
Ht 6ft Wt 12st (74-75)
Career: North Kenton BC, Leicester C. October 1969; Torquay U. (£15,000) November 1974; READING (loan) 29 January 1975; Atherstone July 1975

A centre forward who cost Torquay a club record fee, Dave was troubled with injuries during his career. Although he scored 23 goals in 77 League games for United, Dave suffered a broken leg, dislocated ankle and broken jaw while with them. His loan spell at Reading, that saw Bruce Stuckey go in the opposite direction, was hampered by a back injury and he only managed two games in his one month stay.

Reading Record: Lge 2
League Career Total: 86(1)/24

TELLING Hubert

b. Swindon 2nd qtr 1913
Ht 5ft 9 Wt 10st 11 (35-36)
Career: Swindon Victoria; READING (trial) May 1934; Crystal Palace; Hartlepools U.

Hubert was signed by Reading after a fine performance against Watford reserves during a trial at Elm Park. The slightly built centre half got just one chance in the League but unfortunately that ended in a 6-1 defeat at Southend and Hubert was released soon after.

Reading Record: Lge 1
League Career Total: 5

TERRY Patrick Alfred

b. Lambeth 2.10.1933
Ht 5ft 10 Wt 12st 2 (65-66)
Career: Eastbourne U; Charlton A. March 1953; Newport Co. June 1956; Swansea T. February 1958; Gillingham October 1958; Northampton T. July 1961; Millwall February 1962; READING (£1,800) 21 August 1964; Swindon T. (£5,300) 28 February 1967; Brentford 29 June 1968; Hillingdon Bor. July 1969; Folkestone May 1970; Stevenage Bor. August 1972

A real football nomad, Pat never stayed long with any of his nine League clubs and yet he is well remembered at all of them. An old fashioned centre forward who used his physical strength to the full, Pat was one of the best headers of the ball in the game and it is said that two thirds of his goals were obtained in this way. He scored regularly throughout his career, averaging approximately a goal every other game, yet he only enjoyed one promotion in his League career when he joined Millwall with three months to go in their 1961-62 Fourth Division title win.

At Reading he scored many of his goals from Alan Scarrott's pinpoint crosses and corners and his heading tended to overshadow a very useful left foot. A broken leg in December 1964 interrupted his spell at Elm Park but he still topped Reading's scorers, a feat he repeated the following season. It came as a surprise when Reading sold Pat on for a good profit to Swindon where he became the last player to date to score for and against Reading in the big derby games. A true hard man, Pat was almost 38 when he helped Folkestone to promotion in 1970-71, and was able to carry on playing until he was nearly 40.

Reading Record: Lge 99/41, FAC 6/4, LC 11/6, Total 116/51
League Career Total: 494(1)/229

THOMPSON George Wilfred

b. Sunderland 15.4.1896 d. Sunderland 1976
Ht 6ft Wt 13st (23-24)
Career: Southwick; Norwich C; Croydon Common; Durham C; Norwich C; Aberdare A; Dundee U; Torquay U; READING (£100) July 1923; Coventry C. July 1924; Nuneaton T; Walsall 1926; Caernavon T.

George's career details reveal a player willing to travel the country to play football, having performed for three of the Home Countries before he got his chance in the League with Reading. He started the 1923-24 season at right half, holding his place until December when, after a warning from the club about rough play, he was sent off at Southend. He had a shorter run at left half near the end of that season before continuing his wanderings, although he only managed to play another three League games in his career.

Reading Record: Lge 23/2, FAC 1, Total 24/2
League Career Total: 26/2

THORNHILL Rodney Derek

b. Reading 24.1.1942
Ht 5ft 11 Wt 11st 10 (65-66)
Career: READING amateur 20 August 1960, professional 27 May 1963; Poole T. June 1970

Reading spotted Rod when he played for Berkshire Boys Clubs against London and signed him, initially as an amateur, five months later. A gangling player, Rod was affectionately known as 'Spider' and could play in almost any position. He began his first team career as a half back, but was subsequently used in the forward line or at full back. Although Rod was probably at his best when asked to play in a more defensive role, his greatest moment came in the forward line when, in September 1964, he scored four goals against Watford.

After barely missing a game for 20 months, Rod suffered a damaged retina in November 1969 and never played for the first team again.

Reading Record: Lge 188(4)/19, FAC 11/3, LC 16(2)/1, Total 215(6)/23

THORP Michael Stephen
b. Wallingford 5.12.1975
Ht 6ft Wt 12st (95-96)
Career: READING YTS; Slough T. 1994; READING 12 January 1995 & July 1997; Cheltenham T. (loan) February 1998; Barry T. (trial); Slough T; Basingstoke; Oxford C. 1999

The great grandson of pre-War Reading player, Len Darnell, Michael had a remarkable Reading career, being signed for the club on three occasions by three different managers. Associated with Reading from the age of ten, Michael was released by Mark McGhee, but after a short spell with Slough, he returned as Jimmy Quinn and Mick Gooding's first signing. They released him in May 1997 but two months later he was back at Elm Park, this time as Terry Bullivant's first signing. His first spell with Reading was hampered by a broken leg received in a charity match, but he made a stunning League debut in September 1995, against McGhee's Leicester. Michael played with great composure at the centre of the defence and had excellent distribution but, unfortunately, he was injured after his next game and had to wait two years before he got another first team chance. Released for the final time, Michael had a trial with Barry that included an appearance against Dynamo Kiev in the European Champions League.

Reading Record: Lge 2(3), FAC 1(1), LC 2, Total 5(4)

THORPE Anthony Lee
b. Leicester 10.4.1974
Ht 5ft 9 Wt 12st 3 (98-99)
Career: Leicester C. YTS; Luton T. (free) August 1982; Fulham (£800,000) February 1998; Bristol C. (£1 m.) June 1998; READING (loan) 5 February 1999; Luton T. (loan) March 1999; Luton (loan) November 1999

Tony enjoyed a free scoring spell with Luton that saw him win a PFA Division Two award but two big money moves failed to see him maintain his strike rate. He joined Reading on a month's loan and although he did not greatly impress, Tony's one goal saw him maintain his 100% penalty record with a last minute winner against Preston. On his day he can be a quicksilver striker who is deadly inside the penalty area, and Tony seemed to have finally settled down to life away from Luton when he topped City's scorers in 1999-00 and 2000-01.

Reading Record: Lge 6/1
League Career Total: 180(57)/93

THORPE Edwin
b Kiveton Park 1898 d. ?
Ht 5ft 7 1/2 Wt 11st (23-24)
Career: Sheffield Wed; Lincoln C; Doncaster R; York C; READING July 1923

A left back, Ted spent most of his career in Yorkshire but made all his League appearances with Lincoln before joining Reading. He played just three more League games, all at left back, in September 1923 before quitting League football.

Reading Record: Lge 3
League Career Record: 15

TED'S CLAIM TO FAME: Few players can have made a more controversial statement than Ted. While at Reading he said that he preferred living in the South except that Southerners could not make proper Yorkshire puddings!

THORPE Percy
b. 18.7.1899 Nottingham d. ?
Ht 5ft 8 Wt 12st (28-29)
Career: Sutton T; Blackpool 1924; Connahs Quay summer 1928; READING (£150) October 1928; Sheffield U. June 1930; West Ham U; Accrington Stan; Port Vale

Although a regular in Blackpool's defence for three years, and captain in his final season, Percy dropped into non-League football after failing to agree terms. He soon returned to the League with Reading and hardly missed a game as a solid and reliable right back until the summer of 1929-30, when he moved on to Sheffield United. After over 100 League appearances for them, Percy only made another six with his last three clubs.

Reading Record: Lge 72, FAC 1, Total 73
League Career Total: 294/5

TINDALL Ronald Albert Ernest
b. Streatham 23.9.1935
Ht 5ft 11 Wt 12st 10 (63-64)
Career: Chelsea from jnrs April 1953; West Ham U. October 1961; READING (£11,000) 10 October 1962; Portsmouth (free) September 1964, manager April 1970 to May 1973, general manager 1974

A strong but skilful centre forward, Ron played a major role in the development of a young Jimmy Greaves at Chelsea as well as scoring 67 League goals himself. After representing the Football League, Ron moved to West Ham for a year before costing Reading a record fee.

He made a good start at Elm Park, and also played cricket for Surrey, taking a career total of 150 wickets and averaging 25 runs, so was not available to play for Reading after Easter. There was some disappointment when Ron chose cricket over Reading's 1963-64 relegation battle and that summer he was given a free transfer so he could emigrate to South Africa. As it was Ron decided to stay in England and gave sterling service to Portsmouth, as a player converting to full back and then as a manager. In his later years Ron did emigrate, to Australia, to become director of cricket coaching in Western Australia and then state director of sport in Perth.

Reading Record: Lge 36/12, FAC 2/1, LC 1, Total 39/13
League Career Total: 368(2)/89

TINSLEY Walter Edward
b. Ironville 10.8.1891 d. Ripley 7.3.1966
Ht 5ft 10 Wt 11st 5 (24-25)
Career: Alfreton T; Sutton T; Sunderland 1912; Middlesbrough 1913; Nottingham For. summer 1921; READING summer 1924

The First World War seemed to affect Walter's style of play since he scored 42 goals in 60 games for Middlesbrough in the two seasons prior to the War but he never got close to double figures after that. Despite this, Walter was described as *'a brainy sort of forward and a dangerous man in front of goal'* when he joined Reading. Walter was 33 when he moved to Elm Park but he was a regular for the club and scored a first half hat trick against Brentford in March 1925 before being carried off injured. Reading signed Hugh Davey to replace him but Walter fought back to play a vital role at inside left during Reading's Third Division South championship win. After just one Second Division appearance, Walter retired at the end of 1926-27.

Reading Record: Lge 55/13, FAC 3, Total 58/13
League Career Total: 212/75

TOWNSEND Charles Rogers Noel
b. Tilehurst 1910 d. ?
Ht 5ft 8 Wt 10st 3 (34-35)
Career: Oxford C; READING amateur August 1932, professional January 1933

A local youngster, Charles was a member of the Reading U15 side that reached the final of the 1924 England Schools Shield yet it took another eight years before he was signed by his local club. Charles was an all round sportsman who played tennis and golf as well as winning medals for boxing. At Reading, he played at either full back or wing half although his first team appearances were all at half back, and after missing most of 1935-36 he returned to the non-League ranks.

Reading Record: Lge 11, FAC 3, Total 14

TRAVERS Michael Joseph Patrick
b. Blackwater 23.6.1942
Ht 5ft 9 Wt 10st (65-66)
Career: READING amateur 7 January 1958, professional 26 October 1959; Portsmouth (free) July 1967; Aldershot (free) July 1972; Basingstoke T. August 1973

A product of Reading's youth team, Mick was initially a left half but his powerful shooting saw him moved regularly to the left wing. There he scored some spectacular goals with one of the hardest shots in football and twice this put Mick into double figures for League goals. From 1962-63 Mick spent four years as a first team regular but he lost his place early 1966-67, and was released at the end of that season. After his playing career was over, Mick worked as an accountant, having begun his studies while with Reading.

Reading Record: Lge 156(2)/34, FAC 13, LC 15/2, Total 184(2)/36
League Career Total: 259(14)/42

TUNE David Barrie
b Reading 1.11.1938
Ht 5ft 9 Wt 10st 9 (57-58)
Career: READING from jnrs 1 November 1955

Although David was the regular right half for Reading's reserves for over three seasons he struggled to replace Sylvan Anderton in the first team. His one chance came when Anderton was injured and, although he did well enough in that one game, against Watford in September 1957, David never got another first team chance and was released in June 1960.

Reading Record: Lge 1

TURNER John Graham Anthony

b. Gateshead 23.12.1954
Ht 6ft 1 Wt 13st 2 (75-76)
Career: Easington; Derby Co. from apprentice December 1972; Doncaster R. (loan) January 1974; Brighton (loan) April 1974; Peterborough U. (loan); Huddersfield T. (loan) March 1975; READING (£2,000) 27 May 1975; Torquay U. (£3,000) August 1976; Chesterfield (£30,000) February 1980; Everton (loan); Torquay U. August 1983; Weymouth; Burnley August 1984; Peterborough U. October 1984

A former miner, John spent two and a half seasons with Derby but his only League experience during that time came during several loan spells. He did win two Central League championships and while at Derby, was voted Goalie of the Competition during an U23s tournament in Toulon. John also showed his versatility by scoring a hat trick for the reserves after moving out of goal due to a hand injury. Signed by Reading as cover for Steve Death, John played in the run-in of Reading's 1975-76 Fourth Division promotion season. Although he was never really able to take over the goalkeeper's jersey permanently from the legendary Death, John was popular with the supporters and he actively promoted the club off the pitch. This included coaching a number of local clubs and even being part of the Supporters' Club quiz team that reached the final of a top local sports quiz. John left Reading for a giveaway fee as the first to be transferred under the new freedom of contract rules and was a PFA Fourth Division award winner in 1979-80. His career eventually ended at Peterborough where, as David Seaman's replacement, he suffered a badly broken leg in an FA Cup-tie against Leeds.

Reading Record: Lge 31, LC 5, Total 36
League Career Total: 338

TURNER Stanley Frederick

b. Wokingham 31.5.1941
Ht 5ft 8 Wt 9st 12 (60-61)
Career: READING amateur 17 September 1957, part-time professional December 1960; Bracknell T. manager

A young right winger who combined playing for Reading with a printers apprenticeship, Stan had a run of four first team games a month after signing professional.

Unable to get past the more established first team players, Stan was given a free transfer and emigrated to Australia. He returned to the UK in 1968 and became manager at Bracknell while restoring his connections at Elm Park.

Reading Record: Lge 3, FAC 1, Total 4

TUTTY Wayne Keith

b. Oxford 18.6.1963
Ht 5ft 9 Wt 10st 7 (83-84)
Career: Oxford U. apprentice; Banbury U; READING non contract August 1982, permanent June 1983; Pathos T; Salamina; Witney T.

Released by Oxford, Wayne was working as a removal man when Reading gave him his chance and he repaid them by scoring a late equalizer on his League debut. Although only used occasionally, he was offered a full contract at the end of his first season. Wayne was capable of playing at either right back or in midfield but he suffered a recurring pelvic injury that forced his retirement from League football. He then had a spell with a couple of Cypriot clubs before returning to non-League football.

Reading Record: Lge 11(2)/4, LC 2, AMC 1, FLT 1, Total 15(2)/4

TYSON Nathan

b. Reading 4.5.1982
Ht 5ft 10 Wt 10st 1 (00-01)
Career: READING Youth Academy; Maidenhead U (loan) March 2001; Swansea C. (loan) summer 2001

A lightning fast player, Nathan was one of the first Academy players to make it through to Reading's first team when he came on for the last 10 minutes of their game at Bury in April 2000. Capable of playing on either wing or as a striker, Nathan underlined his promise by scoring against Charlton in a friendly at the start of the following season.

Reading Record: Lge (1) +

UPHILL Edward Dennis Herbert

b. Bath 11.8.1931
Ht 5ft 9 Wt 11st 3 (52-53)
Career: Peasedown; Finchley; Tottenham H. from jnrs September 1949; READING (player exchange) 4 February 1953; Coventry C. (£3,350) October 1953; Mansfield T. March 1957; Watford June 1959; Crystal Palace October 1960; Rugby T. April 1963; Romford; Dartford February 1964; Croxley Casuals October 1967

Dennis joined Spurs after representing the British Army during his National Service and although he rarely got to play in their first team he scored once in two games during their 1950-51 championship season. He joined Reading to replace Johnny Brooks who moved to Spurs in the same deal and proved to be a very productive player with a bustling, unselfish style. Despite this, Dennis was rarely short of a goal himself, being Reading's top scorer in 1954-55, and had been selected for the FA against the Western League the previous season. After leaving Reading, Dennis continued to score regularly, especially at Watford, where he and Cliff Holton were dubbed 'the Terrible Twins' as they scored 72 goals between them in 1959-60, Dennis getting 30 of them. On quitting League football, Dennis hit another 147 goals before retiring in Watford as a bookmaker and Conservative councillor.

Reading Record: Lge 92/41, FAC 6/5, Total 98/46
League Career Total: 344/145

VALLARD Leonard Gerald Harold
b. Sherbourne 6.7.1940
Ht 5ft 7 Wt 11st 6 (60-61)
Career: Portsmouth amateur; Yeovil T; READING 12 May 1958; Chelmsford C. summer 1962; Cambridge U; Basingstoke T. 1966; Sligo R. player manager September 1973 to November 1973

A solid left back, Len had the misfortune to break his arm on his League debut for Reading, at Colchester in September 1959. He won a regular first team spot for the first half of 1960-61 and again at the start of the following season but returned to non-League football in 1962. At Basingstoke he captained them to two Hampshire League titles before his career was ended by a neck injury sustained at Yeovil, 16 years to the day after he had made his debut on the same ground.

Reading Record: Lge 37/2, FAC 1, LC 2, Total 40/2

LEN'S CLAIM TO FAME - In May 1974 Len was named Cricketer of the Month by the Reading Evening Post after he had scored 184 for Tadley in an innings that saw him hit five sixes and a four in one over.

VAN DER KWAAK Peter
b. Haarlem 12.10.1968
Ht 6ft 4 Wt 13st 13 (99-00)
Career: Ajax; Dordecht 90; READING (free) 17 August 1998; Carlisle U. (loan) February 2000; Go Ahead Eagles April 2000

A Dutch goalie, Peter played for Dordecht for four years before signing for Reading on a 'Bosman' after impressing in pre-season friendlies.

He made a horrendous mistake in his debut that saw him let in an Andy Legg back pass, one of seven goals Peter conceded in his first two games. Things improved when he kept a clean sheet during the opening game at the Madejski Stadium but that was to be his last start for Reading and Peter returned to Holland 20 months later.

Reading Record: Lge 3(1), LC 1, Total 4(1)
League Career Total: 5(1)

VAUGHAN Nigel Mark
b. Caerlon 20.5.1959
Ht 5ft 5 Wt 8st 9 (86-87)
Career: Newport Co. from apprentice May 1977; Cardiff C. September 1983; READING (loan) February 1987; Wolverhampton W. (£12,000); Hereford U. (free) August 1990; Newport player manager

One of the smallest players in the League, and the lightest to play for Reading, Nigel never let his size affect his play. Indeed, he began his career as a full back noted for his tough tackling before moving on to the wing. At Newport Nigel won the Welsh Cup in 1980 and won caps at youth and U21 level as well as the first of 10 full Welsh caps. After topping Cardiff's scorers for two seasons, Nigel was loaned to Reading as Dean Horrix went in the opposite direction and scored in the last game of his loan spell with a header, despite being the smallest player on the pitch. A move to Wolves saw him hit a purple patch, winning the Fourth and Third Division titles and Sherpa Van trophy in his first two seasons. In October and November 1987, Nigel scored in six consecutive Wolves games even though he was playing in midfield.

Reading Record: Lge 5/1
League Career Total: 459(25)/86

VIVEASH Adrian Lee
b. Swindon 30.9.1969
Ht 6ft 1 Wt 12st 13 (00-01)
Career: Swindon T. from YTS July 1988; READING (loan) 4 January 1993; READING (loan) 20 January 1995; Barnsley (loan) August 1995; Walsall (free) October 1995; READING (free) 3 July 2000

Originally a winger, Adrian soon developed into a strong defender with Swindon and twice enjoyed loan spells with Reading. He played six games on each occasion, and scored at Bournemouth in their Autoglass Trophy tie, proving to be a steady defender.

Adrian's spell at Swindon was hampered by two broken legs, but his four seasons at Walsall included their Division Two promotion season when his strength in the tackle and heading ability gave him a 'towering presence' in their defence, leading to him twice being named their Player of the Year . Back at Reading for a third time, this time permanently, Adrian immediately settled into their defence again. He also found time to score some vital goals, including the fastest so far at the Madejski Stadium - a header after 40 seconds against Cambridge. Often teamed up in the centre of Reading's defence with namesakes Whitbread and Williams, he became a part of 'Adrian's Wall'.

Reading Record: Lge 51/2, FAC 3, LC 2, AMC 3/1, Play-offs 3, Total 62/3 +
League Career Total: 304(5)/18 +

WAGSTAFF Barry

b. Brampton 28.11.1945
Ht 5ft 11 Wt 11st 1 (69-70)
Career: Don & Dearne BC; Sheffield U. from apprentice June 1963; READING (£10,000) 10 July 1969; Rotherham U. (£10,000) 11 March 1975; Worksop T. 1977; Barnsley youth manager 1996

For over 12 years the Wagstaff brothers shared identical careers although their physiques and styles could not have been more different. Younger but bigger than his brother Tony, Barry was a solid defender who could also play in midfield and would have

made more than 115 League appearances for Sheffield United but for a broken ankle. The Wagstaff brothers became one of Jack Mansell's first signings for Reading, paying £17,500 for the pair, and building his free scoring team around them. Although used in a more defensive role than his brother, Barry scored four times as many goals as him, often heading in Tony's corners and free kicks. Memorable goals included Reading's equalizer against double holders, Arsenal, after having scored for both sides in the previous round.

Keen to move back North, Barry was eventually sold to Rotherham, whom he immediately helped to promotion to the Third Division.

Reading Record: Lge 197(6)/23, FAC 16/3, LC 15/1, Watney Cup 1, Total 229(6)/27
League Career Total: 344(19)/29

BARRY'S CLAIM TO FAME - In January 1970, at Bournemouth, 1970, Barry became the first Reading substitute to score a League goal.

WAGSTAFF Tony

b. Wombwell 19.2.1944
Ht 5ft 8 Wt 9st 7 (70-71)
Career: Sheffield U. from amateur March 1961; READING (£7,500) 10 July 1969; Cheltenham T. April 1974; Hillingdon Bor. March 1975; Hounslow December 1976

Like his brother, Tony made his League debut at 17 and scored 21 first team goals for Sheffield United before moving with Barry to Reading. There, his accurate passing inspired Reading to become the League's top scorers in his first season at Elm Park. This made Tony a marked man and his lack of physical strength sometimes made it difficult to shake off the close attention of less talented defenders. Tony scored Reading's very first goal in the Fourth Division and was virtually ever-present during his first four seasons, before niggling injuries began to affect his form. In 1974 he became the first signing of former Reading favourite, Denis Allen, who had at that time, recently become manager of Cheltenham.

Reading Record: Lge 166(7)/6, FAC 13(1), LC 5/1, Watney Cup 1, Total 185(8)/7
League Career Total: 304(10)/29

WALKER John

b. Beith 8.10.1882 d. Swindon 16.12.1968
Ht 5ft 9 Wt 12st 6 (21-22)
Career: Eastern Burnside; Cambuslang Rngrs; Burnbank A; Raith R; Beith; Glasgow Rngrs 1905; Cowdenbeath 1906; Swindon T. June 1907; Middlesbrough April (£2,000) April 1913; Swindon (Wartime guest); READING May 1921

After playing for numerous Scottish clubs, 'Jock' hit form with Swindon where he became one of their greatest players. A full back, who was 'a dashing and powerful tackler, has nothing to learn as to how to stop a man', Jock barely missed a game at the County Ground in six seasons and made 248 first team appearances. Although he never scored a goal in that spell, Jock helped them win the Southern League in 1910-11 and twice reached the FA Cup semi finals.

His form was such that, as well as playing for the Southern League, Jock was capped nine times for Scotland between 1911 and 1913, being on the losing side only once. Jock ended his career with two seasons at Reading although there was some criticism of the club when he was signed for a second season, at the age of almost 40, and was made captain. However, he continued to display great form, using his experience to save his legs. His last League game was against QPR in March 1923 when Jock was 40 years five months old and, not surprisingly, that makes him Reading's oldest League player. Jock was so fond of his spell at Swindon that he was never happy playing against his old club and requested to play for the reserves rather than play against them at the County Ground.

Reading Record: Lge 58, FAC 2, Total 60
League Career Total: 164

WALKER John Young Hilley
b. Glasgow 12.12.1928
Ht 5ft 8 Wt 10st 11 (58-59)
Career: Campsie Black Watch; Wolverhampton W. August 1947; Southampton (£12,000) October 1952; READING (£2,750) 12 December 1957; Amersham; Wokingham T coach July 1966; Tilehurst amateur September 1969

One of the greatest characters to play for Reading, Johnny has had a lifelong love of football and this was apparent to anyone who saw him play. Although missed by the big Scottish clubs Johnny won honours during his National Service, playing for the British Army and keeping Jimmy Hill out of the battalion side. At Wolves he played in the FA Cup semi final against Newcastle and was a Reading target before moving to Southampton for their record fee. As a skilful inside forward he scored over 50 goals in 186 first team appearances and there was some surprise in Southampton when Johnny was allowed to join Reading.

Aged 30 when he moved to Elm Park, it was hoped that Johnny would be able to give the club a couple of years service, as it was he played for eight seasons, making over 300 first team appearances. Johnny was able to extend his career due to his intelligent, almost crafty, style of play and the fact that he gradually moved back through the team, first to half back and finally as a right back. In addition to his play, Johnny was an inspirational captain - his cry of 'Steady' was famous around Elm Park and settled many a nervous player plus quite a few supporters! It has to be said that, off the pitch, Johnny did not always look like a professional sportsman, and one of his favourite tricks was to try and gain free admission to away games by pretending to be a penniless supporter. On one occasion, at Wrexham, the joke almost backfired when the doorman wouldn't let him in even after he revealed his true identity. In the end, Roy Bentley, Reading's manager, had to be called to explain that the apparent down and out was indeed Reading's captain! After his playing days were over, Johnny assisted Reading, and other local clubs, in several ways and remained a regular supporter of the club he served so well.

Reading Record: Lge 287/24, FAC 21/2, LC 5/1, SPFC 6, Total 319/27
League Career Total: 496/93

WALLACE Raymond George
b. Greenwich 2.10.1969
Ht 5ft 6 Wt 10st 2 (91-92)
Career: Southampton from trainee April 1988; Leeds U. (£100,000) July 1991; Swansea C. (loan) March 1992; READING (loan) 11 March 1994; Stoke C. (free) August 1994; Hull C. (loan); Altrincham 1999

The twin brother of Rod Wallace and one of three brothers to play at the same time for Southampton, Ray made four appearances for England U21 before moving to Leeds along with Rod. At Leeds, Ray rarely got into their first team and was loaned out on a couple of occasions. His spell with Reading saw him play three games at right back in place of the injured Ray Ransom as the club moved towards the Division Two title. Eventually Ray moved to Stoke where he was used more in midfield.

Reading Record: Lge 3
League Career Total: 191(11)/12

WALLBANKS James

b. Platts Bridge 12.9.1909 d. Reading 28.10.1979
Ht 5ft 9 Wt 11st 10 (38-39)
Career: Annfield Plain; Barnsley (£100) March 1929; Norwich C. May 1931; Northampton T. August 1932; Chopwell Institute; Wigan A; Millwall June 1934; READING 7 October 1938; Wartime guest for Consett, Millwall, Wrexham, Fulham & Sunderland; Ramsgate player manager summer 1947; Carlisle U. trainer; Millwall trainer; READING trainer 20 June 1953, then physio

Jimmy came from a footballing family, being one of five brothers who played top class football with three of them making it into the League. It wasn't until he joined Millwall that Jimmy got to play regular League football and it was there that he achieved his greatest success. He was centre half when Millwall became the first Third Division side to reach the semi final of the FA Cup and then won promotion in 1937-38. Described as *a dapper little stopper and a terrier in the tackle',* Jimmy joined Reading as a centre half but was soon switched to right back where he could use the speed that had once earned him extra money as a professional sprinter. After the War Jimmy played one more season then turned to coaching and physiotherapy, assisting managerial newcomer Bill Shankly at Carlisle before returning to Elm Park in 1953. From then on Jimmy was a fixture at Reading, serving under a number of managers and even enjoying a successful three months as caretaker manager himself **(see 'The Managers' for full details)**. At the age of 65 he handed over the on-pitch responsibility to Maurice Evans but continued to treat Reading players and other local sportsmen. Jimmy was awarded a well deserved testimonial game in 1975 and he was a regular at the ground until his death when both the club and town lost a popular and well respected personality.

Reading Record: Lge 48/1, FAC 7, SSC 3, Wartime 48, Total 106/1
League Career Total: 152/1

JIM'S CLAIM TO FAME - When Jimmy was booked by an over zealous referee for running on to the pitch to treat an injured player at Hartlepool in September 1973, he was almost 64, and so is thought to be the oldest person ever to be cautioned in a League game.

WALMESLEY Clifford

b. Burnley 25.11.1910 d. 23.4.1983
Ht 5ft 11 1/2 Wt 11st (32-33)
Career: Burnley; Manchester C. September 1931; READING 30 May 1932; Rochdale summer 1933; Stalybridge Celtic 1935

Trained as a commercial artist, the captain of Burnley Cricket Club and a fine pianist, Cliff earned his living as a goalkeeper but only made five League appearances with his first three League clubs.

Reading beat Leicester for his signature but apart from three games over Christmas 1932, Cliff was unable to oust Dick Mellors from the first team. He moved back to Lancashire after one season at Elm Park where he enjoyed two good seasons with Rochdale.

Reading Record: Lge 3
League Career Total: 66

WANKLYN Edward Wayne

b. Hull 21.1.1960
Ht 5ft 7 1/2 Wt 11st (77-78)
Career: QPR assoc. schoolboy; Bracknell BC; READING from apprentice 21 January 1978; Aldershot June 1981; Basingstoke T. August 1982; Farnborough T; Wycombe W. October 1984; Wokingham T; Staines T. manager February 1992; Windsor & Eton manager; Wokingham T. joint manager 1995; Fleet T. manager 2000; Farnborough T. asst.manager

Wayne's father was capped by Wales at Rugby Union and then played Rugby League professionally with Hull. The family then moved to the Fulham area which led to Wayne playing for Middlesex Boys and for London, for whom he scored all four goals in a 4-0 win over Liverpool. Spotted by Reading player, Gary Peters, while playing for Bracknell Boys Club, Wayne delayed signing for Reading until he had scored the two goals that put Berkshire Boys Clubs into the quarter-finals of the Gillette Cup. Wayne developed into a hard working left sided midfielder but although he had several runs in the first team he was never sure of a regular place. He played 13 times in Reading's 1978-79 Fourth Division championship season and then had the satisfaction of scoring his first League goal, the winner at Hull, the town of his birth. Later, Wayne enjoyed a varied managerial career in non League football.

Reading Record: Lge 47(7)/3, LC 1(2)/1, Total 48(9)/4
League Career Total: 62(10)/5

WATKIN Arthur Dennis

b. Stapleford 11.1911 d. Nottingham 3.1983
Ht 5ft 9 Wt 11st 2 (36-37)
Career: Stapleford; Aston Villa from amateur November 1932; READING June 1936

A fringe player during his three and a half years at Villa Park, Dennis was a fast and tricky winger with a goalscoring knack and *a constant menace to the defence'.* He proved to be all of that at Reading, scoring double figures in his first two seasons, including four against Newport in the FA Cup, and was a member of the side that won the Southern Section Cup in 1938. Dennis was put on the open to offer list in May 1938 but stayed another season at Elm Park before being released.

As well as playing for Reading, Dennis also played cricket for Northamptonshire, being signed to replace the injured Harold Larwood, and in his second County Championship game, took six wickets for 48 runs.

Reading Record: Lge 86/22, FAC 4/4, SSC 6/1, Total 96/27
League Career Total: 107/27

WDOWCZYK Dariusz
b. Warsaw 21.9.1962
Ht 5ft 11 Wt 11st 11 (94-95)
Career: Guardia Warsaw 1973; Legia 1983; Celtic (£400,000) November 1989; Falkirk (trial) July 1994; READING (free) 12 August 1994; Polonia Warsaw player coach July 1998, manager October 1998; Orlen Plock manager November 2000

A classy left footed central defender, Dariusz came to fame with Legia where he made 220 appearances for the Polish First Division side before moving to Celtic. As well as playing in over 140 games in Scotland, Dariusz increased his Polish cap total to 53, 10 as captain, before being given a free transfer. Spotted by Reading while playing in a friendly for Falkirk, he was quickly snapped up and was a regular in the defence as Reading finished second in Division One. Dariusz was a calm, quiet player, but in September 1996 he was involved in a public bust-up with joint manager, Jimmy Quinn, that ended up with the Pole stating he would never play for Reading again. Although the dispute was quickly resolved, Dariusz's words came back to haunt him as a series of injuries saw him only make another five League starts over the next 20 months. On leaving Reading, Dariusz developed into one of Poland's most promising managers, and in 1999-00 he guided Polonia Warsaw to a surprising, but emphatic, Polish championship.

Reading Record: Lge 77(5), FAC 1, LC 7(1), Play-offs 3, Total 88(6)

WEBB Douglas John
b. Stokenchurch 10.3.1939
Ht 5ft 8 Wt 11st 4 (60-61)
Career: Cholsey U18s; READING amateur 24 May 1955, professional 26 November 1956; Cheltenham T. (trial) October 1968; Dartford 1969; Ramsgate November 1970; Hungerford 1971; READING youth team manager 13 August 1973, physio July 1979, reserve team manager July 1980

Few people have demonstrated more enthusiasm for Reading Football Club, either as a player or coach, than Douggie. His early career was interrupted by National service but he used the time to help the RAF win the 1959 Inter Services Championship.

Although he never fully established himself as a first team regular, only playing in more than half of the games in two of his 12 seasons, Douggie was a regular scorer from inside left or left wing. Douggie was one of the club's most energetic players who would chase every lost cause and many of his goals came from such determination. His enthusiasm never waned when in the reserves and as a result he topped the second string's goalscorers for four consecutive seasons, and still holds the club record with 106 reserve team goals. Early in 1967 Douggie began suffering with achilles tendon problems and after several operations he was forced to quit League football. He recovered sufficiently to help Dartford and Ramsgate to promotion before returning to Elm Park as youth team manager. This was a role ideally suited to Douggie as he was able to pass his experience and high standards of character on to Reading's developing youngsters, including his son, Neil. He combined this role with a full time job at Courage Brewery, but had one season full time as Reading's physio. However, Douggie preferred part-time participation and so became the manager of the reserve team. This resulted in him becoming one of the club's oldest players when he came on as sub at Leicester at the age of 42. The sale of his son, Neil, in 1982 heralded Douggie's final departure from Reading, but he is still remembered with affection by local fans.

Reading Record: Lge 178(2)/81, FAC 12/9, LC 8(1)/2, SPFC 3/1, Total 201(3)/93

WEBB Neil John
b. Reading 30.7.1963
Ht ft 11 Wt 11st 6 (81-82)
Career: READING July 1978, professional 3 November 1980; Portsmouth (£87,500) July 1982; Nottingham For. (£250,000) June 1985; Manchester U. (£1.5m.) June 1989; Nottingham For. (£800,000) November 1992; Swindon (loan) October 1994; Inter Direct (Hong Kong) (loan) January 1996; Grimsby T. (trial) August 1996; Aldershot T. October 1996; Weymouth player coach; Merthyr Tyd. November 1999; Reading T. manager May 2001

Although those who saw Johnny Brooks play might disagree, Neil must surely be the best player ever to be born in, and produced by, Reading. Neil's father, Douggie, was a former Reading player and youth coach while his mother, Joan, was the club's commercial manager, so it was inevitable that Neil would join his local club. It was also inevitable that his upbringing would enable him to cope modestly with the fame his talents were to bring. Neil's early progress was sensational - he was the youngest player to be selected for Reading's first team, the second youngest to actually play, while, at 17 years 1 month, he became the club's youngest goalscorer. In addition, Neil was capped 10 times for England Youth, scoring a hat trick against Egypt in the 1981 World Youth Cup.

By 1982 Neil had become Reading's youngest top scorer as well as being one of the best young midfielders in the country, so it was apparent that he would move on although there was some surprise when he went to fellow Third Division club, Portsmouth, albeit for yet another club record. There he won the Third Division championship and a PFA Divisional award before moving to Forest in a deal that earned Reading another £80,000. At Forest he won the FA Cup and League Cup and, having outshone Maradona in the League's Centenary win over the Rest of the World, Neil became England's 1000th international when he came on as substitute for Glen Hoddle. He scored on his full England debut and, after a move to Manchester United, Neil was being widely tipped as England's next captain. Unfortunately, Neil snapped an achilles playing against Sweden and his England career was all but over, having scored four times in 26 internationals. Worse still, Neil was never quite the same player after that long injury and his career slowly declined although he showed great determination to carry on playing. In addition, he followed in the footsteps of his wife, the writer and broadcaster Shelley Webb, by writing a weekly column in a local Reading paper as well summarizing Reading's games for a local radio station.

Reading Record: Lge 65(7)/22, FAC 2, LC 2(2), FLGC 3, Total 72(9)/22
League Career: 438(18)/114

WESTON Harold

b. Birmingham c.1897 d. ?
Ht 5ft 10 Wt 12st 7 (20-21)
Career: Fulham amateur; Chatham; READING (£200) February 1920; Northfleet (£200) summer 1922

A centre forward who could also play in the inside berths, Harry joined Reading after the First World War and although he was never able to command a first team place for long, he stayed at Elm Park for three seasons. He also played in the Southern League inter-division game against the Welsh section. A bad foul on Harry during the 1921 Royal Berks Hospital Charity match against Southampton led to a pitch invasion and some very rough play so the referee 'sent off' both teams for a while to let tempers cool. He played in Reading's first League game, at Newport, but was never a prolific scorer and in 1922 Harry moved to Northfleet, along with Ted Hanney and George Ritchie.

Reading Record: Lge 26/6, FAC 2, SL 11/2, Total 39/8

WESTWOOD Gary Michael

b. Barrow 3.4.1964
Ht 6ft Wt 13st (85-86)
Career: Ipswich from apprentice April 1981; Crystal Palace (loan) 1981; Charlton A. (loan) 1982; READING (loan) September 1983; Peterborough U. (loan) 1983-84; READING (free) July 1984; Wokingham T. July 1988; St Albans 1992; Hayes; Wokingham T.

A former England Youth international goalkeeper, Gary's League career was confined to games played for Reading, first on loan and then as a permanent signing. His loan spell saw him keep three clean sheets in five starts so it was not surprising that Reading jumped at the chance to sign the ginger haired keeper when Ipswich released him. After taking over from Alan Judge in September, Gary never missed a game for two and a half seasons which meant he was ever-present during Reading's runaway Third Division championship win in 1985-86. A dip in form around the following Christmas eventually led to the signing of Steve Francis, and Gary was relegated to second choice. Despite this he was a fine keeper with no noticeable weaknesses so it was surprising that Gary decided to go part-time and quit League football after he left Reading.

Reading Record: Lge 128, FAC 10, LC 9, FMC 2, AMC 2, Total 151

WHEELER Arthur **James**

b. Reading 21.12.1933
Ht 5ft 6 Wt 10st 7 (61-62)
Career: Hunley & Palmers; READING amateur May 1952, professional 5 August 1952; Bradford C. manager June 1968

To a whole generation of Reading schoolboys (the author included), Jimmy was their undisputed hero. A local lad, who won the National Cup with Berkshire Boys Clubs, Jimmy was a livewire player whose bravery and enthusiasm for the Reading cause often outshone, but never outweighed, his skills. Although Jimmy played across the forward line, he was at his best in one of the wing positions and it was from there that he was a prolific scorer. He hit double figures for nine consecutive seasons, top scoring from 1957-58 through to 1960-61 when Jimmy hit a remarkable 35 first team goals. Despite his lack of inches, a surprising number of goals came from 'Jimmy Wee's' head. Jimmy scored in Elm Park's first floodlit game, scored Reading's first goal in the new 'unified' Third Division and only Trevor Senior scored more first team goals for the club than Jimmy's 170. But for a broken leg in September 1964, that effectively ended his career as a forward, Jimmy would undoubtedly hold Reading's scoring record yet, in some ways, that injury lead to Jimmy's greatest moment. Appointed as manager of the reserves, he led and inspired the second eleven to a memorable season as they won the Football Combination Second Division title. Such was Jim's charisma that the reserves were attracting higher gates than the first team and, with him scoring nine goals as football's first wing back, he was runaway winner of the Player of the Year trophy that season, despite only making two first team appearances. Eventually, Jimmy left Reading to manage Bradford City to promotion in his first season, but he resigned after a poor start to the next season, returning to the Reading area where he scouted for a number of clubs.

Reading Record: Lge 404(1)/145, FAC 27/15, LC 8/2, SPFC 13/8, Total 452(1)/170

WHITBREAD **Adrian** Richard

b. Epping 22.10.1971
Ht 6ft 1 Wt 12st 12 (00-01)
Career: Leyton O. from trainee 13 November 1989; Swindon (£500,000) 29 July 1993; West Ham U. (£650,000) 17 August 1994; Portsmouth (loan) 9 November 1995, permanent (£250,000) 24 October 1996; Luton (loan) 2000; READING (loan) 9 February 2001, permanent July 2001

An experienced central defender who had played for both Swindon and West Ham in the Premiership, Adrian established himself at Portsmouth where he was highly regarded and was club captain. He became disillusioned at Fratton Park and, available on a 'Bosman' at the end of 2000-01, Adrian joined Reading on loan for the remainder of that season. It was no coincidence that his arrival saw a return to form for Reading since as well as a solid and reliable defender, Adrian is also a good communicator which is just as well for Reading as he was one of three central defenders named Adrian within the club! There was great disappointment at the club when a last minute change of heart by the League prevented him from taking part in the play-offs, despite the fact that Reading were poised to sign him permanently.

Reading Record: Lge 19 +
League Career Total: 337(9)/5 +

WHITE **Mark** Ivan

b. Sheffield 26.10.1958
Ht 5ft 9 Wt 11st (80-81)
Career: Sheffield U. apprentice; READING (trial) December 1976, professional 10 March 1977; Cape Town Spurs July 1988; Henley T. 1991-92

Mark was one of the best left footed players ever to appear for Reading and but for shocking luck with injuries he would almost certainly be regarded as one of the club's greats. Even so he still played a major role in some of Reading's best moments. Equally strong at left back, central defence or midfield, Mark was ever-present at left back in Reading's 1978-79 Fourth Division championship season that included a League record 11 match run without conceding a goal, and he won a PFA Divisional award. He helped the club to another record in 1985-86 when he played in all of the clubs 13 match winning run at the start of another championship season before suffering a serious knee injury. Mark also scored the goal that won promotion in 1983-84 while, a year later he scored Reading's fastest ever League goal when he netted after just 12.96 seconds against York, a feat even more remarkable since it was the visitors who had kicked off. Several other injuries interrupted his career, the worse being a badly broken leg at the start of 1986-87.

While his broken leg kept him out for a year, the ever popular Mark still enjoyed a successful testimonial. After leaving Reading, Mark had a spell in South Africa, playing in the same team as Kevin Keegan, before returning to the Reading area. Mark won many friends with the brave and cheerful way he coped with his injuries and so it is perhaps typical he should use those experiences to his advantage by qualifying as a chartered physiotherapist.

Reading Record: Lge 265(13)/11 FAC 12(1)/1, LC 20(3)/1, FLGC 3, AMC 3, Total 303(17)/13

MARK'S CLAIM TO FAME - As well as being on Sheffield United's books from 11, Mark was also a ball boy at Bramall Lane. At the end of games, he had to take a corner flag back to the offices but after one game he got half way across the pitch before he realized that extra time was about to start and, much to the amusement of 28,000 fans, he had to make his way back to the corner.

WHITEHEAD Philip Matthew
b. Halifax 17.12.1969
Ht 6ft 3 Wt 15st 10 (99-00)
Career: Halifax T. from apprentice July 1988; Barnsley (£60,000) March 1990; Halifax T. (loan) March 1991; Scunthorpe U. (loan) November 1991 & September 1992; Bradford C. (loan) November 1992; Oxford U. (£75,000) November 1993; West Bromwich Alb. (£250,000) December 1998; READING (£300,000) 7 October 1999

Phil ended an unsettled spell with Barnsley when he joined Oxford, where he developed into one of the best goalies outside the Premiership. He was very popular at the Manor, and only Oxford's financial plight caused his sale to West Brom. A change of manager cost Phil his first team place, and when John Gorman left Albion to become assistant manager at Reading, Phil soon followed him, becoming Alan Pardew's first signing. He quickly established himself as the number one keeper at the Madejski Stadium, but a thigh injury after 12 games cost him his place. Phil was ever-present in the first team for 2000-01, proving himself to be one of the best keepers in the lower divisions.

Reading Record: Lge 57, FAC 5, LC 2, Play-offs 3, Total 67 +
League Career Total: 379 +

PHIL'S CLAIM TO FAME - During 1998-99 Phil let in 10 goals in two games at the Stadium of Light, three for West Brom and seven with Oxford. That total equalled the number that Sunderland's ever-present keeper, Thomas Sorenson, conceded in all of their 23 home games.

WHITEHOUSE James A
b. West Bromwich 19.9.1934
Ht 5ft 9 Wt 10st 3 (60-61)
Career: West Bromwich Alb. from amateur November 1954; READING (£250) 17 July 1956; Coventry (free) August 1962; Millwall March 1964; Hillingdon Bor. August 1965; Hastings U. October 1966

Although he failed to make West Brom's League side Jimmy became a fixture in Reading's first team as soon as he moved to Elm Park. A skilful, classy inside right, Jimmy is best remembered as the creator of chances for his colleagues, particularly Jimmy Wheeler, with whom he seemed to have a telepathic understanding. However, Jimmy was also a regular goalscorer, averaging almost a goal every three games. The blond haired player was popular at Reading so it was a great surprise when he was allowed to join Coventry where he helped them win promotion to the Second Division, and scored twice for City on his return to Elm Park.

Reading Record: Lge 203/61, FAC 15/3, LC 3, SPFC 6/3, Total 227/67
League Career Total: 287/86

WHITEHURST William
b. Thurnscoe 10.6.1959
Ht 6ft 1 1/2 Wt 13st 13 (88-89)
Career: Mexborough; Hull C. (£2,500) October 1980; Newcastle U. December 1985; Oxford U. October 1986; READING (£120,000) 9 February 1988; Sunderland (£90,000) September 1988; Hull C. player exchange November 1989; Sheffield U. (£35,000) February 1990; Stoke C. (loan) November 1990; Doncaster R. February 1991; Crewe Alex. January 1992; Hong Kong; Goole T. November 1992; Frickley A. manager

A bustling centre forward in the old fashioned mould, Billy made his name at Hull where he made 193 League team appearances and scored 47 goals. Strangely, his subsequent career saw him play for another nine League clubs, yet in total they failed to add up to his spell with Hull.

Reading bought Billy to score the goals they needed to avoid relegation from the Second Division and although he netted six in 15 games it was not enough to prevent the drop. Billy had a stormy playing career and it was no different at Reading, who decided to sell him after only seven months following an incident in a night club. Typically, Billy left Reading in spectacular fashion - his late equalizer against Bolton was a long range dipping volley that was one of Elm Park's most memorable efforts. From then on Billy continued his nomadic playing career before settling down to run a pub near Sheffield United's ground.

Reading Record: Lge 17/8, LC 2, Total 19/8
League Career Total: 351(37)/77

WHITHAM Jack
b. Burnley 8.12.1946
Ht 5ft 11 Wt 12 st (75-76)
Career: Holy Trinity; Burnley (trial); Bury (trial); Sheffield Wed. November 1966; Liverpool (£57,000) May 1970; Cardiff C. (free) January 1974; READING (free) 1 July 1975; Worksop T.

Having failed to be taken on by Burnley and Bury as a wing half, Jack joined Sheffield Wednesday where he was developed into a free scoring centre forward. From his debut, when he came on as substitute to score twice against his home town club, Jack tended to score his goals in batches. A hat trick against Manchester United helped him become Wednesday's top scorer in 1968-69 despite several injuries, while at Liverpool Jack hit a televised hat trick against Derby. He was rewarded with a substitute appearance for England U23s in 1968 but the goals had started to dry up by the time he joined Reading. Jack had a varied start at Elm Park as his first five games for the club were made in four different competitions, but he retained his bulk scoring habit as all three of his first team goals came in a hat trick at Hartlepool. Injuries and the form of others meant that Jack was unable to make a major contribution to Reading's Fourth Division promotion season but he did give one memorable display at Elm Park. A talented singer/songwriter, Jack gave a fine performance to a packed Supporter's Club social club before leaving the club at the end of that season.

Reading Record: Lge 13(6)/3, FAC 1, LC 1, Total 15(6)/3
League Career Total: 94(17)/40

WHITLOCK Mark
b. Portsmouth 14.3.1961
Ht 5ft 11 1/2 Wt 12st 2 (89-90)
Career: Salisbury Sparks; Southampton from apprentice March 1979; Grimsby T. (loan) October 1982; Aldershot (loan) March 1983; Bournemouth June 1986; READING (£60,000) December 1988; Aldershot August 1988

Mark began his career with Southampton, making 69 appearances for them, including three in Europe, before moving along the coast to Bournemouth. A solid central defender, Mark helped them into the Second Division for the first time in their history. He was less successful at Reading where the club was in a transitional stage and the emergence of Adrian Williams saw Mark's first team chances reduced. Given a free transfer, he joined Aldershot where he did his best to shore up their defence before their financial problems became too much and he left them just before they folded.

Reading Record: Lge 26(1), FAC 10(2), AMC 5, Total: 41(3)
League Career Total: 228(10)/4

WHITTAKER Percy
b. Rotherham 19.11.1905 d. ?
Ht 5ft 8 1/2 Wt 10st 12 (38-39)
Career: Grantham; Wath A; Wolverhampton W. 1930; READING 7 June 1933

Another in the line of short but brave Reading goalkeepers, Percy came to Elm Park after winning a Central League championship medal with Wolves. He immediately won over the Reading fans with his fearless displays and the way he commanded his area over much taller players. Unfortunately, Percy's bravery cost him a series of injuries so, although he was the club's number one keeper for the six seasons before the War, he always missed half a dozen or so games each season. His worse injury was to his knee that needed an operation to correct and so cost him half of the 1934-35 season. As well as winning the Southern Section Cup in 1938, Percy had another good reason to feel glad he moved to Elm Park since, in 1936, he married to the step-daughter of Joe Smith, the manager who brought him to Reading. Like Steve Death, another small, brave Reading goalie, Percy had an interest in greyhound racing and when he was released by Reading in 1939 he became an owner, and joined the training staff at the town's greyhound stadium.

Reading Record: Lge 185, FAC 16, SSC 12, Total 213
League Career Total: 191

WICKS Alan Hayward

b. Henley 8.2.1933
Ht 5ft 11 Wt 13st 5 (55-56)
Career: READING from amateur 13 May 1952; Tunbridge Wells 1959

Following a spell as an amateur after playing for Reading and Berkshire Boys, Alan signed professional for Reading before serving in Malaya during his National Service. His brother, John, was also a professional with the club, but never made it to the first team. As it was, Alan only made one League appearance, at right half against Colchester in February 1956, for what was Elm Park's first League game under floodlights.

Reading Record: Lge 1

WICKS 'Jim' John R

b. Reading c.1899 d. ?
Ht 5ft 6 Wt 11st (23-24)
Career: Wycombe W; Nottingham For; READING June 1923; QPR 1924

A member of a well known Reading football family, Jim took a roundabout route before making his League debut with his home town team. A steady keeper, Jim was signed as cover for George Irwin but having made a handful of first team appearances he was released at the end of his first season.

Reading Record: Lge 6
League Career Total: 11

WICKS Stanley Maurice

b. Reading 11.7.1928 d Reading 21.2.1983
Ht 6ft 2 1/2 Wt 13st 3 (51-52)
Career: Castle St Institute; READING May 1946; Chelsea (£13,300) 19 January 1954

Another member of the Wicks family that produced three generations of League players, Stan became the best known. Having helped Berks & Bucks win the FA Youth Championship, Stan signed for Reading and had established himself in the first team by 1950. Initially a left back, Stan was used increasingly at centre half where he could use his impressive physique to the full. Representative honours soon followed, starting with an appearance for the FA v Cambridge University, then an England B cap plus a game for the Football Combination in 1953. By then Chelsea had already offered to swap Ron Greenwood plus cash for the Reading captain and after a year of haggling Ted Drake finally got his man.

Stan was impressive as Chelsea won their only championship title in 1954-55 and two games for the Football League, plus one for London against Basle, looked to be leading to full honours when a knee injury put an end to his career in August 1957. From then on, Stan concentrated on the family carpet business in Reading until his death from cancer at only 54.

Reading Record: Lge 168/1, FAC 12, Total 180/1
League Career Total: 239/2

WILDE James P

b. Tinsley c.1891 d. ?
Ht 5ft 10 Wt 11st (20-21)
Career: Rotherham T 1913; Burnley 1914; READING May 1920; Accrington Stan. 1921

Jimmy went to the same school as Elm Park pre-World War One hero, Alan Foster, and Harry Marshall, the manager who brought him to Reading. Although he only made one League appearance for Burnley, Jimmy was highly thought of as a player and he proved a versatile acquisition, playing in both full back roles and the two wing half berths during his one season with Reading.

Reading Record: Lge 24, FAC 3, Total 27
League Career Total: 59

WILDMAN Frank Reginald

b. Pontefract 1910
Ht 5ft 10 Wt 11st (35-36)
Career: South Kirby; Wolverhampton W. 1932; READING 22 February 1935; Swindon summer 1937; Frickley Colliery

After 54 League games for Wolves, Frank was signed by Reading as cover for their injured goalie, Percy Whittaker, and he went straight into the first team. Described as having a *very safe pair of hands and grand anticipation* Frank had to be satisfied with reserve football when Whittaker was fit and a serious bout of pneumonia hit his Reading career still further.

Reading Record: Lge 14, FAC 1, SSC 1, Total 16
League Career Total: 162

WILKIE Arthur William

b. Woolwich 7.10.1942
Ht 5ft 10 Wt 11st (60-61)
Career: READING groundstaff 11 November 1958, professional 8 October 1959; Chelmsford C. summer 1968; Basingstoke T.

Although a fine goalkeeper, Arthur will always be remembered for the hour he spent out of his goal. Injured in a Reading game against Halifax in August 1959, long before the days of substitutes, Arthur went on the wing and scored twice to become the only keeper to get two goals in a League game. A former England Youth international, Arthur's Reading career saw him in competition with Mike Dixon for the first team place for seven seasons with his acrobatic, shot stopping skills just beating Dixon's bravery. Reading never forgot Arthur's goalscoring exploits and in his last season he had a spell on the wing in the reserves, scoring on his outfield debut. More goals were to follow after Arthur was reinstated as an amateur in 1972 when he scored 22 goals in 15 local Reading league games before emigrating to New Zealand.

Reading Record: Lge 169/2, FAC 11, LC 8, Total 188/2

WILKS William
b. Staveley 1917
Ht 5ft 10 Wt 10st 1 (36-37)
Career: Staveley Gas Works; READING summer 1936

A tall, slim wing half, William had three seasons with Reading without ever really being anything more than a reserve player. Despite this, he played in the second leg of the Southern Section Cup at Bristol City and so gained a winners medal.

Reading Record: Lge 3, SSC 3, Total 6

WILLIAMS Adrian
b. Reading 16.8.1971
Ht 6ft 2 Wt 12st 6 (96-97)
Career: Bracknell BC; Wokingham T; READING apprentice 1986, professional 4 March 1989; Wolverhampton W. (£750,000) July 1996; READING (loan) 15 February 2000 & 22 March 2000, (free) 3 July 2000

An extremely versatile player, Adrian was a right winger when introduced to Reading's Centre of Excellence by former Reading defender, Steve Wood, but made his League debut just beyond his 17th birthday at right back. After that he played in midfield and emergency centre forward before settling into his best position at the centre of the defence in 1991-92. During that season, Adrian achieved his ambition by becoming the first Reading born player to captain the side for 30 years, and he quickly developed into a fine player and leader. Strong and determined, Reading's defence was always better organised when Adie played but a series of injuries interrupted his career but not his progress.

In 1993-94 he led Reading to the Second Division title, winning a PFA Divisional award plus the first of 12 Welsh caps, thanks to his Welsh father. A year after scoring in the 1995 play-off final, Adrian moved to Mark Mc-Ghee's Wolverhampton, but his bad luck with injuries continued so that by February 2000 he had only made 27 League appearances for them, well short of the 60 he needed to make to earn Reading another £250,000. There was great delight when Adie returned to Reading, initially on loan, and his spell to the end of the season coincided with the club's upturn in fortunes. Signed permanently in the summer, Adie suffered another injury that kept him out for the start of the new season and then after just five games back, a further knee injury left him on the touchline for seven months until a surprise recall for the play-off semi-final.
See also 'The Managers'

Reading Record: Lge 211(5)/15, FAC 16/2, LC 17/2, AMC 12/1, Play-offs 5/1, Total 261(5)/21 +
League Career Total: 237(6)/15 +

ADIE'S CLAIM TO FAME - When Adie played against Wrexham he wore the number 10 shirt and so became the first player to wear all 14 shirts in League matches, including the keeper's jersey, having gone in goal after Steve Francis was injured at Fulham in April 1992.

WILLIAMS Derick
b. Sunderland 5.10.1965
Ht 5ft 11 Wt 11st 10 (85-86)
Career: Watford from apprentice 1983; READING July 1985

A very promising youth career saw Derick capped at schools level and 12 times for England Youth. Unable to break into Watford's first team, Derick was signed by Reading as cover for goalkeeper Gary Westwood, and within a month of moving to Elm Park he was the only Third Division player in England's squad for the World Youth Cup in Russia.

With Westwood in great form, Derick's only first team game was in the Freight Rover Trophy game at Bournemouth. He was continually troubled by a back injury and at the end of his first season Derick was advised to retire from football at the age of only 21.

Reading Record: AMC 1

WILLIAMS Jeremy Simon

b. Didcot 24.3.1960
Ht 5ft 11 Wt 11st 10 (80-81)
Career: Didcot T; READING apprentice 25 June 1976, professional March 1978; Oulo (Finland) (loan) summer 1980; Gillingham (player exchange) August 1988; Aldershot July 1989; Windsor & Eton; Didcot T. youth coach

A free scoring, pacey centre forward, Jerry averaged two goals a game for Reading's minor side and hit over 30 in his first season as an apprentice. This form earned him a first team call-up but the circumstances could hardly have been more difficult. 3-0 down at home to Bury, Charlie Hurley's last action as Reading manager before resigning at half time was to bring on Jerry as sub. Despite the situation, Jerry turned on a great display, making Reading's goal and nearly scoring. Over the next four seasons he was used intermittently, often as a substitute, but an injury crisis early in 1981 saw him playing at right back. He proved such a revelation in this position that he was Reading's Player of the Year the following season. 1985-86 saw another change for Jerry as he was used mainly as a right winger as the club ran away with the Third Division title, scoring the first goal of Reading's record breaking start.

Although Jerry regarded his best position as full back, he gave his best ever display for Reading on the wing when he gave the, then, England full back, Kenny Samson, a torrid afternoon in Reading's FA Cup-tie against Arsenal. Jerry's penultimate appearance for Reading had been a well deserved substitute appearance in the Simod Cup final at Wembley, especially as he had scored in the semi-final penalty shoot out with the first spot kick of his professional career.

Reading Record: Lge 283(26)/17, FAC 13(1), LC 15/1, FLGT 8, AMC 4, FMC 5 (2), Total 328(29)/18
League Career Total: 354(35)/24

WILLIAMS Martin Keith

b. Luton 12.7.1973
Ht 5ft 9 Wt 11st 12 (99-00)
Career: Bramingham Spitfires; Leicester C. jnrs; Luton T. September 1991; Eu Pa (Finland) (loan) February 1993; Colchester U. (loan) March 1995; READING (free) 13 July 1995; Swindon T. (free) August 2000; Peterborough U. (loan) January 2001

Martin began his League career with Luton, the club for which his uncle, Ray Daniels, had also played. The young winger was used mainly as a substitute at Luton and for much of his first season at Reading until a late run of form earned him an extended contract. Reading's last season in Division One saw Martin played as a striker and it was clear that this would be his best position, a fact borne out by his topping the Reading's goalscorers in 1998-99, even though he was out injured from February. Martin took some time to shake off the effects of that injury and he was no longer a first choice striker by the end of 1999-00 and was released. At Reading Martin was known as 'The Kid' by the players after sleeping in a child's bed on a club tour, and he kept the fans guessing with ever changing hairstyles that ranged from dreadlocks to bright orange.

Reading Record: Lge 99(29)/26, FAC 8(2)/1, LC 10(6)/2, AMC 2, Total 119(37)/29
League Career Total: 144(61)/31

WILLIAMS Richard

b. Newcastle 15.12.1905 d. 27.5.1983
Ht 6ft Wt 11st (30-31)
Career: Jarrow; Stoke C. 1926; READING (£200) June 1930;
Chester (loan) October 1931 then permanent

Dick saved a penalty on his League debut with Stoke
and made 59 League appearances in the last two of his
four seasons with them. At Reading he got a brief run in
the first team after Lance Richardson had conceded
eight at Burnley, but after four games Dick returned to
keeping goal for the reserves and was released after that
one season. Almost seventy years later, Dick's great-
grandson was mascot when Reading made their last
visit to the Victoria Ground.

Reading Record: Lge 4
League Career Total: 65

WILLIAMS Robert Gordon

b. Bristol 17.2.1940
Ht 5ft 7 Wt 10st (70-71)
Career: Bristol C. May 1958; Rotherham U. (£14,000)
February 1965; Bristol R. (£16,000) March 1967; READING
(free) 5 August 1969; Keynsham T. (trial) 1971; AS Ostend
summer 1971; Cheltenham T. (trial) July 1972; Weymouth
August 1972; READING reserve team manager August 1976,
youth team manager 1980; Bristol C. youth scout October
1997; READING scout 1999

Despite going to a rugby playing school Bobby won FA
youth honours, thanks to his father who organised a
team for his son to play in. At Bristol City, he formed a
formidable partnership with John Ateyo and then met
with similar success at Rotherham alongside Les
Chappell. Bobby was reunited with Chappell and his
Rotherham manager, Jack Mansell, at Reading, after a
successful trial period. Playing out on the left of the
attack, Bobby demonstrated his skill of sneaking in
unnoticed to grab goals that had earned him the
nickname 'Shadow', and he finished second highest
goalscorer in his first Reading season, with 16 . 1970-
71 started with Bobby captaining Reading against
Manchester United in the Watney Cup, but ended in
relegation and his release. Bobby's playing career
ended with a serious car crash in September 1973 but he
returned to Elm Park, first as reserve team manager and
then in charge of the youth team. Heavily involved in
the launch of Reading's Centre of Excellence, over 40
players came through Bobby's teams to the first team
including three internationals, Neil Webb, Lawrie
Sanchez and Adie Williams. After a short spell away
from the club, Bobby returned as a scout, much to the
delight of the Supporters' Club for whom the likable
West Countryman had been elected a vice president.

Reading Record: Lge 60(5)/21, FAC 5/1, LC 1, Watney
Cup 1, Total 67(5)/22
League Career: 322(6)/115

WILLIAMS Roderick

b. Wandsworth (some records say Newport) 2.12.1909 d. ?
Ht 5ft 10 Wt 11st 4 (37-38)
Career: Sutton U; Epsom T; Uxbridge T; Norwich C. 1933;
Exeter C. 1936; READING 7 June 1937; West Ham U. (player
exchange) 11 November 1937; Clapton O. summer 1936

A prolific goalscoring centre forward, Rod was capped
by Middlesex before turning professional and scored 36
goals during his one season with Exeter. His move to
Reading cost a record transfer fee and Rod looked worth
every penny as he scored 12 goals in his first 14 League
games. It was, therefore, something of a surprise when
Reading exchanged him for West Ham's Len Young
and Peter Simpson only five months after they had
bought him. Rod's stay at Upton Park was almost as
short, before he ended his career with Clapton Orient.

Reading Record: Lge 14/12, SSC 1, Total 15/12
League Career Total: 118/71

WILSON John Robert

b. Blyth c.1899 d. 1996
Ht 5ft 11 Wt 13st (23-24)
Career: Bedlington U; Portsmouth 1921; READING (£75)
June 1923; Northampton T. summer 1926

Despite being born in Northumberland, John was
always known as 'Jock' at Reading, but it didn't put him
off - not only did he enjoy a fine spell at Elm Park, it was
quoted in the press that *he liked the Reading district
better than the more Southern town'*. That town was
Portsmouth where he had played his first 61 League
games at centre half. The arrival of Alf Messer at
Reading saw Jock move to right half and there he
proved the ideal foil for his left half partner, Dai Evans,
being a solid, consistent player. Virtually ever-present
for his first three seasons, Jock lost his place to Bill
Inglis and played just two games in 1926-27 before
moving to Northampton.

Reading Record: Lge 119/1, FAC 6, Total 125/1
League Career Total: 203/2

WILSON Thomas Bastin

b. Windyates 25.7.33
Ht 5ft 10 Wt 11st 7 (57-58)
Career: Thornton Hibs; READING (£100) 19 March 1956;
Exeter C. July 1957

An outside right, signed by Reading from Scottish
junior football, Tommy had to be content with reserve
football for most of his 15 months at Elm Park.

Tommy was finally given his chance in February 1957 and scored on his debut, but that was not enough to earn him more than a couple of short runs before being given a 'free'.

Reading Record: Lge 8/1 SPFC 1, Total 9/1
League Career Total: 30/3

WITTER Anthony Junior
b. London 12.8.1965
Ht 6ft 1 Wt 13st (96-97)
Career: QPR jnrs; Uxbridge T; Grays A; Crystal Palace (£10,000) October 1990; QPR (£125,000) August 1991; Plymouth Arg. (loan) January 1992; READING (loan) 11 February 1994; Millwall (£100,000) 14 October 1994; Northampton August 1998; Torquay U. November 1998; Welling December 1998; Scunthorpe U. February 1999; Hayes July 2000

Tony proved a doubly expensive player for QPR. After rejecting him as a youngster, they had to pay £125,000 to bring him back to Loftus Road and then he only made one League appearance for them. Tony joined Reading on loan where he proved to be an impressive defender who, having finished fourth in the Rumbelow's Sprint Challenge, was never short of pace. His final game for Reading saw Tony win the Man of the Match award, despite playing the last 38 minutes with what proved to be a broken leg.

Reading Record: Lge 4
League Career Total: 126(6)/3

WOOD Darren
b. Derby 22.10.1968
Ht 6ft 1 Wt 12st 8 (90-91)
Career: Chesterfield from YTS June 1987; READING (£40,000) July 1989; Northampton (player exchange) August 1990

Darren was established as a first team regular for Chesterfield by the time he was 19 and had played 67 League games before joining Reading. A calm, classy central defender, Darren lost his first team place shortly after Ian Porterfield became Reading's manager and although he won his place back he moved to Northampton to replace Keith McPherson. Unfortunately, Darren broke his leg in the act of scoring in his third game for Northampton and although he played once more, his League career was over.

Reading Record: Lge 31(1)/2, FAC 5(1), LC 4, Total 40(2)/2
League Career Total: 96(7)/6

WOOD Stephen Allan
b. Bracknell 2.2.1963
Ht 6ft 1 Wt 12st 7 (85-86)
Career: Arsenal assoc. schoolboy; READING apprentice August 1979, professional 19 February 1981; Millwall (£80,000) 17 June 1987; Southampton (£400,000) October 1991; Oxford U. (free) July 1994; Woking

One of the best modern central defenders to be produced by Reading, Steve relied on his skill and intelligent play rather than physical strength. This meant that he was able to cope with the requirements of top flight defending when with Millwall and Southampton. Steve made his League debut a few days after his 17th birthday and from the start of 1981-82 he was established as a first team regular, as part of a formidable and balanced central defensive partnership with Martin Hicks. Promoted to the Third Division in 1983-84 with Reading, Steve was ever-present and Player of the Year for the next two seasons, the second seeing him win a Third Division championship medal. At Millwall, he helped the Lions into the First Division, eventually ending his career at right back with Oxford. Steve now runs a soccer coaching school in the Reading area.

Reading Record: Lge 216(3)/9, FAC 15, LC 10, FLGT 3, AMC 3, FMC 1, Total 248(3)/9
League Career Total: 382(6)/9

WOODS Christopher Charles Edward
b. Boston 14.11.1959
Ht 6ft 2 Wt 14st 5 (96-97)
Career: Nottingham For. from apprentice December 1976; Norwich C. (£225,000) July 1979; Glasgow Rngrs (£600,000) July 1986; Sheffield Wed. (£1.2m.) August 1991; READING (loan) 27 October 1995; Colorado Rapids; Southampton November 1996; Sunderland March 1997; Burnley July 1997; Birmingham coach July 1998; Everton coach 2000

Understudy to Peter Shilton for both Forest and England, Chris came out of his mentor's shadow to enjoy a memorable goalkeeping career.

Having won a League Cup medal in 1978 before he had even played in the League, Chris moved to Norwich to get a regular game and won the trophy again in 1985, following it with the Second Division title. More silverware followed at Rangers where he won four championship and three Scottish Cup winners medals. By now Chris was playing in goal for England as well, and to some effect. In 24 internationals he only conceded eight goals and kept 19 clean sheets. In fact Chris didn't concede a goal until the closing minutes of his sixth international and is therefore, statistically, England's most successful goalkeeper. Steve had rather a less successful start during his loan spell with Reading since he let in four on his debut, at home to Ipswich. Those goals were not down to Chris and he displayed all his class in the rest of his month at Elm Park.

Reading Record: 5
League Career Total: 406(1)

CHRIS'S CLAIM TO FAME: While Reading's Steve Death holds the League record for 1,103 minutes without conceding a goal, Chris holds the same record in Scotland with a 1,196 minute goalless run with Rangers.

WOOLER Alan Thomas
b. Poole 17.8.1953
Ht 5ft 10 Wt 11st (72-73)
Career: Manchester U. (trial); Alton T; Weymouth; READING amateur January 1971, professional 29 October 1971; West Ham U. (free) August 1973; Aldershot April 1976; Boston Minutemen (loan); HJK Helsinki player coach; Millwall Lionesses manager

A stylish left back or central defender, Alan was Jimmy Wallbank's only signing during his spell as caretaker-taker manager at Reading. He was an attack minded player with a long throw but lost his place in October 1972 and was released. Remarkably for a Fourth Division free transfer, Alan ended up playing in the First Division with West Ham although he only appeared in four League games. Alan had a far more successful spell with Aldershot, making over 280 appearances for them while a loan spell saw Alan help Boston Minutemen win the North American League in 1977. Another success came in 1991 when he guided Millwall's ladies team, the Lionesses, to victory in the Women's FA Cup.

Reading Record: Lge 38, FAC 3(1), LC 1, Total 42(1)
League Career Total: 305(3)/3

WRAY James Herbert
b. Didsbury 17.11.1893 d. Honiton 3.8.1963
Ht 5ft 7 1/2 Wt 11st 6 (20-21)
Career: Norman A; Bolton W; Manchester C. (trial); READING summer 1919; Southport summer 1921; Chorley; Exeter C; Ottery St Mary; Chard T.

Centre forward, Jimmy had several attempts at breaking in to the League before earning his first pro contract when he joined Reading for their last season in the Southern League. Despite a general lack of goals in the club's first League season he was only selected twice, scoring in his second game, the best goals per game ratio of all the 10 centre forwards used that season.

Reading Record: Lge 2/1, SL 16/5, Total 18/6
League Career Total: 20/3

WRIGGLESWORTH William Herbert
b. South Elmswell 12.11.1912 d. Accrington 11.8.1980
Ht 5ft 4 Wt 9st 4 (47-48)
Career: Frickley Colliery; Chesterfield May 1932; Wolverhampton W. December 1934; Manchester U. January 1937; Wartime guest for Walsall, Chelsea & Arsenal; Bolton W. January 1947; Southampton October 1947; READING (£400) June 1948; Burton Alb. player manager summer 1949; Scarborough; Accrington Stan. coach

According to a Carreras cigarette card, Billy's 'value lies in combining cleverness with speed' and it helped him enjoy an 18 year playing career. A tiny left winger, Billy had toured with the FA during the War and often combined playing with giving talks to the troops. He had enjoyed his best spell with Wolves where he had scored 21 times in 50 games, but he was well into the veteran stage when he joined Reading. Billy played the first three games of 1948-49 but apart from a couple of well spaced out games, his League career was over and so fans would no longer see his amusing habit of trapping the ball with his bottom!

Reading Record: Lge 5, FAC 1, Total 6
League Career Total: 141/39

WRIGHT Andrew James
b. Leeds 21.10.1978
Ht 5ft 4 1/2 Wt 9st 12 (98-99)
Career: Leeds U. from YTS October 1995; READING (loan) 8 December 1998; Fortuna Sittard (Holland) summer 1999

Even though he was capped by England at all levels up to U21 and helped Leeds win the 1997 FA Youth Cup, Andy could not break into their first team.

Consequently, Andy's League debut came in a loan spell with Reading where the speedy left winger was used as substitute, although he did start in the Auto Windscreens tie at Bournemouth.

Reading Record: Lge (2), AMC 1, Total 1(2)

WRIGHT Thomas James
b. Belfast 29.8.1963
Ht 6ft 1 Wt 13st 5 (96-97)
Career: Linfield; Newcastle U. (£30,000) January 1988; Hull C. (loan) February 1991; Nottingham For. (£400,000) September 1993; READING (loan) 4 October 1996; Manchester C. (loan) January 1997, (£450,000) March 1997; Wrexham (loan) February 1999; Newcastle U. (loan) August 1999; Bolton W. (loan) January 2001

After three years at Newcastle, a big money move to Forest proved a disaster for Tommy as, after only 10 games in their goal, he suffered a knee injury that needed three operations over two years. After three reserve games he was loaned to Reading and the following day he kept a clean sheet at Wolves. This proved to be the first of a series of brilliant displays over 17 games that made him a favourite with Reading's fans, many of whom regard him as the club's best ever loan signing. Tommy was rewarded by winning a recall into the Northern Irish squad and he was subsequently able to push his total up to 31 caps as well as earning himself a permanent move to Manchester City.

Reading Record: Lge 17
League Career Total: 162(2) +

WRIGHT William Bullock
b. Sheffield 25.12.1899 d. ?
Ht 5ft 8 1/2 Wt 9st 12 (35-36)
Career: Southend U; Bolton W; READING May 1933; FC Rouen coach May 1938; Crystal Palace coach July 1939

Billy was the son of a professional footballer, Jockie Wright, who had played for Bolton and, having appeared in the first game at Burnden Park, he later scored the first FA Cup goal at the new ground. Although Billy also played for Bolton, he joined them via Southend after United's manager, T. Mather, spotted him playing for his regiment and then took Billy with him when he got the manager's job at Burnden Park. He played in five different positions with the club, making 154 League appearances before joining Reading. A polished player, Billy hardly missed a game at left half during his first four seasons at Elm Park, and he was club captain from 1937. That season saw the 38 year old used less regularly and he was released at the end of the season to enable him to start his coaching career.

Reading Record: Lge 173/3, FAC 16/1, SSC 4/1, Total 193/5
League Career Total: 327/24

YARD Ernest John
b. Stranraer 3.5.1941
Ht 5ft 9 Wt 10st 7 (66-67)
Career: Kilmarnock; Partick Thistle (£4,000); Bury (£12,000) December 1963; Crystal Palace (£9,000) May 1965; READING (£4,850) 11 November 1966; Cape Town C. (£1,000) May 1969

Ernie's early career was spent as a centre forward and it was only when he moved to Crystal Palace that he was converted to wing half. His arrival at Reading saw a dramatic change in the club's form and Ernie's skilful but tenacious play turned a struggling team into promotion challengers. His first game saw Reading win 6-0 after going seven games without a victory, and he then became a fixture in the first team for two and half seasons. Then new manager, Jack Mansell, allowed Ernie to leave the club, and he emigrated to South Africa where he helped Cape Town City win the Castle Cup and was named Cape Footballer of the Year in 1970.

Reading Record: Lge 101(3)/6, FAC 7(1), LC 4, Total 112(4)/6
League Career Total: 181(5)/22

YARNELL Herbert George
b. Pontefract c.1888 d. ?
Ht 5ft 9 Wt 12st (20-21)
Career: Blackpool; READING May 1920

Bert had the honour of scoring Reading's first League goal at Elm Park when he netted against Gillingham on 1 September 1920. He had already played in Reading's first League game but by the end of September he faced an operation on his injured knee. Bert's Reading career came to a strange end when he was suspended and put on the transfer list in February 1921 after discipline breaches that included 'misconduct' with a married woman.

Reading Record: Lge 5/1
League Career Total: 14/2

YOULDEN Thomas Frederick
b. Islington 8.7.1949
Ht 6ft Wt 12st 9 (72-73)
Career: Arsenal from apprentice July 1966; Portsmouth April 1968; READING (£4,000) 10 July 1972; Aldershot (£2,500) April 1977; Addleston & Weybridge player coach July 1981; Chelsea Youth Academy coach

Having given up a promising swimming career (he swam for London), to join Arsenal, Tommy became disillusioned at his lack of progress at Highbury and went on the dole before being persuaded to join Portsmouth.

As well as swimming, Tommy had played five times for England Boys, including the 9-1 win over Ireland at Elm Park in March 1964. Later, he returned to Reading when he became Charlie Hurley's first, and one of his best, signings, as the classy central defender shored up the club's defence. But for injuries, Tommy would have been ever-present for his five seasons at Elm Park and he was a vital part of the Fourth Division promotion season of 1975-76. When he asked for a transfer the following season, Reading valued him at £35,000 but were forced to accept a giveaway fee from Aldershot that was set by the League tribunal. Tommy played over 120 games for the Shots but was sent off during an FA Cup-tie on his return to Elm Park. Tommy later took part in the football based film, as an extra in 'Fever Pitch'.

Reading Record: Lge 161(2)/3, FAC 6, LC 14, Total 181(2)/3
League Career Total: 361(15)/5

TOMMY'S CLAIM TO FAME - Hardly a prolific scorer, Tommy actually scored one less than the records show. On the opening game of 1975-76, Tommy hit a free kick into the side netting of the game against Rochdale. Everyone politely applauded the effort except the ref who was convinced that the ball had gone in the net and Reading's promotion season was under way with 'the goal that never was'.

YOUNG Leonard Archibald
b. East Ham 23.2.1912
Ht 5ft 11 1/2 Wt 12st 7 (37-38)
Career: Colchester U; Ilford; West Ham U. 1933; READING (player exchange) 11 November 1937; Brighton (£500) February) 1948; Bata Sports coach

Having played only 12 League games in four seasons at West Ham, Len joined Reading as part of the deal that took Rod Williams to Upton Park. At Reading he played in all three half back positions without really being regarded as first choice in any of them. Len appeared for Reading throughout the War and was a member of the team that won the 1941 London War Cup to add to his success in the 1938 Southern Section Cup. After the War, Len was used in a more defensive role before moving on to Brighton. In 1953 he emigrated to Australia to take up a coaching position in Victoria.

Reading Record: Lge 84, FAC 5, SSC 5, Wartime 116/2; Total 210/2
League Career Total: 104

YOUNG Matthew Sprott
b. Cambois 1st qtr 1901 d. ?
Ht 5ft 10 Wt 12st 7 (24-25)
Career: Preston Colliery; Hartlepools U. 1923; READING June 1924; Workington summer 1925; Preston 1926

Matt's form on the right wing at Hartlepools tempted Reading to sign the youngster and give him his debut on the first day of the season. After four games he lost his place and from then on he was only able to add two more appearances before being released after that one season. He fared no better at Preston and so Matt returned to the non-League game.

Reading Record: Lge 6
League Career Total: 41/3

Les Chappell

Alec Christie

Dean Horrix

Sandy Kane

Billy McConnell

Jim McIntyre

TEAM OF THE CENTURY

Or, more precisely, Team of the last 80 years! During the research and writing of this book I have formed an opinion on many of the hundreds of players who appeared for Reading before I started my visits to Elm Park. So, I thought it might be appropriate, or at least fun, to name the players I consider to be the best to play for the club since its League entry in 1920.

GOALKEEPER – Reading have always been well served by their goalies, right from Syd Crawford through to Phil Whitehead, but it boiled down to a straight choice between Steve Death and Shaka Hislop. In the end, the fact that Shaka has performed consistently well at the highest level gives him the edge – that and the fact that he is nine inches taller than Deathie!

FULL BACKS – Our greatest full back, Herbert Smith, won four England caps while an amateur with Reading but he had retired long before 1920. That leaves the way clear for Irish international, Billy McConnell to just beat Colin Meldrum for the left back role. On the right the wonderfully versatile Gary Peters nearly got the nod but the number two shirt (no squad numbers in my team!) goes to another of our great team of the Twenties, Bert Eggo.

CENTRE BACKS – In his day Alf Messer was regarded as the best uncapped player in the country, as well as being one of Reading's all time greats but my other choice might be more contentious. Martin Hicks had his critics but in my defence (and his) he was ever-present in three of the club's greatest achievements – the 1,103 minutes without conceding a goal, the 13 consecutive wins and the Simod Cup triumph.

MIDFIELD – The easiest choice of all. England internationals Neil Webb and Johnny Brooks plus Wartime cap, Maurice Edelston, would be in virtually every Reading fan's selection while the only doubt about including my boyhood hero, Jimmy Wheeler is whether to play him in midfield or the forward line. Remembering the effort and enthusiasm he put into every game he'd probably play in both!

STRIKERS - Joe Bailey, Hugh Davey, Frank Richardson, Jack Palethorpe, Tommy Tait, Tony MacPhee, Ron Blackman, Kerry Dixon, Trevor Senior and Jimmy Quinn – pick any two and you would have a great partnership. Despite their great talents only one went on to prove himself at the highest level in the First Division and, to a lesser extent, for England, so one place must go to Kerry Dixon. The other almost went to another of my all time favourites, Trevor Senior, but those who saw them both play reckon that Ron Blackman was just, and only just, better than 'Super Trev' so he gets the final place.

THE AUTHOR'S READING TEAM OF THE CENTURY

		SHAKA HISLOP	
BERT EGGO	ALF MESSER	MARTIN HICKS	BILLY MCCONNELL
NEIL WEBB	MAURICE EDELSTON	JOHNNY BROOKS	JIMMY WHEELER
	KERRY DIXON		RON BLACKMAN

The five substitutes would include three of the club's most versatile players – Fred Bartholomew, Denis Allen and Adrian Williams, plus Jimmy Quinn and Trevor Senior. I haven't bothered with a substitute goalie since all five have played as emergency keepers during their Reading careers.

And finally, my side would be managed by 'Mr Reading', the late, great Maurice Evans.

WARTIME GUESTS

This section lists all the players who 'guested' for Reading in the 1939-40 to 1945-46 seasons in competitive games, other than the 1945-46 FA Cup which are included in the general Players' section.

'Pos' (position) is the normal position for which the player appeared for Reading i.e. 'rb' - right back, 'ch' - centre half, 'ir' - inside right, 'lw' - left wing etc. 'Seasons' indicates those played for Reading e.g. '40, 42' shows appearances were made in 1940-41 and 1942-43. 'Club' is the one for which the player was registered with prior to their Reading appearances. Also included are ex Reading players and future players who also made guest appearances.

Every effort has been made to ensure the accuracy of the figures shown but the reduced level of reporting during the War and last minute team changes has, occasionally, made it difficult to verify the accuracy of some line-ups.

(Left) Ron Bishop
(Right) Albert Geldard

Name	Pos	Seasons	App/Gl	Club	Comments
L A Abery	gl	39	1	Amateur	'A' team player from Maidenhead
W Adams	lw	43,44	8 /1	Spurs	
Albert V Aicken	rh	42	3	Brentford	
Robert Allen	lh	42	1	Brentford	
Len Allum	rh	41,44	3	Clapton 0.	Reading born but made his name with Chelsea
Ashton	ch	44	1	Battle Ath.	Local amateur
Joe Bacuzzi	rb	40	2	Fulham	Dave's father;13 War caps; First England player to be subbed.
Fred Bartlett	ch	40,42	3	Clapton O.	Had previously scored og for Reading in game v Clapton O.
William Bates	rw	40	1	Luton	
'Pat' Beasley	lw	41	12 /2	Huddersfield	Won two League titles with Arsenal. 1 England cap
Sgt R Beebe	gl	42	1	Amateur	Army amateur spotted in rep. game at Elm Park.
Bird	il	40	1	?	
Ralph Birkett	rw	42	2 /1	Newcastle	1 England cap plus 1 Wartime cap
Ron Bishop	rb	42,43,45	15	Amateur	Popular local player. Reading Part time pro Post-War
F Bowers	il	45	1	Amateur	
John Bradley	il	40 - 43	49 /32	Southampton	Hitchhiked to games - some missed matches when he failed to get a lift. Ted Bates' best man.
Norman Brooks	lw	40-44	11 /5	Amateur	See entry in 'The Players'.
George Burchell	lb	41,42	2	Brentford	Amateur international on Brentford and Romsey's books
Harry Burgess	il	39	5 /2	Chelsea	4 England caps. Wiith Sheffield Wed in 1930 (League Champs.)
Ron Burgess	lh	43	1	Spurs	32 Welsh caps. Played for Gt Britain v Europe and captained Spurs to 1950 League title.
P M Burgess	gl	44	1	Amateur	Regular for Reading's youth team
Matt Busby	rh	42 - 45	36 /2	Liverpool	See entry in 'Best and the Rest'
Jim Campbell	lw	45	3 /1	Leicester	
Edwin Chapman	lw	41	1	Oldham	Ordered to play by officer friend of Joe Edelston
Allenby Chilton	ch	45	3	Man United	F.A.Cup winner 1948, League Champs. 1952. Scored og for Reading in 1954 FA Cup-tie v United
Ken Chisholm	cf	44	4 /2	Queens Park	Amateur with Queens Park
Stan Clayton	ir	42	1 /2	Notts Co	
Bill Clover	rb	45	19	Amateur	See entry in 'The Players'
A Collier	rb	42	2	Hibernian	
S Cook	rh	41	1	Rotherham	Also played for Man. Utd
Harold Cothliff	ir	39 - 42	59 /15	Torquay	Scored Elm Park's fastest ever goal (10 seconds v West Ham in January 1941.
J H Court	lw	41	9 /1	Aldershot	Amateur with the Shots
Freddy Cox	rw	39 - 43	8 /2	Spurs	See entry in 'Best and the Rest'
Sammy Crooks	rw	39	1	Derby	26 England caps. 22 years at Derby
Arthur Cunliffe	ir	42	2 /2	Hull	2 goals on Reading debut v Chelsea. 2 England caps
John Davie	rw	40,41	4 /1	Brighton	Scored 125 War goals for Brighton
Davidson	gl	41	2	Amateur	
David Davies	ir	44	1 /1	Hull	
Albert Dawes	lb	39	1	C. Palace	

Name	Pos	Seasons	App/Gl	Club	Comments
Alfred Day	il	45	1	Swindon	Won his 1 cap for Wales before making League debut
Gordon Dreyer	rb	43	1	Luton	
George Duke	gl	45	5	Luton	
'Dally' Duncan	lw	39	1	Derby	14 Scottish caps. FA Cup winner 1946
Len Duns	lw	41	9	Sunderland	
George Eastham	il	40	6	Blackpool	Known as 'Diddler'. Father of George - both capped for England
Joe Edelston	ir	42	1	Amateur	Maurice's elder brother
C Ednay	gl	40	2	Battle Ath.	Amateur who conceded 11 goals in 2 games. Also played for Norwich v Reading
L Evans	ir	45	1	?	
William Fagan	rh	44	14 /4	Liverpool	
Robert Ferrier	il	42	1	Grimsby	
Freddy Fisher	rw	44,45	23 /3	Slough	See entry in 'The Players'
Fred T Fisher	rb	44,45	22	Grimsby	
Doug Flack	gl	39,40	3	Fulham	Had already played at Elm Park for Fulham and Brighton
C Fuller	ir	42	1	Amateur	17 year old local player
John Galloway	il	45	7 /1	Glasgow R.	
D Garrie	lw	44	1	Amateur	Served locally in RAF
Edward Gaskell	gl	39	1	Brentford	Kept clean sheet in his only game
Albert Geldard	rw	40	4	Bolton	Youngest ever League player. 3 England caps
'Jack' Gibbins	il	40	1 /2	Tottenham	Amateur and War international
Dennis Gill	lw	40	2	Amateur	16 year old clerical assistant at Elm Park. Died in India in 1946
Gillespie	gl	44	1	CrystalPalace	Possibly Watford's Pat Gillespie
Len Goldberg	rb	41 - 44	80	Leeds	See entry in 'The Players'
W Gorrie	ch	42,43	6	Cowdenb'th	
Joffre Gulliver	lb	45	12	Leeds	See entry in 'The Players'
Almeric Hall	ir	41	4 /1	Spurs	
Willie Hall	il	45	1	Spurs	10 England caps. Scored 5 goals v Ireland
W Hamilton	il	44	1 /1	St Bernards	Scored the winner in his only game
Fred Hampshire	ch	40	3	Amateur	Later a Reading teacher
J R E Hardisty	ir	43,44	26 /2	Hibernian	England Amateur Intl.
George Hardwick	lb	44,45	4	Middlesbro'	13 full and 17 Wartime England caps. Played for Great Britain v Europe
Jim Harrison	lb	43	12	Leicester	
R W Hardwood	il	40	10	Amateur	18 year old 'A' team player
Albert Hayhurst	ch	39	1		See entry in 'The Players'
Wilf Heathcote	cf	45	1 /1	QPR	Reading's last Wartime guest
Foster Hedley	lw	43	5	Swindon	
Les Henley	ir	41,45	7 /6	Arsenal	See entry in 'The Players'
Charles Higgins	lb	45	1	Arbroath	
R Hill	ir	44	1	Amateur	Played for Reading and England Universities
Tom Hinchcliffe	ir	42	5 /2	Derby	
Sam Hodgson	rh	43	2	Grimsby	
John Holliday	lw	43	1	Brentford	Lent by home club for game at Griffin Park

Name	Pos	Seasons	App/Gl	Club	Comments
G Holton	rh	44	1	Amateur	Played for Henley
A H 'Tommy' Hopper	rw	40 - 43	15 /2	Amateur	Member of 1948 Olympic squad.
					Scored first goal in a Wembley Amateur Cup final
Les Howe	rh	40,41	9 /2	Spurs	Scored twice on Reading debut
T Howshall	rh	44,45	3	Stoke	
'Jack' Hurst	rh	40	6 /1	Bolton	
Harold Iddon	il	43,45	2 /2	Preston	Scored twice on Reading debut
Harold Ireland	lw	39 - 44	7 /4	Amateur	Well known player with Reading Tramways.
					Poor eyesight prevented a pro career
Jim Ithell	rh	40	1	Bolton	
A Johnstone	rb	43	1	Partick T.	
Harry Johnston	lh	40	2	Blackpool	See entry in 'The Managers'
William Jones	fb	42,43	2	Liverpool	2 England caps. 1947 League Champs. medal
Philip Joslin	gl	42	2	Torquay	
James	lh	40	1	Amateur	Stationed locally with RAF
H Kelsey	lw	39	1 /1	Maidenhead	Scored winner in his only game
J Kilkenney	rb	40	3	Corinthians	Pilot officer in RAF
Jack ? Knight	lw	43	1	Bolton	Also played for York
Harry Knott	il	40	1	Amateur	Had played for Reading Res. as far back as 1924
J H Laird	il	42	2 /1	St Mirren	
Roy Lambert	lb	43	7	Liverpool	5 full and 4 Wartime Welsh caps.
					Youngest ever player to sign for a League club
Derek Lane	rb	45	4	Amateur	A metallurgist by profession
Billy Lane	il	41	1	Watford	See entry in 'The Players'
W Lawrence	gl	45	9		Reading's first sub in friendly v Fulham Oct. 1939
D Lewis	rh	44	1	Southampton	
Harry Lewis	ir	39	1 /1	QueenofS'th	Scored 5 minutes into debut
E R Litchfield	rw	42	1	Newcastle	
A Livingstone	lh	45	1	?	
George Ludford	cf	39	1 /1	Spurs	
Archie MacAullay	rh	41	1	West Ham	7 full and 5 Scottish War. caps. Played for GB
					v Europe
McClellon	lh	43	1	Charlton	Also played for Falkirk
McColl	il	40	1	Bradford	
Joe McCormack	lh	42	2	Bolton	
Alan McCrohan	lw	44, 45	16 /3	Amateur	See entry in 'The Players'
C McFarlane	ir	43	1	Notts Forest	
J McPhie	rb	40 - 45	33	Falkirk	Played in London War Cup final
Harry McShane	ol	42	1	Blackburn	Man Utd. scout who discovered Andy Ritchie and
					Nicky Butt. Father of Ian 'Lovejoy' McShane
John Mahon	lw	40	2	Huddersfield	Also played for WBA
R Malcolm	ol	43	1	Amateur	Reading Youth team player
Johnny Mapson	gl	39 - 44	188	Sunderland	See entry in 'The Players'
George Marks	gl	45	12	Arsenal	See entry in 'The Players'
Ernest Marshall	il	45	3 /1	Cardiff	

Name	Pos	Seasons	App/Gl	Club	Comments
E A Martin	lw	43	1	Battle Ath.	16 year old local amateur
Arnold Mayes	ch	42	1	Chelsea	
Joe Mercer	rh	42	6 /1	Everton	Played for captained and managed England. Won three League Champs. and the FA Cup
Alfred Miller	rh	43	3	Plymouth	
George Milligan	lh	42	15 /1	Everton	Scored on his Reading debut
Mitchell	ir	42	1 /1	Dundee Utd	
Reg Mogford	il	42,43	23 /7	Newport	Served in RAF at High Wycombe
Robert Morris	ch	43	5	Norwich	
Jimmy Mullen	lw	42	2	Wolves	12 full and 3 Wartime England caps Uncle of Reading's Jimmy Mullen
Ernest Muttitt	lb	41,43	3	Brentford	
H Neilan	rw	40	3 /1	Amateur	Reading Youth player
Vic Niblett	ch	43 - 45	47	Amateur	See entry in 'The Players'
Tommy Oakes	rw	45	1	Man Utd	Amateur on United's books
O'Callaghan	il	40	1	Spurs	Played when Reading were a player short v Arsenal at White Hart Lane
John O'Hare	?	39	1	Chelsea	
Jack Oxberry	lw	41	1		See entry in 'The Players'
H Padgett	il	44	7 /4	Leeds	
Edward Painter	il	42,43	18 /5	Swindon	
George Paterson	il	42,43	34 /9	Liverpool	
John Pattison	rh	44,45	27	Portsmouth	See entry in 'The Players'
H C Penny	gl	42	1	Amateur	Son of former Reading player, Bert conceded 6 goals
H Perkins	il	40	2	Amateur	16 year old 'A' team player
Edward Perry	if	40	1	Doncaster	3 full and 1 Wartime Welsh caps
George Pescod	ch	42	1	Halifax	
Peter Peters	gl	45	2	Amateur	See entry in 'The Players'
Harold Pond	rh	44	7	Carlisle	
Bart Purvis	lb	44	3	North Shields	
R Purvis	lb	45	8	Chelsea	
Bill Ratcliffe	ch	40 - 45	82	Oldham	See entry in 'The Players'
J Rawlinson	lh	43	1	Amateur	
John Roberts	ir	40	1 /1	Bolton	1 Welsh cap
Od Rojahn	rh	43	2	Amateur	Norwegian serviceman recommended by Matt Busby
Robert Ross	lh	42	3	Glasgow R.	
W H Sainsbury	gl	42	1	Spurs	Amateur loaned from opponents 'Spurs after Mapson hospitalized
P J Sarney	cf	44	1	Amateur	On Army home leave from Iraq
Hedley Schwabb	lw	44	1	Amateur	Local Army cadet
Horace Sheppard	ch	39, 42, 45	3	Aldershot	
Simpson	ir	42	1	East Fife	
Tommy Sinclair	if	40	2 /2	Bolton	Scored twice on Reading debut
Edward Smith	lb	43	1	Millwall	Later managed Benfica to League and Cup victories
Les Smith	lw	44	1	Brentford	Reading game abandoned after 40 minutes. Played in Amateur Cup final at 17.

Name	Pos	Seasons	App/Gl	Club	Comments
'Reg' Smith	rh	43	1	Millwall	2 England and 1 Wartime cap. Real name Schmidt. Son of South African rugby international
'Smith'	gl	43	1	Amateur	Nom de plume for well known local keeper who conceded 5 goals in his only game
Ken Smith	il	44	1	Bolton	Amateur with Bolton
Frank Soo	cf	42, 43	3	Stoke	9 England Wartime caps
Joe Stephenson	il	41	2 /1	Leeds	2 England caps. Killed in Burma campaign
Lloyd Stone	cf	39	1	Amateur	Son of former Reading director
Billy Strauss	lw	42	1	Aberdeen	South African international
M Sturgess	rw	45	2	Amateur	Regular for Reading reserves
Frank Swift	gl	43	4	Man. City	19 full plus 14 Wartime England caps. Died in Munich air disaster
Tommy Tait	ir	39, 40	2	Torquay	See entry in 'The Players'
Albert Tennant	rh	41	1	Chelsea	
James Todd	rh	45	4	Blackpool	Capped for North. Ireland below full international level
T Townsend	cf	43	1	Amateur	Scored 126 goals for local side Earley Utd
Walburton	lw	40	1	Aston Villa	
D Walker	lh	40	1	?	
Henry Waller	ch	42	1	Arsenal	
Jock Watson	lb	43	1	Leyton	Amateur. Also played for Brentford
Eric Westwood	fb	40	4	Man. City	Capped at England B and FL level
C J Wicks	il	44	1	Amateur	Local youngster
L R Wicks	lb	40	4	Amateur	Played for local club, Early Minors
George Wilkins	ir	39	2 /1	Brentford	Father of England international Gerry Wilkins
Cyril Williams	lw	43, 44	39 /16	Bristol City	
Stan Williams	lw	42, 43, 44	16 /1	Aberdeen	Scottish international
W Williams	ch	45	1	Amateur	Local player from Caversham
Daniel Winter	rb	40	5	Bolton	Scored own goal on Reading debut
Robert Wright	lh	41	3	Charlton	Captain in Royal Armoured Corps
R J Yardley	cf	44	1	Amateur	Local player
R Yates	cf	44	9 /2	Chester	Turned up at ground asking to play
Ben Yorston	il	39	1	Middlesboro'	1 Scottish cap

(Left) Freddy Cox, (Middle) Joe Mercer, (Right) Billy Strauss

'BEST & THE REST'

Featuring all first team players in a Who's Who should be sufficient to cover all of a club's important players but that is not the case with Reading, hence this special section.

As well as those players unlucky enough to have a Reading career restricted to the three games of the abandoned 1939-40 season this section also features the footballer thought by many to be the greatest British player of all time, plus the manager who discovered him, again another British great.

Others who fall into this category are a double Olympic gold medalist, a goalie who had a street named after him and the player who went on to have a more varied influence on League football than anyone else in the Twentieth century.

(Left) Vic Woodley
(Right) Jimmy Hill

BARTRAM Samuel

b. Simonside 22.1.1914 d. Harpenden, 17.7.1981
Ht 6ft 0 1/2 Wt 12st 5 (37-38)
Career: Bolden Villa; North Shields; Chester le Street; Jarrow; READING (trial) 1931; Bolden Villa April 1933; Easington Colliery; Bolden Colliery Welfare; Charlton A. September 1934; York C. manager March 1956; Luton manager July 1960

Generally reckoned to be the best uncapped goalie in British football, Sam is a legend at Charlton. There he made over 600 first team appearances winning numerous honours, culminating in an FA Cup winners medal in 1947; even having a street named after him, and Reading missed him! However, manager Joe Smith can hardly be blamed as Sam came to Reading as a left half and never played in goal during his spell in the reserves. It was only when he returned to the North East that he got to play in goal and was spotted by Charlton three years after leaving Elm Park.

League Career Total: 579

BEST George

b. Belfast 22.5.1946
Ht 5ft 8 1/2 Wt 10st 3 (69-70)
Career: Manchester U. from apprentice May 1963; Stockport Co. (loan) November 1975; Los Angeles; Fulham September 1976; Hibernian; Golden Bay Earthquake; Hong Kong; Bournemouth March 1983; READING (guest) 29 October 1985

In his day George could justifiably claim to be the most talented British footballer the game had seen. An Irish international at 17, Footballer of the Year, European Footballer of the Year, European Cup winner in 1968, but by 1973 it all started to go wrong. Despite being marked out of the game by Will Dixon in his one visit to Elm Park, when Manchester United played Reading in the 1970 Watney Cup, George went on to score the very first penalty shoot-out goal in the final of that competition. His next visit to Elm Park could have been in 1975, shortly after he had moved to Stockport, but his agent insisted on a share of the gate for him to appear so he missed the game.

What is less well known is that Maurice Evans tried to sign George for Reading in October 1982 after he had seen him play for a Hong Kong side in a friendly at Oxford. Unfortunately, George was still contracted to Golden Bay Earthquake and the deal fell through so Reading fans had to wait another two years to see him. By that time the great man had been reduced to making guest appearances, and it was on that basis that he played for Reading in a friendly against New Zealand on 29 October 1985.

Although a shadow of his former self with his pace reduced by the extra weight he was carrying, George still showed the occasional flashes of skills that had made him the legend he still is.

Reading Record: Friendly 1
League Career Total: 411/147

GEORGE'S CLAIM TO FAME - Despite his many achievements with Manchester United and Northern Ireland, there can be little doubt that his proudest achievement must have been that his one appearance for Reading was in the first game ever to be sponsored by a firm of solicitors!

BLISSETT Luther Lloyd

b. Jamaica 1.2.1958
Ht 5ft 11 Wt 12st (88-89)
Career: Watford from jnrs July 1975; AC Milan (£1m) 1982; Watford August 1984; READING (guest) 10 August 1988; Bournemouth November 1988; Watford August 1991; West Bromwich Alb. (loan) October 1992; Bury August 1993; Mansfield T. (loan) December 1993

One of Watford's all-time greats, Luther was part of the Graham Taylor team that rose up through the divisions to qualify for European football. This earned him a £1 million move to Italy and 14 England caps. He was the first black player to score for England and the only one to date to score a hat-trick. A hard working striker whose pace and strength were a constant threat to defences, Luther was available for transfer from his second spell at Watford when he made a guest appearance in Martin Hicks' testimonial game against Spurs at the start of 1988-89. He marked this game by scoring the winner with a sensational right foot drive, but Ian Branfoot was put off by the £100,000 asking price so this proved to be Luther's only game for Reading and three months later he joined Bournemouth.

Reading Record: Friendly 1/1
League Career Total: 505(49)/207

BUSBY Matthew William

b. Orbiston 26.5.1909 d. 20.1.1994
Ht 5ft 10 Wt 11st 8 (43-44)
Career: Alpine Villa; Denny Hibs; Manchester C. February 1928; Liverpool (£8,000) March 1936; Wartime guest for Chelsea, Middlesbrough, Brentford, Bournemouth, READING 16 May 1942 to 19 September 1945; Manchester U. manager 1945, admin manager June 1969, caretaker manager December 1970, director June 1971 to August 1982, Club President March 1980.

It is easy to forget that before he became one of, if not the, greatest British manager, Matt was a great player who gave tremendous service to Manchester City and Liverpool. With City he made two cup final appearances, winning in 1934, and was capped by Scotland, once in peacetime and seven times in Wartime internationals. During the War he was stationed for much of the time at Sandhurst and played for Reading on a number occasions during that period. Although near the end of his playing career he became a great favourite at Elm Park, turning in a series of sterling performances at right half. When it became known that he was looking to go into management, Reading offered him the position of assistant manager to Joe Edelston, but then Manchester United offered him their vacant manager's role, and the rest, as they say, is history. Matt's last game was for Reading against Crystal Palace and, such was the respect and affection with which he was held at Elm Park, he was made captain for the game. He chose that match to make about his only mistake in a Reading shirt - his wayward backpass led to Palace's late winner, but that did nothing to dampen the reception he received at the end of the game. As Matt moved towards the legendary status he richly deserved, he never forgot his time at Reading, using Elm Park as a training base when he managed the 1948 British Olympic football squad and bringing his full first team for a benefit match in the Fifties.

Reading Record: Wartime 36/2 plus 3 friendlies
League Career Total: 317/14

MATT'S CLAIM TO FAME - The great Sir Matt Busby's managerial career did not get off to a very auspicious start. In May 1944 he was asked to form and manage a Matt Busby XI to play Reading to raise funds for the 'Salute to a Soldier' campaign. Played at the Royal Military College, Sandhurst, the game achieved its aim in raising funds but must have given Matt second thoughts about his suitability in management as Reading beat his team 6-1.

COX Frederick James Arthur
b. Reading 1.11.1920 d. Poole 17.8.1973
Ht 5ft 7 Wt 11st 7 (54-55)
Career: St Georges B.C; Northfleet; Tottenham H. August 1938; Wartime Guest for Fulham, Manchester C, Swindon, READING November 1939 to December 1943; Arsenal September 1949; West Bromwich Alb. player coach then asst. manager July 1953; Bournemouth manager April 1956; Portsmouth manager August 1958 to February 1961; Gillingham manager June 1962; Bournemouth manager April 1965 to June 1970

Few players were more local to Reading than Freddy who attended Battle School which was 100 yards from Elm Park and yet, apart from a handful of Wartime guest appearances, he never played for his home town side. He progressed from Spurs' nursery club, Northfleet, to make his League debut for them before the War. He scored twice for Reading on his Elm Park debut, a 6-3 win over Bournemouth, but as his War duties involved flying transport planes in the Far East, his appearances were greatly restricted. After the War he was a regular on Spurs' right wing before a move to Arsenal saw him score in the 1950 and 1952 FA Cup semi-finals and so make two Cup Final appearances, winning in 1950. After his playing career was over, Freddy had a successful managerial career where he built up teams that were very difficult to beat.

Reading Record: Wartime 8/2
League Career Total: 182/25

EDWARDS Len
b. East Ham 1920. d 1985
Ht 5ft 8 Wt 10st 10 (38-39)
Career: Fulham; READING 20 June 1939

Len was another player who lost out on a League career because of the War. He had been capped at schoolboy level at the age of 14 and then joined Fulham where he was part of Joe Edelston's successful reserve side. When Edelston became Reading's manager, Len was one of his first signings and made his League debut at left half in the home game against Southend that saw Reading go to the top of the Third Division South. Unfortunately for both Reading and Len, War was declared the next day, and apart from one game for Reading in 1941-42, his career was over.

Reading Record: Wartime 2

FENWICK Alfred L
b. Northumberland 1916
Ht 5ft 11 Wt 12st 2 (39-40)
Career: Sheffield Wed; READING 20 June 1939

After five years at Sheffield Wednesday without making a first team appearance, Alf must have thought that his fortunes were about to change when he joined Reading, his father having played with Reading manager, Joe Edelston, at Hull. He was a well built full back and went straight into Reading's team for their first League game of the 1939-40 season at Bristol Rovers.

Of course, even that one appearance was about to be scrubbed from the record books when League football was suspended after War was declared a week later. Len joined up with the Northumberland Regiment and apart from one further appearance in a friendly against Chelsea, he never played for the club again, nor did he get to play in a League game.

Reading Record: Wartime 1

GALE George Warrington
b. 1st qtr 1916
Ht 6ft 1/2 Wt 12st 5 (39-40)
Career: Cardiff C; Bangor C; Northwich Vic; New Brighton 1938; READING 17 August 1939

George was a promising young goalie who had made his League debut with New Brighton during the 1938-39 season and had joined Reading less than three weeks before War was declared. Consequently, his two appearances in Reading's League side never counted as the season was abandoned, although he did have the satisfaction of keeping clean sheets in both games. He also played in three Wartime friendlies and, injured against Fulham, he became the first Reading player to be substituted.

Reading Record: Wartime 2
League Career Total: 18

HILL James William Thomas
b. Balham 22.7.1928
Ht 6ft Wt 12st (51-52)
Career: Fulham jnrs; Denmark Hill Police; Boys Brigade; READING amateur November 1948; Brentford May 1949; Fulham March 1952; Coventry C. manager November 1961 to September 1967; Fulham commercial manager March 1973; Coventry C. chairman & managing director April 1975 to May 1983; Charlton A. director November 1984 to May 1985; Fulham chairman April 1987 to 1997

Now far more famous for his varied career after his playing days, Jimmy played for Reading at the start of his career. Ted Drake spotted him playing for his regiment and offered Jimmy an amateur contract that saw him play regularly for Reading's third team in the Hampshire League, often forming an inside forward partnership with Johnny Brooks. Jimmy rarely made it to the reserves and was told by Drake that he did not have the necessary skills to make it as a professional.

After making his name as a player with Fulham, where he scored a club record five away goals at Doncaster in 1958, and, as PFA Chairman, threatening strike action before the maximum wage was abolished, Jimmy turned to management. He revolutionized Coventry on and off the pitch before doing the same for ITV's football coverage. In later years, Jimmy was involved in several controversial decisions - making Highfield Road all seater, moving Charlton away from the Valley, and trying to sell Craven Cottage.

League Career Total: 359/51

IBBOTSON Frank
b. 1920 d. Normandy 6.6.1944
Ht: 5ft 8 Wt 11st (38-39)
Career: Leeds U; Portsmouth 1938; READING 10 May 1939

Frank is probably the least known player in Reading's history. An outside left who had not made a first team appearance with either Leeds or Portsmouth, Frank signed for Reading two months before he was called up and posted to Birkenhead. He never got to attend a training session at Elm Park, indeed, it is thought that he may never even have visited the ground. Sadly, Frank was killed during the D Day invasion at the age of 24.

PETERS Martin Stanford
b. Plaistow 8.11.1943
Ht 6ft Wt 11st 10 (73-74)
Career: West Ham U. from apprentice November 1960; Tottenham H. (£200,000) March 1970; Norwich C. (£50,000) March 1975; Sheffield U. player coach August 1980; READING (guest) October 1985

Sir Alf Ramsey once famously described Martin as being 10 years ahead of his time. But when he guested for Reading, alongside George Best in a friendly against New Zealand, Martin was probably a few years after his time! Even so the class that had won him 67 England caps was still apparent. As well as his goal in the World Cup final, Martin won the Cup Winners Cup with West Ham plus the FA Cup, twice, with Spurs, who had paid the first £200,000 fee to secure his services.

Reading Record: Friendly 1
League Career Total: 720(2)/175

STANFORD Paul

b. 1960
Ht 5ft 9 Wt 11st 7 (83-84)
Career: West Reading, READING (trial) August 1983

A chunky striker, well known and respected in local football in the Reading area, Paul was a former Reading Chronicle Player of the Year. He was asked to play for injury hit Reading in a pre-season friendly against Brentford in August 1983. Towards the end of the game, with Reading 2-1 down, Paul got into his stride with devastating effect. Within 14 minutes he had scored a hat trick, helping Reading to a 5-2 victory, yet, despite this remarkable debut, Paul never played for Reading again. Although Paul won the matchball, he lost a signet ring during the game.

Reading Record: Friendly: 1/3

THOMPSON Francis Morgan 'Daley'

b. Notting Hill 30.7.1958
Ht 6ft 0 1/2 Wt 13st 12 (94-95)
Career: READING August 1994; Wimbledon October 1994; Mansfield T; Ilkeston T. March 1996; Kingstonian February 1997; Wycombe W. fitness coach March 1999; Farnborough fitness coach summer 1999

Arguably Britain's greatest ever all round athlete, and he played for Reading! Admittedly, Daley's few weeks with Reading was primarily to make a documentary of him training with the club but his infectious enthusiasm proved a great asset to the club. With a hatful of decathlon triumphs to his credit, including two Olympic golds, a World title, two European and three Commonwealth wins plus four World records, Daley was an imposing physical presence on the pitch. He scored with his second touch after coming on as a half time sub in a friendly at Leatherhead, in what was his first game for 15 years. His only other Reading appearance was for the last seven minutes in another friendly, during which his pacey and aggressive forward play managed to create havoc in the normally well organised defence of Spanish giants, Real Sociedad. Daley continued to make the occasional appearance for various clubs, including a game for Wimbledon reserves, alongside Gladiator, Wolf.

Reading Record: Friendly (2)/1

WHITTAM Ernest Alfred

b. Wealdstone 7.1.1911
Ht 5ft 8 1/2 Wt 11st 12 (39-40)
Career: Huddersfield T. from jnrs November 1929; Chester May 1933; Mansfield T. summer 1935; Wolverhampton W. February 1936; Bournemouth May 1936; READING 26 June 1939; Bradford C. (War guest) Rotherham U. April 1945; Leeds U

After averaging five games a season with Wolves, Ernie took his chance at Chester where his strong inside forward play during his first season with them brought him 12 goals in 34 League games. Later, at Bournemouth, he scored 28 goals in 108 games and was a Reading target long before he eventually moved to Elm Park. He played in the first game of 1939-40 but that season was abandoned after three games so that was to be Ernie's only competitive game for Reading, although he did play in four Wartime friendlies before War duties took him away from the area.

Reading Record: Wartime 1
League Career Total: 202/57

WILSON Joseph William

b. Newcastle 10.12.1911 d. 1996
Ht 6ft Wt 13st (38-39)
Career: Stanley U; Newcastle U. September 1928; Southend U. August 1930; Brentford July 1937; READING 14 August 1939; War guest for Consett, Gateshead & York C: Barnsley May 1946; Blyth Spartans

After spending a year in Newcastle's juniors, Joe signed professional and played one League game for them at centre half in December 1929. He then made over 170 appearances for Southend before moving on to Brentford and then Reading. Joe cost the Elm Park club a substantial fee but, as his move to Reading was just three weeks before War was declared, he only managed the three games in the abandoned 1939-40 season, all at right back.

Reading Record: Wartime 4
League Career Total: 245/6

JOE'S CLAIM TO FAME - Joe's birth details are a matter of some confusion as the major statistical sources quote three different dates and three different North Eastern towns - the one shown appears to be the most popular.

WOODLEY Victor Robert

b. Cippenham 26.2.1911 d. 23.10.1978
Ht 6ft Wt 12st 4 (38-39)
Career: Cippenham; Windsor & Eton; READING (trial) 1931; Aldershot (trial); Chelsea May 1931; Derby Co. March 1936; Bath C. player manager summer 1947 to December 1949

Having played for Berks & Bucks, Vic was offered a trial with Reading but despite a series of fine displays for the reserves Reading let the young keeper slip through their fingers. Within three months of joining Chelsea, Vic was in the first team and became England's keeper up to the War, winning 19 caps. Although not spectacular, Vic was unusual amongst pre War keepers in that he was one of the first to come off his line for crosses. Despite his tremendous form for club and country, Vic only won one major honour, when he helped Derby win the 1946 FA Cup.

League Career Total: 282

(Above left) Matt Busby (Above right) Joe Wilson
(Below left) Daley Thompson, (Below right) George Best

MANAGERS

Harold Marshall	Feb 20	-	Dec 20
Jack Smith	Dec.20	-	May 22
Board of Directors	May 22	-	Jan. 23
Arthur Chadwick	Jan.23	-	Oct 25
Harold Bray	Oct 25	-	Jul.26
Angus Wylie	Jul 26	-	June 31
Joseph Smith	Jun 31	-	Aug 35
William Butler	Aug 35	-	Mar 39
John Cochrane	Mar 39	-	Apr 39
Joe Edelston	Apr 39	-	May 47
Ted Drake	June 47	-	Jun 52
Jack Smith	Jun 52	-	Oct 55
Fred May/James Carter	Oct 55	-	Nov 55
Harry Johnston	Nov 55	-	Jan 63
Roy Bentley	Jan 63	-	Feb 69
Ray Henderson	Feb 69	-	Apr 69
Jack Mansell	Apr 69	-	Oct 71
Jimmy Wallbanks	Oct 71	-	Jan 72
Charlie Hurley	Jan 72	-	Feb 76
Maurice Evans	Feb 76	-	Jan 84
Ian Branfoot	Jan 84	-	Oct 89
Lew Chatterley	Oct 89	-	Nov 89
Ian Porterfield	Nov 89	-	Apr 91
Eddie Niedzwiecki	Apr 91	-	May 91
John Haselden	May 91	-	May 91
Mark McGhee	May 91	-	Dec 94
Committee	Dec 94	(1 game)	
Jimmy Quinn/Mick Gooding	Dec 94	-	May 97
Terry Bullivant	Jun 97	-	Mar 98
Tommy Burns	Mar 98	-	Sep 99
Alan Pardew	Sep 99	-	to date.

MARSHALL Harold

Career: Rochdale secretary-manager; READING secretary-manager 23 February 1920 to 23 December 1920

There has been considerable confusion over Reading's early League managers with many records showing Harry Matthews in charge for the 20 years up to 1922. In fact Matthews resigned in February 1920, although he stayed on as a director until November 1922, with Harry Marshall guiding the club into the League. Having previously gone to the same school that had produced Reading players, Jimmy Wilde and Alan Foster, Harry had held a similar post at Rochdale He clearly ruffled a few feathers at Elm Park, being described as *'a trifle heavy handed but that is the way of Northerners.'* In November 1920 the club suspended four players for undisclosed indiscretions and a month later Harry was dismissed for failing to fulfill his duties and he returned to the Rotherham area amidst much acrimony.

Reading League Record: P19 W6 D2 L11
For 21 Against 28

SMITH Jack

See entry as a player
Career (managerial): READING player manager 23 December 1920 to 11 May 1922

Having played for Reading for 10 years, Jack took charge just before Reading faced Chelsea in the FA Cup and it took the First Division side three attempts to knock Jack's team out of the competition. Jack retired as a player soon after taking charge but met with little success as a manager, particularly on the goalscoring front, where Reading averaged less than a goal a game during his managerial spell. Jack was in charge of team matters while Harold Bray became the club secretary, the first time the club had split the roles. Jack's elevation to manager earned him another £1 a week, but when his contract expired in May 1922 Jack quit football to run the local pub he had taken over a year earlier. Despite this he continued to advise the club for several years. Until now Jack has been Reading's 'forgotten manager', as he has never been acknowledged in any previous record books.

Reading League Record: P 66 W 20 D 15 L 30
For 61 Against 78

BOARD OF DIRECTORS

Career: 12 May 1922 to 8 January 1923

Although Reading advertised for a manager after Jack Smith left, the club went eight months before making an appointment. During this period the board, led by chairman, J. E. Phillips, continued to pick the team, as they always had done; the secretary, Harold Bray (see later entry) dealt with the players and trainer Billy Beats, a former Reading player and England international, kept them fit. By November 1922 the team's performances were drawing criticism in the press and when Harry Matthews, who had managed the club for 18 years up to 1920 and played a major role in securing new players for them, resigned from the board, the time had come to appoint a permanent manager.

Reading League Record: P24 W 4 D 8 L12
For 20 Against 38

CHADWICK Arthur

b. Church summer 1875 d. Exeter 21.3.1936
Career (player): Church; Accrington; Burton Swifts 1894; Southampton May 1897; Portsmouth May 1901; Northampton June 1904; Accrington Stan. summer 1906; Exeter C. April 1908
(managerial): Exeter C. 1910; READING 9 January 1923 to 24 October 1925; Southampton October 1925 to April 1931

A powerful centre half, Arthur won Southern League championships with both Southampton and Portsmouth, as well as playing in the 1900 FA Cup final for the Saints. This form earned him two England caps at the turn of the century. After 12 years in charge at Exeter, Arthur took over at Reading and signed the nucleus of their 1925-26 Third Division South championship side, and for the first time the Reading directors allowed him to pick the team. Despite his success, there was some friction between Arthur and others within the club which culminated in trainer, Jerry Jackson, asking to resign. The board also received concerns from senior players and decided to ask the manager to resign instead. He soon joined Southampton and he guided them to the FA Cup semi final in 1927 before retiring in 1931 to live in Exeter. There, he collapsed and died while watching a game at St James Park.

Reading League Record: P 115 W 39 D 31 L 45
For 124 Against 127

ARTHUR'S CLAIM TO FAME - Not only was he the first person to play for and manage Southampton, Arthur was also the first Saint to become a sinner when, in 1899, he became their first player ever to be sent off.

BRAY Harold S

b. c.1872 d. Reading 1935
Career (managerial): READING secretary 9 January 1921 to 1935, caretaker-manager October 1925 to July 1926

A schoolteacher at a number of Reading schools and prominent member of Reading Athletic Club, Harry had been a well known local player until a knee injury forced him to take up refereeing. In 1921 he became the club secretary and took over responsibility for the team when Arthur Chadwick resigned. In fact the players asked the board not to appoint another manager immediately and they were proved right as Harry was able to keep Reading on course throughout the season, aided by club trainer, Jerry Jackson. Between them they held their nerve in the tight run in that saw Reading win the title by one point. Unfortunately both Harry and Jerry died young, Jackson in 1927, and Bray in 1935 after a long illness, but they had been rewarded by being given two of the 15 championship medals awarded to the club.

Reading League Record: P 29 W 17 D 5 L 7
For 58 Against 37

WYLIE Andrew 'Angus'

b. c.1887 Scotland d. ?
Career (managerial): Bo'ness 1923; READING 9 July 1926 to June 1931; Guildford C; Glentoran; Hamilton Acc.

Without a playing career of any note, Angus had 14 years of management experience when he joined Reading. He managed the club throughout its five year spell in the Second Division, although team selection was still made by the directors. Although he guided the club to its highest position in Reading's first 65 years of League football, and to their only FA Cup semi final appearance, both in his first season, he suffered criticism for the number of Scottish players he brought to the club. Significantly, of his many signings from his country of birth, only Bill Johnstone could be considered a success. He was however in charge for two of Reading's greatest FA Cup victories, over Manchester United in 1926-27 and against League champions, Sheffield Wednesday three years later. A strict teetotaler and member of the Sons of Temperance, Angus survived two no confidence votes before choosing to resign, after Reading were relegated in 1931 and he moved to Guildford, signing several Reading players and winning nine of his first 10 games in charge.

Reading League Record: P 210 W 66 D 47 L 97
For 306 Against 396

SMITH Joseph

b. Dudley Port 25.6.1899 d. Blackpool 12.8.1971
Career (player) Newcastle St Lukes; Bolton W. (£10) May 1908; Chelsea (Wartime guest); Stockport Co. (£1,000) March 1927; Darwen player-coach summer 1929; Manchester Central summer 1930; Hyde U. September 1930
(managerial) READING 3 July 1931; Blackpool 12 August 1935

A brilliant goal scoring inside left for Bolton, Joe was said to have had the hardest shot in football, and in 1920-21 he scored 38 League goals for the team, still a club record and the highest total before the offside law was changed. Joe won five full caps, played in three Victory internationals and toured South Africa and Canada before becoming the first player to walk up Wembley's famous 39 steps when he captained Bolton to their 1923 FA Cup win. He added winners medals in 1926 and 1928 before moving to Stockport, where his debut inspired a 20,000 gate and an FA fine as his registration was not in order. Ending his playing career with 254 goals in 440 League appearances, Joe turned to management with Reading.

At Elm Park he was the first manager to have full control over all playing aspects and he rewarded the club with two second places, a third and a fourth in his four years at Reading. Unfortunately, only the champions of the Third Division South were promoted. Joe proved a fine judge of players, signing several former Bolton teammates, and was an excellent motivator, a skill that was demonstrated by Reading's home record during his time in charge that saw them average three goals a game and lose only three League games in four seasons. However, he was hardly a hands-on manager and his lack of pre-match talks was legendary - on one occasion at an away game he is reported to have told the players that he had specific match instructions for the game. The players were stunned, but attentive - Smith's rare tactical order was to make sure they got changed quickly after the game so they could catch an earlier train! In 1935 he took charge at Blackpool and guided them back to the First Division two years later.

He kept 'Pool in the top flight until retiring in April 1958, the third longest managerial career in League history. Of course, Joe will always be remembered as a cup manager, having guided Blackpool to the final three times. In 1953 his team finally won the Cup when Stanley Matthews, along with other great Smith signings, Stan Mortensen and captain Harry Johnston beat Bolton in the competition's most famous final.

Reading League Record: P 168 W 84 D 45 L 39
For 381 Against 253

BUTLER William C

See entry as player

Career (managerial): READING 28 August 1935 to 31 March 1939, caretaker-manager April 1939; Guildford C. June 1939; Torquay U. summer 1945; Johannesburg 1946; Pietermaritsburg F A coach; Rhodesian FA coach

Signed by former Bolton colleague Joe Smith, Billy took over when his boss moved to Blackpool and immediately retired as a player. Like Smith, he kept Reading high in the table but was never quite able to make it to the top spot. Billy was an innovative manager who, as well as being the first to write his own programme notes, introduced a wide variety of training methods and had a gymnasium built in the club. In 1937-38, Billy guided Reading to victory in the last Southern Section Cup. He signed some fine players, none better than Bill Layton and Tony MacPhee, and it came as a complete shock when he tendered his resignation in February 1939. Billy had agreed to carry on to the end of the season if necessary and, although he left the club when Johnny Cochrane was appointed, he returned two weeks later to take charge of one more game after Cochrane's shock departure. After the War, Joe emigrated to South Africa where he played a major role in developing football in that area.

Reading League Record: P 162 W 82 D 33 L 47
For 297 Against 238

COCHRANE John

b. Paisley

Career (player): Johnstone Thistle; Elderslie; St Johnstone (managerial): St Johnstone secretary; St Mirren 1916; Sunderland May 1928; READING 31 March 1939 to 13 April 1939

An unspectacular playing career was followed by success as a manager for Johnny, first at St Mirren where he guided them to their first ever Scottish Cup triumph in 1926. His move to Sunderland saw him become a successful dealer in the transfer market and gradually they improved to become the top club in the country. This culminated in a League Championship win in 1935-36, breaking Arsenal's three year run, and the following year they won the FA Cup. Johnny appears to have been similar in managerial style to Joe Smith - laid back, a good judge of player, who produced attacking, entertaining sides but not a great tactician. With these credentials, when he applied for the vacant Reading job the directors could not believe their luck. He was given a three year contract at a massive £1,000 a year, yet after only four games, one of which he missed due to flu, his contract was terminated. No reason was ever given but the town was rife with rumours, and the War meant that Johnny's otherwise successful managerial career was over.

Reading League Record: P4 W 1 D 2 L 1
For 4 Against 4

EDELSTON Joseph H

b. Appley Bridge 27.4.1891 d. London 10.3.1970

Career (player): St Helens Rec; Nelson; Hull C. March 1913; Manchester C. June 1920; Fulham November 1920 (managerial): Fulham reserve team coach 1925, asst. manager 1927, caretaker manager February 1934 and February 1935; Brentford coach and scout 1937; READING 18 April 1939 to 29 May 1947; Leyton O. asst. manager 1947-1951

A fine defender, Joe spent 17 years at Fulham in various positions, serving under six managers, and it was surprising that he never got a chance to manage the club. He left Craven Cotttage in strange circumstances - Joe's reserves were top of the Combination while the first team were bottom of their division when the manager accused Joe of countermanding his tactical instructions. FA Secretary, Stanley Rous, recommended Reading appoint Joe and he proved the ideal man to guide the club through the War years. One of the first FA qualified coaches, he had helped train the 1936 Great Britain Olympic squad, and was well organised. Joe made Elm Park a centre of activity during the hostilities.

Not only did he keep the club playing, often with famous guest players, winning the London War Cup in 1941, Joe also opened the ground to a variety of activities. Elm Park staged events ranging from American Football to fitness training for the forces, and even staged a boxing match that included Joe Louis. Despite suffering an attack of pneumonia in 1946, Joe was able to steer Reading through the first season after the War that included the club's record 10-2 League win. In addition to the work he did for Reading, Joe's family also played a major part with son Maurice being one of the club's all-time great players and his daughter acting as club secretary, before Joe handed over to Ted Drake.

Reading League Record: P 44 W 17 D 11 L 16
For 84 Against 76

JOE'S CLAIM TO FAME - While on his way to South Africa with an FA touring party in 1920, Joe became, surely, the only League player to be transferred on the high seas when he signed for Manchester City.

DRAKE Edward James

b. Southampton 16.8.1912 d. 31.5.1995

Career (player): Winchester C; Southampton from amateur November 1931; Arsenal (£6,000) March 1934; Wartime guest for West Ham U, Leicester C. & Fulham (managerial): Hendon 1946; READING 2 June 1947; Chelsea 2 June 1952 to September 1961; Barcelona asst. manager January to June 1970; Fulham reserve manager November 1972, chief scout summer 1975, club president mid 1980's

Ted was a free scoring, direct centre forward who won the League Championship in 1935 and 1938 plus the FA Cup in 1936, all with Arsenal, as well as several Wartime honours. He was only capped five times for England which was particularly surprising as he scored six goals in those games. After 171 goals in 239 League games, including a First Division record six in one game at Villa Park, a back injury, sustained at Elm Park of all places, hastened his retirement. One of his first acts as Reading manager was to set up a structure to develop young players and it was a system that was to stand the club in good stead long after he had left. A clever and imaginative manager, Ted produced attacking sides that achieved two runners-up spots and a third while, in 1951-52, they scored a club best of 112 League goals. This brought him to Chelsea's attention, and in 1952 he moved to Stamford Bridge where he was soon joined by Reading defender Stan Wicks and trainer Jack Oxberry. He was soon setting up the same youth system he had established at Reading, and Chelsea's youngsters began to rival those of Manchester United, becoming known as Drake's Ducklings. In 1954-55 he guided Chelsea to their only League title to date and, in doing so, became the first man to play in and manage a Championship winning side. Ted left Chelsea following a dispute over the appointment of Tommy Docherty as coach and spent some time out of the game before giving great service to Fulham. A former County cricketer with Hampshire, Ted described his time with Reading as *'the happiest years of my life'*, so it was particularly poignant that he should die the day after the club lost in the 1995 play-off final.

Reading League Record: P 218 W 107 D 42 L 69
For 403 Against 285

SMITH Arthur John 'Jack'

b. Aberaman 27.10.1911 d. Weymouth 7.6.1975
Career (player): Aberaman; Aberdare A; Merthyr; West Bromwich Alb; Wolverhampton W. June 1930; Bristol R. summer 1934; Swindon T. May 1935; Chelsea (£4,000) March 1938
(managerial): Wolverhampton W. trainer/coach 1945; West Bromwich Alb. July 1948; READING 1 June 1952 to 7 October 1955

But for ill-health at the time of his exams, Jack might have become a dentist rather than enjoying a 25 year career in football. An intelligent full back who played throughout the thirties and the War years, Jack turned to coaching in 1945 before becoming West Brom's first team manager. There he had immediate success, guiding them back to the First Division in his first season, before replacing Ted Drake at Reading.

Drake would always be a hard act to follow and Jack was not helped by the fact that he was forced to sell many of the club's most popular players to help the club's ailing finances. Although Jack put the club on a stronger footing, Reading were never able to challenge for promotion and the highlight of his spell at Elm Park came in the FA Cup when, in January 1955, Reading came within eight minutes of beating Manchester United. Two months later, Jack was given the honour of managing the Third Division South side against the North. Unfortunately, the strain of trying to produce a winning club side on a reduced budget took its toll on Jack's health, and after being given a month's leave of absence in September 1955 he resigned and quit football to run a pub in Weymouth.

Reading League Record: P 147 W 54 D 33 L 60
For 234 Against 229

JACK'S CLAIM TO FAME: In 1941-42, Jack was picked to play for England but two days before the game it was realized he was born in Wales! He eventually got his international call, playing for Wales against England.

MAY Fred/ CARTER E James

May: b Ash Vale 1907 d Reading 14.11.1990
Career: Wokingham T. secretary 1922; READING secretary August 1947, joint caretaker manager 20 September 1955 to 14 November 1955, secretary-manager 14 January 1963 to 31 August 1977, club adviser to October 1981
Carter: b. c.1900 d. Reading 23.5.1963
Career: READING director 5 September 1938, vice chairman, chairman May 1954 to May 1963, joint caretaker-manager 20 September 1955 to 14 November 1955

During the period of Jack Smith's leave, and up to the appointment of Harry Johnston, the club was managed by secretary Fred May and chairman Jimmy Carter. Fred was one of the most respected figures in football both locally and nationally. As a referee he had controlled many games at Elm Park and was to have a 34 year association with Reading. He was also president of the Berks & Bucks FA and, after his death, the Vice Presidents lounge at Elm Park was named after him. Jimmy Carter was a long standing local businessman who was one of the driving forces behind the formation of the Third and Fourth Divisions in 1958. Assisted by senior player Bobby Campbell and trainer Jimmy Wallbanks, they held the fort during a very difficult time.

Reading League Record: P 10 W 3 D 1 L 6
For 9 Against 17

JOHNSTON Henry 'Harry'

b. Manchester 26.9.1919 d. Blackpool 12.10.1973
Career (player): Droylsden A; Blackpool October 1935;
READING (Wartime guest)
(managerial): READING 15 November 1955 to January
1963; Blackpool chief scout April 1967, caretaker-manager
April to May 1969

A great one club man, Harry captained both Blackpool
and England and was Footballer of the Year in 1951.
A reliable wing half and inspirational captain, Harry
will always be remembered as the man who finally
lifted the Cup in the 1953 'Matthews' FA Cup final
having also led them during their two previous final
defeats. Harry played 386 games for Blackpool and
won 10 full caps, despite losing six years of his career
due to the War. During the War, Harry played twice
for Reading while stationed locally and he was to
return to the club as manager. The skilful Johnston
was horrified at the style of play at Elm Park and set
about putting a greater emphasis on skill as well as
reinstating the youth scheme. The club's financial
plight of that period prevented him from strengthening
the side so Reading were never able to mount a
sustained promotion challenge during Harry's time.
He found more success in the Southern Professional
Floodlit Cup, guiding Reading to the final in 1957 and
1958, but it was not enough and, midway through
1962-63 he was told that his contract would not be
renewed. Despite this, the honest, hardworking Harry
remains Reading's longest serving League manager.
On leaving Reading, Harry returned to his spiritual
home in Blackpool, serving his old club for many
years.

Reading League Record: P 327 W 133 D 70 L 124 For
558 Against 507

BENTLEY Roy Thomas Frank

b. Bristol 17.5.1924
Career (player): Portway; Bristol R. amateur 1937; Bristol C.
from amateur August 1941; Newcastle U. (£8,500) June
1946; Chelsea (£12,500) January 1948; Fulham (£8,600)
September 1956; QPR May 1961
(managerial): READING 14 January 1963 to 11 February
1969; Bradford C. scout 1969; Swansea T. August 1969 to
October 1972; Thatcham T, READING secretary 31 August
1977 to 23 February 1984; Aldershot secretary January 1985
to 1986

Roy was a pacey player who was capable of playing in
any forward position, although he was best know as a
somewhat unorthodox centre forward. His skills
earned him some big money moves after the War and
12 England caps, won over a six year period.

Included in his nine England goals was the winner that
earned them their first World Cup finals place, and
when he scored a hat trick against Wales in 1954, he
became the first player to score all three goals in an
England victory. At Chelsea he captained the team to
their 1955 League Championship and towards the end
of his playing career he was converted to a defender.
Appointed as Reading's manager in the middle of the
'Big Freeze', Roy had to wait six weeks to see his side
play, and then they lost after taking the lead four times.
He steered Reading away from the relegation zone
that season and soon established the club as consistent
if unspectacular performers. A tremendous run in the
second half of 1966-67 saw Reading just miss out on
promotion and the fourth place finish was as close as
Roy got in the League. Under him, Reading regularly
got to the third round of the Cup, going out to First
Division opposition on four occasions. The last of
these was a defeat at one of Roy's old clubs,
Newcastle, but the following month he paid the price
for his lack of League success and was sacked.
However, Roy was always a well respected personality at Reading and it was a popular decision when he
was named as club secretary eight years later, having
earlier managed Swansea to promotion in 1970.

Reading League Record: P 280 W 117 D 68 L 95
                        For 442 Against 302

HENDERSON Raymond

See entry as player
Career (managerial): READING caretaker-manager 11
February 1969 to 14 April 1969, asst. manager May 1970 to
31 May 1971; Halifax T. August 1971 to May 1972; Everton
reserve coach July 1973; Southport May 1976 to March 1977

Within four months of being appointed as Reading's
player coach, Ray was replacing Roy Bentley as
caretaker manager. Although never a real contender
for the permanent position, Ray kept things going and,
when Jack Mansell was appointed he provided
valuable assistance to the new manager. Ray lost his
job at Reading after the club's relegation and enjoyed
little success later in his managerial career. At
Halifax, they were knocked out of the Cup by a non-
League side, while Southport had to seek re-election at
the end of his season with them.

Reading League Record: P 15 W 4 D 6 L 5
                        For 23 Against 26

MANSELL John 'Jack'

b. Manchester 22.8.1927
Career (player): Manchester U. amateur; Brighton March 1949; Cardiff C. October 1952; Portsmouth November 1953 to summer 1957
(managerial): Telstar (Holland) coach; Eastbourne U. coach February 1958; Blau Wit (Holland) 1962; Sheffield Wed. coach 1964; Telstar (Holland); Ajax coach; Rotherham U. summer 1965; Boston Beacons summer 1967 to 1968; READING 14 April 1969 to 14 October 1971; West Ham U. scout; Hercules (Greece) July 1972; QPR asst. manager March to April 1974

A classy full back and deep thinker, Jack won two England B caps and took part in Football League tours of South Africa and Hungary before commencing a varied managerial career. A qualified coach, Jack built up a reputation of encouraging his sides to play stylish, attacking football at all times. He seemed the ideal candidate to revitalise Reading and after a slow start that saw the club go out of the FA Cup at Brentwood, everything suddenly clicked. Reading began scoring regularly as his small, nippy forward line took the Third Division by storm. Top for a while, the club ended the season with an 8-0 win to become the League's top scorers, with a League aggregate of 87 for and 77 against. By the start of the next season, Jack had replaced every player signed by Roy Bentley and had made major changes behind the scenes. Reading were favourites for promotion, but the defence, never a strong point of Mansell's teams, became increasingly brittle. The goals dried up, and the club's centenary season ended with its first relegation to the Fourth Division. A poor start brought Jack's inevitable dismissal, and although he never managed another League club he was in constant demand all over the world as a coach.

Reading League Record: P 106 W 39 D 24 L 43
For 143 Against 181

WALLBANKS James

See entry as a player
Career (managerial); READING caretaker-manager 14 October 1971 to 16 January 1972

A wonderful club servant for Reading, it was understandable that the club should turn to their most loyal employee to steady the club after the volatile Mansell period. Jimmy went back to an older style of play and improved the players' motivation to restore some pride. In addition, Jimmy got the club through a tricky FA Cup run that saw his last game in charge earn the club, and new manager Charlie Hurley, a home tie against double winners, Arsenal. Although only in management for 15 games, few Reading managers enjoyed more popularity than Jimmy.

Reading League Record: P 12 W 6 D 1 L 5
For 21 Against 20

HURLEY Charles John

b. Cork 4.10.1936
Career (player): Arsenal (trial); West Ham U. (trial); Millwall October 1953; Sunderland (£20,000) September 1957; Bolton W. June 1969
(managerial): READING 13 January 1972 to 26 February 1976

A legend at Sunderland, where he was voted their Player of the Century, Charlie was reckoned to be one of the best centre halves in the country during his spell with them. An inspirational captain, he played almost 400 games for the club and was similarly impressive for Eire during his 40 international appearances. Charlie had even managed his country for a couple of games but his appointment as boss at Reading was his first in the League. Not surprisingly, for such an accomplished defender, Charlie soon sorted out Reading's defence and in his first full season they conceded a club record low of only 38 goals, a total he lowered to 37 the following season. After three near misses, Charlie led Reading to third place in the Fourth Division in 1975-76, for the club's first promotion in 50 years. Part of Charlie's success was in harnessing the wayward talents of Robin Friday, but the following season Charlie began to lose the support of some of his players. By February the team were in the relegation zone, and 3-0 down at the interval, at home to Bury, Charlie resigned at half time, quitting football for good. It was a sad end to a wonderful career but he will always be fondly remembered at Reading as an impressive and likable character.

Reading League Record: P 238 W 92 D 70 L 76
For 302 Against 169

CHARLIE'S CLAIM TO FAME - The Sunderland Gazette once described Charlie as *'the greatest human being who ever lived'* and *'constructed entirely from pre-cast concrete, he often played when fatally injured with his head missing'*!

EVANS Maurice George

See entry as a player
Career(managerial): Andover player coach 1967; Shrewsbury coach summer 1968, manager October 1972 to December 1973; Wrexham scout July 1974; READING coach 15 July 1974, caretaker-manager 27 February 1977, manager 27 May 1977 to 23 February 1984; Oxford U. chief scout 1984, manager June 1985, general manager March 1988; READING chief scout November 1999

A very popular playing career at Reading was exceeded by a successful managerial career which have combined to make Maurice one of the most popular personalities the club has known.

Maurice returned to Elm Park as coach with Charlie Hurley and when the latter resigned, Maurice took over. Although he could not prevent relegation that season he was given the job permanently. In his second full season he guided Reading to an impressive Fourth Division championship that culminated in a League record run of 11 games without conceding a goal, and was named the division's Manager of the Year. Maurice was a steady, thoughtful man and manager, who was respected throughout the game and his speaking out against the proposed merger with Oxford in 1983 proved a rallying call for the fans. Although he could not prevent relegation in the face of so much off-field distraction, Maurice inspired the players to battle for an immediate return to the Third Division. By January 1984, Reading were third in the division so it was a great shock when Maurice was sacked. Many Reading fans found it hard to forgive the club for this action and the Supporters' Club highlighted the fans' feelings by immediately making Maurice a Life Vice President.

Maurice then moved to Oxford where he, reluctantly, became their manager and guided them to a League Cup triumph in 1986. That win came the day after Reading had clinched promotion to the Second Division and, despite his sacking at Elm Park, Maurice described it as the best weekend of his life. Whichever club he was with, Maurice was always a Reading fan at heart and there was great pleasure throughout the club when he returned as chief scout. It seemed an ideal role for one of the best talent spotters in the country - his signings included Kerry Dixon, Trevor Senior, John Aldridge and Dean Saunders, but nine months later Maurice died suddenly, having been working at the Madejski Stadium earlier in the day. The town of Reading and the game of football mourned the loss of a man who disproved the football adage that nice people cannot be winners.

Reading League Record: P 317 W 125 D 91 L 101
For 462 Against 403

BRANFOOT Ian Grant
b. Gateshead 26.1.1947
Career (player): Gateshead; Sheffield Wed. July 1965; Doncaster R. December 1969; Lincoln C. July 1973
(managerial) Lincoln C. coach 1978; Southampton youth coach, reserve coach; READING asst. manager July 1983, manager 26 January 1984 to 23 October 1989; Crystal Palace asst. manager November 1989; Southampton June 1991 to 1994; Fulham summer 1994 to 1996 then general manager; Sunderland Academy coach 2000

A dependable full back in the lower divisions, Ian was ever present as Lincoln won the 1975-76 Fourth Division title, later becoming their coach. After filling several roles at the Dell, Ian joined Reading as assistant manager before taking over from Maurice Evans. This proved a difficult time as many fans were angry at the dismissal of Evans, but Ian kept the side on track to maintain the promotion spot his predecessor had reached. 1985-86 saw his team win their first 13 League games, a League record, as they won the Third Division title in style, and Ian won the Manager of the Year award. His team was built on a hardworking, direct style that wasn't always pretty to watch but was effective. However the sale of top scorer, Trevor Senior, saw the team struggle in the Second Division and relegation was inevitable from early in the season. Amazingly, while the team couldn't beat Second Division opposition they overcame six First Division sides in cup games, and won the Simod Cup amidst great excitement in the town. An indifferent start to the 1989-90 season back in the Third soon saw the board bow to pressure from the fans and Ian was dismissed. He soon found a position at Crystal Palace and they reached the FA Cup final in 1990 before he took charge at Southampton. Again, Ian did well in cup games, reaching the final of the Zenith Data Cup, but his direct style and the constant struggle against the drop led to a vicious campaign by some Southampton fans. Despite gaining great credit from the way he conducted himself in the face of such behaviour, Ian was eventually sacked. Although Reading fans are still split on their opinion of Ian, he remains the club's most successful manager with two promotions and a cup win to his credit.

Reading League Record: P 256 W 100 D 69 L 87
For 462 Against 403

CHATTERLEY Lawson 'Lew' Colin
b. Birmingham 15.2.1945
Career (player): Aston Villa from apprentice February 1962; Doncaster R. (loan) March 1971; Northampton T. September 1971; Grimsby T. February 1972; Southampton March 1974; Torquay U. player coach February 1975
(managerial): Chicago Sting coach 1978; Southampton coach 1979; Sunderland coach July 1985; Poole T. June 1987; READING coach June 1988, caretaker-manager 23 October 1989 to 14 November 1989; Southampton youth development Jan 1990, coach July 1991 to 1996

Lew was a former youth international and played for Villa in the 1963 League Cup Final when only 18. At Doncaster he teamed up with Lawrie McMenemy for the first of four spells with this charismatic manager.

Ian Branfoot brought him back from non-League football to be his coach at Reading and it was Lew who took over in a caretaker role when Ian was dismissed from Elm Park. Branfoot obviously did not bear a grudge as he appointed Lew as his assistant at the Dell in 1991.

Reading League Record: P 4 W 1 D - L 3
For 2 Against 9

PORTERFIELD John 'Ian'

See entry as a player
Career (managerial): Rotherham U. December 1979; Sheffield U. June 1981 to March 1986; Aberdeen November 1986 to May 1988; Chelsea asst. manager November 1989; READING 14 November 1989 to 18 April 1991; Chelsea June 1991 to February 1993; Zambia; Ittihead (Saudi Arabia) summer 1994; Bolton W. coach; Worthing summer 1996; Zimbabwe October 1996; Trinidad & Tobago 2000

The most successful manager to be appointed by Reading, Ian Porterfield had three promotions to his credit when he joined the club. His first success came at Rotherham where he won the Third Division title in 1980-81, and he followed this by taking Sheffield United from the Fourth to the Second in three seasons. Ian then took over from Alex Ferguson at Aberdeen, who lost on penalties to Rangers in the 1988 Scottish League Cup final. He had a strange start with Reading in that his first four games were against Bristol clubs, and after 10 weeks he had been in charge of seven League games plus 13 Cup games. His first signing, Mick Gooding, proved a great one for the club but his next big fee, for Craig Maskell, nearly bankrupted Reading. Results on the pitch were erratic but it was still a surprise when he was dismissed after only 18 months in charge, shortly after a drink driving charge and concerns that he had not been keeping the board advised of offers for players. After a spell in charge at Chelsea, Ian was in demand as a manager in developing football nations. He came close to getting Zambia to the 1994 World Cup finals after they lost most of their squad in a plane crash, later guiding them to the final of the African Nations Cup.

Reading League Record: P 69 W 26 D 20 L 23
For 87 Against 83

IAN'S CLAIM TO FAME - When Ian was dismissed by Chelsea in 1993 he became the first Premiership manager to be sacked.

NIEDZWIECKI Andrew Edward

b. Bangor 3.5.1959
Career (player): Wrexham from apprentice July 1976; Chelsea (£45,000) June 1983
(managerial): Chelsea youth coach 1988; READING coach summer 1990, asst. manager, caretaker-manager 18 April 1991 to 1 May 1991; Chelsea reserve coach 1991 to 1996

A promising goalkeeping career, that saw 'Steady Eddie' twice capped for Wales, was ended in 1986 by a serious knee injury. After a spell coaching for Chelsea, Eddie became Ian Porterfield's number two at Reading where his vocal and animated touchline displays made him a popular figure at Elm Park. At the beginning of April 1991, financial restraints forced the club to give Eddie a month's notice but a couple of weeks later he was made caretaker manager for four games, although he refused the club's offer to stay in charge to the end of the season. His short spell in charge was not without incident and he was given a police warning at the end of a stormy game at Brentford.

Reading League Record: P 4 W 1 D 0 L 3
For 3 Against 5

HASELDEN John James

b. Doncaster 3.8.1943
Career (player): Denaby U; Rotherham U. February 1962; Doncaster R. September 1968; Mansfield T. (loan) February 1972
(managerial): Mansfield T. coach; Sheffield Wed. physio; Huddersfield T. physio January 1976, caretaker-manager April to October 1977; READING coach/physio October 1986, caretaker-manager 1 May to 9 May 1991; Nottingham For. physio July 1994

Another player whose career was cut short by injury, John was a centre half who was also capable of leading the attack. He qualified as a coach at 23 and as a physio at 29, using both skills in his later career, especially at Mansfield where he helped them to the Fourth Division title in 1974-75. At Reading, John acted as coach and physio, taking over as caretaker manager when the club was in disarray and suffered two heavy away defeats, before handing over to Mark McGhee. John stayed at Elm Park to help McGhee guide Reading to the Division Two title before moving on to Forest.

Reading League Record: P 2 W 0 D 0 L 2
For 1 Against 9

MCGHEE Mark Edward

See entry as a player

Career (managerial): READING player manager 10 May 1991 to 14 December 1994; Leicester C. December 1994; Wolverhampton W. December 1995 to November 1998; Coventry C. scout summer 2000; Millwall September 2000

Appointed as Reading's player manager on the recommendation of Alex Ferguson and Jim Smith, Mark steadily turned round the club from the previous unsettled period. He introduced a more cultured style of play and made several shrewd signings, the most important being the appointment of influential coach, Colin Lee, as his number two. Midway through 1992-93 everything began to gel, and although his team had left it too late to mount a serious challenge, the stage was set for the following season. Playing slick attacking football without jeopardising the defence, Mark produced one of Reading's best sides, as the team took the Division Two title, while his bargain signing, Jimmy Quinn, was the country's top scorer.

Not surprisingly, Mark was the division's Manager of the Year. Mark maintained the momentum in Division One and he was being hailed as Reading's greatest manager, when he shook the club by quitting to move to Leicester, having only just committed his future to Reading. What made matters worse was that Mark took his backroom team with him. He failed to keep City in the Premiership, and within a year had left them for Wolves in similar circumstances. Despite spending a lot of money, and buying several Reading players, Mark failed to get Wolves promoted and spent a long time out of the game after losing his job at Molineux. The manner of his departure from Elm Park guaranteed him a 'warm' welcome whenever he returned, and Reading always seemed to raise their game against his sides so, despite inevitably being the underdogs, Reading only lost twice in nine meetings with Mark's teams. However, Mark had his most recent success when his Millwall team beat Reading to the automatic promotion spot as they won the 2000-01 Division Two title.

Reading League Record: P 160 W 70 D 45 L 45
For 231 Against 177

COMMITTEE (Jimmy Quinn, Mick Gooding, Adrian Williams, Jeff Hopkins, David Armstrong)

Mark McGhee's sudden departure, along with his backroom staff left Reading without an obvious replacement so chairman, John Madjeski, took the unusual step of naming a committee of senior players plus Community Officer, Dave Armstrong, to take charge of the next game.

Dave made over 600 appearances for Middlesbrough and Southampton, winning two England caps, and had been at Elm Park since July 1994. The committee proved a great success as they inspired the team and fans to achieve an unlikely televised 4-2 victory over Graham Taylor's high flying Wolves in one of Elm Park's most memorable games. Armstrong was an unsuccessful applicant for the vacant manager's position and left Reading the following March.

COMMITTEE'S CLAIM TO FAME - Apart from their success on the field, the committee also created a League record. Adrian Williams was 23 years 4 months old which made him the League's youngest manager - even if it was only for 20% of one game!

QUINN James Martin /
GOODING Michael Charles

See entries as players

Career (managerial): READING joint caretaker player managers 20 December 1994, permanent 5 January 1995 to 9 May 1997

Quinn: Swindon T. October 1999 to May 2000; Northwich Vic. September 2000 joint caretaker player manager

Gooding: Plymouth A. coach March 1998; Southend U. player coach July 1998, caretaker manager September 2000

Despite having almost 30 years playing experience between them, Jimmy and Mick did a remarkable job in the first few months of their managerial career. Not only did they maintain Mark McGhee's momentum, but by switching to a slightly more direct style they took Reading to second place in Division One. This was Reading's highest ever League placing but it was the only season that century that the second place team in this division did not get automatic promotion and, with a shortage of fit players in the play-off final, Reading went down 4-3. The club had a small consolation of winning the Berks & Bucks Senior Cup for the first time in 100 years, but with several key players moving on in the summer, Jimmy and Mick had little chance of repeating their success. The next two seasons both saw relegation battles but the duo had the ability to raise their teams for the big games so Division One status was maintained. Although Jimmy's style was seen by some players and fans as occasionally abrasive, there is little doubt they did as well as could be expected, so there was some surprise when their contracts were not renewed. Both carried on playing into their forties, while Jimmy had another shot in charge at Swindon, but their dire financial circumstances gave him no chance of success.

Reading League Record: P 116 W 33 D 33 L 42
For 231 Against 177

BULLIVANT Terence Paul

b. Lambeth 23.9.1956
Career (player): Fulham from apprentice May 1974; Aston Villa (£220,000) November 1979; Charlton A. (£90,000) July 1982; Brentford July 1983; READING (loan) March 1984
(managerial): Fulham youth coach 1988; Barnet coach 1994, caretaker-manager August 1996 and April 1997, permanent summer 1997; READING 30 June 1997 to 18 March 1998; Brentford coach July 1997

A skilful, industrious midfielder, Terry played for Brentford in the first Associate Members Cup final at Wembley in 1985. He had previously had a month on loan with Reading, whose manager, Ian Branfoot, described him as *'not a bad passer and can also tackle'*. Unfortunately, injuries and suspension restricted his Reading career to just one reserve game. Terry returned to Reading with the initial task of keeping the club in Division One, pending the move to the Madejski Stadium, but after taking just one point from his first six games it was clear this was going to be difficult. While the team struggled in the League, Terry found some relief in cup games, guiding Reading to their first FA Cup fifth round tie in sixty years, while an away win at Leeds then saw Reading go out to a controversial late goal in the League Cup quarter finals. These successes were followed by a run of five defeats and after a couple of protests by disillusioned fans, Terry resigned.

Reading League Record: P 38 W 10 D 9 L 19
For 36 Against 66

BURNS Thomas

b. Glasgow 16.12.1956
Career (player): Maryhill Celtic; Celtic 1975
(managerial): Kilmarnock player manager December 1989; Celtic summer 1994 to April 1997; Newcastle U. youth coach June 1997; READING 25 March 1997 to 16 September 1999; Celtic coach February 2000

Tommy was one of Celtic's all time great players. A naturally gifted, creative player, he won six championships and six cups with them in 440 appearances and was capped eight times for Scotland. He enjoyed immediate managerial success in his four years at Kilmarnock as he took them from the Second Division to the Premiership before returning to Celtic. There, Tommy failed to break Rangers' domination and almost joined Reading in June 1997, before teaming up with Kenny Dalglish at Newcastle. Nine months later, Reading went back to him with an offer he could not refuse, but he was unable to prevent the club being relegated, despite signing a League record seven players on transfer deadline day.

Reading lost eight of their first nine League games under his charge, and apart from a run in March 1999, his team rarely looked comfortable. Another bulk signing on the 1999 transfer deadline did little to change things and by September, with no sign of improvement on the pitch, he was dismissed. Tommy had put a lot of faith in Scottish players, having spent almost £4 million during his time at Reading, but few of his many signings proved successful and a number were released without bringing in a fee.

Reading League Record: P 59 W 18 D 14 L 27
For 66 Against 87

PARDEW Alan Scott

b. Wimbledon 18.7.1961
Career (player): Whyteleafe; Corinthian Casuals; Dulwich Ham. September 1984; Yeovil (£5,000) February 1986; Crystal Palace (£7,000) March 1987; Charlton A. (free) November 1991; Barnet July 1995; Dulwich Ham. September 1999
(managerial): READING reserve coach 30 June 1997 to May 1998, caretaker manager 18 March 1998 to 24 March 1998; Aston Villa scout; READING caretaker-manager 16 September 1999, manager 13 October 1999 to date.

As a player, Alan is best remembered for scoring Palace's winner in their epic FA Cup semi final against Liverpool in 1990 but he was always a reliable attacking midfielder throughout his career. He spent several seasons with Terry Bullivant at Barnet and when Terry became Reading's manager, Alan joined him to take charge of the reserves. After Terry left, Alan took charge of one game, at home to Huddersfield, before the appointment of Tommy Burns. When Tommy announced the disbanding of the reserve side, Alan was redundant but he had made a good impression and was asked to return as caretaker after Burns' sacking. After a month, Alan beat off some strong opposition to get the position permanently, and he set about reorganizing the side. Initially, the results did not improve and Reading went 13 games without a win, but Alan had got the team playing consistently well by the end of the season. A calm, thoughtful manager, Alan found his ideal assistant in Reading born former West Ham, QPR and Portsmouth midfielder, Martin 'Mad Dog' Allen. Between them they produced a free scoring side for 2000-01, but the season ended in a double disappointment when they first just missed out on automatic promotion, and then lost in extra time in the play-off final. However, for the future, things look positive under Alan's control, especially as he has demonstrated fine judgment in his transfer dealings, all of his signings proving a success.

Reading League Record: P87 W 40 D 24 L 23
For 134 Against 103 +

Jack Smith

Ted Drake

Roy Bentley

Charles Hurley

Mark McGhee

~ Yore Publications ~

Established in 1991 by Dave Twydell, Yore publications have become the leading publishers of Football League club histories. Nearly thirty have been produced, and although many are now out of print, some clubs for which copies are still available include - Scarborough, Wycombe Wanderers, Lincoln City, Notts County, Barnsley, Bury and Scunthorpe United. Each history is a large page quality hardback with dustjacket and contains a well illustrated written history, full statistics and line-ups for at least all Football League seasons are included, with many named team groups.

A number of Football League Who's Who books (biography and statistics of every League player) have also been produced, including Chesterfield, Mansfield Town, Portsmouth, and Hull City .

Non-League football is another feature of our publications, especially the 'Gone But Not Forgotten' series (published twice yearly), each of which contains around six (written and illustrated) abbreviated histories of defunct clubs and/or former grounds (also Videos available).

Compilation histories of former Football League and Scottish League clubs (plus a video), and Unusual titles (e.g. 'The Little Red Book of Chinese Football') are also included in our stocks.

Two or three free Newsletters are posted each year. For your first copy, please send a S.A.E. to:
Yore Publications (Ref R/W),
12 The Furrows, Harefield, Middx. UB9 6AT.
Or visit our web sites:
www.yorepublications.sageweb.co.uk...   or   .....www.yore.demon.co.uk/index.html